The Limiting Principle

THE MIDDLE RANGE SERIES

THE MIDDLE RANGE SERIES

Edited by Peter S. Bearman, Emily Erikson, Christopher Muller, and Catherine Turco
Co-Founding Editor: Shamus R. Khan

The Middle Range Series promotes studies that link theory to richly textured empirical contexts to produce innovative paths of inquiry and new solutions to intriguing and substantively important problems.

The Middle Range, a term coined by and represented in the work of Columbia sociologist Robert Merton, is a style of social research that links theory with observation to produce empirically novel and theoretically generative research. This approach yielded significant advances in the social sciences over the last half century. The Middle Range series builds on that tradition, publishing works that are as innovative theoretically as they are empirically.

The series is most interested in projects that seek explanations of substantively important, intriguing phenomena and puzzles from the real world, whether contemporary or historical. Exemplary projects tend to span micro and macro levels of analysis, incorporate qualitative and quantitative data, and engage theory with richly textured empirics. The series supports authors attempting to discover innovative new paths of inquiry and creative new solutions to old problems.

Markets with Bureaucratic Characteristics: How Economic Bureaucrats Make Policies and Remake the Chinese State, Yingyao Wang

Judge Thy Neighbor: Denunciations in the Spanish Inquisition, Romanov Russia, and Nazi Germany, Patrick Bergemann

Trade and Nation: How Companies and Politics Reshaped Economic Thought, Emily Erikson

The Corsairs of Saint-Malo: Network Organization of a Merchant Elite Under the Ancien Régime, Henning Hillmann

Working for Respect: Community and Conflict at Walmart, Adam Reich and Peter Bearman

Concepts and Categories: Foundations for Sociological and Cultural Analysis, Michael T. Hannan, Gaël Le Mens, Greta Hsu, Balázs Kovács, Giacomo Negro, László Pólos, Elizabeth Pontikes, and Amanda J. Sharkey

The Conversational Firm: Rethinking Bureaucracy in the Age of Social Media, Catherine J. Turco

THE
LIMITING
PRINCIPLE

How Privacy Became a Public Issue

MARTIN EIERMANN

Columbia University Press
New York

Columbia University Press
Publishers Since 1893
New York   Chichester, West Sussex

Library of Congress Cataloging-in-Publication Data
Names: Eiermann, Martin author
Title: The limiting principle : how privacy became a public issue / Martin Eiermann.
Description: New York : Columbia University Press, 2025. | Series: The middle range series |
Includes bibliographical references and index.
Identifiers: LCCN 2025001315 | ISBN 9780231218870 hardback |
ISBN 9780231218887 trade paperback | ISBN 9780231562478 ebook
Subjects: LCSH: Privacy—United States | Privacy—History | Privacy in literature
Classification: LCC BF637.P74 E44 2025 | DDC 155.9/2—dc23/eng/20250516

Cover design: Elliott S. Cairns
Cover image: Berenice Abbott, *Tempo of the City: II* (1938), detail.
New York Public Library Digital Collections.

GPSR Authorized Representative: Easy Access System Europe,
Mustamäe tee 50, 10621 Tallinn, Estonia, gpsr.requests@easproject.com

From the counterplay of these two interests, in concealing and revealing, arise variations and fates of human interactions that permeate them in their entirety.

GEORG SIMMEL

Contents

Preface   *ix*

Introduction: Privacy for a New Age   1

1   Under the Eaves of the Home: Domestic Privacy and
    the Cultivation of Self   24

2   In the Glare of the Calcium: Privacy in the
    Early Information Age   48

3   The Chief Curse of the Tenement: Moral Anxieties
    and the Codification of Privacy in Urban Life   77

4   Inviolate Personalities: Individual Privacy in an
    Era of Informational Persons   105

5   A Modern Legal Fact: How Privacy Gained a
    Foothold in American Jurisprudence   132

6   Governance by Exception: Bureaucratic Rule and
    the Limits of Privacy   161

    Conclusion: Privacy in an Age of Surveillance   189

    Methodological Coda   *207*
    Acknowledgments   *223*
    Notes   *227*
    Bibliography   *293*
    Index   *329*

Preface

The technosocial realities of the present can appear as so unprecedented as to render any historical analysis beside the point. This
is one reason why many books on privacy and surveillance focus
strictly on the here and now. Yet their subjects are anything but neo-
teric. Already at the turn of the twentieth century, American newspapers
denounced invasive data collection efforts and proclaimed that the privacy
enjoyed by prior generations had become illusionary in an "era of publicity."[1] Several decades later, the novelist Malcolm Bradbury turned the protagonist of his novel *The History Man*—the sociologist Howard Kirk—into
a committed midcentury nullifidian. There are "no more private corners in
society," he asserted, "there are no concealments any longer, no mysterious
dark places of the soul. We're all right there in front of the entire audience
of the universe."[2]

From the vantage point of the 2020s, such passages appear less like arti-
facts of the twentieth century and more like clear-eyed anticipations of
the twenty-first century, where we often appear to stand "nude and available" before society.[3] But they also suggest that elegies to privacy are best
understood as iterations of a recurring swan song rather than dispassion-
ate appraisals of the status quo. This choir of lament sings loudest amid
rapid change and social dislocation, when privacy is cast as the antidote
to a wide range of social problems but also appears to be at the brink of
extinction.

Yet I would like to think that the fictional Mr. Kirk and his real-life fellow travelers are wrong on two counts. First, they are wrong to believe that technological innovations and new techniques of governance have made privacy impossible, like an antiquated idea that is now destined for the dustbin of history. Rather than asserting the impossibility of privacy and accepting the ubiquity of surveillance as social fact, it is better to ask: What grievances, values, or ideologies motivate public demands for privacy or defenses of surveillance? How is the scope of privacy protections reshaped by political conflict over the limits of institutional power? And who benefits?

Second, however, they are also wrong to put so much faith in the power of concealment. Privacy can be a privilege but also a source of deprivation—because visibility is often a prerequisite for trust, accountability, and social inclusion—and it has long been placed in the service of reactionary politics and carved up by exceptions that legitimate the disproportionate surveillance of specific people, spaces, and types of information. We ought to be clear about privacy's liberatory potential, especially during periods of turmoil and inflection.

The decades around the turn of the twentieth century were such a period. In a nation that was searching for order amid rapid sociotechnological changes and frequent moral panics about the ills of modern society, the logic of privacy was prodigiously applied to emerging social problems and began a long march through the institutions of American governance. It became increasingly embroiled with the institutional exercise of power and the experiences of millions of people who participated in social life as citizens and consumers.

The privacy architecture that took shape during this tumultuous period had a profound impact on the organization and functioning of society, and some of its core features have remained with us ever since: the sheer breadth of privacy claims in politics and public life; the tight coupling of privacy and public morals; the sectoral fragmentation and selectivity of privacy protections; and the reconciliation of those protections with the prerogatives of governments and corporations. If we want to grasp the contours, promises, and limitations of privacy—to sharpen our understanding of a notoriously elusive idea, to recognize how it has transformed American society, but also to guard against misplaced faith—the Early Information Age is a good place to start.

The Limiting Principle

Introduction

Privacy for a New Age

n 1885, after a lifetime of work as a teacher and administrator in public
schools throughout the Midwest, Josiah Hurty eased into retirement by
accepting a series of short-term appointments in the American South
that would allow him to spread the gospel of childhood education for a
little bit longer. He was on leave from his most recent posting and staying with his wife Ann and daughter Julia in Cincinnati when he died on
October 1, 1889, at the ripe age of seventy-nine. Upon finding her father
dead, Julia wrote to her four siblings and to the local parish in Paris, Illinois, where her parents had lived for twenty years and where Josiah Hurty
desired to be buried. As the self-appointed historian of the family, she also
organized her deceased father's papers, which included a scrapbook, an
album with a short autobiographic account of his life, and newspaper clippings from the various school districts where he had served.[1]

Much of what we can learn about Josiah Hurty's life comes from these
personal papers and from oral family recollections. There are no standardized birth or death certificates; no documents about retirement benefits
or life insurance policies; no detailed financial records. Despite his relative prominence in educational circles, news about his life and death did
not travel easily or very far. The reason for this is simple: Josiah Hurty
belonged to the last generation of Americans who could spend their lives
largely without appearing in official databases and without regular access

1

to telephones and nationally syndicated news. The American state already tracked Civil War veterans who were owed a military pension and each decade merged millions of census forms into a rudimentary statistical mosaic of the United States.[2] But for the most part, Josiah Hurty's personal data stayed within the tight circles of his community or traveled in sealed letters along the network of postal routes that connected urban centers and gradually penetrated the American interior. At the time of his death, the informational infrastructure of the United States was still closer in scope and sophistication to the early days of the republic than it was to any recognizably modern administrative and mass media state.

Yet in the decades that followed, his son John helped to build a world that differed profoundly from the one Josiah Hurty had inhabited. John Hurty joined a growing movement of physicians, social reformers, bureaucrats, politicians, statisticians, publishers, and business magnates that fashioned a society awash in information and, in so doing, "brought a new kind of man into being," a person "whose essence was plotted by a thousand numbers."[3] This marked the beginning of what I will call the Early Information Age: a period that predated the invention of electronic computers by over half a century but that was already characterized by step changes in the complexity of administrative apparatuses, the volume of information that routinely circulated through the social body, the salience of such information as a technology of governance, and the influence of institutional actors that collected and disseminated it.[4]

John Hurty was a pharmacist by training and trade, and in 1896, he took over as the secretary of the Indiana State Board of Health.[5] The board was still in its infancy, having convened its first meeting only in 1892, and it lacked the power and funding to accomplish much of anything.[6] John Hurty set out to change this by combatting the spread of infectious diseases like cholera, smallpox, and typhoid fever, which killed around one in forty urban residents around the turn of the twentieth century.[7] He helped to turn the public health bureaucracy from an administrative backwater into an organized sanitation police, demanding the mandatory reporting of infectious disease outbreaks by local physicians and ordering that buildings with potentially contagious patients be placed under twenty-four-hour police surveillance.[8]

But his ambitions extended far beyond such local "sentinel surveillance" campaigns. Before one could argue about the causes of death and disease, John Hurty reasoned, it was "evidently necessary" to acquire accurate data about infections, births, deaths, and other crucial stages of an individual's life course and health history.[9] Reflecting on this work during a 1910 speech to the American Medical Association, he remarked: "The accurate collection, tabulation and analysis of records of births, still-births, deaths, marriages, divorces, and sickness may be said to constitute the bookkeeping of humanity. The bookkeeping of dollars is very important, but of far greater importance is the bookkeeping of those events in the lives of human beings which are fundamental to an understanding of the movements of mankind. . . . Without vital statistics, a nation cannot know its vital latitude and longitude, its national time of day on the great ocean of time."[10] John Hurty was adamant that the systematic collection of personal and statistical data could put public administration in the United States on a more scientific and more efficient footing. Just as the ability to record one's latitudinal position with ever-improving sextants had allowed prior generations of sailors to pilot their ships safely across the vast expanses of the Atlantic Ocean, such data collection would allow political leaders and a growing cadre of government bureaucrats to steer the ship of state through the unsteady waters of the Progressive Era.

The prerequisite infrastructure grew quickly. In the closing decades of the nineteenth century, bureaus of health and labor statistics were established in most U.S. states; the U.S. Postal Service added thousands of miles of mail delivery routes; and the Census Bureau found a permanent home in the federal Department of Commerce.[11] The Census Bureau also modernized its efforts to collect and disseminate statistical knowledge, replacing manual counts of census forms with newly developed tabulating machines that could keep track of forty different data points and sort tens of thousands of census records in a few hours. At the local level, idiosyncratic and haphazard systems of record-keeping were replaced with standardized birth and death certificates; and police departments began to assemble "rogues' galleries" of mug shots. These were then disseminated through publications like *Professional Criminals of America*, an 1886 collection of photographs and biographical blurbs compiled by the former New York police chief Thomas Byrnes.[12] For the first time in the nation's history, individuals and populations became systematically legible to government officials and trackable across place and time.

In the private sector, the confluence of emerging technologies and growing consumer markets likewise increased the circulation of personal data, the capacity to collect and analyze it, and the incentives for doing so. The contract with the Census Bureau allowed Herman Hollerith, the inventor of the tabulating machine, to establish one of the first major computing companies in the nation's history, simply known at first as the Tabulating Machine Company and several mergers later renamed as International Business Machines, which is commonly abbreviated as IBM.[13] In addition, 2.3 million workers found employment in the transportation and communication industries between the Civil War and the early twentieth century as companies like the American Telephone and Telegraph Company—now better known as AT&T—blanketed the United States with a network of telephone lines that democratized long-distance communication. In 1890, almost no American household had access to a telephone landline. By 1920, a majority did.[14] And corporations in the growing retail economy experimented with consumer credit ratings and thereby decoupled financial solvency from interpersonal trust, spawned new conceptions of quantified financial risk and subsidiary industries focused on credit reporting, and catalyzed a boom in private consumption.[15] To an unprecedented degree, Americans began to experience the circulation of personal data and the exercise of informational power, that is, the ability of "scripting into a database" the lives and life histories of specific individuals and entire populations.[16]

Other facets of everyday life changed as well, turning the United States from a relatively contained "society of island communities" into a modern mass society.[17] Publishers like William Randolph Hearst and Joseph Pulitzer built media empires with so-called "penny press" newspapers that reported on political corruption, the crimes of the poor, and the indulgences of the rich. Photographic film replaced silver-plated glass, reducing costs and taking photographers from their studios into the streets of American cities. And the country developed into a majority-urban society for the first time in its history, driven in part by a steady influx of immigrants into industrial cities that also more than quadrupled the U.S. population and the number of foreign-born residents between 1850 and 1920.[18] As one contemporary observer noted, society was transformed "with such amazing rapidity" that the future appeared wide open, filled at once with great possibility and great uncertainty.[19]

Collectively, this farrago of transformations led to new ways of being *in* the social world; new techniques of collecting information *about* the American populace and specific individuals; and new relationships *among* citizens, consumers, firms, and governing agencies. Even as the so-called "cult of the individual"—that is, the view of individuals as agentic, autonomous, and morally sovereign elementary units of society—was cemented as a cornerstone of the American imagination, social interdependence and the threat of unwanted exposure also increased.[20] Citizens and consumers became more venerated than in the past but also more exposed: not just objects "of a sort of religion," in the words of Emile Durkheim, but also subjected to "the pressures of living in a complex world."[21] As the *Chicago Daily Tribune* noted in 1902, the far-reaching changes that made John Hurty's America so profoundly different from the world inhabited by his father Josiah meant that primary school teachers, marriage license clerks, municipal health officials, gas inspectors, janitors, landlords, police officers, pawnshop owners, mortgage lenders, grocery store clerks, tabloid journalists, photographers, urban neighbors, factory employers, and morgue workers could all affect the privacy of the individual through their observations and examinations.[22]

PRIVACY FOR A NEW AGE

Amid this cascade of events that threatened "to deprive us of even the quietude of a less advanced period," as one observer noted in 1898, privacy became a distinctly public issue for the first time in American history. It assumed wide social significance and attracted large public audiences, was deemed to be worthy of political attention and legal codification, and thereby began to affect the institutional exercise of power and the functioning of American society at scale.[23]

For earlier generations of Americans, the logic of privacy had primarily featured as a potpourri of informal cultural norms that gave voice to underlying norms of domesticity and propriety.[24] It applied almost exclusively to relationships among family members and close acquaintances, and it often extended only as far as the outer walls of the home. Until the middle of the nineteenth century, for example, the word "privacy" largely appeared in novels like Nathaniel Hawthorne's *The Scarlet Letter*, in which the protagonist refuses to meet "in any narrower privacy than beneath the open sky" to prevent eavesdropping onto intimate conversations, or Charles Dickens's *Barnaby Rudge*, in which an unexpected visitor "knocked with his knuckles at the chamber-door" and intruded "in this extraordinary manner upon the privacy of a gentleman" who had just withdrawn into his room.[25] Even overtly political mentions of privacy—like the 1806 claim by the Virginia politician Thomas Mann Randolph Jr. that "privacy of debate on certain occasions is not only consistent with the spirit of popular government, but is demanded by its most essential principles"—largely focused on nearby eavesdroppers who sought to gain a political advantage by listening into confidential deliberations.[26] Such understandings of privacy differed markedly from those of later decades. Framed in terms of intimate spaces and social roles, they captured a conception of privacy among blood relatives, peers, and colleagues. It was almost entirely absent from legislation and jurisprudence and still had little to say about the relationships among individuals, institutional actors, and society writ large.

The subsequent shift was directly informed by emerging social and technological realities and reactive to their attendant moral panics. In a rapidly changing society, what could be known about someone, by whom, under what circumstances, and toward what ends? And what were the rules, procedures, and exceptions that helped to delineate a realm of privacy against a society with an increasing (and increasingly institutionalized) will to knowledge? These were precisely the questions that imposed themselves with greater urgency and new significance.

The logic of privacy became *broad* amid such changes as a growing number of social, legal, and political debates were subsumed under its conceptual umbrella, making use of a common language and a shared set of ideas to confront new technological realities and the real and imagined social challenges of a new age. It also became *sticky*, taking up permanent residence in the halls of Congress and finding its way into legislation and the into the annals of jurisprudence.[27] Moral entrepreneurs, credentialed professionals, political operatives, and state officials formed communities of thought and forged temporary coalitions around an ascendant idea. They helped to tie it into "a whole web of discourses [and] special knowledges" in American law, politics, capitalism, and culture and thereby embedded it more deeply than ever before in the institutional fabric of American society.[28]

Several features of the privacy architecture that emerged from this period have remained with us ever since. This is why a return to history can help us understand how we have, of all possible worlds, ended up in this one. In international comparison, the United States now stands out in part for the wide range of political hopes and moral imaginaries—about bodily integrity, sexual self-determination, liberal governance, workers' rights, the consumer economy, and so forth—that are articulated through the language of spatial access and informational self-determination. Yet the privacy architecture of the United States is also uniquely fragmented and reliant on a byzantine patchwork of sectoral bills and regulations. And it is characterized by an approach that I call *governance by exception*, imposing limits on the informational reach of governing agencies but also legitimating the disproportionate surveillance of some populations and some types of information in the name of infectious disease prevention, reactionary morals, and national security. This is the privacy architecture of what one nineteenth-century observer dubbed a "wire fence" society: sundered by many rigid but permeable barriers.[29]

PERIL AND PROMISE

My emphasis on privacy in the Information Age runs against a common refrain: that privacy becomes impossible when technological innovations enable the mass collection and analysis of personal data.[30] Such critiques already proliferated in the early 1900s, when newspapers and magazines warned about the deleterious effects that new technologies had on the privacy of individuals and families. But they are especially common in the twenty-first century because the volume of personal data that circulates through digital systems and is aggregated by governing agencies and corporations has increased exponentially. New technological capacities beget new forms of surveillance, feeding the growth of what Oscar H. Gandy Jr. has called a "panoptic sort," that is, an entrenched system of intersecting and overlapping technologies that facilitate "the collection, processing, and sharing of information" across virtually all areas of life.[31] Individuals often have little choice in the matter because the rules of data aggregation are largely dictated by companies and governing agencies. Perhaps we are therefore witnessing the "disappearance of disappearance," since it has become increasingly difficult for individuals "to maintain their anonymity, or to escape the monitoring of social institutions."[32] Our agency over data sharing and our control over personal information appear irrevocably diminished; invisibility and inscrutability seem destined for extinction. We find ourselves in an age of "prying, digging, peering, and poking."[33]

New technologies have additionally encouraged new habits of voluntary self-exposure that offer a peek into private lives even to relative strangers. For example, having an active online presence has become such a central aspect of adolescent sociability and adult networking that it has significantly altered conceptions of information sharing and bred fatalism regarding control over sensitive or embarrassing personal information.[34] The apparently inescapable collection of behavioral data is therefore matched by practices of proactive self-promotion and voluntary confession.[35] As a result, privacy seems not only less attainable than in the past but also less valued—a historical oddity and a holdover from bygone times, to be pushed into oblivion by the twin forces of technological progress and changing social custom. The "privacy war is long over," *The Atlantic* therefore concluded in 2018, "and you lost."[36]

An idolization of the preindustrial or precomputational past often lurks in the conceptual shadows of such arguments. Before the invention of modern technologies and the growth of the federal bureaucracy, during an imagined "golden age" of privacy, "the mania of governments for information was still in a nascent state," according to Edward Shils, while "the isolation of villages from each other meant that if anyone did come into one from the outside, his past remained his own possession."[37] In a similar vein, the privacy scholar Robert Ellis Smith declared (with more than a dash of hyperbole and parochialism) that "the people of early nineteenth-century America had more privacy than any other culture before or since."[38] This is the logic of zero-sum games recast as historical analysis: advances in technological capacity and social complexity must precipitate the disappearance of privacy from technological systems and everyday life.

Yet it is also difficult to imagine a world without privacy. Much has been made of the so-called "privacy paradox"—the claim that consumers acquiesce to data collection in practice even if they reject it in principle—but recent research suggests that consumer behaviors are not quite as paradoxical as once thought.[39] Popular sensibilities toward privacy are also more pronounced today than they were before the emergence of digital technologies.[40] And even the propensity to share highly personal information online is less an indication that we have collectively given up on privacy than a strategy for exercising agency over personal narratives in an increasingly digitized world.[41]

Corporate strategists have evidently received the memo. In and around California's Silicon Valley, the birthplace of informational capitalism, highways are regularly flanked by billboards that elevate the promise of privacy into a sales pitch by asserting that hardware and software are "designed from the ground up to protect your privacy," ostensibly by baking data protection and consumer choice into the basic architecture of technological products.[42] Politicians and bureaucrats have also shown renewed interest. Legislatures from Virginia to California have passed new consumer privacy laws, and federal agencies from the Federal Trade Commission to Customs and Border Protection are incorporating the language of privacy into their enforcement proceedings and operational routines. It is a sign of widespread appeal that even a prominent lobby group of the technology industry operates under the name "Privacy for America," campaigning against data misuse while also opposing many consumer protection bills. Indeed, privacy talk has become so commonplace that it often flies under the radar. In 2020, one investigation by *The Washington Post* found that the combined length of privacy notices on a reporter's phone topped one million words, although few consumers will ever read them, according to another study by the Pew Research Center.[43] Embedded into the practices of myriad organizations, encoded into the design of informational systems, and wrapped into layers of legal language, the logic of privacy is sometimes advertised with great fanfare and sometimes relegated to the fine print. But it is undeniably, and consequentially, *present*.[44]

Indeed, the social significance of privacy may have reached a maximum in the twenty-first century, when the tug-of-war between privacy and visibility often involves powerful institutions.[45] Contemporary struggles over privacy require us to consider not just the eavesdroppers lurking behind a closed door but the actions of a vast number of people clothed in the privileges of officialdom, the collection of personal data in ostensibly public or semipublic settings far beyond the home and the bedroom, and the automated aggregation and analysis of such data through interconnected technological systems.[46] Far from withering away, the logic of privacy has, over the past 150 years, come into its own as the central "limiting principle" of modern society: it constrains our visibility to governing agencies and digital corporations and now structures the terrain upon which a wide array of conflicts plays out over the exercise of power, the rights of individuals, and the organization of society.[47]

This is not just an empirical assertion. Often, it also serves as an expression of faith. Already in 1928, U.S. Supreme Court Justice Louis Brandeis declared privacy to be the right "most valued by civilized men" and suggested that a firmer commitment to privacy could protect the core tenets of liberal democracy.[48] More recently, those same hopes have buoyed campaigns for abortion access and consumer rights and have sparked hopes that a resolute defense of the "right to be let alone" could stem the creeping enlargement of executive power and break the stranglehold of "surveillance capitalism."[49] Perhaps, the argument goes, a strengthened commitment to the privacy of citizens and consumers will curb the collection of consumer data, reign in the American state, and thereby reinforce the agency and autonomy of the individual.

Even in a polarized political climate, those debates do not map neatly onto partisan lines. In fact, the range of political issues and hopes that have become attached to privacy is so vast that the common thread is sometimes hard to detect. Some issues are thinly linked at best, dangling precariously from the conceptual scaffolding like bulbous holiday ornaments from the branches of a tree. But far from being left for dead and abandoned, privacy may in fact be more relevant than ever before because the concept's reach and the underlying potential for exposure are much greater than in the past.

These are the two antipodes that now shape discussions of privacy. One is a view that is steeped in the pessimism of the head and rooted in understandings of privacy as a holdover from a bygone era. The other is a view that is buoyed by the optimism of the heart and recasts privacy as a constitutive principle of liberal societies, fit for the challenges of the Information Age.[50] Both perspectives are motivated by the challenges of the present, and both contain an element of historical truth. But their pitfalls are significant. References to an alleged golden age of privacy in the distant past do not stand up well to empirical scrutiny. To the contrary, conceptions of privacy in the modern United States are much more varied and institutionalized than anything that existed in the young American republic. Far from being overtaken by the realities of the Early Information Age, the logic of privacy was profoundly shaped and energized amid the social and technological changes of that period.

Yet the impact of this transformation has rarely been as liberatory as lofty rhetoric would suggest.[51] In many instances, the contours of privacy have simply reflected the power struggles and prejudices of a given time and place, encoding reactionary moral imaginaries and government prerogatives into law and social custom and facilitating rather than eroding the exercise of informational power. Privacy has been pushed and pulled into one direction or another and occasionally tasked with bearing a larger burden than it could bear; shaped by struggles over the power of the expanding American state and the social problems of America's expanding cities; placed in the service of Victorian prudery and illiberal politics; and carved up by a patchwork of exceptions and conditionalities. Indeed, privacy frequently resembles a negative space: defined not primarily by what it protects, but by those types of information, populations, and actions that are placed outside the umbrella of privacy. The history of privacy in the Information Age is a history of gradual becoming and growing institutionalization but also of exaggerated expectations and stunted potential.

PRIVACY WITHIN SOCIETY

Privacy is sometimes cast as the antithesis of the social: it seemingly diminishes whenever the unencumbered individual has to tolerate the company of others. Our sociality comes necessarily at the expense of our privacy. This book takes a very different perspective. It would be wholly misleading, I think, to conceptualize privacy as something that is defined and found outside society. At a most basic level, the norms that govern spatial or informational access are not predetermined by the rules of logic. They are rooted in lived experience and the organization of social systems, which explains why those norms vary across time and place.[52]

Second, privacy norms are not simply rules of noninterference but specify certain conditions that allow for the meaningful realization of privacy in practice.[53] For example, privacy within the home has historically been secured by proactively erecting walls and doors that did not exist in older, communally organized dwellings. Similarly, to speak of "privacy against the state" is a call to action rather than a narrow demand for governmental restraint.[54] It insinuates a need for codified restrictions on the discretionary conduct of state officials and urges a distinction between legitimate and illegitimate interventions in the lives of citizens.[55] The protection of actually existing privacy is as much about *doing* something as it is about *not doing* something.

But privacy norms are deeply social in a third sense as well: they allow us to manage societal obligations by circumscribing a sphere that is protected, by social custom and by physical barriers like walls and curtains, against unauthorized or inappropriate intrusion.[56] This reflects a ground truth, already articulated by Georg Simmel in 1906, that our ability to form complex communities is predicated both on the sharing of personal information and the simultaneous ability to safeguard some aspects of the self against unwanted exposure.[57] Privacy offers a temporary reprieve from the judgment of others, enabling us to put down the proverbial masks we don in public without requiring us to abandon social life altogether.[58] It is, in other words, a socially sanctioned way of "repudiating the claims that civil society [makes]" of us.[59] There is no privacy on a deserted island because "the need for privacy is a socially created need."[60]

This is why privacy norms are often seen as essential to any reasonably complex community. Anthropologists have empirically tracked such norms across a vast range of tribal and industrial societies, laying to rest any speculation that privacy is a uniquely Western invention.[61] But specifically in the Francophone and Anglophone worlds, scholars have traced privacy norms to discussions of sexual relations and prayer in the late Middle Ages, letter-writing and diary cultures during the Renaissance era, the rise of humanist and liberal thought, and the revaluation of domestic space among the early modern bourgeoisie.[62] The cultural history of privacy predates the Early Information Age by many generations.

It is therefore a seductive proposition that, as the Bible states in Ecclesiastes 1:9, "that which is done is that which shall be done: and there is no new thing under the sun." Some canonical works on privacy suggest as much, arguing that "human nature is fundamentally the same today" as it was in the distant past, and leveraging this logic to assert that privacy norms have permeated social life in a relatively stable fashion for a very long time.[63] Privacy may have "basically always meant the same thing."[64]

In the continuum of permanence and change, this view places a heavy emphasis on the former, and not without reason. The "great dichotomy" of public and private has existed in one form or another since the demarcation of *oikos* (the household) against *polis* (the community) in ancient Greece.[65] When Diogenes masturbated in the city square of Athens in the fourth century BC, it was the conflation of public space and private conduct that allegedly upset Greek sensibilities.[66] During the early modern period, the public/private dichotomy then reflected a gradual emancipation from ecclesiastical authority—which was relegated to the realm of "private life" and reconstituted as personal faith—and informed a reappraisal of governmental power.[67] As Benjamin Constant wrote in 1814, the separation of a "public sphere" from a "private sphere" of familial life was nothing less than a precondition for political liberalism.[68] In contrast to absolute monarchies, it implied explicit limits to the exercise of state power and positioned civil society as an essential counterweight to the state apparatus. At the same time, the conceptual differentiation of private economic exchange and public administration also mystified the nature and thereby veiled the exercise of power in emerging capitalist societies, partly by insinuating that politics expressed some illusory "common interest" rather than the narrow (i.e., private) class interests of an ascendant bourgeoisie.[69]

Indeed, three signals of a massive shift in social organization since the late Middle Ages are the transition (as John Stuart Mill put it) from communities that sought "the regulation of every part of private conduct by public authority" toward communities that "prevented so great an interference by law in the details of private life"; the rising importance of market exchanges among nominally private persons; and the concurrent rise of what Norbert Elias has called the *homo clausus*, a conception of the individual as "a little world in himself who ultimately exists quite independently of the great world outside."[70] In revolutionary France, Louis Antoine de Saint-Just thus declared that "the freedom of the people is in their private life," and Alexis de Tocqueville observed in the United States that the revolution that had birthed the country had also allowed Americans to "enjoy the pleasures of private life" by drawing a clear distinction to the "public life" of political engagement.[71] The danger that Tocqueville foresaw in the United States was not a renunciation of the public/private distinction but an embrace of the latter at the expense of the former—an atomistic society that neglected to reactivate its associational glue.[72]

This bifurcation of the modern self—and, by extension, the bifurcation of the modern world more generally—remains at the heart of American culture and politics. The growing salience of privacy during the Early Information Age may therefore constitute merely the latest chapter in a much longer history of public/private distinctions. What shifted, perhaps, was simply the boundary dividing the private from the public. Spatial boundaries may have been replaced by informational ones as the focus moved from the privacy of bedrooms to the privacy of personal data, lessening the importance of physical boundaries in everyday life and increasing it for legal (and, later, electronic) barriers to informational access.[73] Practices from sexual intercourse to personal hygiene and data management may have also been reallocated across that boundary and thereby reclassified as newly private or newly public.[74] For example, shifts in sexual norms since the 1960s have led American courts to conclude that revealing a person's sexual orientation invites less stigmatization and carries less social risk in the twenty-first century than in the past and is therefore no longer a violation of privacy.[75] Deep dives into the legal history of the automobile also reveal that cars were initially understood as wholly public spaces—akin to smaller versions of a transit bus—and thereby subjected to the discretionary powers of police officers before becoming governed by a more restrictive set of rules that aimed to protect cars as privately owned spaces through procedural guardrails.[76] In short, the social history of privacy may simply be the history of shifting conceptual boundaries or of shifts across a preexisting boundary.

But this is where we must wedge an analytic crowbar into the narrow gap between privacy and the private. Privacy began to matter in the Early Information Age in "private" as well as ostensibly "public" areas of life, frustrating efforts to confine it to only one side of this dichotomy.[77] It attracted widespread attention and invited legal and political action not only because people valued the sanctity of an intimate realm but also because personal data regularly circulated through decidedly nonintimate corporate and governmental systems. Information that "was once private through obscurity" became widely accessible, and information "that was once merely accessible" received "wide publicity."[78] Privacy in private life was merely one-half of the story.[79]

Simply equating privacy and the private also forces us to abstract so far away from sociohistorical particularities and to gloss over so many fissures that any insight thus obtained would inevitably come with too long a litany of caveats. As a central part of the political imagination and the legal and administrative infrastructure of American society—that is, as a decidedly *public* issue—privacy first had to be internally constituted and externally demarcated; its growing prominence was inseparable from technological shifts, moral panics, and political mobilization; and its meaning and structure derived not from the juxtaposition to any single antipode but from the amalgamation and sublimation through which various ideas about power and social organization were gradually assembled into a minimally coherent whole.[80]

Strictly speaking, privacy in the singular remains a misnomer. It does not resemble a clearly bounded idea but "a complicated network of similarities overlapping and cross-crossing," in Ludwig Wittgenstein's words, whose unity comes from drawing on a common pool of concepts and concerns.[81] What emerged in the late nineteenth century was therefore no simple thing called privacy but a jumble of different interpretations, increasing in social significance but varied in their articulation. But if privacy was not reducible to a single *thing*, it was nonetheless thing-*ish*. It is no accident that the terminology of privacy migrated into so many different domains of social life at roughly the same time. This was *e pluribus unum* in action: the emergence of a shared set of concerns and solutions, drawn from a patchwork of parallel approaches and enacted "across long reaches of the social world," about the problems of governance and social order in the modern United States.[82] What should be known about whom, by whom, under what circumstances, and to what ends? These were the questions to which privacy offered an answer.

This thing-*ish*-ness means that I have generally avoided definitions of privacy that lean heavily on semantics and instead have defined it (and thereby defined my explicandum) in terms of its social significance and societal function. At one time, privacy referred to a set of relatively informal cultural norms that imposed structure on social relations among peers and around the family home. In the Early Information Age, it evolved into a public issue by becoming *broad* and *sticky*. The book is an attempt to analyze this transformation and the impact it had on American society.

PRIVACY AS A PUBLIC ISSUE: A CONCEPTUAL FRAMEWORK

For a long time, social scientists treated privacy primarily as a tool for managing exposure in everyday life.[83] This has changed with a younger generation of scholars who place greater emphasis on analyses of institutional power and social inequality.[84] Many of their studies will make appearances in the coming chapters, and I have usually chosen to discuss them whenever they overlap most closely with my own. But it is useful to highlight one particularly compelling historical account at the outset, if only to put the aims of this book into starker relief. In *The Known Citizen*, Sarah Igo documents how Americans thought about privacy between the mid-1800s and the early 2000s.[85] The book offers eight periodized snapshots of a shifting collective conscience and demonstrates that the kinds of things that people wanted to keep private—bedrooms, Social Security numbers, electronic records, and so forth—and the versions of themselves they sought to present for public scrutiny and appreciation have been exceptionally pliable. Whereas the legal scholar Judith Jarvis Thomson once lamented that "nobody seems to have any very clear idea what [privacy] is," the reader of Igo's book might now respond that this is precisely the point.[86] The salience of privacy in modern American society derives in part from these protean characteristics. Igo's book also offers a welcome corrective to fatalistic accounts that forecast the death of privacy in the modern United States by showing that American culture has always made room for solitude and secrecy alongside transparency and self-promotion because our lives are neither fully public nor fully private but contain what Christena Nippert-Eng has called "islands of privacy"—areas of our lives and selves that are carefully and selectively shielded against unwanted or unauthorized intrusions.[87]

This book will inevitably till some of the same empirical ground, but we shall seek to harvest a different crop. Studying the history of privacy primarily as a centuries-long daisy chain of cultural moments—as an evolving repertoire of those facets of life that were to be shielded against a rotating cast of intruders, or alternatively presented before a changing set of audiences—trivializes the most remarkable inflection in the modern history of privacy: the transformation from a relatively informal set of social norms about domestic relations into a public issue and a limiting principle of modern American society—that is, into something that was not merely a familial concern but generated political and judicial attention, invited codification and regulation, and ultimately had consequences for the functioning of society at large. The logic of privacy became a prominent perch from which a vast array of arguments about social and political order could be made in a compelling way. Its diffusion and institutionalization in public life demand our attention and deserve an explanation.

It is useful to sketch my conceptual framework at the outset. Having it clearly in focus may not deliver us safely across "the great ocean of time," as John Hurty wrote in 1910, but it can clarify the stakes of the argument and help to navigate the muddy waters of historical idiosyncrasy. First and foremost, I pivot from the study of collective sentiments toward analyzing rules of access and disclosure in specific domains of social life and institutional contexts.[88] Such rules—mezzo-social phenomena, if you will—can popularize, stabilize, and legitimate particular visions of the social world. They can be highly informal or formally codified; and they have a habit of getting "in the way" of history by introducing new bends and temporary dams into the ceaselessly flowing stream of events.[89] In doing so, they shape the organization of society and the space of historical possibility.

These rules must also be generally "appropriate to [a specific] context and obey the governing norms" within it.[90] This was not lost on Georg Simmel, who argued well over one hundred years ago that social relations among colleagues, friends, family members, or romantic partners are predicated on distinct (and distinctly different) patterns of reciprocal "revelation and concealment."[91] But many of the most consequential struggles over privacy that have occurred since the late nineteenth century did not just play out among peers or social acquaintances. They involved large organizations and governing agencies because these often have the greatest capacity to gather and utilize information and because the scope of such data collection remains contingent on regulatory and legislative guardrails.[92] Shifting the focus toward institutionally specific rules of access and disclosure reinterprets Simmel's emphasis on contextuality for an increasingly bureaucratized world.

The codification of such rules is in turn influenced by coalitions of support and opposition that emerge in the political domain during periods of uncertainty and moral panics. There is "endless potential for categorical conflict" over the meaning of privacy and the proper balancing of potentially competing social goods, and the twists and turns in the history of privacy are inextricably tied to particular moments of political mobilization and the information politics of specific organizations.[93] Social movements, professional organizations, legislators, and officials all influence whether, when, where, and how a retreat from the front stage of social life is possible. Prior developments can impose constraints on such struggles, but those are best understood as probabilistic nudges rather than logic gates. They structure the terrain of struggle without necessitating any particular outcome.[94] They load the dice but do not roll them.

This implies a departure from the common view that the scope of privacy is largely determined by technological circumstance or simply imposed from above upon an unsuspecting populace.[95] That is not true. The social history of privacy is a history of contingent developments, persistent struggles, and abandoned alternatives. During periods of social dislocation, when conditions become sufficiently destabilized to make the existing cultural and legislative toolkit seem inadequate, decisive shifts can—and do—occur.[96] But in other instances, the logic of privacy incorporates rather than upends vested political interests and social norms, often through exceptions that push some populations or types of information beyond its protective umbrella.[97]

The competing claims about spatial access or informational self-determination that surface during those struggles are often animated by competing visions of the American social order. Perspectives on privacy are views "from somewhere," shaped by the social positions, values, and ideologies of their proponents.[98] Already in antebellum America, the conceptual distinction between domestic privacy and public life was a gendered distinction that helped to justify the confinement of women to the home.[99] Similar moral and ideological connotations explain why privacy has historically been experienced differently by those at the margins of society or at the bottom of the ethnoracial hierarchy. For example, before the Emancipation Proclamation in 1862 (which freed slaves in the Confederate states), and at the time of the Browning Ruling of 1896 (which denied indigenous parents the right to determine what school their children would attend), Black enslaved people and Native Americans enjoyed very little of the domestic privacy that was concurrently afforded to white society. In the American West and Southwest, Indigenous children were regularly removed from their biological kin as a matter of government policy, breaking familial bonds as well as cultural bonds to tribal communities and physical bonds to ancestral lands.[100] On southern plantations, to be enslaved was to *be* private property but not to *deserve* privacy because, from the perspective of the slave-owning class, there was no independent self that deserved protection against outside interference.[101]

Individuals or groups can enjoy qualitatively different types of privacy as well as quantitatively different degrees of privacy, relative to other individuals and groups, in ways that are directly contingent on political ideology and imagined hierarchies of deservingness and belonging. In other words, the contours of privacy—the burdens and benefits that come with it or the ability to claim it in the first place—have long been inseparable from the promises and prejudices of American society. Privacy thus resembles what Michael Freeden has called a "thin-centered" logic: it does not appear in pure unencumbered form but is hitched to a multitude of other ideas and values.[102] This tendency toward entanglement is easily obscured when moral and ideological connotations are recoded in spatial, psychological, or informational terms. Privacy can then appear as a concept that is largely unburdened by social status and prejudice and stripped of unpalatable connotations. But whenever it is placed under the empirical microscope and examined as a feature of the social world (as opposed to a purely intellectual construct or a basic psychological need), the convictions and commitments embedded within privacy claims become visible.[103] Shaping those claims is a way of exercising social control.

When I characterize the diffusion and institutionalization of privacy as salient correlates to the growing power of information, I therefore specifically have in mind the ways in which the governance of privacy can legitimate particular visions of—and particular institutional arrangements within—the social world. This is especially relevant when the life courses and life chances of individuals hinge directly on being "seen" by the state or the market,[104] and when the opportunity structures encountered by various populations that find themselves "under scrutiny" depend to a considerable degree on the precise ways in which personal data are collected and subsequently deployed at the bureaucratic frontline.[105] In the Information Age, visibility has become a common prerequisite for access to state assistance and socioeconomic inclusion, while obscurity can breed institutional suspicion.[106] For that reason, privacy norms now have considerable "second-order" effects on the structure and functioning of society and the distribution of social (dis)advantage.[107]

Unfortunately, the conceptual link between data collection and social stratification has become overshadowed in recent years by theories that place a one-sided emphasis on the leveling effects of seemingly ubiquitous surveillance systems. When personal data are routinely collected from almost everyone and about virtually all aspects of life, it is tempting to conclude that qualitative differences in visibility are reduced to subtle differences in degree as a heavy blanket of social control begins to cover the entire body politic.[108] The effects of surveillance are felt everywhere all at once. However, this perspective risks underestimating the variability of privacy protections and the uneven bureaucratic use of personal data, and it risks overestimating the newness of new surveillance infrastructures. Historically, the ability to claim privacy protections has hinged directly on citizenship, race, ethnicity, gender, marital status, and sexual orientation.[109] But even today, seemingly total surveillance systems are characterized by a significant amount of targeting and slack. The collection of personal data and the deployment of such data in bureaucratic settings is rarely as indiscriminate and expansive as technological and organizational capacity would allow them to be.[110] In fact, it is often the selectivity of such data collection efforts—rather than their ubiquity—that should give us pause.

THE ROAD AHEAD

The following chapters focus on processes and events that are sometimes obscure and idiosyncratic. This is not a sweeping macrosocial history, and there are two reasons for it. First, historical change neither obeys general laws nor follows a course that has been set for us in times immemorial. It meanders and generally frustrates efforts to predict it with any degree of certitude. The study of such change must therefore begin close to the ground "with social activity in its immediate contexts of social time and place."[111] Second, it is precisely in those scattered activities and contexts that macrosocial realignments become manifest, rarely detectable at first but undeniable in the ultimate instance. Focusing on them enables us to discern "the thunder of world history more clearly than anywhere else," as the Austrian economist Joseph Schumpeter once wrote.[112] Our task, then, is to resist the allure of teleology and the siren song of historicism. We must keep our ears tuned to the whispers of discontinuity that can, in the aggregate, herald the new.

Chapter 1 begins with a discussion of privacy *before* the Early Information Age. Using the tools of computational text analysis and data from thousands of newspaper articles, hundreds of magazines essays, and dozens of novels, I demonstrate just how differently privacy was understood and operationalized before the late nineteenth century. It referred to a set of informal social norms about solitude and propriety that structured interpersonal relations within families and tight social circles and created space (literally and figuratively) for the cultivation of the solitary self. Social-psychological views on privacy are still rooted in this view. But starting in the late nineteenth century, claims about familial and domestic privacy were subsumed into a broader discourse that was oriented toward a much larger set of public audiences and specifically applied the logic of privacy to the emerging social problems and informational realities of the United States.

Chapter 2 zeroes in on this ascendant discourse by identifying shifts and ruptures across a fifty-year period between 1870 and 1920. The chapter shows that the capacious understanding of privacy that is familiar to a twenty-first-century audience first emerged during the final decades of the nineteenth century. There was no simple shift from spatial to informational conceptions of privacy. Instead, amid rapid technological changes and emerging social problems, the logic of privacy was applied to a wide range of previously disconnected debates about social life and institutional power even as it remained rooted in traditional moral imaginaries about domesticity and virtue. It became a lens through which different constituencies made sense of their moral anxieties and political grievances about urbanization, mass media, telecommunications, and state power.

Taken together, chapters 1 and 2 demonstrate that privacy became *broad* around the turn of the twentieth century. Chapters 3 to 6 build on this argument but show how the logic of privacy became *sticky*: it was written into legislation, anchored in jurisprudence and bureaucratic practice, and thereby became an important and durable fixture of the institutional infrastructure of modern American society.

Chapter 3 investigates how older conceptions of spatial privacy were applied to the emerging "social question" and codified through legislative action. The growth of tenement districts galvanized concerns about the deleterious effects of urban life on physical health and moral virtue. Moral entrepreneurs identified the management of visibility as an important remedy against perceived moral decay, helped to turn privacy into a key pillar of the social reform movement, and then built a political coalition that could translate their demands into legislation. The result was a measurable (if necessarily incomplete) transformation of the urban landscape as middle-class conceptions of privacy were encoded into the architecture of tenements and the organization of residential space, affecting the lives of millions of Americans at scale.

Chapter 4 zooms out from the city. The development of powerful telephone companies and the rise of tabloid newspapers increased possibilities for institutional invasions of privacy and tilted the balance of power in favor of corporate and governmental actors. The so-called "informational person" was born during this period, yet concerns about the precarious state of privacy also became more prevalent. In this unsettled time, American writers and legal scholars began to tie the logic of privacy more closely than ever before to the tenets of liberal individualism. They argued that a sphere of inviolability had to be rigorously defended against emerging forms of institutional surveillance, thereby updating older conceptions of American individualism for an age of exposure and preparing the stage for the so-called "rights revolution" of the twentieth century.[113] The result was a tension that has remained with us ever since: states and markets apprehend people through the collection of personalized data, yet the individualism of those people is simultaneously rooted in their ability to exercise informational control and evade involuntary exposure.

Chapter 5 explains how this inviolable self was cast into legal terms by retracing how the right to privacy evolved from a nebulous concept into a clearly defined—and clearly bounded—legal fact. My argument departs from common retellings of legal history. Using a social network analysis of legal citations and a qualitative analysis of historical legal opinions, I show that privacy was first integrated into the judicial canon through the ad hoc reasoning and judicial experimentation of lower-court judges. Communities of insurgent legal thought developed around an ascendant idea, hoping to address a perceived mismatch between existing legal principles and new social realities. Initially, their arguments were almost always focused on private entities, including advertising companies and newspaper publishers. But over the course of several decades, and especially after World War I and the Prohibition era, the right to privacy took a distinctly constitutional and state-centric turn. Citizens' claims against the expanding American state—rather than consumer claims against private companies—became the focus of privacy jurisprudence, which was increasingly tied to the Fourth Amendment, consecrated by the federal judiciary, and thereby severed from divergent schools of legal reasoning.

Chapter 6 turns directly toward the expanding American state. Governing agencies began to rely to a greater degree than ever before on the collection and administrative use of personal and statistical data, triggering campaigns against governmental overreach and excessive state power. Using two large and powerful agencies—the Public Health Service and the Post Office Department—as case studies, I show that these conflicting forces resulted in a patchworked regulatory approach that anchored a commitment to citizens' privacy in administrative regulations but also classified some types of personal data as public records and codified the unexceptional uses of exceptions to render some populations uniquely legible to state officials.

In the conclusion, I tie these historical developments to discussions of privacy and surveillance in the present. Institutional and legal path dependencies mean that the contingent developments and settled struggles of prior decades can cast a long shadow over the privacy architecture of the United States. Contemporary American approaches to privacy still reverberate with echoes of the past in their reliance on sectoral legislation and the routine use of exceptions. More generally, an engagement with history allows us to discover the entanglement of privacy with public morals and ideologies, as well as the uneven landscapes of visibility that often arise from moral panics and political struggles during periods of rapid change and social dislocation.[114]

How can we come to know this history, seemingly so pertinent yet simultaneously so far removed? Years ago, an Assyriologist described to me the challenge of assembling a representation of ancient cultures from cuneiform texts. He compared it to "wringing water from stones," thus capturing both the effort required to extract meaningful information from limited data and the fears about obtaining none at all.[115] But scarcity of evidence is not the only roadblock. Isolating patterns of continuity and change is also complicated by the basic fact that, as Andrew Abbott once observed, "the social process moves on many levels at once."[116] Interannual continuity can obscure changes that unfold over decades (and vice versa), and changes in one domain of social life—economics, technology, culture, politics, and so forth—can be stunted or accelerated by things happening, or not happening, in adjacent domains.

Fortunately, two recent developments have become true force multipliers in historical social science. First, the digitization of historical data and the development of new computational tools have progressed rapidly. The chapters that follow make use of this development by combining years of archival research with the computational analyses of digitized datasets. The close readings of historical documents, excavated from the boxes that fill miles of shelf space at the National Archives and other university archives, can uncover historical developments with a granularity that simply cannot be matched by computational approaches. Yet computational work can capture latent patterns that are only detectable from a distance and identify subtle shifts that might otherwise go unnoticed. I discuss these methods and data sources in a methodological coda at the end of this book.

Second, institutional processes, networked constellations of actors, and mezzo-social mechanisms of change have become load-bearing elements of the theoretical scaffolding in historical social science.[117] According to this view of the social world, general social realities can be reflected in localized dynamics and conflicts—this is also the Schumpeterian creed—and it is often by tracking them over time and across institutional domains that we can begin to isolate meaningful signals from the inevitable noisiness of the world.[118] I adopt the same perspective in this book.

Still, the pursuit of knowledge is a bit like rain on a roof: you never know where the water might come through. In the best case, each chapter will spark ideas that I have failed to discuss and raise questions that I have not answered. The plugging of those holes is what we call science.

1

Under the Eaves of the Home

Domestic Privacy and the Cultivation of Self

In the summer of 1879, the novelist Robert Louis Stevenson boarded the steamship *SS Devonia* near Glasgow in Scotland. He had received word that his lover Fanny Vandegrift was about to divorce her first husband, and he endeavored to join her on the West Coast of the United States. But the journey taxed Stevenson's spirit and health. The immigrants he encountered aboard the vessel were driven by despair rather than lofty ambition—"family men broken by adversity, elderly youths who had failed to place themselves in life, and people who had seen better days," who also appeared bent on displacing Native Americans from their "own hereditary continent"—and were forced to crowd below deck into "eight pens of sixteen bunks apiece" without private compartments or elbow room.[1] Stevenson eventually arrived in California after an extended train journey from New York City, carrying little money and a severe case of bronchitis. But by May 1880, Fanny Vandegrift had finalized her divorce, Stevenson had recuperated, and his father had agreed to cover the costs of their wedding. They got married and set off for a honeymoon in the Mayacamas Mountains north of San Francisco, taking up residence in an abandoned mining camp. "Here there was no man to intrude," Stevenson later recalled, and "the sense of privacy . . . was complete."[2]

What was this sense of privacy, so readily apparent in a mountain retreat and so scarce on crowded ships and trains? Stevenson continued: "It was not only man who was excluded: animals, the song of birds, the lowing of cattle, the bleating of sheep, clouds even, and the variations of the weather, were here also wanting; and as, day after day, the sky was one dome of blue, and the pines below us stood motionless in the still air, so the hours themselves were marked out from each other only by the series of our own affairs."[3]

To him, and to many of his contemporaries, privacy signaled isolation and solitude, the ability to focus on one's own affairs by avoiding encounters with neighbors and passersby, and the possibility of gathering one's thoughts and cultivating one's mind. It was closely tied to a quest for spiritual rejuvenation. But, unlike more modern renditions, this conception of privacy had little to say about the inquisitive tendencies of powerful institutions; and it cast physical distance and material barriers like walls and doors as the primary means of managing access. Unlike other social and political liberties to which privacy is commonly linked today, it also did not yet allude to an individual right.[4] When Stevenson invoked the language of privacy in the 1870s, he likely did not have citizens' privacy against the state or consumer privacy in a market economy at the forefront of his mind. Instead, he drew on a repertoire of cultural norms that already existed on both sides of the Atlantic and captured a desire for privacy within relatively tight social circles and the home.

Social-psychological perspectives on privacy still echo this view. Their arguments are threefold, focusing on the solitary cultivation of self, the functional significance of privacy for the management of social relations, and the cultural repertoires available for these two purposes in a given time and place.[5] First, privacy allows us to evade judgment and the pressure to meet social expectations by presenting a socially sanctioned escape route or, in the words of Barrington Moore, a social safety valve.[6] The wholly unencumbered individual has neither a need nor a desire for privacy, since such a desire presupposes feasible alternatives "where actions or words can be either withheld or disclosed, where a space can be inviolate or intruded upon."[7]

The work of Erving Goffman contains perhaps the most famous articulation of this view. Beginning from the premise that the "presentation of self" in everyday life is always a carefully managed performance, Goffman suggested that a person could be one version of themselves in public and quite another behind closed doors.[8] The key to this performance was a deliberate back-and-forth movement between the "front stage" and the "back stage" of social life. The "back stage" was where the dramaturgy ceased, Goffman argued, where the performer "forgo[es] speaking in his lines, and step[s] out of character."[9] This bifurcation between two spheres of life illustrates why the constitution of the self is commonly regarded as a dual process of socialization and individuation. We are molded by the world that surrounds us and by the entanglements of our personal life with the lives of others, yet we also grow through "opportunities for reflection" and the solitary cultivation of the self.[10] The informal rules that govern privacy in everyday life thus constitute a "common bond" that renders relationships sustainable and ties interdependent communities together by "providing for periodic suspensions of interactions."[11] Hitting the pause button can even make social relationships stronger in the long run, although maintaining relations and reputations can also be more difficult in atomistic societies that prize personal privacy over mutual trust and social solidarity.[12]

Second, privacy norms permeate the cultural fabric of almost any community because the selective management of exposure and access is a feature of *any* relationship. The self-knowledge we share with others is necessarily partial. As Georg Simmel once observed, whatever we say "is never an immediate and faithful presentation of what really occurs in us." It is instead "only a section," stylized "by selection and arrangement."[13] On the front stage of social life, everyone has *something* to hide.[14] In fact, it is precisely by veiling some aspects of the self and stylizing other aspects—by becoming partially mysterious to the surrounding world—that we cultivate our individuality alongside our sociality.

Third, however, any "panhuman" need for privacy is inevitably expressed through cultural repertoires that vary across time, place, community structure, and relationship type.[15] Privacy norms among romantic partners or siblings differ meaningfully from norms among casual acquaintances or professional colleagues. More generally, different structures of social organization can result in different expectations of privacy and visibility, which in turn affect the types of behaviors that are either encouraged or stigmatized.[16] Small tribal communities engender different needs than metropolitan life, and societies that place a greater emphasis on the nuclear family tend to cultivate different privacy expectations than societies where child-rearing and labor are communally organized.[17] In some clan-based societies, for example, there was historically "no space, not just physically but psycho-socially, to withdraw into the privacy of one's own self-estimate."[18] It was only with the retreat of the community that the privacy of the nuclear family, and the individual within it, rose to the fore—a development that was aptly captured by Norbert Elias's insistence that the growing complexity of modern societies went hand in hand with an increasing focus on the internal cultivation of the individual self.[19] Privacy therefore stands as one example of the tight link between sociogenesis and psychogenesis: new patterns of social organization can lead to new expectations and psychological needs, which in turn shape cultural norms and the presentation of self in everyday life.[20]

It is useful to state this view at the outset, since it still permeates sociological writings on privacy.[21] Even studies that specifically focus on privacy in the age of "surveillance capitalism" and "Big Data surveillance" often broach the topic by identifying cultural norms that "prohibit or permit observability" in everyday life and by studying the quotidian strategies through which individuals balance their privacy against concurrent desires for publicity and exposure.[22] The same emphasis on the situational management of visibility also drives many corporate approaches to privacy in the digital realm. One must only look no farther than privacy tools on social media platforms, which are steeped in the language of choice and consent but have generally focused on giving users greater control over who can see the content they share or interact with, while those same tools give users much less control over the collection and utilization of their data by platform providers.[23]

The social-psychological view also comes closest to capturing how Americans or visitors like Robert Louis Stevenson wrote and talked about privacy in the id-1800s. However, around the turn of the twentieth century, the logic of privacy was then folded into a much more capacious public and political discourse that foregrounded the emerging challenges of the Early Information Age, highlighted the need for legislative action and judicial interventions, and pushed the limits of privacy beyond the nuclear family and the home. But to understand these remarkable changes, we first need to examine what came before. So this is where we must begin: by establishing a historical baseline that can be juxtaposed against the novelty of later decades.

STUDYING THE PAST: A SHORT NOTE

When we peer back into history, we frequently encounter reflections of the present. The writer V. S. Naipaul called this the "enigma of arrival": thrust into an unfamiliar setting, our initial glance is colored by an existing stock of knowledge.[24] We judge what is foreign against what is familiar. The risk is that we bend historical explanations until they corroborate the common-sensical and conform to presentist explanations. For example, a history of privacy "from Plymouth Rock to the Internet" draws on the diary entries of Benjamin Franklin as evidence that informational privacy was already "a crucial element" of the statesman's view on governance.[25] But what did Franklin actually write in those diary entries? He praised several virtues that "occurr'd to [him] as necessary or desirable" for a good and productive life, including silence, tranquility, justice, order, frugality, temperance, and moderation. Arguably, it is something of an interpretive stretch to see echoes of a recognizably modern notion of privacy in this eighteenth-century list, and it illustrates the perpetual danger of historical casuistry.

In a slightly different vein, the legal scholar Amy Gajda has suggested that American courts have "always" recognized a right to privacy, although judges relied almost exclusively on the language of "truthful libel" before the 1890s.[26] This is undoubtedly true in a general sense (libel law and common law have offered remedies to reputational damage for several centuries, and the importance of precedent in Anglo-Saxon legal systems means that emerging concepts are inevitably anchored in those older legal genealogies). But it also risks coercing centuries of jurisprudence and distinctly different schools of legal reasoning into a single analytic category. Broad references to "cultures of privacy" invite similar critiques, especially when the term "culture" is used as a blanket explanation that masks the importance of more concrete institutional arrangements and specific sets of actors for bringing about an outcome of interest. The burden is therefore on us to understand the facets of history in their specificity and on their own terms—to search for gradual changes and sudden ruptures in the historical record and to reckon with the diversity and malleability of ideas, norms, and practices that proliferate in society at different historical moments.

But estrangement can also breed insight. It leaves us less susceptible to the power of custom and thus able to see things that would otherwise be obscured by the forces of habit and convention.[27] From the vantage point of the twenty-first century, we also enjoy the benefits of historical hindsight and accumulated scholarship. We can observe the sometimes-twisted ways in which historical contingencies echoed through time and across American society, and we have a rich set of explanatory models at our disposal to analyze their effects. We shall leverage these to understand the social significance and consequences of events that may have seemed rather obscure in their own time but that subsequent history has revealed as hallmarks of the old or harbingers of the new.

The printed word offers a window into this history, especially since the volume of printed materials increased rapidly during the nineteenth century. In the early years of the American republic, public and political discourses depended heavily on the transmission of ideas through pamphlets and personal letters, which is one reason why the historical record from that period overwhelmingly captures ideas that circulated among the elite.[28] Everyday discourses were rarely preserved for posterity, except in diaries, which also tended to be kept by (and were preserved in the estates of) relatively affluent Americans. However, new printing technologies, the rise of press syndicates, and the expansion of postal delivery routes contributed to a steep increase in newspaper production and circulation.[29] Between 1850 and 1870, the annual number of newspaper copies tripled, and the number of subscribers quadrupled. Between 1870 and 1930, they each increased more than tenfold again. Illiteracy rates continued to decrease, especially among minorities, enabling a greater percentage of Americans to consume printed content directly.[30] For the first time in American history, it made sense to speak of a media-rich society that linked a large swath of the American populace into a common information-sharing network. As a republic of letters gave way to publishers with national reach and an increasing number of local newspapers, the printed word came to occupy an ever more central role in public discourse.[31]

DOMESTICITY AND PRIVATE SPACE

Newspapers devoted comparatively few column inches to discussions of privacy before the mid-1800s. During the eighteenth and early nineteenth centuries, readers would have most commonly encountered the language of privacy in serialized romance novels or other works of literary fiction that discussed the "privacy of the domestic circle" and the "conspicuous sphere of domestic privacy," the privacy of apartments and summer retreats, and the privacy of bathrooms and boudoirs.[32] They would have read that privacy implied solitude and reflective contemplation; enabled the flourishing of artistic and romantic sensibilities; and allowed for the development of one's moral faculties and the true realization of one's character that were otherwise overshadowed by "the glare of public life."[33] They would also have learned that women in particular deserved to be enveloped in a veil of privacy "like the white drapery of the Veiled Lady" and thereby protected against the world of politics and sinful temptation.[34]

But it wasn't just that the venues where privacy was mentioned and discussed were quite limited. The scope and audience of privacy claims were much more limited as well. During this earlier period of American history, "a life of privacy and seclusion" commonly implied a retreat "from every scene of gaiety" and "the pleasures of social life."[35] Americans of all social strata had long balanced social activities with private and solitary pursuits, and writings from this period are rife with praise for "the loneliness of the country" and "the ennui of long, burning, empty days" where "no village bell ever summoned."[36] In her novel *The Waves*, the writer Virginia Woolf expressed this sentiment when she wrote that "after the day's pursuit and all its anguish, after its listenings, and its waitings, and its suspicions. . . . I need privacy—to be alone with you, to set this hubbub in order."[37] The abolitionist writer and women's rights campaigner Lydia Maria Child captured a similar view in her novel *Philothea*: a "simple-hearted maiden" had decided to withdraw into "the privacy of domestic life" where she "loved to prepare her grandfather's frugal repast of bread and grapes, and wild honey; to take care of his garments; [and] to copy his manuscripts."[38] In each of these literary scenes, a life of privacy implied seclusion and quietude, and it allowed for a person's attention to be turned inward toward the self or the immediate family. When writers lamented the loss of their privacy and chastised others for invading it, their attention was most frequently directed toward their peers, relatives, children, or other acquaintances—in other words, the audience for their grievances was a local audience, composed of those with whom they maintained relations of spatial or social proximity.

For persons of renown, privacy could additionally mean a break from official duties and public scrutiny. Already in 1761, John Adams—then a recent Harvard graduate and budding pamphleteer, and later a signatory to the Declaration of Independence and second U.S. president—had remarked in his diary that "I shall be pleased with my solitude" after attending a town meeting, and he later expressed his displeasure with political opponents who tried to glean his "sentiments, actions, desires, and resolutions" by observing his conversations and written correspondence.[39] Some fifteen years later, during the Revolutionary War, George Washington (the commanding general of the American forces) was sufficiently fed up with his improvised field quarters that he dispatched a construction crew to his mansion at Mount Vernon, instructing them to erect a private suite so that he, upon returning from his military duties, would no longer have to endure the constant presence of guests and dignitaries.[40]

Adams' diary and Washington's orders highlight that privacy was primarily sought and found in private *spaces*. While the entanglement of privacy and private property is largely a product of more recent times, the ability to demarcate personal space has long been central to the management of privacy in everyday life. As Oliver Wendell Holmes Sr.—the father of the prominent Supreme Court justice—argued in the *Atlantic Monthly* in 1859, a person could find privacy simply by closing doors and drawing curtains, and thereby shield themselves against the pressures of social obligations and the "idle curiosity" that drove members of one's social circle to ask prodding questions about "personal appearance" or "even most sacred feelings."[41] This is why doors that regulated access to homes or bedrooms were among the most widely used tools for privacy management.[42] They constituted physical barriers as well as social-psychological ones because they separated the home from the world beyond it and granted selective access to a person's domestic circle and intimate life. As Georg Simmel once noted, "precisely because [the door] can also be opened, its closure provides the feeling of a stronger isolation against everything outside." The wall was mute, "but the door speaks."[43]

The family home had particular significance as a sanctuary from public scrutiny and social obligations and was guarded by architectural means as well as cultural custom.[44] To enter a home uninvited was widely considered an affront, and an unauthorized intrusion into a bedroom constituted a grave faux pas. In an essay published in the *Atlantic Monthly* in 1879, the writer Richard Grant White admitted feeling "some shyness and hesitation" whenever he crossed another person's doorstep "as if I were intruding upon household privacy."[45] Further spatial subdivisions (which were simultaneously social divisions laden with symbolic meaning) existed on the inside of many American homes. In upper-class domiciles, visitors such as White usually entered a ground-floor reception area and would need to pass through multiple doors or climb a staircase before reaching personal studies and bedrooms, which were often located toward the rear of a building or concentrated upstairs. Parlors and living rooms in such homes still provided easily accessible spaces where guests could be entertained, yet those who desired to escape social situations had the option of retreating from view by moving to a different part of the house. Children sometimes had access to dedicated playrooms even as they were expected to convene with the rest of the family around the dinner table.[46] Spaces dedicated to sexual intimacy or personal hygiene were particularly sequestered as well, thereby helping to make eros disappear from the lives of children and the social life of the so-called "respectable society" in nineteenth-century America.[47] The spatial organization of bedrooms and bathrooms in middle- and upper-class society thus reflected the proclivities of a society that already balanced sociality and solitude, frequently treated sexuality as a taboo topic, and enveloped carnal desires and bodily functions in material enclosures and restrictive social norms.[48]

This vision of domestic life was partially at odds with the lived experience of poorer communities. One salient difference between working-class living quarters and those of privileged social strata had long been the ability to earmark certain rooms as "private" by subdividing residential space.[49] But in the communities that sprung up around mills and factories in places like Lowell, Massachusetts, or in the immigrant quarters of coastal cities, families, boarders, and other temporary guests generally crowded into relatively constrained domestic spaces. Living quarters doubled as family workshops and improvised hostels, and beds were treated as communal furniture long after the once-widespread practice of nightly cohabitation had fallen out of fashion among wealthier Americans. Girls who were sent off at a young age to contribute to the family finances by working in textile mills or as domestic servants and maids also enjoyed little of the solitude and seclusion that domestic privacy was supposed to protect.[50] In those instances, economic constraints prevented the permanent division of residential space into explicitly public and private domains, although practices like the widespread use of hanging sheets (to divide communal spaces into smaller semiprivate enclaves) indicate that aspirations of domestic privacy were shared across socioeconomic lines—even if the ability to encode such aspirations into the basic architecture of everyday life remained limited for some populations.

The strong emphasis on the privacy of the nuclear family was also not reflected in the customs of many Native American communities, which tended to subsume individual families into "a much larger network of kin and marital alliances" and, in parts of the country, eschewed permanently settled homes in favor of nomadic lifestyles. In contrast to Anglo-American households that reinforced "obligations and rights through a rigid system of hierarchy" within the family and an equally rigid separation of the nuclear family from the rest of the community, Native American kinship systems extended communal obligations and privileges much more widely through rules of reciprocity, mutual child-rearing, or "supplementary institutions such as ceremonial friendships, games, and hospitality rules."[51] The outer boundaries of these communities were also less intensely marked through spatial barriers than through ritualistic experiences, especially in nomadic tribes that followed the seasonal migration of bison and caribou. Tragically, this lack of permanent settlements among native tribes on the Great Plains—which ran counter to European expectations of domesticity—became a direct justification for the forcible relocation of children during the Indian Removal campaigns of the mid-nineteenth century and for assimilationist policies that aimed to integrate Indigenous children into Western models of domestic life.[52] From the perspective of those who administered tribal lands and the American frontier, the cultivation of sheltered domesticity was a racialized ideal that justified state interventions in the lives of native children as well as their subsequent reeducation in the proper ways of domestic life in so-called "Indian schools."[53]

The lives of many Black Americans also differed profoundly in the degree and structure of everyday exposure, especially once economic dependencies in the southern plantation economy had been recast as explicitly racialized domination.[54] Enslaved Americans were granted little of the personhood that motivated many privacy claims in the nineteenth century. Their value was measured in monetary rather than moral terms, and their needs were often reduced to whatever nutritional intake and medical care were necessary to sustain their economic output. On the 1850 census, for example, enslaved people were still listed under the name of their owners and sequentially numbered—an administrative demonstration of denied personhood. Precisely at a time when the social valuation of family life increased in Anglo-American society, Black families were also systematically and forcibly separated at slave auctions. It was common practice to remove enslaved children from their families (in part to interrupt the formation of kinship networks), essentially reducing child-bearing mothers to surrogates for the reproduction of labor power.[55] As one former enslaved person later recounted, "we lived in constant fear that we would be sold away from our families."[56]

On southern plantations, a strict surveillance regime also turned solitude and private spaces into hard-won achievements. These achievements included slave cabins built out of view from the "big house," as well as footpaths and meeting sites where men and women could temporarily escape the watchful eye of their overseers and the routines of forced labor.[57] Rich cultural repertoires still developed in these interstitial spaces (spirituals being the most well-known examples). Yet the ability to move freely and with agency between the front stage and back stage of social life was profoundly constrained and contorted within a system of economic exploitation and racial domination. But even in northern states, former enslaved people and free-born Black Americans were treated with considerable suspicion; their presence in the community was duly recorded; and night-watch patrols continued to monitor and control their movements long after such forms of lateral peer-to-peer surveillance had fallen out of fashion among Anglo-American settlers. In everyday life as well as in early systems of institutionalized social control, the "surveillance of blackness" was a common and characteristic feature.[58]

The lived experiences of many Americans thus remained in tension with conceptions of privacy that were predicated on white middle-class conceptions of intimacy, femininity, and the nuclear family.[59] But by the 1870s, and in a stratified society, those conceptions had nonetheless become widespread as a "common language" of privacy.[60] It is possible to get a sense of this by turning from individual texts toward an entire corpus of historical records, and from specific mentions of the term "privacy" toward its so-called semantic "neighborhood": the list of terms with most-similar word embedding spaces.[61] Words that have similar embedding spaces are not usually printed in the *same* texts. Instead, they are used in *similar* texts. Linguists sometimes refer to this as "distributional similarity" and commonly use it as an approximation of semantic similarity.[62]

Table 1.1 shows the semantic neighborhoods—the list of words with most-similar embedding spaces—of the term privacy from 1870 to 1919. It is based on data from the *Chronicling America* collection of historical newspapers maintained by the Library of Congress, which includes close to ninety thousand mentions of "privacy" across five successive decades. These data demonstrate that the close alignment of privacy with domesticity and quietude was a core feature of privacy discourse in the middle to late nineteenth century. In the 1870s and beyond, privacy commonly alluded to "seclusion" or to a "sanctuary" that protected the "inner" aspects of a person's life and created room for "unmolested" endeavors and "tête-à-tête" conversations about personal and "confidential" matters. This was a (physical and mental) space into which a person could "retire" after a

Table 1.1 Words with most similar embedding spaces to "privacy," grouped by decade and ranked by cosine similarity

1870s		1880s		1890s		1900s		1910s	
Term	Similarity	Term	Similarity	Term	Similarity	Term	Similarity	Term	Similarity
Seclude	0.659	Intrude	0.654	Strict	0.607	Strict	0.628	Absolute	0.614
Intrude	0.597	Sanctity	0.616	Secrecy	0.604	Seclude	0.591	Seclude	0.612
Secrecy	0.579	Seclude	0.592	Publicity	0.573	Absolute	0.589	Strict	0.561
Sanctity	0.576	Comfort	0.554	Seclude	0.569	Publicity	0.575	Inviolable	0.481
Retirement	0.568	Secrecy	0.554	Absolute	0.564	Comfort	0.551	Sanctity	0.477
Publicity	0.551	Bedchamber	0.543	Intrude	0.551	Intrude	0.519	Leisurely	0.465
Obtrude	0.514	Invade	0.541	Attendant	0.550	Assure	0.517	Comfort	0.461
Sanctuary	0.513	Obtrude	0.539	Obtrude	0.539	Uninvited	0.513	Boudoir	0.449
Quietude	0.508	Apartment	0.527	Comfort	0.524	Sanctity	0.499	Leisure	0.443
Sacred	0.507	Publicity	0.520	Boudoir	0.514	Secrecy	0.485	Quietude	0.439
Invade	0.501	Ostentation	0.516	Sleeping	0.511	Admittance	0.483	Openness	0.436
Decorum	0.496	Private	0.507	Inviolable	0.509	Confidential	0.477	Intrude	0.435
Inviolability	0.493	Tete-a-tete	0.504	Sanctity	0.506	Ensure	0.476	Neatness	0.430
Indelicacy	0.490	Decorum	0.496	Compartment	0.504	Boudoir	0.469	Soundproof	0.429
Retire	0.488	Impertinent	0.492	Invade	0.493	Access	0.469	Mainfloor	0.428
Restraint	0.482	Incompatible	0.492	Utmost	0.474	Inconvenient	0.456	Solitude	0.427
Unmolested	0.481	Etiquette	0.486	Innermost	0.472	Locked	0.450	Obtrusive	0.423
Infelicity	0.476	Homelike	0.482	Bedchamber	0.466	Utmost	0.449	Invade	0.422
Private	0.475	Privileged	0.476	Confidential	0.463	Stuffy	0.448	Detention	0.418
Inner	0.454	Boudoir	0.473	Luxury	0.461	Nouns	0.442	Confidence	0.417

Source: Chronicling America.

social engagement or a day's work and thus trade "publicity" for "quietude" and social engagements for "solitude." It was also a precarious "luxury," coming under threat through "invasion" and "intrusion" by inquisitive and "uninvited" others.

Yet the list of similar terms also suggests that privacy was balanced against "publicity," "openness," and social exchange.[63] Especially among higher social strata, there was a growing pressure to perform a particular vision of private family life in full view of one's social peers: maintaining an active social life and entertaining visitors at the home became, in certain social circles, the somewhat counterintuitive strategy through which middle-class families could assert their place within respectable society and showcase the sheltered domestic spaces they had built for themselves.[64] Having one's personal affairs known to the surrounding community was certainly problematic if it occurred as the result of "wanton" intrusions, but a person could still decide to seek public exposure without relinquishing their claims to privacy altogether. This is why its pursuit was commonly a matter of managing "access" and not a complete retreat from social settings: doors that could be "locked" and walls that were "soundproof" offered "confidentiality" to those who had chosen to seclude themselves, but without confining any individual permanently to the "bedroom," the "bedchamber," or the "boudoir." The task, then, was not to sever the links between the front stage and the back stage but to control the flow of people and information and maintain an air of mystery about some aspects of the self.

How was this achieved? The semantic neighborhoods of privacy suggest an answer. Before the 1890s, privacy norms were prominently encased in informal rules of "etiquette" and "decorum" and the social stigmatization of "indelicate" and "infelicitous" behavior rather than any formalized legal code. Eavesdropping was, as one novelist noted, "not quite an honorable practice" and laden with such stigma that those who were caught in the act risked social ostracization. Inversely, exhibiting "fine judgment and excellent taste" usually meant that a person "always maintained their distance" and did not inquire too closely into the affairs of distant relatives or casual acquaintances.[65] Because perceived violations of privacy were usually perpetrated at close range or by members of the same community, they were also dealt with through local responses and communal sanctions. Something as simple as the closing of a door or as complicated as the severing of social ties could put an end to invasions of privacy and forestall future infractions. Indeed, it was often "the person who discovered the culprit" who was most adequately positioned to deal out a punishment.[66] If they did not act directly, the community could inflict punishment by shunning suspected offenders or designating someone to set them straight.

Local courts occasionally dealt with suspected home intruders and eavesdroppers, but those cases were rare and tended to turn on the application of English common law and laws against physical intrusions and "repeating [gossip] to the disturbance of the neighborhood."[67] They also mostly involved theft or actions that rose to the level of defamation or libel—two legal concepts that presupposed demonstrable material and reputational harm from the unauthorized *publication* of potentially incriminating information but had little to say about the unauthorized *intrusion* into personal spaces and papers. In one such case, adjudicated in 1829 in Washington, DC, the travel writer Anne Royall was tried for being a so-called "common scold"—a highly gendered legal charge that had historically been applied to women who were deemed to be habitually quarrelsome or verbally abusive. Royall had attracted considerable attention as a single, self-supporting woman who produced acerbic writings about individuals she considered distasteful.[68] She was eventually sentenced to a fine for malicious slander. Yet such common-law disputes "faded from the legal horizon" as the nineteenth century wore on, as one contemporary observer noted.[69] In disputes about physical intrusions that did not involve theft, magistrates usually remained altogether at the sidelines, and legal remedies were correspondingly scarce.[70] With few exceptions, the governance of privacy in nineteenth-century America remained the governance of physical intrusions into personal space on the basis of unwritten rules and through the social stigmatization of infelicitous behavior.

Those unwritten rules are examples of what Ann Swidler has called "culture in action": they provide a set of resources from which individuals and the communities into which they are embedded can draw to structure their actions and interactions.[71] The "shyness and hesitation" a person could experience upon entering a stranger's home are stress responses activated by a cultural stock of knowledge about commonly acceptable social behavior, as well as by physical markers like doorsteps and door frames. Unspoken but widely understood conventions and physical barriers incentivized people to act in particular ways—especially when deviations were subject to social sanctions and risk of pariah status—and also helped to justify socially desirable behaviors and spatial arrangements.[72]

THE COLONIAL ORIGINS OF FAMILIAL PRIVACY

For much of the nineteenth century, the governance of privacy was characterized by this dual focus on domestic spaces and quotidian social relations, expressed through relatively informal social norms and the spatial layouts of the home. This combination of features made nineteenth-century privacy markedly different from more recent periods—but also from life in the American colonies, where the social and spatial organization of everyday life had often blurred the distinction between family units and their communal surroundings, shared social obligations had dominated over personal affairs, and defenses of solitude and seclusion had been concentrated among a narrow set of social elites.

Physical isolation had provided a strong natural barrier to the spread of information in colonial America and along the western frontier, but privacy *within* small communities had been relatively scarce. For example, before 1750, most Americans lived in a settlement with fewer than fifteen hundred inhabitants where "everyone [was] known, more or less, by everyone."[73] The spatial arrangements of family life in the American colonies also betrayed a lack of emphasis on individual privacy. Early log cabins and frontier homes protected people from the elements but not from ears and eyes within the home—they were "well suited to people who had a strong sense of family and a weak sense of individual privacy."[74] Such homes were commonly organized around a central communal area with fireplace and chimney that did quadruple duty as a daytime workshop, kitchen and dining room, place for religious instruction and rudimentary schooling, and nighttime sleeping quarters. Even relatively minute details of architecture and furniture design exemplified an emphasis on communal living. Many early American homes maximized porch space around the house (which allowed people to gather in a semipublic place) instead of maximizing the number of individual studies and bedrooms inside.[75] Chairs and individual bedframes were also uncommon as people sat on communal benches that were not entirely dissimilar from church pews and slept in beds that were shared by multiple household members.[76]

Conceptions of marital privacy were also less widespread in colonial America, where multiple persons often crowded into the same bed, partly to keep warm and partly because the sharing of sleeping quarters was not considered untoward.[77] Even among the well-to-do, it was not uncommon for visitors to end the day by climbing into bed with their host to enjoy a bit of (nonsexual) "late courteous entertainment."[78] The social distinction between a family's offspring and lodgers and servants of a similar age was less pronounced, too, since they were all expected to contribute their respective labor power.[79] And when pregnancy and childbirth limited the labor contributions of mothers, neighbors and extended kin commonly stepped in (and physically moved into the home), further blurring the distinctions between family units and the larger communities into which they were embedded.

This comparative lack of familial and individual privacy was reinforced by ecclesiastical authorities. Religious communities during the eighteenth century were primarily organized around the church, with church figures as the spiritual as well as political and cultural leaders of the community.[80] This was especially true in Puritan communities—prominently described by Max Weber in *The Protestant Ethic*—which considered good personal behavior a prerequisite for communal cohesion in this world and for salvation in the next. Keeping a watchful eye over "the sin of one's neighbor" was therefore an indispensable part of living in accordance with religious doctrine.[81] Joining the church often involved a ritualistic (although voluntary) confession and character assessment known as "the Relation," during which a person would submit to questioning by church elders and parish members. Church attendance was usually mandatory, and clerical leaders organized volunteer night watches that enforced the church's strict morality code after dusk and actively encouraged their flock to "all watch one another, and try out our wickedness."[82] In one Calvinist church, the pulpit was even decorated with a painting that depicted the all-seeing eye of God, lest anyone forget that secrecy and heresy went hand in hand.[83] After having visited such communities, one observer from Britain noted with consternation that the desire to discover "every little irregularity in the neighborhood" was a standout feature of tight-knit religious communities in the American colonies that put the prudery of the British to shame and embedded families into a dense network of communal relations of social control.[84]

Yet gradually, imperfectly, and unevenly across American society, the "nuclear [family] escaped the surveillance and supervision of neighbors and grandparents" and emerged as a more self-contained unit of social organization.[85] Some of these changes were rooted in the changing compositions of households. Communal homestead settlements and the hosting of temporary lodgers and servants became less widespread in the 1800s, so that the spatial boundaries of the home increasingly coincided with the genealogical boundaries of the family. The once-widespread practice of having "servants living in our home by day and night, confronted with our strange customs and new ideas, [and] having our family affairs always before them" had presented "a condition as far removed from privacy as could be imagined," in the words of the feminist writer Charlotte Perkins Gilman.[86] But such conditions became less common, as did the practice of accepting young apprentices as temporary houseguests. Working-class families and childless couples continued to accept paying lodgers. But as factory-based mechanized production grew in importance, apprentices and temporary laborers increasingly secured rooms in dedicated workers' accommodations instead of moving in with the families of craftsmen.[87]

The influence of Puritanism also declined, and Americans who immigrated to the United States after the colonial period maintained a more distant relationship with religious authorities.[88] In many of these emerging communities of faith, religion featured less prominently as a form of ecclesiastical interference in family life and more prominently as a set of shared ritualistic experiences. The basic organizational structure of these communities was usually the family, with the head of the patriarchal household as the primary authority and each home as a proverbial castle unto itself. During the Second Great Awakening of the early nineteenth century, so-called "revivalists" additionally began to emphasize the importance of personal encounters with God's grace as catalysts for spiritual transformation and rebirth.[89] To a greater extent than in the past, the relationship with the divine became a matter of personal faith that was not directly supervised by local clerical leaders. The gradual decline of ecclesiastical power thus lessened the grip of the church over everyday life and allowed a secularized commitment to domesticity, mystery, and moral refinement to be wrapped into cultural custom rather than theological doctrine.[90]

Such cultural custom increasingly emphasized the family home as a uniquely protected physical space and also as a gendered moral space: men performed public service and economically productive work outside the home, while women worked within the home to create space for the moral education of children and the cultivation of a distinctly feminine self.[91] As one nineteenth-century proverb proclaimed, "the woman, the cat, and the chimney should never leave the house."[92] Coding the home as a space that was uniquely suited to the cultivation of *female* virtue—and coding intrusions into "female" spaces within the home as grave threats to the virtue and virginity of women—was a way of protecting women from the surrounding community but also a way of justifying their confinement to the home.[93] In the so-called "cult of true womanhood" that prevailed in nineteenth-century America and was communicated through women's magazines and the seminars of a budding "home economics" movement, women were frequently "the hostage in the home."[94]

Within the home, spatial divisions also increased throughout the nineteenth century. Bedrooms and bathrooms were partitioned off, sometimes by simple curtains and often by walls and doors. In more affluent homes, bedrooms and parlors were increasingly placed at opposing ends of a building or, when more than a single story was constructed, separated by a staircase. This growing spatial differentiation—and the gradual sequestering of bodily functions and sexual intercourse—gave material form to the social valuation of the nuclear family and the different roles assigned to various family members. While it had not been uncommon in the eighteenth century for children to be physically present while their parents engaged in marital intercourse or extramarital adultery, the sex life of adults gradually receded from view and the practice of bed-sharing among adults became less common.[95] Writing in 1890 in *Scribner's Magazine* under a pseudonym, the American essayist Alice French captured these cultural currents when she noted that privacy was "one of the luxuries" of modern society because it presupposed a shift from communal living arrangements toward subdivided single-family homes. To French, the "addition of sleeping-rooms, and afterward of withdrawing-rooms" had made it possible to "escape from the noise and publicity" by segregating families from the wider community, family members from guests, and children from their parents.[96]

THE MORAL CULTIVATION OF SELF

Privacy claims during the nineteenth century therefore differed meaningfully from those found in colonial America. They spoke to the spatial differentiation and cultural veneration of domestic life, and were in turn reified by emerging social and architectural custom. Increasingly, the family was regarded as the basic organizational unit of society and the family home as the site where the spiritual uplift of women would naturally occur and where children were transformed into little adults.[97] The privacy of the family thus mattered for two reasons. On the one hand, it protected the social integrity of entire family units. On the other hand, it provided a sheltered space for the moral and character development of specific individuals. Freed from the observation and judgment of one's peers, a person could pursue their own refinement through deliberate introspection and maintain a sense of mystery about some aspects of the self.[98] As one writer noted at the time, "the world, the state, the church, the school, all are felons whensoever they violate the sanctity of the private heart."[99]

One of the most well-known enactments of this creed was Henry David Thoreau's 1845 residence at Walden Pond, during which he used physical isolation to achieve spiritual rejuvenation.[100] But Thoreau was far from the only one to embrace such a perspective. Across the United States, writers and poets began to emphasize the autonomous development of the human soul and the unknowability of the self and treated solitude as an important prerequisite for the cultivation of one's conscience. Going in part against an established social-constructionist view of human psychology (which treated people more or less as the products of their social environments), this generation of writers drew a direct link from solitude to self-actualization and the coming-into-being of autonomous persons.[101]

American literature from this period is rife with celebrations of isolated existences and the solitary pursuit of moral virtue. One widely circulated collection of aphorisms was aptly titled "Fruits of Solitude," originally written by William Penn (the prominent Quaker and founder of the Pennsylvania colony). To Penn, shutting out "noise and talk" provided "opportunity for reflection" and "direction and advantage" for personal refinement.[102] In his epic poem *The Recluse*, William Wordsworth captured similar sentiments when writing:

> Of the individual Mind that keeps her own
> Inviolate retirement, subject there
> To Conscience only, and the law supreme
> Of that Intelligence which governs all
> I sing:—"fit audience let me find though few!"[103]

In the cultural imagination of the 1800s, the path to privacy therefore ran through such idealist notions of the solitary self rather than materialist conceptions of private property. Privacy was ultimately "a migration to solitude," as Sue Halpern has more recently written, "to that place where we are fundamentally by ourselves."[104] Even those who did not subscribe to the overt mysticism of transcendentalist thinkers—preferring, perhaps, the "frontier individualism" that took hold in the western United States— would have found recognizable elements in this celebration of introspection, unknowability, and self-reliance.[105]

EAVESDROPPERS AND GOSSIPMONGERS

The embedding spaces discussed above have already hinted at the persons against whom such a sense of privacy had to be defended: the "perennial foes" of privacy were commonly found among a person's peers. In addition to neighbors, they included spouses, friends, "the eavesdropper and the gossip-monger," and "local busybodies" who could inflict their harm only in close physical proximity and through direct personal interaction.[106] Quite literally, one had to stand "within the drip from the eaves of a house" to intrude on a person's privacy.[107] As one writer thus noted, the biggest threats to privacy came from persons who happened to pass by during inopportune moments and from "near friends [who] are too apt to assume the power of prying into and criticizing each other's hearts."[108] The *Atlantic Monthly* later summed up this view by analogizing invaders of privacy to the literary character Paul Pry, who had made his debut in a London theater in 1825 before appearing on American stages and in magazines. Paul Pry was an "inquisitive, gossiping, meddlesome gentleman," who "climbed garden walls, listened at keyholes, entered bedrooms unannounced, carried tales, and displayed a genius for upsetting the best-laid plans of the other persons in the play; and when they reproached him he suavely replied: A spirit of inquiry is the great characteristic of the age we live in."[109] Yet such eavesdropping still ran against the widespread desire "to have the temptation to talk and to look about us removed," as one writer observed in 1876 in *Scribner's Magazine*.[110] He concluded that, even in the age of Paul Pry, "we all like privacy sometimes."

Similar concerns had already existed during the eighteenth century, especially among social elites. In 1729, Benjamin Franklin had authored an article (under the pen name "The Busy-Body") for *The American Weekly Mercury* in which he recounted the story of a neighbor who "of late . . . makes her visits so excessively often, and stays so very long every visit, that I am tir'd out of all patience." Franklin continued: "Every person has little secrets and privacies that are not proper to be expos'd even to the nearest friend," yet, finding himself in the near constant companionship of others,

"I have no manner of time at all to my self."[111] The story itself was likely fictional, and Franklin never systematically discussed the concept of privacy. Yet his writings highlight that cultural norms which blossomed during the nineteenth century grew from pre-existing seeds when concerns that had formerly been concentrated among American elites found an audience among a wider swath of the American populace.

As we shall see in the coming chapters, intergenerational transfer and audience expansion are recurring themes in the history of privacy: when the logic of privacy was applied to emerging social problems, the arguments that were put forth about the importance and precarious state of privacy in a changing society were often rooted in the moral codes and concerns of prior generations or derived from the narrow preoccupations of social elites. The case for privacy was anchored in the past and in class-specific moral imaginaries even as it became oriented toward the future and found a larger public audience.

Occasionally, privacy carried connotations of secrecy rather than mere seclusion. Regents and rulers have long insisted that so-called *arcana imperii*—secrets of state known only to the sovereign—require close protection.[112] Since the founding of the American republic, the presumption of a public sector that is "in fact a private sector about which knowledge must not be made public" has therefore been central to legislative politics and political diplomacy.[113] Secrecy and privacy were in turn sufficiently close in meaning that Samuel Johnson's *Dictionary of the English Language* already defined them reciprocally: privacy was the "state of being secret; secrecy," while secrecy was "privacy; state of being hidden."[114]

This understanding carried over from sovereign politics into popular culture, and from the eighteenth into the nineteenth century. In William Gilmore Simms's novel *Beauchampe*, for example, the eponymous title character was accused of having "forced yourself upon my privacy . . . to fathom my secrets" and made to "bear the penalty of forbidden knowledge."[115] Yet, crucially, such affronts were unlikely to have been committed by someone acting in an official capacity. Expectations of secrecy were usually undermined by local gossip. And as long as most Americans were only "subject to the close scrutiny of friends and neighbors" and reciprocated that scrutiny "with lively interest," as the *Atlantic Monthly* noted in its article on Paul Pry, such gossip remained a relatively harmless amateur sport and "may even have a salutary social effect."[116] Gossip, like privacy, had a distinctly social function by tying together communities on the basis of whispered news.[117]

When Americans worried about intrusions by state officials and distant others before the middle of the nineteenth century, such concerns were commonly motivated by a desire to guard against theft rather than by fears of surveillance. Postal carriers were the most frequent point of contact with the world of officialdom for many Americans, and the payroll of the Post Office Department accounted for a considerable percentage of the nonmilitary federal budget. But postal delivery nonetheless remained a relatively disjointed endeavor until the 1870s. Letters sent across any meaningful distance were usually loaded into unlocked mail bags in one location, handed off to private train or carriage operators, transported into the general vicinity of their intended destination, and then left for collection at a local tavern or inn. It was not uncommon for innkeepers to read correspondence before passing it to the intended recipient, although they would likely have found little gossip-worthy material: the majority of letters written and sent in the United States during that time were filled with business correspondence, in part because those who could fluently write often confided their more intimate thoughts to personal diaries. Still, some letter writers resorted to creative measures to conceal the contents of their mail by using shorthand, coded language, and extra layers of opaque wrapping paper that made it difficult to determine the contents of a letter or package from the outside or to decipher the business information contained therein.[118]

Prominent Americans had regarded this system of postal delivery with considerable suspicion for a long time. Not without reason, Ralph Waldo Emerson had judged it unlikely that "a bit of paper, containing our most secret thoughts, and protected only by a seal, should travel safely from one end of the world to the other, without anyone whose hands it has passed through having meddled with it."[119] Many of America's early political leaders—including Thomas Jefferson, Alexander Hamilton, and George Washington—had also voiced concerns about the ability of political foes to exploit the lack of postal safeguards to gain insight into their political strategies.[120] Partly at their urging, and also at the initiative of Postmaster General Benjamin Franklin, the sanctity of the mail was anchored in postal regulations at a very early date. Post Office Department provisions that forbade its employees from tampering with sealed letters date back to the British takeover of postal administration in the American colonies in 1710 and the official founding of the Post Office Department in 1792. Yet those provisions were not regularly enforced and carried relatively low fines before the middle of the nineteenth century. When enforcement actions increased in the mid-1800s (by imposing higher fines and by introducing locked mailbags and personal post office boxes), those changes were largely motivated by a desire of postal officials to secure personal property against quick-fingered thieves. One agent of the Post Office Department thus remarked, in a book that recounted his work on the front lines of postal administration, that "the thought of robbing a letter of its pecuniary contents" sparked greater concern than "an idle or malicious inquisitiveness."[121] Many Americans who defended the sanctity of the sealed letter before the 1850s worried less about the privacy of their written communications than about crimes of opportunity as mail bags passed unguarded through the hands of postmasters, postal clerks, railroad workers, local couriers, and innkeepers.[122]

On the whole, therefore, the perceived *role* of government officials before the end of the nineteenth century was to protect interpersonal communications against theft, while the perceived *threats* to privacy came primarily from persons who already knew each other or at least found themselves in close physical proximity. The logic of privacy already structured social and spatial relations within individual families and social circles, yet it rarely spoke to the routine and illicit collection of personal data by officials, publishers, or unacquainted strangers.

CONTINUITY AND CHANGE IN PRIVACY DISCOURSE

Spatial, familial, and situational understandings of privacy survived into the Early Information Age. At no point was privacy stripped of its spatial connotations or its implicit reference to seclusion and solitude, and it lost neither its moral undertones nor its perceived relevance to the cultivation of moral virtue. This claim contradicts the common view that concerns about spatial privacy were simply replaced by concerns about informational privacy.[123] Yet no such straightforward replacement ever occurred. This becomes evident when we compare the semantic neighborhoods of privacy during successive decades, using so-called cosine similarity scores (figure 1.1). The more similar two semantic neighborhoods are, the closer the resulting cosine similarity score will be to 1. There are no hard thresholds for what constitutes a "stable" word meaning, but values around 0.9 are commonly considered appropriate.[124] (Again, those interested in the methodological details will find them at the end of this book.)

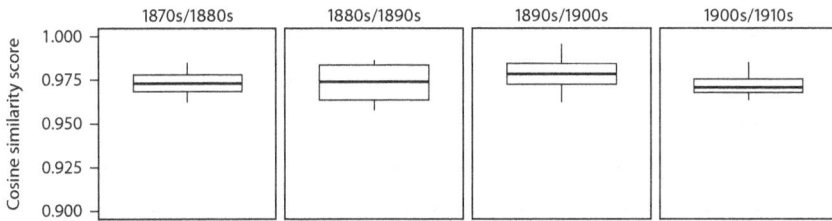

FIGURE 1.1 Cosine similarity scores comparing embedding spaces for the term "privacy" across adjacent pairs of decades. *Source*: Chronicling America.

The cosine similarity scores in the dataset of historical newspaper content easily exceed that threshold. Scores for adjacent pairs of decades—indicating, for example, how much semantic neighborhoods changed between the 1870s and the 1880s—are all above 0.95. Even comparing periods at opposing ends of the selected time window shows a relatively high degree of semantic stability, with a cosine similarity score above 0.9. The basic contours of meaning remained intact across fifty years of societal, technological, and political change.

What, if anything, changed? As this chapter has shown, privacy discourse during the nineteenth century largely sidestepped a direct engagement with structural constraints and institutional power. It foregrounded domestic spaces and the moral cultivation of self, and it focused on the sensibilities of persons and families "whose privacy is invaded" rather than on "the exercise of power," the "groups that undertake it," and the involuntary exposure of entire populations.[125] But, gradually, privacy was linked to a wider range of social phenomena (and was thereby also linked into a wider set of specialized discourses and expert knowledges) and applied to the moral and political anxieties of the Early Information Age. The capacious qualities of privacy discourse that are so familiar from the vantage point of the present—the appearance of the logic of privacy in a wide array of contexts, the focus on institutional actors and constitutional protections, and the juxtaposition of privacy against competing economic and political priorities—first took shape at the dawn of the twentieth century. This is the period to which we must now turn. As the second chapter will show, privacy became *broad* through this transformation. It remained wedded to the cultural repertoires and moral imaginaries of prior decades but was also applied to new social problems, to a wider set of problems, and to the problems of institutional action and governmental power.

2

In the Glare of the Calcium

Privacy in the Early Information Age

The new age arrived in Chicago under skies that were thick with clouds and heavy with rain. But as the city came to life on May 1, 1893, the rain stopped, the clouds thinned, and the void left by the receding mist was filled by hundreds of thousands who had arrived by foot, cart, or ferry to witness the opening ceremonies of the Chicago World's Fair.[1] Four hundred years after Christopher Columbus had claimed the Americas as a colonial possession for the Spanish Crown, the 1893 exhibition declared nothing less than "man's victory over air, earth, fire and flood" by showcasing the marvels of modern technology and the power of industry.[2] It aimed to signal, to the world but also to America's own citizens, that the United States had risen from its settler-colonialist origins and had fashioned a modern society from the raw materials of ingenuity and industriousness. At 12:20 P.M., President Grover Cleveland officially opened the fair by depressing the lever on a telegraph box, which was connected by wire to switchboards and relay stations across the fairground. A leviathan steam engine sprang to life in the nearby Palace of Mechanic Arts and soon powered thousands of incandescent light bulbs through the world's largest dynamo as the fairground began "throbbing with the pulse of the new time."[3]

Signs of this "new time" were everywhere as cities expanded, novel technologies upended many areas of life, and the United States evolved into an "increasingly knowing society" where personal information was collected more frequently by an expanding set of institutions, traveled more easily and across greater distances, and carried greater practical significance than in the past.[4] But could privacy still exist in such a society? In a two-column article, the *Chicago Daily Tribune* answered in the negative: the "veil of privacy" was precariously thin for many Americans because "tab is kept on [them] from cradle to grave."[5] To illustrate this point, the newspaper recounted the life course of a typical urbanite. Having just exited the womb, this person was immediately entered into municipal birth records. Health officials began to demand immunization against smallpox and the measles. The Department of Education sought proof of such vaccinations and tracked the young person's progress through the public school system. Degree in hand, employers began to ask for references, and landlords and life insurance agents requested financial records. Banks came calling with credit offers, made conditional on a background check. If financial hardship struck, pawn brokers recorded in-kind deposits and sometimes forwarded the information to the police department's stolen property unit. City clerks scrutinized family histories before issuing marriage licenses. Public prominence and notoriety could attract the attention of photographers and yellow press journalists, and neighbors could try to steal a glance through apartment windows. Once a year, a doctor performed a medical examination, and once a decade, a federal enumerator appeared with a census schedule. And when this person had drawn their final breath after a lifetime of examinations, the Health Department would once again appear by their bedside to duly record the moment and cause of death—the final data point of a life lived "in the glare of the calcium."[6]

The article in the *Chicago Daily Tribune* was published at the turn of the twentieth century, yet it also foreshadowed discussions of privacy from more recent decades. In 1932, the *Atlantic Monthly* echoed many of the same concerns when it linked the struggle for privacy in the modern United States not just to eavesdroppers and inquisitive peers but to a multitude of officials and professionals who had "been exalted to power as tabloid reporters, radio gossips, Sunday-supplement writers, cameramen, wire-tapping dry agents, blackmailing shysters, and back-fence biographers."[7] Forty years later still, in 1974, *The New York Times* argued that privacy was jeopardized by a cavalcade of representatives from police departments, regulatory agencies, the Internal Revenue Service, boards of health, newspapers, and human resource departments.[8] Across more than seven decades, these articles betrayed a common theme: The significance of privacy in modern life was remarkably broad, and its conceptual umbrella roomy.

This remains true today. In international comparison, the United States stands out in part for the vast range of political issues that are negotiated—and for the myriad hopes and fears that are thus articulated—through the logic of privacy. These include debates about free speech, bodily integrity, sexual self-determination, the inviolability of personal space, freedom from governmental and corporate surveillance, protections against reputational harm and mistrust, and due process rights. This "sweeping" scope of privacy claims has often made it difficult to define what privacy even *is*, since the concept itself has become "so complex, so entangled in competing and contradictory dimensions" that it often appears elusive and remains exceedingly abstract.[9] More than one hundred years after the Early Information Age, privacy seems less like a clearly bounded concept than "a many splendored and complicated thing" that is perhaps best left "undefined."[10] It carries "a galaxy of connotations" and usually defies attempts to confine it to one narrow category or another, "cannot be satisfactorily defined," and can appear to be in "hopeless disarray."[11] It therefore also has the "protean capacity to be all things" to all observers, which is why more than two hundred competing definitions of privacy now exist in the anglophone literature.[12] Privacy is, in the words of author Deborah Nelson, "curiously vital but deeply paradoxical."[13]

This "hodgepodge" of perspectives is partly a product of the division of labor, as different industries and academic disciplines have pursued idiosyncratic approaches.[14] Privacy is now anchored in so many specialized bodies of knowledge that the conversation is necessarily fragmented. But the breadth of privacy claims in the contemporary United States also serves as a reminder that, as Karl Mannheim wrote, "the same concept in most cases means very different things when used by differently situated persons."[15] Privacy looks different from the perspective of a scandal-plagued politician than it does from the perspective of a welfare recipient or the executive at a technology company, and it can be placed in the service of vastly different political ideologies and partisan agendas. Views on privacy reflect the exigencies and challenges of life rather than first principles—they are constructed "from the bottom up" in ways that bespeak "concrete, historical, and factual circumstances" or strategically leverage the logic of privacy to achieve personal, corporate, or political aims.[16]

As a result of this capaciousness, the things that privacy is tasked with accomplishing are highly varied, as are the rules and customs that govern the collection of personal data, the settings where such data collection occurs, the types of information that are being collected, the populations from whom data are collected, and the motivations and justifications for doing so.[17] Definitional coherence is often only imposed from the vantage point of the present upon an unruly past, and the "collective singular" implied by the term privacy can rub uneasily against the irreducible plurality of social experience and against the manifold demands on privacy that percolate in the social world.[18] Seen from this angle, the difficulty of nailing down a general definition is a signal rather than noise. It tells us something important about the kaleidoscopic qualities of privacy in the contemporary United States and the vast number of concerns and hopes it is expected to address.

But as chapter 1 has shown, such a capacious understanding of privacy would have been relatively unfamiliar to many nineteenth-century Americans for whom privacy was commonly secured by closing window blinds and doors, thus putting a stop to potential eavesdropping and preventing unwanted intrusions by casual observers and overeager visitors. To these earlier generations, privacy primarily expressed social norms "that set and fortif[ied] the boundaries around [their] intimate lives."[19] Yet talk about domestic spaces, solitary contemplation, and rules of decorum captured merely a sliver of privacy discourses that began to proliferate in the late 1800s. As the United States evolved into an information-rich society— where the dynamic density of social exchanges increased, personal data traveled more freely, and individuals came into more regular contact with private-sector organizations and government officials—the logic of privacy seeped into discussions of urbanization, tabloid journalism, telegraph and telephone records, and medical and financial information. It related to a large range of social problems and was aimed at a varied set of public audiences.

This chapter traces the gradual diffusion of privacy across five decades, tens of thousands of historical texts, and hundreds of congressional speeches. It demonstrates how privacy became a salient public issue that incited political debate and invited legislative and judicial intervention. Discussions of privacy still touched on physical space and patriarchal understandings of the home as a protected space of moral purity and womanhood. However, at the advent of the new age that had been so proudly proclaimed at the Chicago World's Fair—and at a time when many Americans and American institutions were actively "searching for order" amid rapid change and social dislocation—it also began to offer a template for confronting the problems of modernity and the exercise of informational power by government officials and private companies.[20] As one observer noted in 1898, "numerous inventions" and "growing intrusions" had made it imperative to reimagine privacy, redefine the forces and actors that could place it in jeopardy, and manage the visibility of Americans through novel legal and political means.[21]

This diffusion occurred not just in newspapers and magazines—where the "first rough draft of history" is commonly written—but also in an epicenter of political power: the U.S. Congress.[22] Senators and representatives had long invoked the language of privacy to discuss backroom negotiations and confidential political dealmaking in "the committee room." But after the 1870s, the language of privacy additionally began to appear in congressional debates about the governmental collection and publication of income data, the enforcement of liquor laws, and the disclosure of telegraphic messages. The privacy of the home, personal data, and interpersonal communications began to echo through the halls of Congress as "a matter of momentous importance," lest the legislature allow for "the Constitution to be trampled under foot" and "for the most sacred rights to be outraged and disregarded."[23] Privacy emerged in the specialized and often theatrical environment of the U.S. Congress as a language—a rhetorical and political resource of sorts—through which questions about individual rights, bureaucratic power, American federalism, and antitrust action could be understood and addressed.

PRIVACY BECOMES BROAD

The meaning and application of many terms are considerably more fluid than their dictionary definitions would suggest. Changes in cultural custom and social organization can directly affect how those terms are understood and applied, while the act of naming and classifying social phenomena can also reorder social realities even as it describes them.[24] *How* such changes happen can be revealing. Discursive shifts can be swift or gradual, and they can come from the invention of new terms or the adaptation of existing ones to new sociopolitical circumstances. For example, public discourse sometimes evolves through vocabulary expansion, whereby new terms

enter common use and either replace existing ones or are applied to hith-
erto unnamed phenomena. The conflict that was fought in the muddy
trenches of Verdun and Ypres was generally known as the Great War until
1941 but as World War I thereafter.[25] From the vantage point of the early
1940s—after the United States had joined the Allied war effort—the years
between 1914 and 1918 appeared less like a singular "great" battle and
more like the first of several episodes of mechanized warfare that could
be sequentially numbered. Inherited designations were cast aside for new
ones that reordered the past in light of the present.

Existing vocabularies can also be adapted to new social realities. The
term "computer" was once applied to people—often female and underpaid
in comparison to male "engineers"—who solved advanced calculations
with pen and paper.[26] But with the advent of electromechanical calculating
machines in the 1950s and 1960s, "computer" gradually became decoupled
from the concept of manual labor and was instead invoked to describe the
work of machines.[27] Shifts in technological capacities compelled linguistic
shifts as new meanings were grafted onto existing terms, usually relegating
their earlier connotations to the dustbin of discursive history.

But not all evolving terms shed their preexisting meaning. Social
reformers who advocated for "public welfare" programs in the 1800s drew
on century-old discourses in economics and theology about the material
"welfare of nations" and the "spiritual welfare" of souls and applied them to
the social problems of the Industrial Revolution.[28] The concept of welfare
evolved when it was applied to new problems and introduced into new contexts.[29] It became more capacious, acquiring new connotations and new
use cases without necessarily losing the original ones, and thereby it serves
as a reminder that language does not generally follow the rule of having
"one form for one meaning, and one meaning for one form."[30] Concepts
that were once tightly bounded can become roomy.[31]Privacy, too, falls into
this category. In the late nineteenth century, something did change, and
profoundly so: the language of privacy appeared in novel contexts—and
in a much larger range of contexts than ever before—was tied to emerging
social issues, and was recast as a matter of political and legal concern.

The tools of computational text analysis allow us to parse tens of thousands of individual utterances until such a shift becomes discernible, to
specify its timing within the constant undulations of public discourse, and
to identify specific thematic associations. But whereas the analyses of the
previous chapter focused on the similarity of privacy to other terms—that

is, on identifying words that were joined together into one semantic family—the goal now is to examine shifting thematic contexts across multiple decades. Instead of identifying most-similar terms, we want to analyze the words that appeared alongside privacy on the printed page.[32]

In every decade between the 1870s and the 1910s, privacy appeared in texts about physical space and particularly about domestic space (table 2.1). There was the privacy of the "home," the "house," the "room," and the "chamber." Each of these co-occurring terms represented a physical location that offered temporary refuge from the wider world, its social obligations, and the gaze of inquisitive neighbors and relatives. There was also talk of families and friends, men and women, and wives, representing the different constituencies who could have their privacy invaded or invade the privacy of their peers and relatives. These close associations of privacy, space, and familial relationships are among the most long-standing features of privacy discourse in the United States. To a newspaper columnist or subscriber in the early twentieth century—or, for that matter, to a judge, legislator, or bureaucratic official—they would have been just as intelligible as they were to prior generations. (Supreme Court cases that affirmed the right to privacy during the twentieth century still relied on this understanding of the home as a protected space, although by then, the judicial focus had shifted from gawkers and busybodies to law enforcement officers and state officials.) Even in the Early Information Age, the language of privacy remained tethered to discussions of physical space.

However, the list of co-occurring terms also hints at a gradual broadening of privacy discourse. This process is well-known to linguists, who have shown that a single term or concept can take on several layers of contextually specific significance.[33] Before the end of the nineteenth century, privacy was discussed almost exclusively in reference to domesticity and family relations. During the 1870s and 1880s, for example, newspaper passages were filled with references to houses, homes, rooms, chambers, and doors or, more generally, places. A lady might "retire" into her room during the night. A person or an entire family might value the privacy offered by the "domestic" realm, protected by the "door" and the "lock." Discussions of privacy during this time were still closer in emphasis and scope to the conversations that had dominated during the eighteenth and early nineteenth centuries. But by 1900, privacy also appeared in passages that discussed physical spaces beyond the home and the collection of personal data. Privacy was no longer merely sought (or violated) in private homes but in "offices," "banks," and "boxes"—a reference to mailboxes that shielded letters not just from inclement weather and thieves but increasingly from prying eyes as well. It showed up in the context of "cures," "examinations," "prescriptions," "treatments," "loans," and "money." During the first decade of the twentieth century, seven of the twenty most frequently co-occurring terms listed in table 2.1 referred to medical examinations or financial transactions. Newly invented and widely adopted technologies also began to make an appearance. The telephone first entered the list of co-occurring terms in the 1900s and became a more frequent companion of privacy in the 1910s, when landlines had become widely accessible to American families.

We can pinpoint the timing and estimate the magnitude of this shift by using cosine similarity scores to compare thematic contexts across consecutive decades, shown in figure 2.1 and subset by content type (newspapers, magazines, literary fiction). Chapter 1 already introduced such scores: they are scaled between –1 and 1, with –1 indicating total dissimilarity and 1 indicating a perfect match. While scores measuring the degree of change in semantics (from chapter 1) were high across the five decades from 1870 to 1920—hovering around 0.95 for each pair of consecutive decades—scores measuring the similarity of thematic contexts were considerably lower before the turn of the twentieth century. In historical newspapers, the thematic contexts of privacy discussions shifted most strongly between the 1870s and 1890s. By 1900, new (and considerably broader) thematic contours had become settled. In historical magazines, interdecadal change was generally higher and was greatest between the 1880s and 1900s. In other words, the period of the greatest thematic fluidity came slightly later in American magazines than in newspapers. Whereas newspapers were unrivalled in the immediacy of their coverage—especially once syndicated news could be transmitted to newspaper offices across the United States through the telegraph network—magazines focused more heavily on social commentary that lagged behind breaking news and was oriented toward "translocal" communities of thought (and of thinkers) rather than local audiences.[34] Notably, cosine similarity scores were highest, and the variability of those scores was lowest, for literary fiction (ranging from 0.67 in 1870/1880 to 0.78 in 1900/1910). This underscores that changes in privacy discourse were driven primarily by an engagement with the acute (or perceived-to-be-acute) problems of modern life, as newspaper and magazine

Table 2.1 Words that appear alongside the term "privacy," grouped by decade and ranked by co-occurrence odds

1870s Term	Odds	1880s Term	Odds	1890s Term	Odds	1900s Term	Odds	1910s Term	Odds
Man	0.160	Loan	0.189	Home	0.426	Home	0.296	Home	0.292
Room	0.107	Room	0.135	Cure	0.174	Cure	0.219	Room	0.145
Home	0.097	Man	0.128	Woman	0.162	Room	0.152	Woman	0.140
Public	0.087	Home	0.119	Perfect	0.124	Woman	0.130	Cure	0.133
Intrude	0.070	Company	0.092	Room	0.116	Strict	0.111	Loan	0.129
House	0.069	Guarantee	0.089	Consultation	0.111	Absolute	0.101	Treatment	0.107
Day	0.066	Value	0.088	Relief	0.101	Rate	0.083	Absolute	0.083
Family	0.063	Reasonable	0.088	Confidential	0.097	Treatment	0.082	Box	0.080
Place	0.059	Advance	0.088	Mail	0.087	Wine	0.078	Man	0.070
Sacred	0.055	Rate	0.086	Case	0.082	Man	0.075	Strict	0.064
Life	0.054	Promptness	0.086	Physician	0.081	Loan	0.069	Case	0.056
Time	0.053	Cash	0.077	Lady	0.074	Office	0.065	Right	0.054
State	0.046	Article	0.075	Man	0.069	Private	0.064	Company	0.054
Invade	0.046	Storage	0.074	Private	0.063	Confidence	0.052	Medical	0.052
Lady	0.043	Silverware	0.070	Treatment	0.063	Floor	0.050	Examination	0.051
City	0.041	Public	0.069	Attention	0.058	Street	0.050	Office	0.051
Comfort	0.038	House	0.066	Convenience	0.058	Guard	0.049	Trouble	0.051
Secure	0.038	Diamond	0.065	Traveler	0.056	Painless	0.049	Bank	0.051
Business	0.037	Time	0.063	Insure	0.056	Case	0.047	Assure	0.051
Door	0.036	Family	0.061	Care	0.054	Letter	0.047	Pay	0.050
Word	0.035	Lady	0.055	State	0.053	Day	0.046	Telephone	0.049
Woman	0.035	Life	0.052	Strict	0.051	Doctor	0.045	House	0.048
Open	0.034	Intrude	0.051	Confinement	0.051	Time	0.044	Time	0.045
Private	0.034	Place	0.051	Female	0.050	Assure	0.043	Day	0.043

Word		Word		Word		Word		Word		Word	
Care	0.033	Woman	0.044	Family	0.050	Hotel	0.042	Special	0.041		
Faithful	0.033	Private	0.043	Address	0.049	Secure	0.042	Prescription	0.039		
Service	0.033	Day	0.040	Loan	0.049	Service	0.041	Service	0.037		
People	0.032	Mail	0.040	Time	0.046	Guarantee	0.041	Hair	0.036		
Party	0.032	Secure	0.039	Car	0.045	Trial	0.038	Floor	0.036		
Friend	0.032	Perfect	0.038	Doctor	0.045	Professional	0.036	Family	0.036		
Desire	0.032	Comfort	0.037	Disease	0.045	Family	0.035	Money	0.035		
Domestic	0.031	Address	0.035	City	0.043	House	0.035	Question	0.033		
Night	0.031	Invade	0.035	Absolute	0.043	Examination	0.034	Public	0.033		
Retire	0.030	Office	0.034	House	0.041	Open	0.033	World	0.033		
Country	0.030	Fee	0.033	Adopt	0.041	City	0.033	Trial	0.033		
Hotel	0.028	President	0.031	Comfort	0.041	Life	0.033	Place	0.032		
Lock	0.028	Consultation	0.031	Rate	0.040	Pierce	0.032	Amount	0.031		
Right	0.027	Strict	0.031	Require	0.040	Comfort	0.032	Work	0.031		
World	0.026	Open	0.031	Day	0.039	Telephone	0.031	Lady	0.031		
Street	0.025	People	0.029	Desire	0.039	Physician	0.031	Jewelry	0.031		
Chamber	0.025	Night	0.029	Aid	0.038	Car	0.031	President	0.030		
Letter	0.025	Order	0.029	Hospital	0.038	Term	0.031	Doctor	0.029		
Strict	0.025	Confidential	0.028	Disorder	0.036	Perfect	0.031	Hemorrhoid	0.029		
Contract	0.025	Desire	0.028	Avoid	0.035	Relief	0.030	Advice	0.029		
Wife	0.024	State	0.028	Place	0.033	Work	0.030	Porch	0.029		
Paper	0.024	Hotel	0.028	Secure	0.033	Insure	0.030	Paper	0.029		
Hand	0.024	Present	0.027	Sympathy	0.033	Public	0.030	Guarantee	0.029		
Secret	0.023	World	0.027	Funeral	0.033	Confidential	0.030	Rate	0.028		
Name	0.023	West	0.027	Letter	0.032	Package	0.030	Open	0.028		
Young	0.023	Door	0.027	North	0.032	Hold	0.029	Rectal	0.028		

Source: Chronicling America.

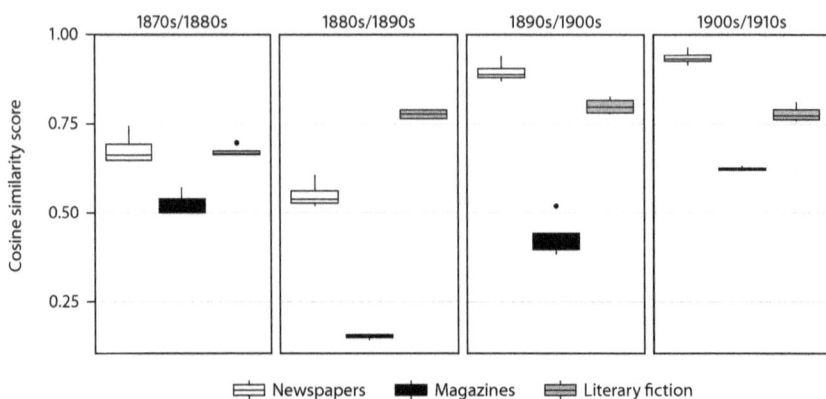

FIGURE 2.1 Cosine similarity scores comparing co-occurrence spaces for the term "privacy" across adjacent pairs of decades. *Sources: Chronicling America; Corpus of Historical American English.*

writing tends to engage more speedily and more directly with such issues than literary fiction.

The shift was gradual but undeniable. At the turn of the twentieth century, privacy was still linked to the physical space of the home and the social space of the family. But it also had a greater bearing on visibility *outside* the home and the personal data of *individuals.* In a world where such data traveled more easily, more widely, and through a greater variety of channels than in the past, the struggle for privacy was neither merely a family affair nor simply a matter of closing doors and windows.

This shift was amplified by structural changes in the newspaper industry. The prominence of classified ads increased during the late nineteenth century as the economics of retail capitalism and for-profit journalism evolved. A growing number of consumer-facing businesses began to rely on mail-order catalogues and classified ads to expand their customer base, gradually integrating regional markets and turning participation in the consumer economy from a hyperlocal affair into a long-distance endeavor. In Chicago, for example, Richard W. Sears and Alvah C. Roebuck transformed a local jewelry business into a powerful retail machine that sold anything from household goods and kitchen appliances to bicycles and groceries and generated $750,000 in annual sales by 1895 (equal to around $28 million in 2024): the Sears Corporation. At the same time, news publishers began to shift their primary source of revenue from newspaper sales to advertisements, and total advertising volume in the print industry increased more than 50 percent between 1890 and 1900 alone.[35]

Starting in the 1880s, such advertisements made increasingly liberal use of the language of privacy to sell anything from home loans and mailboxes to miracle cures and tinctures that could be taken in "the privacy of the doctor's office" to address a wide range of ailments, including socially stigmatized venereal diseases, female wrinkles, and male baldness. A doctor in San Francisco offered to cure "the liquor habit" while also promising "strictest privacy" about an addiction that was commonly regarded as a sign of irresponsibility and immorality. A real estate developer in the "most ideal residential section of Brooklyn" advertised "all of the privacy of the one-family house" but the conveniences of a larger apartment building. Union Pacific Railroad sold "excursions to California and Oregon" with the comfort and "utmost privacy" of partitioned railcars. And banks across the United States began to emphasize the "strict confidentiality" and "privacy" of their financial transactions and credit offerings, suggesting that "business privacy is an essential element of success both for the small organization and the larger undertaking" (figure 2.2).[36]

It is perhaps tempting to dismiss such advertisements as data noise because they do not fall into the category of public discourse as it is commonly understood: they do not craft an elaborate argument and may not appeal to the faculties of reason. But advertisements provide an important signal nonetheless. Framing products or services in terms of privacy only made sense if potential customers were already attuned to such claims or at least willing to accept their plausibility because public claims generally presuppose the existence of a *Publikum*, that is, of an audience that takes the basic terms of debate for granted.[37] Companies could not stretch the imagination of their customers too far because people do not endlessly generate new meanings but generally invoke "shared meanings from the cultural resources available to them."[38] Advertisements tend to appeal to a shared cultural stock of ideas and ideologies and usually maintain rather than subvert the commonsensical.[39] They are lagging indicators that the logic of privacy had broadened considerably from its midcentury incarnation. It may not have offered tangible material benefits for a majority of Americans, as the *Atlantic Monthly* noted in 1900, but it could certainly be put into service by entrepreneurs who correctly read the prevailing cultural currents and pitched their services accordingly.

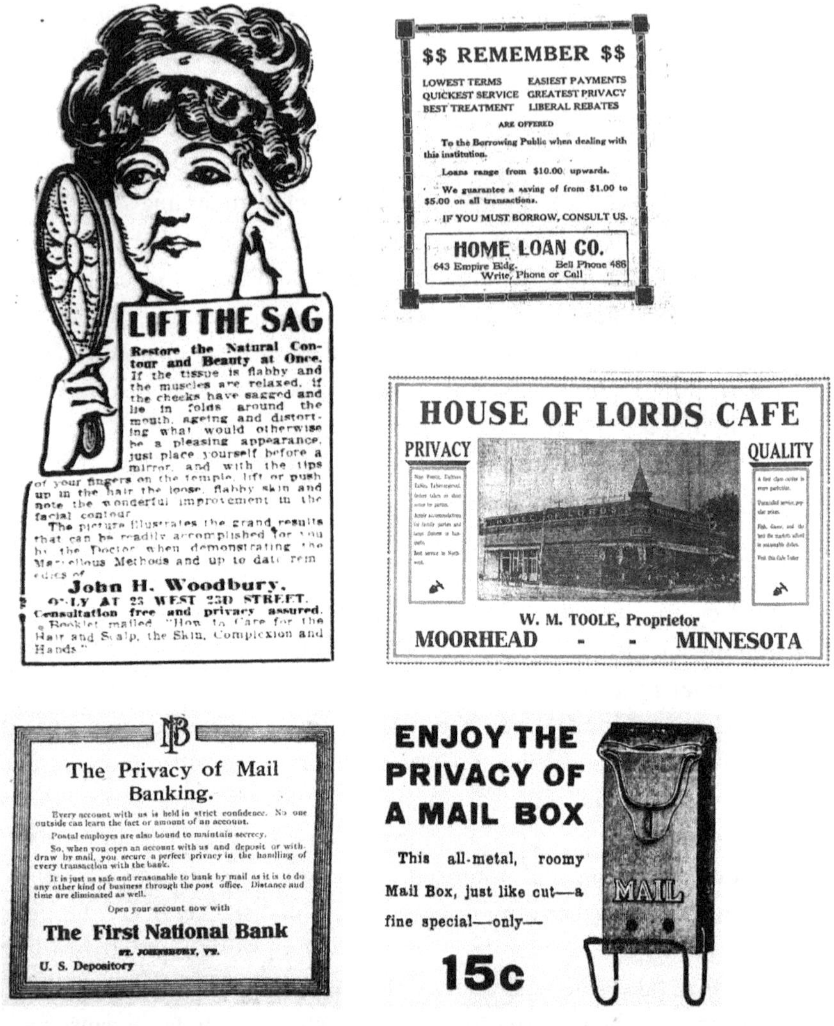

LIFT THE SAG

Restore the Natural Contour and Beauty at Once. If the tissue is flabby and the muscles are relaxed, if the cheeks have sagged and lie in folds around the mouth, ageing and distorting what would otherwise be a pleasing appearance, just place yourself before a mirror, and with the tips of your fingers on the temple, lift or push up in the hair the loose, flabby skin and note the wonderful improvement in the facial contour.

The picture illustrates the grand results that can be readily accomplished for you by the Doctor when demonstrating the Marvellous Methods and up to date remedies of

John H. Woodbury,
ONLY AT 23 WEST 23D STREET. Consultation free and privacy assured. Booklet mailed "How to Care for the Hair and Scalp, the Skin, Complexion and Hands."

$$ REMEMBER $$

LOWEST TERMS   EASIEST PAYMENTS
QUICKEST SERVICE GREATEST PRIVACY
BEST TREATMENT LIBERAL REBATES

ARE OFFERED

To the Borrowing Public when dealing with this institution.

Loans range from $10.00 upwards.

We guarantee a saving of from $1.00 to $5.00 on all transactions.

IF YOU MUST BORROW, CONSULT US.

HOME LOAN CO.
643 Empire Bldg.   Bell Phone 488
Write, Phone or Call

HOUSE OF LORDS CAFE

PRIVACY   QUALITY

W. M. TOOLE, Proprietor
MOORHEAD   -   -   MINNESOTA

The Privacy of Mail Banking.

Every account with us is held in strict confidence. No one outside can learn the fact or amount of an account.

Postal employes are also bound to maintain secrecy.

So, when you open an account with us and deposit or withdraw by mail, you secure a perfect privacy in the handling of every transaction with the bank.

It is just as safe and reasonable to bank by mail as it is to do any other kind of business through the post office. Distance and time are eliminated as well.

Open your account now with

The First National Bank
ST. JOHNSBURY, VT.
U. S. Depository

ENJOY THE PRIVACY OF A MAIL BOX

This all-metal, roomy

Mail Box, just like cut—a

fine special—only—

15c

FIGURE 2.2 Classified advertisements from *The New York Tribune* (*top left*), *The St. Johnsbury Caledonian* (*bottom left*), *The Clarksburg Daily Telegram* (*top right*), *The Jeffersonian* (*center right*), and *The Chattanooga News* (*bottom right*). *Source: Chronicling America.*

Other changes in privacy discourse were precipitated by emerging technologies. Already in 1853, twenty different companies had operated more than twenty-three thousand miles of telegraph wire in the United States, and the first transcontinental connection was completed in 1861.[40] Adoption of the telegraph then proceeded rapidly as the number of annually sent telegrams increased from nine million in 1870 to sixty-three million in 1900 and Western Union established a de facto monopoly over long-distance electronic communications (figure 2.3).[41] The telegraph became a powerful technology of long-distance communication and commerce, but one that could also be powerfully abused by a government that, in the words of U.S. Senator James Bailey, "interposes in our domestic life and enters into the very privacy of our homes" and "regulates the relations of husband and wife, of father and child, of neighbor and neighbor."[42]

Across the United States, newspapers argued with greater frequency and urgency that remote communications were vulnerable to wiretapping by government authorities, editorialized that "it is difficult to imagine how a more complete system of government surveillance could be established" than through the tapping of telephone wires, and even recommended that some international cables be severed, "rather than have the privacy of dispatches hence invaded even by official eyes."[43] As the union publication *The Telegrapher* noted, "If the privacy of communicating by telegraph is to be invaded on every pretext, letters and every other mode of communication are liable to the same treatment. If private communications are thus to be proclaimed upon the house tops, if the privilege of interchange of thought is to be abridged, the liberties of the people are endangered. The secrecy of the telegraph wire must remain inviolate. It is now the great medium of communication in all matters of pressing importance. But its value lies largely in the fact of the privacy of messages."[44]

Some historians have therefore argued that informational understandings of privacy simply replaced spatial ones as Americans began to worry

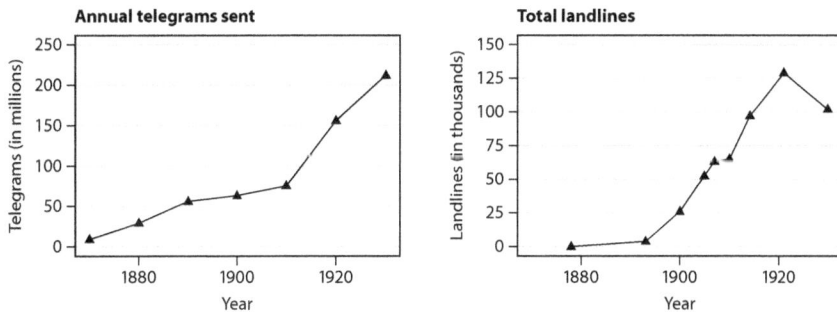

FIGURE 2.3 Telegraph and telephone adoption. *Sources*: U.S. Bureau of the Census; Hochfelder, *The Telegraph in America*; Mueller, "Universal Service in Telephone History"; Fischer, "The Revolution in Rural Telephony."

less about the sanctity of the home and began to worry more about protecting their personal information.[45] But this is not quite correct. As the lists of co-occurring terms have already suggested, privacy remained closely wedded to debates about physical space and domesticity even in the twentieth century, and the family home was widely expected to provide physical *as well as* social and moral shelter at a time of rapid social change and prevalent social dislocation—as it had for Americans in the nineteenth century. Discussions of telegraphic messages and informational privacy were additive features of twentieth-century privacy discourse: they did not replace earlier concerns about the privacy of residential space but introduced the language of privacy into new domains of public discourse (and introduced it to a new set of audiences) as Americans wrestled with the technological realities and social questions of the Early Information Age.

Yet domestic life at the turn of the twentieth century also differed substantially from prior decades. In 1850, only around 3.5 million Americans (out of 23 million) lived in urban areas. But cities grew rapidly during subsequent decades as millions of immigrants arrived in the tenement neighborhoods of Boston, Baltimore, Philadelphia, or New York. Some moved further westward, finding a home near industrial hubs like Chicago and St. Louis. New York City had around one million inhabitants in 1870; Chicago and Philadelphia surpassed the one-million mark in 1890 (figure 2.4). And

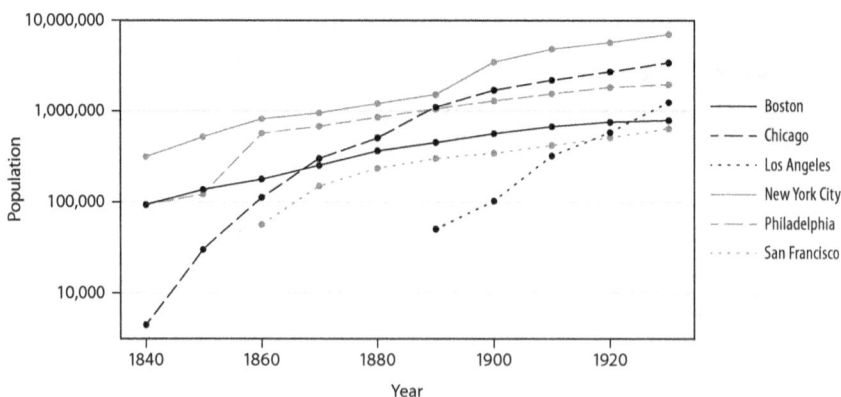

FIGURE 2.4 U.S. urban populations (with y-axis in log scale). *Source*: U.S. Bureau of the Census.

by 1920, the United States had become a majority-urban society with more than fifty-four million people living in cities.[46]

The urban apartment building became a common substitute for free-standing single-family homes. In the 1860s, for example, around 15,000 buildings in New York City were classified as multifamily tenements. But by 1900, the housing stock had expanded to 82,562 tenement buildings that collectively housed 2.4 million people—almost three-quarters of the city's total population.[47] This changed not just the distribution of populations across the vast expanses of the North American continent—more people became more concentrated in metropolitan areas—but the conditions of everyday life. "To live in a crowd has become a habit," the magazine *Galaxy* noted, as a growing number of Americans could no longer find "that secluded nook in the country profitable to mind and body" but opted "to live in communication with the public."[48] This shift in residential life was a major reason why *The Washington Herald* declared that "[we] leave each other too little opportunity to be and to act alone," or why the editorial board of *The Washington Times* noted that publicity had become "a necessary condition of existence" in the modern United States.[49] As the article continued, "Our fathers might live in a country farmhouse a mile away from their nearest neighbor and if they chose to locate their pig-sty hinder their parlor window, it concerned no one but themselves. We live in fourteen story apartments where whole communities use the same entrance and elevator and it is a matter of public concern how the house-wife cooks her dinner and hangs her clothes out to dry."[50]

Some writers welcomed the density and high drumbeat of urban life insofar as it created new possibilities for self-expression and reinvention. It offered an escape from small communities "in which everybody's life is very carefully inspected and registered by a small circle of neighbors."[51] But many came to regard the American city as the harbinger of increased and involuntary exposure that subjected its residents to the pressures of overcrowding and the casual gaze of a community that was often orders of magnitude larger than in a small town. The growth of cities had placed an increasing number of Americans in the immediate vicinity of relative strangers, breaking the bonds of familiarity and kinship that tied together many rural communities. As one observer later noted, the possibility of privacy in such cities hinged not simply on the ability to hide sensitive and intimate discussions behind closed doors but on "the present social conditions" more generally.[52]

In this social environment, the case for privacy was often a conservative one. It analogized privacy and domesticity and linked domesticity to
a sense of moral purity that appeared to be under siege by the forces of
modernity. Writing in an 1889 edition of *Scribner's Magazine*, one observer
suggested that the "removal from immoral tendencies" was best pursued
through the "adornment of domestic life."[53] Or as *The Kenosha Telegraph*
from Wisconsin argued, "in the great ocean of humanity that floods our cities, thousands upon thousands have no home, no family ties, no hallowed
recollections to render near the family fireside." The article continued: "A
true family . . . reposes upon love and religion; it is nurtured by traditions
of honor and virtue; and the symbol of its permanence is the home owned
and transmitted from generation to generation. The poor and the laboring
classes of our great cities have no homes. Hired rooms which are changed
from year to year are not homes. The operative's cottage, without yard or
garden, without flowers or privacy, is not a home."[54]

If the home and the routines of domestic life represented "the nucleus
and source of all inward happiness and higher development of character,"
the buzz of city life and the itinerant lifestyle of urban residents were not
just byproducts of progress or (less favorably) conduits for the spread of
infectious disease. They also posed a threat to the moral fabric of American
society by undermining the integrity of the family home and the privacy
of domestic life. *The Bossier Banner*, a Louisianan newspaper, thus noted,
"One of the saddest features of our modern life is the tendency which
it creates to shatter and scatter these precious home jewels. Fierce and
destructive excitements and the constant friction of outward business and
social activity are slowly consuming the sanctity and the sweetness of the
retirement and the privacy of home."[55] As more and more people crowded
into each city block—particularly in places like New York City's Lower East
Side or around the stockyards and factories of Chicago's Bridgeport neighborhood—it became difficult to ignore the challenge of securing privacy
in distinctly urban spaces. While the right to personal property remained
"stoutly defended against all forms of attack from without," life within the
home was allegedly "crumbling to ruin from the deadly influences which
are permitted to spring up and grow inside the inclosure."[56]

As the previous chapter has already shown, this idolization of the home
as the sanctum of privacy and a source of moral purity had historically
been gender-biased, with a disproportionate emphasis on female sensi-
bility and moral purity. The gendering of privacy did not end with the

advent of the Early Information Age. Writers continued to claim that the home was a "woman's kingdom" and should be "the choice garden spot of the soul, the nursery of every virtue, public and private, and the earthly paradise of affection and refined enjoyment."[57] This moralizing association of femininity and domesticity was also still reflected in the organization of economic activity, with men "[producing] goods in the public sphere downtown" while women "reproduced labor in the private sphere of the home."[58] Especially at a time when female labor force participation rates were increasing and calls for women's public representation and voting rights grew louder, privacy thus continued to proffer a logic that could be drawn upon to defend the confinement of women to the domestic realm.[59] When viewed from the perspective of wives and daughters, privacy was therefore as much about offering protection against unwanted social obligations as it was about limiting their public visibility under the guise of moral worth and spiritual refinement. As the social reformer Thomas Wentworth Higginson wrote in an 1881 essay in defense of women's education and literacy, "the opinion dies hard that [the woman] is best off when least visible."[60]

However, women featured in the privacy discourse of the Progressive Era not just as precarious creatures in need of shelter and protections but also as potential intruders into male-dominated physical and social spaces, allegedly giving men "no chance to escape from the persistence of feminine society."[61] William Conant Church, who rose to fame as an enterprising journalist before cofounding both the National Rifle Association and the Metropolitan Museum of Art in New York, made liberal use of this argument in an essay against the suffragette movement.[62] Condemning competition for the audience's attention as "an insolence which is only worse in a woman than in a man," he argued that political speeches by women constituted a double affront: they forced women out of the domestic realm for which they seemed to be predestined, and they forced female agitation upon an unsuspecting (male) audience that had to consume it in public. The logic of privacy may have been applied to the emerging social realities of an urbanizing nation—and may have promised to liberate Americans from the gaze of their peers and neighbors—, yet the "sacred privacy of women" in the modern American city was often the antithesis of female liberation.

There is, however, a caveat to this story. Around the turn of the twentieth century, the language of privacy remained clearly *gendered*, but it also lost some of its female *gender bias*. We can capture this subtle difference by considering the gender association of privacy discourses and their so-called embedding bias across five decades. Gender associations measure the average vector distance of the term privacy to an explicitly gendered list of vocabulary words like woman, man, wife, husband, female, male, and the like. Embedding bias then subsets this list by gender (which during the late nineteenth century implied a binary distinction of "male" and "female"), comparing the similarity of privacy to male-coded and female-coded terms. A positive embedding bias therefore suggests that privacy was predominantly associated with discussions of women, femininity, and female gender norms.

The data, shown in figure 2.5, suggest a continued *association* of privacy with gendered terms, coupled with a decreasing female gender *bias*. As privacy became broad, it became tied to the lived experience and visibility of men as well as women. As the presumed heads of households in a patriarchal society, men provided much of the information that was increasingly sought by local officials and business owners. Financial loans and rental contracts required them to give testimony about their finances, and census forms had to be filled out. Given the gender norms and uneven distribution of labor within the average American family, the politics of visibility and the collection of data about individuals and families were experienced very differently, but in a similarly acute manner, by men and women. Privacy therefore became broad in a double sense: it was linked to a wider range of issues—from concerns about familial privacy in an increasingly urban society to debates about medical and financial information and

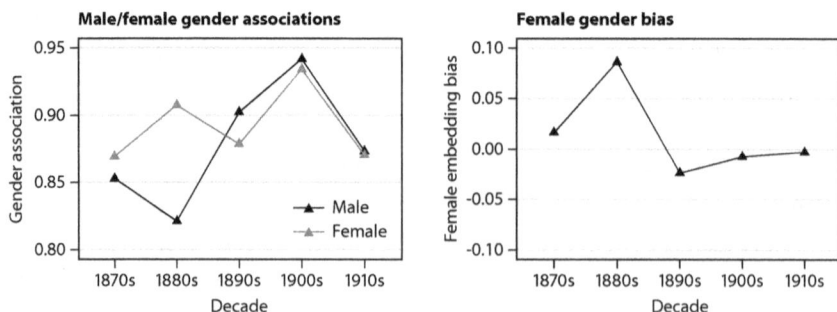

FIGURE 2.5 Gender associations and female gender bias of the term "privacy" by decade. *Source: Chronicling America.*

telecommunications technologies—and also spoke explicitly to the lived experiences of, and social expectations for, a more diverse public.

PRIVACY BEFORE CONGRESS

The diffusion of privacy was mirrored in the halls of American political power.[63] Before the mid-1870s, references to privacy in congressional debates were relatively rare and usually limited to casual mentions of the "privacy of the committee room" and of representatives' offices. Politicians claimed privacy primarily for themselves—rather than debating privacy in society writ large or framing it as an issue of constitutional significance—especially when sensitive political negotiations and information related to national security and diplomatic relations had to be shielded against political rivals and when newspaper articles about political horse-trading and secret backroom deals could have exposed members of Congress to unwanted scrutiny. Senator Allen G. Thurman spoke for many of his colleagues when he argued in 1873 that the art of politics "can only be done in the privacy of a committee room or of a library or a closet" and not in the "open Senate."[64] Yet during subsequent decades, that same language increasingly appeared in discussions of telegrams (in the late 1870s), government invasions of private homes through warrantless searches (starting in the 1880s and continuing through the 1920s), and income data collection by the Internal Revenue Service and the Census Bureau (also in the 1880s).

Debates over telegraphic privacy were an early example of this shift. Already in 1861, the Lincoln administration had ordered the seizure of telegrams in many American cities—especially those located along the military frontier—to suppress the spread of treasonous information and guard military secrets during the Civil War.[65] But back in Washington, Lincoln faced a divided Congress, where charges of executive overreach and usurpations of power spilled into the open and alliances largely broke down along partisan lines. Republicans loyal to Lincoln defended the use of extraordinary measures during a time of national crisis. But antiwar Democrats like the Ohioan Representative Clement Vallandigham—widely known for arguing that antislavery legislation violated the basic principles of American federalism—also rose before Congress to condemn "this wide breach of the Constitution" and attacked Lincoln for having "seized and carried away [telegraphic messages] without search warrant, without probable cause, without oath and without description of the places searched or the things to be seized." Vallandigham warned of a slippery slope that began with governmental violations of telegraph privacy but could end with searches and seizures "of the public mails" and the "drawers and the secretaries of the private citizens" that were as tyrannical "as in the worst days of English repression."[66]

Such arguments tied "the privacy of the telegraph" and "the sanctity of the person" to constitutional principles rather than the self-interest of politicians bent on avoiding public scrutiny. They articulated a vision of privacy that was less concerned with the Paul Prys of this world and more concerned with governmental excess and the prerogatives of executive power. And they highlighted that debates about informational privacy were, in fact, about much more than privacy itself. Those who supported Lincoln's agenda could point towards the exigencies of wartime governance and expansive theories of presidential power to justify the seizure of the telegrams; while those who supported the Confederate cause could invoke claims about the privacy of telecommunications to advance a more general defense of Southern self-determination. From the moment it entered the lexicon of American politics, defenses and critiques of privacy were hitched to a multitude of political ideologies and partisan agendas.

Governmental efforts to seize telegraphic messages were initially limited to wartime emergencies, and laws against wiretapping even came to be "regarded as obsolete" in the immediate wake of the Civil War, according to an 1866 report published in *The New York Times*.[67] However, this began to change as telegraph networks expanded during the 1860s and 1870s. Initiatives that were pioneered during a military emergency became templates for the handling of sensitive or personal data during peacetime and concerns over the privacy of personal communications spilled over into the postwar era. During the impeachment trials of President Andrew Johnson in 1968 and of Secretary of War William Belknap in 1876, members of the House of Representatives demanded access to personal messages in the hope of finding evidence of illicit dealmaking. In 1873, Congress also sifted through three-quarters of a ton of telegrams in search of incriminating evidence about the sudden and destabilizing bankruptcy of the railroad and lumber financier Jay Cooke during the Panic of 1873.[68]

These congressional attempts to force the "wholesale seizure" of telegrams partially reflected attempts by the Senate and the House of Representatives to reclaim power from the executive branch in the wake of the Civil War through the establishment of investigative committees.[69] But they also evinced a growing sentiment that the inviolability of the telegraph was, politically speaking, a double-edged sword. On the one hand, the privacy of interpersonal communications had been deeply engrained since the establishment of the U.S. Postal Service under Benjamin Franklin in 1775 and the ratification of the Fourth Amendment in 1791. But on the other hand, congressional delegates became increasingly concerned that rival politicians and industrial titans could invoke this privacy doctrine to evade unwanted oversight and protect themselves against congressional investigations of fraud and misconduct. During the impeachment hearings of Andrew Johnson, for example, only a single member of the House of Representatives lodged a complaint against congressional seizure of telegraphic messages, which he condemned as an "outrage upon private life and liberty."[70]

The argument that politicians could have *too much* privacy and invoke the privacy of their telecommunications as a protective shield against democratic oversight became particularly significant during investigations of electoral fraud after the 1876 presidential election. The election had pitted the Democratic candidate Samuel Tilden against the Republican Rutherford B. Hayes, and it had been extraordinarily close. Three days after the polls closed, Tilden had seemed like the likely victor, falling one vote short of a majority in the Electoral College. But up to twenty electors were contested, and accusations of electoral fraud and bribery were widespread. In response, Congress established a bipartisan commission to probe for irregularities in Oregon and Louisiana. One of the claims the commission sought to investigate—also fanned by the publication of several articles in *The New York Tribune*—was whether party officials had used coded language in telegrams to promise bribes and extract favors from state officials who oversaw the election. To do so, members of the commission proposed the seizure of telegrams that had been sent and received by those officials.

Local telegraph operators and Western Union's leadership initially refused to furnish the relevant messages, arguing that they were "strictly private and confidential" and could not be disclosed.[71] Attention soon turned to whether Congress could force Western Union to comply with the commission's request for access, and partisan splits emerged during a congressional debate in January 1877. On one side of the aisle were politicians like the Oregonian Senator James K. Kelly, who argued that "there is no reason why telegraphic communications should not be made public," since "it is a wellknown principle of law that written communications, however confidential they may be, can be required to be produced in a judicial tribunal." The "new-fangled sentimentality about the sanctity of telegraphic messages" needed not prevent the investigation of potential crimes and the uncovering of political rot.[72] But on the other side were congressmen like Senator John Sherman from Ohio, who warned that "the Senate of the United States will not be the first to break down the ordinary barriers which respect the privacy and rights of private individuals" and argued that, at most, Congress had the authority to seek disclosure of "specific telegrams or letters that bore distinctly on the matter in issue."[73] The dispute also echoed beyond Congress, and newspapers generally sided with Western Union. They defended the "inviolable sanctity of telegrams," noted that "every person using the telegraph . . . assumes that a telegram is as free from exposure as a letter," and speculated that governmental attempts to seize telegraph messages would be "repulsive to the people in general" and violate the "most cherished" right of the people "to secrecy and privacy in inter-communication."[74] As *The Baltimore Sun* proclaimed in its editorial, "the world simply cannot afford to have the privacy of the telegraph violated."[75] While opinions were split within the U.S. Congress, the American press largely regarded the seizure of telegrams as "an outrage upon the liberties of the citizen which no plea of public necessity can justify."[76]

In the decades that followed, congressional discussions of privacy broadened further. Sometimes the occasions were rather arcane. In 1880, Congress took up a bill about water management in Washington, DC. The city had made plans to expand its sewer system, but municipal administrators had become concerned that an estimated fifteen million gallons of daily throughput would overwhelm the mainlines and drain local reservoirs. One solution, written into a draft bill, was to install water meters (so that residents could be charged for the amount of water they consumed) and to endow police officers with the authority to investigate water waste through unannounced inspections of taps and spigots in private homes. As the city's chief civil engineer suggested, a dose of administrative paternalism and a strengthened police corps could prevent "water thieving" and convince citizens to "cease to infringe on the [water] rights of others."[77]

Yet the bill was met with strong opposition. Senator Daniel W. Voorhees rose before his colleagues to proclaim that "I should not want a policeman to come to my room" and "invade the privacy of my home on his mere volition and will."[78] He concluded that water waste policing would "insult and outrage the sense of propriety, decency, and security of every family in the city." The controversy was eventually defused when Senator Roscoe Conkling proposed to amend the bill to specify that "no such entrance shall be made into any dwelling-house without the consent of the occupant."[79] Conkling's amendment resolved an emerging tension between administrative authority and citizens' privacy claims through the expansion of procedural guardrails. But it also exemplified a growing recognition that privacy could be placed in jeopardy not just by the actions of eavesdroppers and busybodies but through interventions in private life by public authorities, most notably the American state.

Similar concerns echoed through other congressional debates. In July 1880, a proposal in the House of Representatives to abolish the Internal Revenue Service as a "relic of the war and no longer necessary" almost immediately sparked calls for additional amendments that would dismantle other forms of taxation as well, including "any internal taxes on spirits distilled from apples, peaches, and other fruits." The federal government had taxed liquor production in one form or another since the introduction of the whiskey tax in 1791 (which helped to finance military expenditures during the Revolutionary War), but the taxes had remained highly unpopular. Picking up on such popular discontent, the proponent of the brandy tax repeal framed his amendment as a way of lessening financial burdens on farmers and fruit growers. Yet William H. H. Cowles, a Democrat from North Carolina, also cast the case against the brandy tax more generally as a defense of limited governance. He suggested that enforcement of such a tax required the expansion of the government's "inquisitorial branches," and he reported that his constituents had "complained of spies entering their houses and domiciles and the most intricate nooks and corners, without regard to the privacy of the home of the citizen."[80] In 1894, during another debate on liquor taxation, another member of Congress similarly complained that the "inquisition and returns of the liquor tax collector" would receive a new lease on life unless Congress abandoned plans for such taxation and thereby affirmed the "absolute privacy and secrecy" of distillers' financial records.[81] In 1902, the same logic was even applied to the governmental regulation of butter production. At a time when attention to food and workplace safety increased—this was merely three years before Upton Sinclair published his novel *The Jungle*, an indictment of poor working conditions and poor hygiene in Chicago's meatpacking plants—congressional delegates argued that legislation still had to make exceptions for at-home manufacturing, lest inspectors "go into the privacy of the home and dictate to the American citizen in what color, form, or shape he shall put his food on the table." In debates such as this one, the logic of privacy was largely divorced from concerns about eavesdropping and state secrets. Instead, it was tied into a larger set of arguments about limited governance that would, as one member of the House of Representatives put it, "keep the long, meddlesome, and greedy fingers of the United States Government out of the lard cans and butter dishes of the domestic housewife."[82]

Accusations of governmental overreach also touched on what was arguably the most ambitious administrative undertaking of the federal government during the nineteenth century: the U.S. Census. Starting with the 1870 and 1880 censuses, federal officials worked to decrease the amount of missing census data, imposed higher penalties for nonparticipation, and expanded the range of data points that the federal government collected about each American resident. The backlash was swift. As *The New York Times* noted, the newly expanded Census administration had engendered "universal suspicion," and many Americans did not trust enumerators to handle their personal data with the requisite care.[83] When the Census Bureau considered adding questions about medical conditions in the 1890 enumeration, concerned lawyers even organized a nationwide campaign that advised Americans to simply ignore the questions.[84] Congress weighed in as well, with representatives branding the collection of medical information and the introduction of census questions about poverty and criminal records by the Census Bureau as "unwarranted and unconstitutional" extensions of federal power that could be used toward illegitimate ends, such as the prosecution of petty crimes among their constituents (figure 2.6).[85]

But the most severe opposition generally arose in response to attempts by the Census Bureau to collect and disclose financial information. When census officials proposed to combat income tax evasion by making some financial records public, the initiative was quickly satirized by the press as the "new inquisition" and condemned as "a piece of offensive impertinence" and "a monstrous oppression."[86] Texas Senator Joseph W. Bailey was one of the most vocal opponents within Congress, painting a dark picture of government overreach: "I am not willing to see it said that an enumerator, too often without judgment and discretion, can be sent into every home in this land with an impudent inquiry as to the private affairs of the citizen. Such a proposition twenty years ago would have brought

THE CENSUS.

CENSUS-TAKER. "Good-morning, madam; I'm taking the census."
OLD LADY. "The what?"
C.-T. "The c-e-n-s-u-s!"
O. L. "For lan's sake! what with tramps takin' everythin' they kin lay their han's on, young folks takin' fotygrafs of ye without so much as askin', an' impudent fellows comin' roun' as wants ter take yer senses, pretty soon there won't be nothin' left ter take, I'm thinking."

FIGURE 2.6 "The Census." *Source: Harper's Weekly*, June 14, 1890.

every man in America to his feet. It would have been regarded as an invasion of the privacy of his home and his business."[87]

Bailey's counterfactual history was predicated on an anachronism: As the previous chapter has shown, defenses of familial privacy were, for most of American history, aimed at managing access by casual observers and acquaintances rather than agents of the American state. Yet his intervention still captured an evolving sense of unease about governmental data collection—which extended from the federal census all the way down to local provisions requiring "a tavern keeper to disclose the names of the lodgers or boarders in his house." That system, Bailey claimed, "is almost as unreasonable as a search and seizure without warrant."

The pushback against census enumeration was sufficient to kill not just the practice of public disclosure of census records but the entire income tax system, which was not reconstituted until the early twentieth century.[88] (Notably, congressional delegates were much less concerned about capitation taxes, which were widely implemented during the 1890s as a prerequisite for voting. These so-called "poll taxes" did not require the collection of income data and had the practical effect of de facto disenfranchising Black voters in the former Confederacy—two aspects that made them palatable, and often attractive, to legislatures during the Reconstruction era.)[89] The Census Bureau also began to exercise tighter control over the flow of census data within the federal bureaucracy. Historically, the Director of the Census had enjoyed considerable discretionary power to share records with the Internal Revenue Service, social service organizations, or the Department of Defense. Yet the bureau began to interpret its discretionary authority in a more limited fashion after the 1880s and 1890s, largely due to concerns that public mistrust in the Census Bureau's handling of personal data would reduce the accuracy of reported information. When preparing for the Thirteenth Census Act in 1909, officials still advised that "all branches of the Federal Government should have access to census schedules" but added two caveats that continue to define the approach of federal agencies to data confidentiality in the twenty-first century. First, data should only be supplied for "statistical purposes" and could no longer be used to identify individual respondents. Second, data "should not be used to detriment of persons or organizations furnishing them." As the chief statistician of the census later wrote, "as a matter of policy we ought carefully to guard against giving any one the impression that the information collected by the Census under the assurance that it will be treated as confidential is not as carefully safeguarded as it ought to be." Any requests that were not explicitly authorized by the law were henceforth treated as impermissible—an interpretation of statutory law also known as *expressio unius est exclusio alteriu*.[90] What the Census Bureau implemented and also advertised through pamphlets and even through a traveling exhibition in the 1910s and 1920s, was therefore an improved safeguarding of personal records that were already in governmental custody, rather than a reduction in data collection.

Many of these congressional debates turned on the privacy of individual citizens and small business owners. However, in several instances—less common, but not necessarily less consequential—congressional debates elevated the alleged privacy of *corporate* records to the fore of political discourse, especially during several waves of antitrust legislation in the late nineteenth and early twentieth centuries. During debates about the Interstate Commerce Act in 1887, which relied on the Constitution's interstate commerce clause to regulate railroad rates and thereby curtail the price-setting power of private-sector monopolists, several delegates condemned governmental interference in the rail industry as the beginning of a "system of espionage upon all of our business enterprises" that threatened to "destroy all the sacred attributes and privacy that belong to the business of the successful people in this country."[91] Similar arguments reappeared during subsequent discussions of the Hepburn Act, which expanded federal oversight of railroad pricing (and attracted the ire of wealthy industrialists, who worried about political interference in rate-setting and the mandatory disclosure of railroad finances), although, by that time, Progressives like Idaho Senator William Borah were ready to counter that "the plea of business privacy has been driven too hard. . . . The men who have wealth must not hide it from the taxgatherer and flaunt it on the street."[92] But at a time when the modern American corporation emerged as a distinct economic and legal entity—and also at a time when courts routinely wrestled with questions about corporate personhood and the extension of individual rights to firms—claims about the "inquisitorial powers" of the American state extended not just to family homes and personal communications, but also to corporate financial records. (A similar conflation of personal and corporate claims also proliferated in other areas of jurisprudence: In the 1890s, American courts adjudicated cases based on the Fourteenth Amendment—which spells out the right to due process and the equal protection clause—largely without differentiating between the rights of individuals and the rights of firms, backed in part by legal theories "that emphasized corporate connections to natural persons.")[93]

This corporatist interpretation of privacy ultimately receded into the background. Especially after the turn of the twentieth century, judges and politicians became more receptive to the argument that privacy rights were specifically bestowed upon individual persons, who enjoyed a reasonable expectation of privacy in relation to personal writings, interpersonal communications, and images.[94] Firms had control over proprietary information but no corresponding right to privacy.

Nonetheless, discussions of privacy in the American press and among members of Congress had by the 1920s become more varied in their form and more expansive in their scope than ever before. They touched not just on domestic life and the illicit behavior of casual observers but problematized the deleterious consequences of urbanization, technological innovation, and bureaucratic rule for the privacy of individuals. New possibilities for exposure bred salient concerns about privacy. The following chapters will scrutinize the intellectual, political, and judicial struggles that arose in response to this tension. Such struggles pushed claims about the inviolate nature of the individual self to the fore of privacy discourse, anchored social reform movements, triggered legislative action, attracted growing interest and scrutiny from judges, and affected how the American state leveraged personal information to govern through tumultuous times. Privacy still spoke to the organization of physical and social space in everyday life. But across several transformative decades, it also evolved into a durable feature of the institutional fabric of American society.

3

The Chief Curse of the Tenement

Moral Anxieties and the
Codification of Privacy in Urban Life

T he Early Information Age was marked by great optimism and an almost fervent belief in the possibility of progress. But as the nineteenth century drew to a close, the newfangled forces of modernity also left American society with enduring inequalities and pervasive anxieties about the future. This was a time when, in the prescient words of Karl Marx, everything seemed "pregnant with its contrary."[1] The salience of the so-called "social question" increased as prosperity and poverty became concentrated at opposing ends of the social spectrum, and the modest gains experienced by Black Americans during the Reconstruction era were partly reversed through new forms of legally sanctioned exclusion that fueled a first wave of Black migration from the rural South into northern cities.[2] To the "tired climbers" who had immigrated to the United States in search of a better life or had escaped the shackles of slavery, the proverbial promised land of Canaan often remained "dim and far away."[3]

These contradictions were particularly apparent in New York City, where the glamour of the Gilded Age contrasted starkly with rapidly expanding tenement districts. Life in these tenements was sufficiently destitute "to send a chill to any heart," as the journalist Jacob Riis observed in his 1890 book *How the Other Half Lives*, a landmark account of poverty and immigrant life in the American city. Tenement life jeopardized public and personal health and often locked residents into economic deprivation and dependence. Yet "the chief curse of the tenement," wrote Riis, was a nearly complete lack of privacy that touched "family life with deadly moral contagion" and undermined the principles of good citizenship.[4] In most buildings, families and paying lodgers crowded into small apartments that lacked internal subdivisions and private bathrooms. Walk-through bedrooms opened directly into a central hallway that was "a highway for all the world by night and by day."[5] And windows faced each other across narrow alleys and air shafts, so that neighbors could barely avoid becoming intimate witnesses to each other's lives. The spatial realities of urban residential life thus turned "the smallest happenings [into] great events" as families and individuals risked becoming "lost in the group."[6]

On the morning of April 12, 1901, the representatives of New York's 124th State Assembly convened in Albany to enact a potential remedy by passing the Tenement House Act of 1901. The law was one of the first comprehensive attempts to regulate inner-city housing and would, in due time, come to serve as a template for tenement regulation across the United States. It demonstrated that the modern city was shaped as much by private investment and public infrastructure projects as it was molded by new zoning and building codes. It also marked a turning point in the history of privacy. Following years of agitation by social reformers, the 1901 law aimed not only to improve ventilation and fire safety but also to address the apparent moral ills of urban life. It mandated that apartment layouts be modified to shield bedrooms against sudden intrusions, divided residential spaces from public hallways, and forced developers to ensure the privacy of bathroom facilities. Using the stilted language common to legislative acts, it translated talk *about* privacy into the regulation *of* privacy in the modern American city, folding it into the realm of issues that were explicit targets of political mobilization and subject to governmental regulation. Privacy and public life coexisted in the modern American city not only because many Americans pursued lives of selective visibility rather than total invisibility, but also because the layouts of ostensibly private spaces were shaped by popular anxieties and legislative interventions.

Privacy became broad around the turn of the twentieth century. But through legislation like the 1901 Tenement House Act, it also became sticky.[7] The historian Richard Hofstadter has fittingly referred to this period as the "age of reform": a time when "all of society was felt to be threatened . . . by moral and social degeneration" amid rapid social change, sparking moral panics and reform campaigns that in turn fueled political mobilization and legislative action.[8] In this unsettled time, it became apparent that the protection of privacy in the modern United States required more than the closing of doors. Social reformers helped to lift the logic of privacy from the pages of American newspapers into the halls of political power, aiming to make the enjoyment of privacy—or, more specifically, the enjoyment of a particular middle-class conception of domestic privacy—less contingent on informal rules of decorum by anchoring it in legislation and in urban space itself.

This integration of privacy claims into the governance of space is an example of what we may call "moral institutionalization": the process through which normative claims about social organization are encoded in legislation and quite literally "built into the world" and thereby insulated from recurring challenges and endowed with the power to impose lasting transformations at scale.[9] Yet the passage of the 1901 Tenement House Act was far from inevitable. The bill that was placed before state legislators was the first of its kind—and one of the first attempts to codify a commitment to privacy in any kind of legislation, anywhere in the United States (two exceptions being a short-lived California law from 1899, which related to the publication of portraits and caricatures, and a congressional bill from 1887 that would have criminalized the unauthorized publication of photos of women but stalled out in the Judiciary Committee)—and it needed to clear many hurdles before it was ever debated in Albany.[10] Social reform advocates had attempted for decades to pass comprehensive tenement legislation, but each attempt had either resulted in complete failure or deferred ambitious regulation until an unspecified future date. Earlier bills also included no references to privacy but regarded improved sanitation, access to fresh air, and improved fire safety as the central pillars of the social reform agenda. What, then, accounts for the success of the privacy-focused 1901 bill?

The answer lies at the intersection of moral anxieties, collective action, and political leadership. This chapter shows that the legislative uptake and architectural codification of privacy hinged on two groups of actors that first popularized middle-class visions of domestic privacy during periods of increasing urbanization and moral panics and then forged a temporary coalition that could translate those visions into parliamentary action. In the first group were moral entrepreneurs like the journalist Jacob Riis and urban planners like the architect Ernest Flagg, who popularized privacy as a central pillar of the tenement reform agenda and propagated the management of visibility in the modern American city as a remedy to the perceived ills of urban life. In the second group were political operatives like the city bureaucrat and social reformer Lawrence Veiller and New York's governor Theodore Roosevelt, who circumvented municipal opposition and helped to secure a legislative victory at the state level. The result was a measurable—if necessarily partial—transformation of urban space. Starting in 1901, tenements in New York City began to resemble miniaturized versions of middle-class apartments, with internal subdivisions between bedrooms and shared living spaces, private toilets, and windows that interrupted sightlines between adjacent buildings. The campaigns that sparked those changes thus stand as crucial links between the cultural valuation of domestic privacy in the nineteenth century and the institutionalization of privacy in the twentieth century. They still drew on traditional understandings of domesticity to confront an uncertain future, but they also transposed privacy norms onto new social problems and catalyzed their encoding into legislation, thereby affecting the organization of space in America's expanding cities at scale.

URBAN REFORM AS A MORAL CRUSADE

Managing privacy is partially a matter of managing physical proximity and spatial access in a world that is already saturated with moral meaning. The arrangements of rooms, doors, and windows within buildings—as well as the layouts that group such buildings into campuses, neighborhoods, and cities—are snapshots of society because the built environment encases not only people and things but also a social and moral order.[11] Spatial arrangements also encourage specific ways of being in the world. They affect individual and collective behavior, shaping how we move through daily life and sustain social relations, since the layout of homes, transportation systems, and coffee houses can improve social integration or erect obstacles to meaningful participation in civic and cultural life.[12] Spatial arrangements can even leave an imprint on our sense of self. Encoded in the grandiosity of medieval cathedrals was a message about the smallness of man before God, whereas modern prisons and factories are rife with architectural features that encourage docility and deference. We are creatures not merely of habit but also of the material and social spaces we habitually encounter, which is why the built environment has the power to shape social relations and conceptions of the self through spatial arrangements, architectural forms, and the "symbolic meanings of place."[13]

The sociality of physical space helps to explain why political struggles have long incorporated claims about access to, exclusion from, or movement through the built environment.[14] Many social movements—from working-class resistance against the enclosure of the commons to campaigns against racially segregated lunch counters in the 1960s and twenty-first-century fights over transgender bathrooms—are at least in part oriented toward the ability "to lay claim to certain types of space and the power to shape space."[15]

In the waning decades of the nineteenth century, a plethora of initiatives sought to address the social problems of industrialization and urbanization by remaking the American city. Below ground, New York City's sewer networks had already grown to include thousands of miles of pipes, replacing cesspools and privately funded sewage pipes with a centralized public hygiene infrastructure.[16] Above ground, copper wires carried electrical power and artificial light into more neighborhoods, while skeletons of steel beams allowed the city to stretch farther into the sky than ever before.[17] Reform advocates within the so-called "City Beautiful" movement also aimed to remedy the real and perceived ills of urban life by upgrading streets and parks and by treating access to aesthetically pleasing "broad open space" as a catalyst for moral uplift and good citizenship.[18] But massive improvements notwithstanding, millions of lives were still spent in overcrowded tenement buildings—a term that generally referred to multiunit buildings where apartments or individual rooms were available for rent and that provided housing to many working-class and immigrant families (figure 3.1).[19]

Such accommodations existed, in varying forms, across the American continent: from the immigrant neighborhoods of South Boston and predominantly Black neighborhoods in Baltimore to the working-class districts of Chicago's West Side and parts of St. Louis. But the tenement population and the urgency of the "tenement question" were highest in New York City. Living conditions on New York's Lower East Side were abominable even by the standards of the time, leading the architect and tenement reform advocate Ernest Flagg to describe them in 1894 as the "worst curse which ever afflicted any great community."[20]

So-called "railroad tenements" had become the default model of construction in New York City after the middle of the nineteenth century.

FIGURE 3.1 New York City tenement life around the turn of the twentieth century. *Source*: Library of Congress.

A central corridor ran down the center of each narrow floor, with rooms on either side that were arranged like compartments in a railroad carriage and with shared kitchens and toilets located at opposing ends of the building.[21] Yet those railroad tenements soon became infamous as hot spots of disease, especially as the population density of tenement neighborhoods continued to increase. Early reform campaigns therefore focused on "abominable smells" and "kennel-stagnant refuse waters" and aimed to reduce the spread of infectious diseases in the city's most densely populated districts, leading to the passage of New York's first tenement laws in 1867 and 1879.[22] The most immediate consequence of these laws was the emergence of "dumbbell tenements" (named after their footprint, which vaguely resembled a dumbbell), which replaced the earlier railroad model and incorporated small interior air shafts through which air and light could reach the lower floors (figure 3.2). Yet the narrow shafts quickly turned into receptacles for trash, thereby negating their original purpose and undermining the intended improvements in air quality, while overcrowding also continued to worsen.

FIGURE 3.2
Dumbbell tenement designs introduced by the Tenement House Act of 1879. *Source*: New York Public Library.

The long-term shortcomings of the 1879 law became especially glaring when the ambitions of social reform advocates expanded despite municipal inaction. In the 1880s and 1890s, tenement reform evolved from a public health campaign into a broader moral crusade as reform advocates went into battle not just against invisible germs but against "baleful" exposure to crime, gambling, prostitution, liquor abuse, and sexual activity. If the American family was forced to "[herd] together from morning to night in almost barbaric fashion," suffering "vulgar intrusion" and showing "no respect for each other's individuality," the argument went, one could scarcely expect that immigrants would grow into good citizens, or children into upstanding adults.[23] As one prominent journalist, E. L. Godkin, concluded in 1890, "in no way does poverty make itself more painfully felt . . . than in the loss of seclusion and the social promiscuousness that it entails."[24] Or, in the words of Jacob Riis, "there is scarce a room in all the [Lower East Side] district that has not one or more [lodgers], some above half a score, sleeping on cots, or on the floor. It is idle to speak of privacy in these 'homes.'"[25]

Such views cast tenements as the anathema of decency, foregrounded the moral (rather than physical) hazards of urban life, and sought to safeguard the perceived character units of society—the family and the individual within it—by remaking residential space. To the extent that architecture and building codes mapped moral imaginaries onto this space and thereby determined the "moral condition of the family," the struggle over tenement reform was therefore not simply about space itself, but about the capacity of spatial layouts—and of urban residential space in particular—to produce certain kinds of people.[26] At stake was the moral development of millions of people in tens of thousands of buildings across New York City, who were exposed to conditions that seemingly rendered them susceptible to "moral disease," "perversions or neurasthenic tendencies," and "perverted citizenship" and thereby undermined both the "dignity of the individual" and the "security of the threshold."[27] This led *The New York Times* to conclude in an 1894 article that the success or failure of tenement legislation had begun to serve as "a propitious indication of progress toward a higher morality."[28]

Residential privacy took on particular significance in this moral crusade because the family home was a site where the tension between the "inescapable propinquity" of social life and the concurrent moral veneration of privacy was most immediately felt.[29] The rise of the modern city had brought this tension to a head. Historically, most Americans had lived in relatively small communities, and even major cities had been less densely populated. Many immigrants who arrived during the second half of the nineteenth century had a rural background as well, having left villages in western Ireland, Bohemia, or the Palatinate to seek a different life in America. In contrast, tenement residents found themselves surrounded "by streams of unknown strangers."[30] The mass movement of people into cities in the closing decades of the nineteenth century meant that people who lived in proximity or even in shared residential spaces were less likely to be linked through kinship ties or multigenerational family histories than in the past.

On the one hand, this created new possibilities for self-expression. Rural communities often blurred distinctions between private and public life because people tended to be well-known to their neighbors and faced a choice between self-regulating their presentation of self according to prevalent social norms and facing social stigmatization. (This is arguably still the case today: I grew up in a village in Germany's Rhine Valley, where a sign in a neighbor's front yard proudly proclaimed that "the Good Lord knows everything, but the neighborhood knows more.")[31] Greater degrees of spatial and social privacy—and a greater freedom to explore and express different facets of one's personality—are sometimes achievable in larger communities because "the eye of the other is less often a factor in how we behave" when social relations are more anonymous and social organization is more atomistic.[32]

This is one reason why the so-called "cult of the individual" is tightly linked not just to the increasing division of economic labor in society but also to the rise of the modern metropolis. Large and geographically concentrated communities facilitated social interdependence and supported the reconstitution of the socially situated self as an *individual self*.[33] Walter Benjamin thus wrote approvingly during the early twentieth century about the so-called "flâneur" as a creature of the modern city who could vanish amid the crowd and revel in their newfound anonymity.[34] Georg Simmel similarly observed in 1903 that the modern city "grants to the individual a kind and an amount of personal freedom which has no analogy whatsoever under other conditions."[35] For Simmel, the immersion in metropolitan life and the experience of transient urban relations allowed a person to "maintain the independence and individuality of his existence against the sovereign powers of society" to a degree that would have been impossible in smaller rural hamlets.[36]

On the other hand, the modern city also created new possibilities for involuntary exposure.[37] Multiple families commonly lived on each floor of a tenement building and multiple generations within each apartment. Kitchens and bathrooms were shared among all occupants; bedrooms were easily accessible from such semipublic spaces and from interior hallways, and economic necessity forced many families to run workshops out of their apartments during the day and to accept rent-paying lodgers at night. These spatial arrangements were a far cry removed from idealized notions of the family home as a social sanctuary, discussed in chapter 1. According to the architectural trade publication *Real Estate Record and Builders Guide*, as long as the bedroom was "next to the parlor and having no door between, but only an archway, and both bedrooms being continually used as a passageway between the parlor, and the dining-room, kitchen and bathrooms," there could be "no privacy whatsoever."[38] *The New York Times* similarly opined in 1894 that "flimsy partitions" and dual use of domestic spaces made "privacy out of the question," since "the turmoil in one family is common property of, and a most dangerous infliction upon, the rest."[39]

Two years later, the newspaper doubled down on this stance. Conditions in the city's tenements were such that "if [all residents] stood with arms out-stretched they would touch one another"—a state of affairs that entailed serious "moral ills."[40] Sexual intercourse, the beating of children, and the routine practices of everyday life could all be seen and heard from adjacent rooms and sometimes from communal areas as well, threatening to undermine moral decency among millions of urban residents. Such concerns led one writer to conclude, in an article published in the *Atlantic Monthly*, that city life should "keep as much privacy as it can; else it becomes broken and purposeless and unsatisfactory, and at the mercy of idlers."[41]

THE MANAGEMENT OF VISIBILITY AS A REMEDY AGAINST MORAL DECAY

Historians who have studied social reform campaigns of the late 1800s mainly emphasize demands for access to fresh air, daylight, and sanitation.[42] However, social reform advocates in New York City specifically demanded increased protections of tenement residents *from* indiscriminate exposure to the surrounding community, rather than merely improved access *to* better amenities. Their campaigns juxtaposed the apparent moral decay of the city against the family home as an idealized site of moral refinement, cast the management of visibility as a viable remedy against such moral decay, and thereby elevated the struggle over domestic privacy into an important pillar of the tenement reform agenda. By enclosing the social unit of the family within the spatial confines of the home and by subdividing the home internally, reform advocates hoped to create little "islands of privacy" that would protect moral virtue and the integrity of the nuclear family.[43] In the context of tenement reform, privacy became the political language through which the moral anxieties of the late nineteenth century were articulated.[44]

We can catch a glimpse of the close association between privacy and urban development by returning, briefly, to word co-occurrence patterns from chapter 2. Co-occurrence odds of "privacy" with the "city" doubled between the 1880s and the 1890s, and co-occurrence odds with "tenements" increased by one-third. These numbers are derived from models that ingest all historical newspaper data; that is, they capture patterns across hundreds of papers that often circulated far from America's major cities. This means that they likely underestimate just how closely privacy was associated with discussions of urban space.

To get a second—and more direct—window into moral anxieties and the so-called "tenement house problem," we can also turn toward the proceedings of the National Conference on Social Welfare (NCSW).[45] First convened in 1874, and then annually after 1878, the conference was one of the largest gatherings of social reformers in the United States and brought together charitable organizations, social reformers, and welfare providers from most states and many of the country's major cities.[46] By the 1880s, it had become the primary forum where questions of urban reform were discussed. It also provided an important stage for moral entrepreneurs: individuals who leveraged their often-privileged social position to speak up—with great fervor and emotional appeals—against the suffering and exploitation of those with lower social or economic status and whose voices were critical to the dramatization of social problems as moral ones, the popularization of those moral concerns, and the creation of communities of concerned observers and advocates.[47] The proceedings of the NCSW therefore provide a uniquely comprehensive window into the reform initiatives that percolated in American cities during the Progressive Era and also into the arguments through which the social problems of fin-de-siècle America were framed as urgent moral concerns.

In 1885, one speaker appeared before the conference plenary to outline the basic paradigms of tenement reform. "It is well to remember," he argued, "that the government considerations should be: first, domestic privacy, the foundation of morality; second, sanitary condition, the mainspring of health; third, comfort, convenience, attractiveness."[48] This privacy-first perspective shaped conversations about tenement reform during the 1880s and 1890s. It also focused attention on the alleged link between urban densification and moral decay. A representative from the labor organization Knights of Labor noted that thousands of working men and their families were "herded together like cattle; that children are born, live, and die in these narrow homes, where there can be no privacy, and where only by the most earnest efforts can children be saved from moral death."[49] Others echoed this sentiment, linking the "privacy of our chamber" to protection against crime and temptation and treating the "lack of family privacy, and promiscuous toilet arrangements" as architectural features that "[invited] moral temptation" and led tenement residents to "suffer from mortal disease as well as moral decay."[50] In the words of James H. Tufts, who appeared at the NCSW while also serving as Chair of the Philosophy Department at the University of Chicago, "the lack of privacy, decency, comfort, and resources" in tenement districts posed "a far stronger menace" to childhood development and familial harmony than even "the frequency of divorce."[51] In speeches such as this one, concerns about familial privacy outranked concerns about poor health and urban beautification, highlighting just how far moral entrepreneurs had pushed the tenement reform agenda beyond the scope of earlier public health campaigns and the City Beautiful agenda. By the late nineteenth century, the tenement problem was no longer understood as (merely) a matter of insufficient hygiene and sanitation but as "an evil thing from every standpoint, social, industrial and hygienic," and one of the worst features of this problem was "the demoralizing lack of privacy."[52]

If this lack of privacy was a catalyst of moral decay, spatial reorganization was an obvious remedy. Social reform advocates aimed to reorganize urban residential space at two levels: the micro-spatial layouts within buildings and the mezzo-spatial concentration of people within neighborhoods. Tenement buildings constructed in the common "railroad style" had walk-through bedrooms so that any person hoping to reach the far end of the apartment (or exit the apartment in the reverse direction) first had to pass through them. Some bedrooms were also directly accessible from hallways, with no foyer or kitchen to provide a buffer between private and public spaces. The "dumbbell style" design of the late 1870s had offered little improvement. It still had only basic internal subdivisions, and the narrow air shafts it introduced presented yet another challenge to domestic privacy. The distance between windows that had by law to be placed in air-shaft walls to improve circulation was "so slight that domestic privacy [was] destroyed."[53] When the city Tenement Commission took stock in 1900 of the causes of "grave immorality" in New York City's impoverished neighborhoods, the privacy-destroying features of the dumbbell tenement ranked high on the list: a person could easily hear "the sounds that occur in the rooms of every other family in the building, and often in these narrow shafts the windows of one apartment look directly into the windows of another apartment not more than five feet away."[54] The architect Ernest Flagg offered a similar critique, writing that "perhaps the worst feature of this vicious type of dwelling is that there can be no privacy for the family, for all the bedrooms have windows opening upon the narrow light wells, and when the houses are built side by side, each bedroom window is directly opposite to and only about 4 feet distant from another bedroom window in the adjoining house."[55]

Reform advocates proposed several remedies. They suggested that tenement construction could be modeled on middle-class apartments in which "the dining room and kitchen, together with the pantry" were grouped together at one end of the apartment while "[throwing] the family bedrooms all to the rear, giving them far better light and air as well as greater privacy."[56] One social reformer summed up the advantages of such layouts by stating that "each apartment is entered from a short private hall. No bed-rooms open into each other or into the living rooms, thus securing complete family privacy."[57] Reformers also proposed giving each apartment access to its own interior toilet—instead of having a shared toilet between adjacent apartments or one toilet per tenement floor—and to make this toilet accessible directly from the kitchen and the parlor, so that a person did not have to pass through public hallways or another person's bedroom to relieve themselves or take care of personal hygiene.[58] This would impose additional costs on developers who not only had to budget floor space but also had to run additional fresh- and wastepaper pipes. Yet to progressively minded reformers like Mary Ellen Richmond—who emerged as a prominent figure in the charitable organization movement in Philadelphia before taking over as a director of the Russell Sage Foundation—relocating toilets into individual apartments and making additional "provisions for privacy, such as inside locks [in bathrooms]" were important steps toward "health and decency" in tenement life.[59] As the head of New York's Department of Tenements later noted, "the privacy provided by the individual toilets . . . guarantees absolute seclusion."[60] Indeed, there was a pervasive belief among social reformers of the 1890s that "a private bathroom . . . and a grass-filled court would make model citizens out of juvenile delinquents and drunkards,"[61] since they helped to confine people within the "self-contained territory" of the home and the cultural bosom of the family.[62]

The second set of concerns among social reformers focused on the concentration and distribution of people in tenement neighborhoods more broadly. The journalist Jacob Riis had already identified overcrowding as a core problem of tenements in 1890, arguing that the "drift of the population to the cities is sending ever-increasing multitudes to crowd them." Where once two families had lived, "ten moved in."[63] This concern, which was less about the subdivision of space in individual apartments than about the total number of people who resided in any given part of the city, was echoed by other social reformers. Elgin Gould, a statistician who had served in the Department of Labor and the Bureau of Labor Statistics before becoming involved in tenement reform efforts in New York City, observed that "in the general herding process every member of the family, from earliest childhood, becomes an easy prey to the forces which drag down."[64] He drew a direct connection between the protection of the single-family home, which Gould regarded as the "character unit of society," and the ability to prevent "social degeneration and decay."[65] Appearing at the NCSW in 1895, the Reverend Malcolm Dana from New York likewise proclaimed that "all the privacy and sacredness that belong to home life are simply impossible in the tenements of the more densely populated wards of our cities."[66] The "herding together of such vast numbers of people" did not just enable infectious diseases to spread quickly among the urban poor but "[engendered] a train of evils" and "perversions" that undermined privacy in urban life and seemed to threatened the moral fabric of American society.[67]

Reform advocates who took this mezzo-spatial perspective generally focused on dedensification through suburban developments, where freestanding single-family homes still offered "prospects of greater privacy."[68] Ostensibly, the mass relocation of people to outer boroughs would allow the working class to pursue a life that avoided "the changed relation of the sexes, the absence of privacy, the intrusion of strangers upon the family life, the use in common of facilities of living where propriety and decency demand their restriction to a single family, [and] the constant sight and sound of debasing influences from which escape is impossible."[69]

In articulating their visions for the management of visibility in urban life, the social reformers quoted on the preceding pages responded to the specific exigencies of tenement life in the late nineteenth century. Yet they also drew more broadly on socioeconomically "situated" views of the moral hazards of the modern city and on the opinions of a newly professionalized class of urban planners that were sometimes at odds with the lived experience and practical constraints faced by the tenement population.[70] A mass relocation from densely populated inner wards toward the city's outer boroughs was economically unfeasible, given the lack of a transportation infrastructure that would have allowed workers to commute to factories and workshops. The trend was still toward a greater *concentration* of working-class people in urban centers of production rather than their *dispersion* into the urban periphery. Many working-class families also relied on additional income that they could generate from taking in boarders or by converting living rooms into daytime workshops. Yet such a calculus of economic necessity was "antithetical to middle-class notions of domesticity" and the visions of urban planners, who treated the management of visibility—rather than the eradication of economic deprivation—as a preferred remedy to the perceived ills of urban life.[71] Many working-class and immigrant residents had additionally been unaccustomed to individual bedrooms and en suite bathrooms because rituals of bodily cleaning, expectations of sociability and solitude, and distinctions between the "front stage" and the "back stage" of social life differed across cultures and class lines.[72] In practice, many spaces of tenement life were hybridized spaces that functioned as bedrooms, living rooms, or workshops depending on the time of day.

This does not mean that tenement residents opposed social reform efforts entirely. To the contrary. As the New York Department of Tenements later noted in its annual reports, private bedrooms and bathrooms became highly popular once mandated by law and even attracted visitors who marveled at the new possibilities for "privacy in city life."[73] Yet the gap between reformers' perceptions of moral ills and residents' experience of city life highlights the undeniable class dynamics of moral institutionalization. Leaders of the social reform movement and the urban planning community—the latter of which had begun to coalesce with the rise of professional training programs, starting in 1865 with the founding of the School of Architecture and Planning at the Massachusetts Institute of Technology—overwhelmingly came from backgrounds of social and economic privilege. The architect Ernest Flagg had studied at the École des Beaux-Arts in Paris; New York's first Tenement House Commissioner Robert W. DeForest served as a company trustee before pursuing public office; and "model tenement" advocate Alfred T. White was sufficiently wealthy to bequeath fifteen million dollars to his daughter upon his death in 1921. Their moral imaginaries and political demands frequently reflected the "tastes, prejudices, and worldview" of the upper social strata and romantic notions of the home "as a haven from the apparent evils of the industrial city."[74]

The "mixture of demographic types" that characterized the tenement reform movement—a privileged and increasingly professionalized cadre of moral entrepreneurs, reformers, architects, and bureaucrats setting out to uplift the immigrant working masses—catalyzed the application of such class-specific moral imaginaries across class lines.[75] This class dimension was occasionally made explicit. One social reform advocate pleaded his case at the NCSW by juxtaposing the "standards of decency you and I know of in our homes" against "the vulgarity, the sordidness, the cheapness of life where there is neither privacy nor sunlight," while the executive secretary of the Better Housing League (whose resumé included university degrees from Cornell University and the Sorbonne in Paris) contrasted the habits of the "average man" who "sits down to a good dinner, reads, plays cards, dances, goes to the theater, or listens to music until he is sleepy" against the dispositions of the "slum-dweller" who "has no peace and no privacy" and "sees no beauty and has no repose."[76] Jane Addams, an American suffragette and social worker who later became the first American woman to be awarded the Nobel Peace Prize, was most explicit: the "lower-class environment" of the tenements needed to be "made more like a middle- or upper-class neighborhood" to secure the all-important social good of privacy and thereby prevent moral degeneration among the urban poor.[77] (Several decades later, U.S. Secretary of State Henry L. Stimson still invoked this sense of bourgeois propriety when he remarked, shortly after shutting down the cryptanalytic Cipher Bureau, that "gentlemen do not read each other's mail.")[78]

Derived from the cultural norms of a bourgeois stratum of American society, Addams's comparisons suggested a vision of propriety that foregrounded mental life rather than material security and often deflected blame for destitute living conditions away from structural economic and social forces and toward "inanimate objects and the poor themselves."[79] In those instances, the so-called "age of reform" revealed itself as an age that remained prominently patterned by social class. America's privileged elite appeared intent not only on protecting its social and economic status against populist challenges from below but also on transposing its moral codes and credentialed expertise onto a differently situated populace.

FROM MORAL CRUSADES TOWARD LEGISLATIVE ACTION

By the turn of the twentieth century, moral entrepreneurs had succeeded in popularizing tenement reform as a matter of urgent moral concern; had elevated the quest for domestic privacy into a central pillar of the tenement reform agenda; and had identified the management of visibility as a remedy to the perceived moral ills of urban life. But their concerns still had to be translated into targeted political campaigns and legislative action, overcoming resistance from commercial developers. In the years and months preceding the passage of the 1901 law, social reform advocates and political operatives succeeded in building a temporary coalition that supported tenement reform at the state level and helped to generate the required legislative support. This coalition was large and diverse, but two individuals stood out for their institutional knowledge, political influence, and decisive interventions: Lawrence Veiller, the leader of New York City's tenement reform coalition, and Theodore Roosevelt, then the governor of the State of New York. Their actions (and interactions) help to explain how the logic of privacy found its way from the bully pulpit of social reform conferences into the language of the law, and thence into the built environment.

Lawrence Veiller had been raised in a devout Episcopalian household, but his political views placed civic responsibility—rather than religious faith—at the heart of American public life. After graduating from the City College of New York in 1890, Veiller had put this principle into action by joining New York's Charity Organization Society (COS) and, later, the city's Buildings Department. The work gave him firsthand knowledge of the politics of urban development and also exposed him to the deleterious conditions encountered by tenement residents. Unlike some veteran social reformers (including Jacob Riis), who had experienced decades of governmental inaction and remained skeptical that the cause of tenement reform could be advanced through existing institutions, Veiller relished the "technicalities of the political process," and he remained specifically committed to initiatives that could counter the influence of land developers over New York City's Buildings Department.[80]

He received a chance to put this approach into practice in 1898, when a new city charter established a municipal commission to revise the building code. Veiller hoped that changes to this code could become catalysts for tenement reform but also feared that the municipal commission would be subjected to extensive lobbying from land developers. In April 1898, at the annual meeting of the COS, he thus proposed the establishment of an advocacy committee that could "present united opposition to bad legislation arising either at Albany or in the Municipal Assembly and affecting the tenement house question."[81] The idea was initially voted down, but in December 1898, the COS endorsed the creation of a subsidiary tenement house committee. Veiller became its secretary and executive officer.[82]

Veiller's concerns about the influences of the developer lobby proved correct. The Building Code Commission included powerful landowners but "no representative of the tenement house interest," and it ignored COS recommendations.[83] Yet after years of consciousness-raising and campaigning by social reform advocates like Riis and Flagg, and also due to the work of organizations like COS, public support for tenement reform was high. As long as victory remained elusive in City Hall, Veiller was determined that the best path toward "restrictive legislation" and "the application of state power to enforce justice" ran through the court of public opinion and the state government in Albany.[84] His pivot toward public advocacy and state-level campaigning soon bore fruit with the city's first Tenement House Exhibition, held in February 1900 at the Sherry Building at Thirty-Eighth Street and Fifth Avenue. The exhibition proved highly popular and the ten thousand visitors who visited the Sherry Building during the exhibition's month-long run were treated to photographs, maps, and statistical graphs that illustrated "the close relations between bad housing, bad health, bad morals, and bad citizenship."[85] One of the attendees was the state's governor himself, Theodore Roosevelt.[86]

Roosevelt was no stranger to the problem of urban reform. He had first taken an interest in the "tenement problem" while serving as a state assemblyman from 1882 to 1884, when he had toured New York City's tenements and had thrown his weight behind a bill that outlawed unlicensed cigar manufacturing in residential buildings. The Court of Appeals had invalidated the bill as unconstitutional, which convinced Roosevelt that progressive reformers could not rely solely on the courts to advance the cause of urban reform. As he later wrote, "the courts were not necessarily the best judges of what should be done to better social and industrial conditions" because judges "knew nothing whatever of tenement-house conditions; they knew nothing whatever of the needs, or of the life and labor, of three-fourths of their fellow-citizens in great cities."[87] The initiative had to come from reform-minded politicians rather than judges.

After a temporary break from politics (during which he tried his hand as a cattle rancher in North Dakota) and a failed mayoral campaign, Roosevelt had returned to New York politics as the city's police commissioner and ex officio member of the municipal Board of Health from 1895 to 1897. The experience put him into regular conversation with reform advocates like Jacob Riis and also convinced him that things "were wrong, pitifully and dreadfully wrong, with the tenement homes," which he regarded as incompatible with the "exacting duties of American citizenship."[88] It also strengthened Roosevelt's impression that New York City's politicians often stood in the way of ambitious social reforms that could combat municipal corruption and lessen the misery of the masses.[89] After another stint away from New York (this time to serve as assistant secretary of the Navy and colonel of the Rough Riders regiment during the Spanish-American War), he returned in 1898 to campaign for the governorship, which he won by a narrow margin. For the first time, municipal reform advocates had a potential ally in the gubernatorial mansion who was sympathetic to their cause, attuned to the various interest groups and institutions that stood in the way of New York tenement reform, and willing to whip the state legislature to implement a progressive political agenda.

At the turn of the twentieth century, long-term social reform campaigns and a temporary opening in New York's political opportunity structure thus converged to pave the way for a new tenement law that was considerably more ambitious than earlier reform efforts.[90] Roosevelt was specifically sympathetic to Veiller's moralizing view on the tenement question.[91] The next hurdle was to convince state legislators to adopt a similar stance. Although city politicians did not openly oppose new initiatives—because they were highly popular among New York's electorate—they nonetheless exerted pressure on state legislators behind the scenes, stalling progress.[92] And there was an additional complication. Under New York state law, bills that pertained to a single city were qualified as "local measures" even if they were drafted by the state assembly. Before being put up for a vote in Albany, these bills first had to be endorsed by city assemblymen. Municipal politicians in New York planned to use this procedural quirk to their advantage, delaying consideration of any bill until the end of the state assembly's legislative session and thereby killing it.

Veiller and Roosevelt worked in tandem to navigate this problem: Veiller rewrote the tenement reform bill, while Roosevelt used his influence within the Republican Party to build support in Albany. The revised version of the bill covered all "cities of the first class" (of which there were only two: New York City and Buffalo), thereby turning it into a true state measure and eliminating the possibility of municipal stalling tactics. One lesson Veiller took from this legislative maneuvering was that "getting legislation passed to which there was opposition was very much like warfare and needed generalship."[93] An initial bill was passed in 1900 and established a state Tenement House Commission under the chairmanship of the lawyer Robert DeForest. Between June 1900 and February 1901, the commission compiled a detailed overview of past tenement reform attempts and a survey of current tenement conditions. It also organized conferences, public forums, and walking tours of tenement districts for New York City journalists.[94] By the spring of 1901, the commission published its report. Veiller was once again tasked with translating its recommendations into a second legislative bill, which he did by April 1901. The bill passed in Albany, was adopted without amendments, and was signed into law by Roosevelt's successor as New York governor—and close political ally—Benjamin Odell Jr.

The Tenement House Act of 1901 reflected the ambitions of the tenement reform movement to a greater degree than previous legislation in 1867 and 1879. Instead of focusing solely on air circulation and fire safety, it aimed more generally to contain the deleterious effects of tenement life on the physical and moral constitution of residents. The law specifically protected privacy in urban life alongside access to fresh air and safe building egress routes. Section 2 led with a conceptual distinction between public halls and private apartments. Sections 59 and 62 addressed concerns about narrow air shafts and interior courtyards, mandating minimum dimensions for each. Sections 60 and 68 regulated the placement and layout of windows in apartments that faced each other directly across internal air shafts. Section 95 mandated the inclusion of "a separate water-closet in a separate compartment within each apartment" for all newly erected tenements, and Section 100 specified that "no tenement house shall be used for a lodging house." But the most explicit defense of urban privacy came in Section 75, aptly titled "Privacy." It established that "in every apartment of three or more rooms in a tenement house hereafter erected, access to every living room and bedroom and to at least one water closet compartment shall be had without passing through any bedroom." The law spelled an end to the railroad and dumbbell layouts that had dominated in New York City since the middle of the nineteenth century by grouping rooms into self-contained apartments that could be accessed through a single front door, while doors between public hallways and private bedrooms were eliminated. Future tenement buildings would resemble miniaturized versions of middle-class apartments. Upon entering an apartment, a person would not face a string of interconnected walk-through rooms but a small foyer or parlor from which doors led into adjacent chambers (figure 3.3).

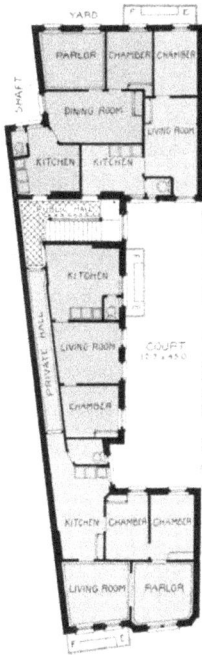

PLAN OF UPPER FLOORS

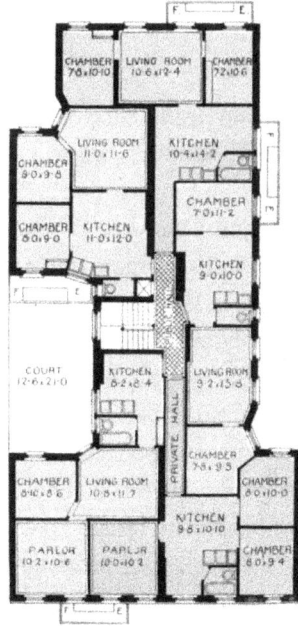

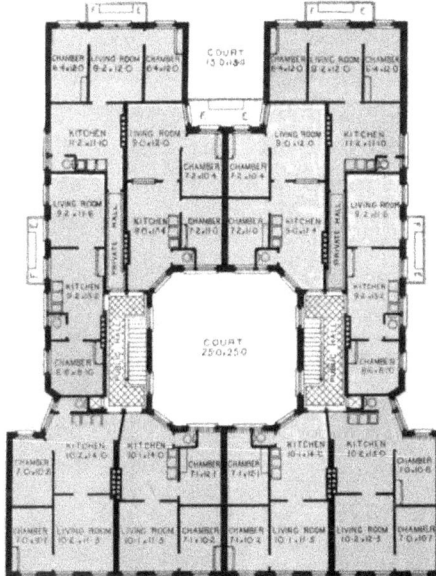

PLAN OF UPPER FLOORS

PLAN OF UPPER FLOORS

FIGURE 3.3 "New law" tenement plans submitted after the Tenement House Act of 1901. *Source*: New York Public Library.

RESHAPING URBAN SPACE

Within a decade of the adoption of the 1901 Tenement House Act, almost thirty thousand buildings were erected in accordance with the law's provisions (figure 3.4). However, it is one thing to elicit symbolic acts of compliance and quite another to ensure that legal provisions are enforced in practice because organized resistance can frustrate implementation efforts and street-level bureaucrats retain considerable discretion over the enforcement of government regulation.[95] As a final step, we must therefore assess the actual impact of the 1901 Tenement House Act on the micro-spatial organization of apartments and the mezzo-spatial concentration of people in tenement districts.

One central provision of the Tenement House Act was the mandatory inclusion of bathroom facilities within each newly built apartment. Private bathrooms can therefore serve as a useful indicator of enforcement efficacy, especially because the required underground sewage infrastructure had already been available since the late nineteenth century in almost all tenement districts; thus, any post-1901 changes in the prevalence of private toilet facilities were unlikely due to expanded sewer systems. Comprehensive construction data on bathroom facilities were only collected after 1901 by the Department of Tenements, but irregular municipal surveys from the late nineteenth century show that only a small percentage of tenement projects included private toilet facilities prior to 1901. One survey, dating to 1894, shows in-unit toilets in only 1 percent of New York City tenements.[96] Yet this number jumped immediately after 1901. By 1910, private

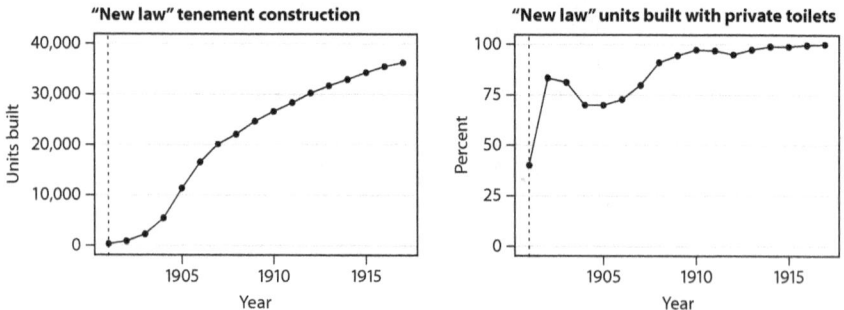

FIGURE 3.4 "New law" tenement construction. *Source*: New York Department of Tenements.

toilets had become nearly ubiquitous in newly built tenements and were present in more than a quarter of all New York City tenements. As post-1901 tenements began to account for a greater percentage of all New York City tenements, the spatial layouts of tenements began to imitate (except in overall size) those of middle-class apartments.

However, the ambitions of some reform advocates had extended beyond such micro-spatial changes. Their aim had also been to replace the "promiscuity in human beehives" with "the privacy of the single-family detached home," as Elgin Gould had put it in 1900, by facilitating the movement of tens of thousands of families from the city's most densely populated neighborhoods into the urban periphery.[97] Yet the 1901 law largely side-stepped this issue, and high residential density remained a problem. Developers also generally responded to newly mandated spatial subdivisions by shrinking the average room size in tenement apartments rather than by increasing the total square footage—even going so far as to accompany tenement inspectors with tape measures to convince them that all rooms met minimum requirements, although not "the fraction of an inch" more.[98]

Residential density estimates show that the 1901 law did not lead to a dedensification of the inner city. According to data collected by the 1894 Tenement House Committee and published in its 1895 report, wards on the Lower East Side commonly had between five hundred and nine hundred residents per acre before the turn of the twentieth century, with the densest wards having up to a thousand (figure 3.5). The Department of Tenements did not conduct systematic ward-level population surveys after 1901, but we can combine population counts from the U.S. Census with ward-specific area estimates from the National Historical Geographic Information System (NHGIS) to estimate residential density during subsequent decades. The data (also shown in figure 3.5) reveal that the same Lower East Side census wards that were surveyed by the Tenement House Committee in 1894 had between 607 and 894 residents per acre in 1910 and between 393 and 465 residents per acre in 1930. Overcrowding in the most densely populated parts of the city only lessened during the 1920s with the development of citywide public transportation infrastructures and a decrease in the annual number of newly arriving immigrants.[99]

In addition to calculating the number of persons residing in a given ward (a measure that does not account for the total available livable space in that area), we can also calculate the average floor area per person (FAPP)—a more micro-spatial measure of residential crowding. This requires some

Ward-level population per acre (1894)

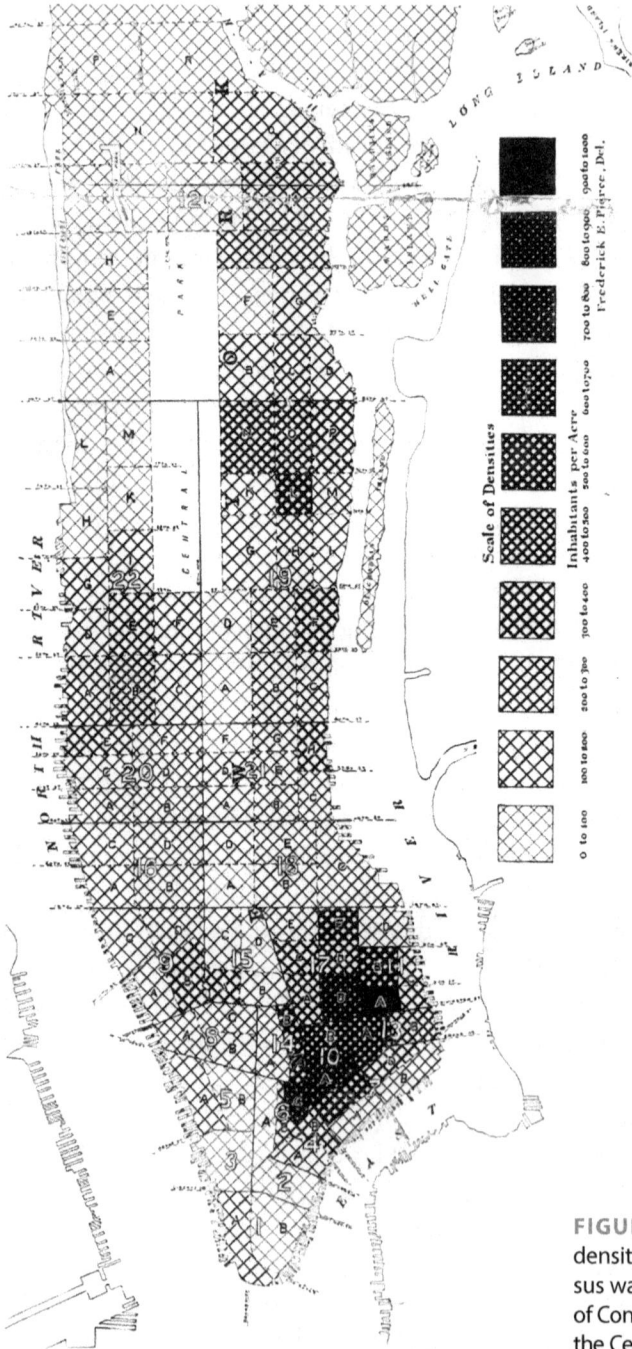

FIGURE 3.5 Population density estimates by census ward. *Sources*: Library of Congress; U.S. Bureau of the Census; IPUMS NHGIS.

Ward-level population
per square kilometer (1910)

Ward-level population
per square kilometer (1930)

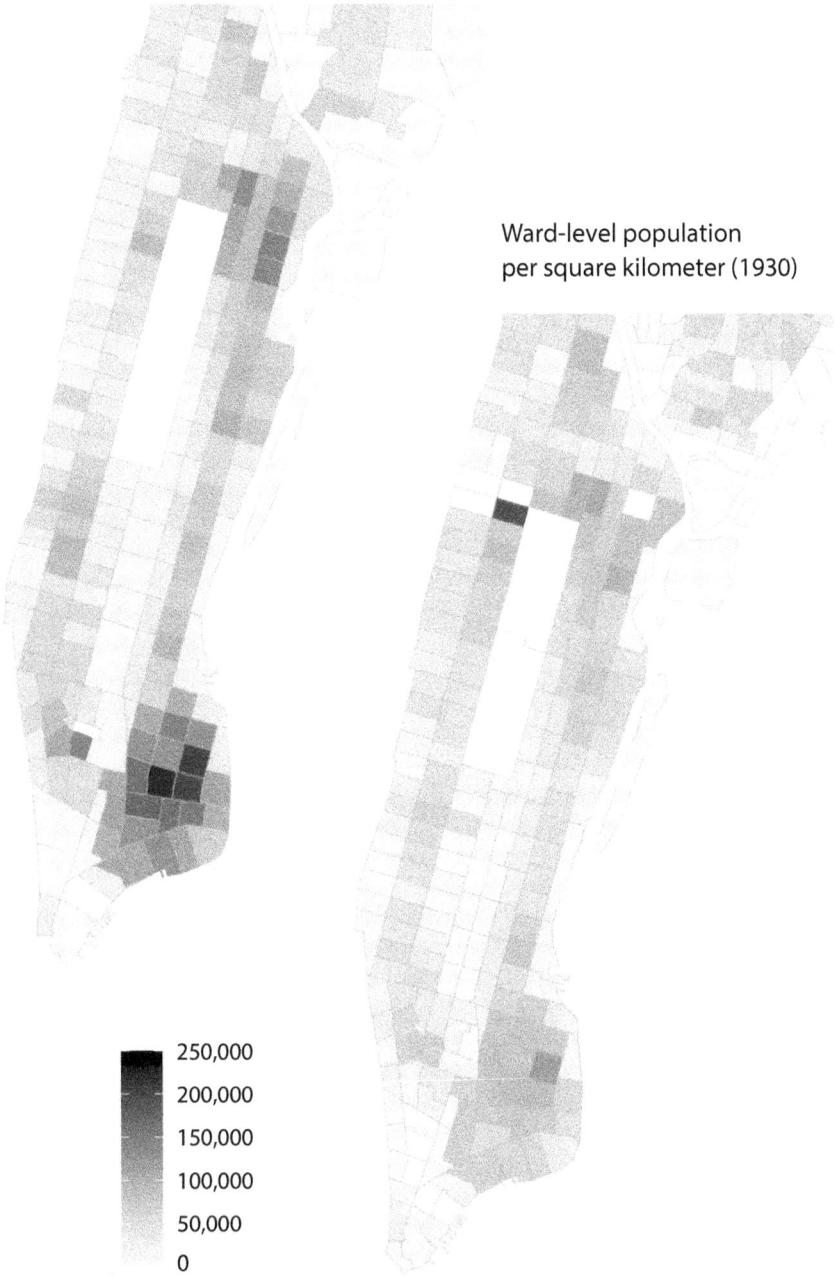

250,000
200,000
150,000
100,000
50,000
0

FIGURE 3.5 *(continued)*

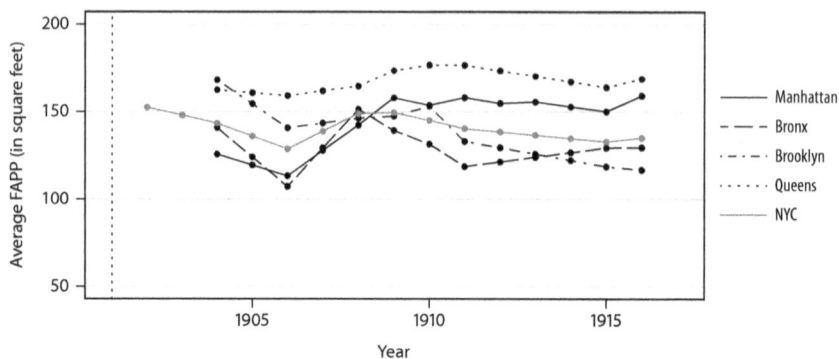

FIGURE 3.6 Average floor area per person (FAPP) by New York City (NYC) borough. *Sources*: New York Public Library; New York Department of Tenements; U.S. Bureau of the Census.

basic assumptions about tenement construction (which are given in detail in the methodological coda) and makes it necessary to aggregate data for each borough rather than for specific census wards. But it reveals a concordant picture: FAPP in Manhattan increased from 125 square feet in 1904 to 155 square feet in 1916. But in Brooklyn, where hundreds of additional tenements were constructed between 1900 and 1920, it decreased from 170 square feet to 120 square feet (figure 3.6). As long as "the proximity of the neighbors compels man to withdraw into his conscience for privacy," as one reform advocate claimed at the NCSW in 1921, idealized notions of domesticity ran into very real obstacles in the form of continued residential crowding. It was only with the rise of suburban communities in the mid-twentieth century that the single-family home took center stage again, and middle-class visions of domestic privacy were democratized across a wider swath of the population.

THE FEDERALIZED INSTITUTIONALIZATION OF PRIVACY

The 1901 Tenement House Act was an early example of legislation that codified privacy by folding it into a larger bill—in this case, a bill that addressed the perceived physical and moral hazards of urban life. It also became a template for tenement reform elsewhere. The Civic League in Yonkers and social reform advocates in Pittsburgh took a page out of Veiller's playbook by staging their own tenement exhibitions, and cities from Baltimore to San Francisco established tenement committees and commissions. By 1912, thirty-eight American cities had sought advice from representatives of the New York Tenement House Committee.[100] At the municipal level, Boston, Cleveland, Jersey City, Syracuse, and Kansas City all developed legislation that was modeled on the New York state law, and twenty additional cities amended existing ordinances.[101] At the state level, Kentucky passed a tenement law modeled on New York's 1901 law in 1910, followed by Massachusetts in 1912, Indiana and Pennsylvania in 1913, California and Minnesota in 1917, and Iowa in 1919. In each of those places, attempts to lessen the impact of the "social question" focused on "subdividing our houses and so giving each family a certain degree of privacy."[102] Before the right to privacy was codified through national legislation, and in a federalized political system, the moral institutionalization of privacy therefore began in municipal assemblies and state legislatures.

This general approach—pushing for the inclusion of privacy protections in bills that also included swaths of unrelated paragraphs—also foreshadowed subsequent legislation that shifted attention from tenement developers to advertising executives and from the nuclear family toward the emerging informational society. New York was once again at the forefront of such efforts. In 1902, a year after the passage of the Tenement House Act, the New York Court of Appeals considered the case of a teenager whose photographs had been used without consent in advertising materials for a flour company. The teenager's family had sued, and the ruling had turned on a new and largely untested legal idea: Could a person claim a right to privacy that protected against the unauthorized appropriation of their likeness? The judges answered in the negative, arguing that privacy was too vague a concept and too divorced from precedent to serve as the basis for an enforceable legal right. But they left the back door slightly ajar: legislators were free to establish such a right by statute.

The decision—in *Roberson v. Rochester Folding Box Co.*—generated national news and was widely met with derision from the press. But it did have one intended effect. Newspaper editorials built a case for the legislative codification of privacy in the absence of judicial intervention, and legislators in the New York State Assembly found themselves under growing pressure to act. They reconvened in Albany to pass a civil rights law that included two novel paragraphs: Section 50 established a right to privacy at the state level by making it a crime to use the name, portrait, picture, or voice of any living person in commercial advertisements without their explicit consent, and Section 51 created a right to sue for an injunction and damages when the aforementioned right to privacy was violated.

The laws of 1901 and 1902—one about tenement reform, the other about advertising—hinted at a future where the logic of privacy appeared not merely as an informal social norm but occupied center stage in political struggles over visibility and power in the modern United States and in the legislation that sometimes resulted from such struggles. If the "most important strategy of politics is concerned with the scope of conflict," as Elmer Eric Schattschneider has argued, these developments marked a step change.[103] The most consequential debates about privacy in the Early Information Age no longer played out within small groups of people but involved organized interest groups and professional associations, newspapers, and legislators. How was a changing society to be protected against social and technological forces that threatened to unsettle existing custom and widened the gap between existing regulatory frameworks and the challenges of modernization? The political conflicts that arose in response to these questions were addressed through institutional action. Their effects were felt at scale, even if they remained premised on more traditional understandings of social roles and public morals.

Considerable efforts were often required to advance the institutionalization of privacy, in part because privacy claims competed for attention with other economic and political imperatives. But as the political dynamics that preceded the passage of the 1901 Tenement House Act law illustrate, moral entrepreneurs could, in coalition with political operatives, dramatize social problems as moral crises and forge temporary alliances that translated moral imaginaries into legislative action. The history of privacy in the United States is, to a considerable degree, the history of moral claims-making, political mobilization, and institutional intervention during periods of dislocation, when existing schemas and informal norms come to be seen as insufficient or outdated. In the tenement reform movement, and later in other political settings, arguments about the precarious state and public significance of privacy often found an eager audience and provided an appealing framework to confront popular anxieties and social problems by affirming the rights of citizens and consumers in a modernizing society.

4

Inviolate Personalities

Individual Privacy in an Era of Informational Persons

E dwin Lawrence Godkin became the first editor of *The Nation* at
a time when the dominance of established publications was being
challenged by so-called "penny press" tabloids: newspapers whose
business often consisted of minting salacious stories from the residue of
everyday life. Founded by a group of abolitionists in 1865, *The Nation* was
something of an upstart as well. But Godkin soon let it be known how he
felt about his ascendant competitors. They published "wildly sensational,
vulgar, and slangy" articles, he argued in 1869, and thereby pursued "about
as demoralizing a business as a young man can engage in."[1] Yet it remained
a lucrative business, nonetheless. Tabloid publishers like Joseph A. Pulitzer
and William Randolph Hearst built veritable business empires, and it took
only two years for Pulitzer's *New York World* to eclipse all other papers
in the city in daily circulation. By the 1890s, Godkin had become convinced that the widespread appeal of the tabloid press was evidence of a
society that had failed to unify after the Civil War and was instead fraying
under the centrifugal forces of social atomization and populist agitation.[2]

These tensions manifested in the political arena, where Godkin observed
that "only a remnant, old men for the most part, still uphold the Liberal
doctrine."[3] But the social disorientation that Emile Durkheim contempo-
raneously described as "anomie" also affected Americans in their everyday life. While the "desire of social approval and the corresponding fear

of social reprobation" may have formerly acted as powerful social glues, Godkin now saw the spread of "barbarous instincts" and mistrust.[4] As he argued in *Scribner's Magazine* in 1890, "a disposition to attack reputation" by "[intruding] on privacy" had become a main source of social conflict.[5] It had reached an unprecedented level with the spread of the tabloids, which had "converted curiosity into what economists call an effectual demand, and gossip into a marketable commodity." There was good money to be made by disseminating personal and potentially incriminating or embarrassing information to an inquisitive public.

While the previous chapter has shown that the rapid growth of tenement districts engendered concerns about the apparent moral ills of modern life and the precarious state of domestic privacy in the modern American city—which in turn catalyzed the adaptation of older cultural norms to new social problems through political mobilization and legislative action—Godkin's criticism hints at a different kind of social conflict. In a society where personal data could unlock benefits, foreclose opportunities, and attract greater public interest than in the past, privacy had to be defended not just amid the fracas of urban living but against institutional actors that turned the collection of personal data into a central part of their operations and the publication of private information into a source of profit.

Newspapers were not the only offenders. The invention of cellulose nitrate film in the late 1880s made photography more portable (by eliminating the need for large photographic plates and correspondingly large cameras), more instantaneous (by reducing exposure times), and more accessible (by reducing costs). While photography had previously been confined to controlled studio settings or carefully orchestrated shoots, amateur photographers—"young knights of the camera" armed "with a dangerous weapon," according to one contemporary account—ventured into the streets of American cities to record candid snapshots of everyday life.[6] Telephones changed how Americans communicated across great distances but also raised the specter of wiretapping and governmental surveillance; and the collection of personal data became central to a consumer economy that relied on standardized measures of creditworthiness.[7] As local interdependences gave way to nationally integrated markets and translocal communities, technologies of distance were required to facilitate interpersonal or economic exchanges. Those exchanges increasingly involved what Colin Koopman has called "informational persons": people who were "inscribed, processed, and reproduced as subjects of data" by organizations with whom they often had little personal interactions (or none at all).[8] Privacy became "more and more strongly entrenched" in the public and legal consciousness in this evolving society, as contemporary observers noted. Yet it was also threatened by information flows far beyond the family home.[9]

One historical text about this transformation stands out in particular. In 1890, two young Boston lawyers published an essay about the "right to privacy" (or, as they also called it, the "right to be let alone") in the *Harvard Law Review*, highlighting the discrepancies between established legal doctrines and rapidly emerging technosocial realities.[10] This essay by Samuel Warren and (future Supreme Court justice) Louis Brandeis is widely seen as a landmark contribution to American jurisprudence. Chapter 5 will challenge its centrality to the legal institutionalization of privacy, arguing that experimentation and contestation in lower courts had a far greater impact on judicial reasoning. Yet the writings of Warren and Brandeis—and also of contemporaries like the journalist E. L. Godkin, the legal scholar Thomas M. Cooley, and others—still reveal something meaningful about the transformation of privacy around the turn of the twentieth century: They amplified and extended ideas about the tight connection between privacy and individualism that had already circulated through American culture in embryonic fashion but had historically been overshadowed by an emphasis on the domestic sphere and the family. But as one writer noted in 1908, the struggle for privacy in the modern United States gradually evolved into a struggle for the "decent seclusion of the individual" rather than the spatial isolation of entire families.[11]

This conjoining of privacy and individualism is often seen as a conceptual necessity—a seemingly natural affinity exists between the two, and so *of course* privacy circumscribes a sphere of inviolability around the rights-bearing individual. For example, Edward Bloustein has argued that privacy protects "the individual's independence, dignity and integrity" and thereby "defines man's essence as a unique and self-determining being."[12] According to this view, which has come to dominate legal scholarship as well as philosophical accounts, privacy violations are "demeaning of individuality" by breaking down an invisible but essential boundary between the public-facing and private parts of the self, be removing important limits on what is possible to know about another person, and by leaving the individual exposed to the tyrannical powers of public authorities.[13] Without privacy, the argument goes, there can be no inviolate personhood and thus no independent self.[14] And without such a self—often understood as the source of human dignity, agency, and morality—the entire liberal edifice of individual rights begins to crumble.[15] As the U.S. Supreme Court therefore declared in 1992 in *Planned Parenthood v. Casey* (which affirmed a constitutional right to abortion as an extension of privacy rights), "at the heart of liberty is the right to define one's own concept of existence, of meaning, of the universe, and of the mystery of human life."[16] The individual's right to privacy hence appears as one of the foundational and "antitotalitarian" principles of liberal societies, traceable to the writings of liberal thinkers and revolutionaries during the eighteenth century—people like Benjamin Constant and Alexis de Tocqueville—and later affirmed by the American federal judiciary during the twentieth century.[17] By defending the individual's right to privacy, liberal-democratic societies reinforce the principle that personal liberty is paramount.

Yet insisting that privacy is derived from the principles of liberal individualism—or, alternatively, critiquing those individualistic roots as unavoidable limitations that distract from "the political power of the state and the social power of capital" and thereby inhibit considerations of the "social significance of privacy" more generally—misses the historically contingent nature of this association. The strongly individualistic interpretation of privacy is a conceptual sprig that came into bloom specifically during the Early Information Age.[18]

Of course there were antecedents, although they generally emphasized "the private" (a term that already appeared more frequently in Adam Smith's *The Wealth of Nations* than the term "wealth") rather than privacy or wrapped discussions of the individual self into spiritual conceptions of the human soul. But as the nineteenth century gave way to the twentieth, an energized community of thinkers tied privacy more closely than ever before to the tenets of liberal individualism and aimed to reify the autonomy of the so-called "private citizen" at a time of increasing interdependence and institutional inquisitiveness. Their arguments erected a conceptual scaffolding that would inform critiques of monopoly capitalism during the Progressive Era and governmental overreach during World War I and ultimately braced the "rights revolution" of the mid-twentieth century, when federal courts expanded the recognition and protection of individual rights. Yet the alliance of privacy and liberal individualism also fueled a tension that has remained with us ever since: economic inclusion and bureaucratic governance in the modern United States often necessitate the sharing and collection of personal data, yet the autonomy of citizens and consumers is simultaneously rooted in their ability to control flows of information or avoid exposure.

The first half of this chapter analyzes how institutional violations of privacy evolved into a central concern during the waning decades of the nineteenth century, even as those concerns were balanced against a concurrent desire for visibility and exposure. The second half of this chapter then discusses the increasingly close association of privacy and liberal individualism that was triggered by these developments. It foregrounds the work of relatively prominent persons to a greater extent than the rest of this book, not because such persons were the only ones who thought and wrote about privacy but because their ideas and decisions have often endured through time, becoming recognized in the twentieth century as lodestars of privacy discourse and serving as anchors for myriad conflicts over privacy and informational power. At a crucial historical juncture, advocates of an individualistic interpretation of privacy sought to defend established social goods and new ideas about the proper relationship between citizens and the state and between consumers and corporations.[19] They expounded an ideational foundation that could, they hoped, bear the weight of a changing society. Building on earlier conceptions of rights-bearing individuals and solitary selves, those writers and thinkers placed a theory of the inviolate personality at the core of the informational person and, in doing so, tied privacy more closely than ever before into a web of liberal ideas about the modern individual. These were the "old men" in Godkin's articles (although they were sometimes quite young, as in the case of the recent law school graduates Samuel Warren and Louis Brandeis), willing not only to uphold "the liberal doctrine" inherited from prior generations but intent on contesting the emerging challenges of the Early Information Age.

"EVERYBODY'S RIGHT TO ANYBODY'S PRIVACY"

The number of newspapers and subscribers increased throughout the nineteenth century but especially so after the 1870s (figure 4.1). Advances in printing technology and the expansion of postal delivery routes made it cheaper to produce and disseminate printed content at scale and across the United States. By the turn of the twentieth century, around twenty thousand newspapers delivered close to ten billion print copies annually

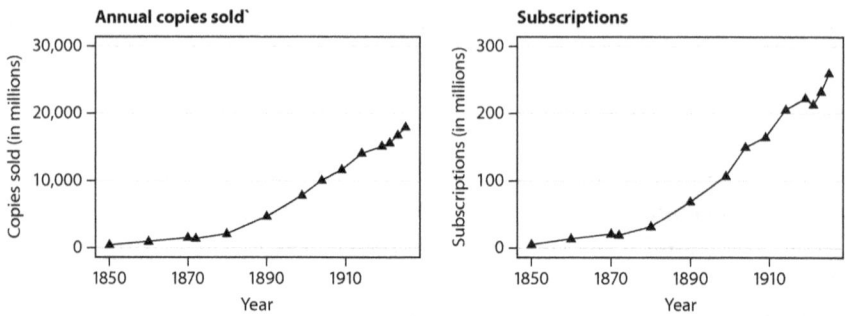

FIGURE 4.1 The U.S. newspaper industry. *Sources*: Dill, *Growth of Newspapers in the U.S.*; Field, "Newspapers and Periodicals."

to American households.[20] Some of these were large metropolitan papers, with the Sunday editions of the forty largest newspapers each having a circulation over a hundred thousand. But the bulk of news coverage was provided by local publications that mixed syndicated national content with coverage of local events; by tabloid newspapers that relied heavily on human-interest stories; and by special-interest publications that served niche markets or provided foreign-language coverage to recent immigrants in their respective mother tongues. Never before in American history had it taken less time for more news to reach a larger number of people.[21]

Journalistic practices also evolved. Tabloid papers pushed a particularly hard editorial line that often blurred the lines between fact-based reporting and creative embellishment. Muckraking journalists began to flex their investigative muscles to report on prominent elites and sordid characters with equal zeal and gritty realism. Through the cultivation of backroom sources in urban centers of power and by closely following police patrols into the poorer parts of town, they aimed to expose the hidden underbelly of American society but also to wage moral crusades against corruption, crime, and poverty. Additionally, the invention of flexible photographic film during the mid-1880s by George Eastman—who would go on to cofound the Eastman Kodak Company—allowed photographers to leave their controlled studio settings and venture into the streets. Instead of asking clients to sit still for prolonged periods in front of a daguerreotype camera, an emerging class of professional photographers could use portable cameras and candid shots to document urban poverty and glamour during the Gilded Age.

Those changes allowed publishers to build large media empires but also generated considerable pushback and criticism. In 1901, for example, Philadelphia city tabloids caused a minor scandal by printing halftone photographs of women in their bathing suits, taken surreptitiously at a beach in Atlantic City.[22] The public outcry captured a growing unease with "Kodakers lying in wait" who seemed to be "in league with some evil spirit" and had seemingly fallen under the influence of a technology that was as seductive—and just as likely to lead to ruin—as "opium, hasheesh, [and] even the fascinations of Monte Carlo."[23] By freezing in time what the photojournalist Henri Cartier-Bresson would later call "the decisive moment", instantaneous photography promised to capture unmediated truths that were otherwise lost to the unyielding passage of time. The true nature of things—the character of individuals, and the problems of society—seemed to reveal itself in tenths or hundredths of a second and in the unguarded expressions on a person's face.[24]

The publication of the Atlantic City photographs marked a strikingly egregious departure from austere journalistic custom, yet it also epitomized broader changes in the publishing industry that engendered criticisms of the tabloid press. Those criticisms came partly from other editors who objected in principle to the new style of journalism but also had economic reasons for voicing their displeasure (they were outcompeted and outsold), and who repeatedly couched their critiques in the language of privacy. Readers of newspaper editorials were informed that the aggressive practices of tabloid reporters had stripped "life of refinement and [diverted] the attention of their readers away from the serious and significant things of life to the personal affairs of their neighbors" and that henceforth "there was no home whose sanctity [tabloid reporters] would not invade if opportunity offered and there was material for a headline in it."[25] An editorial in the *Martinsburg Daily Gazette* from West Virginia observed an "increasing invasion of privacy by the newspapers, so that it almost becomes necessary to ask each stranger at a private gathering, 'Are you a reporter?', and each new visitor at one's door, 'Are you an interviewer?'"[26] And in the *Herald and News* from South Carolina, the editorial board likewise opined that tabloid publishers had established "everybody's right to anybody's privacy" as American society was flooded with "triviality, gossip, and scandal" by yellow press journalists who used "deception" and "blackmail" to extract personal data and intimate confessions from their subjects to further their "vulgar and sordid business."[27]

Conflicts over the publication of potentially incriminating or embarrassing information were nothing new. As far back as ancient Mesopotamia, cuneiform tablets had been baked into an exterior layer of clay to form a physical seal and hide the message within.[28] In seventeenth-century Europe, the nobility and the clergy replaced clay seals with wax but exhibited a similar preoccupation with the sanctity of their personal letters. And in 1770, the American revolutionary leader John Adams complained about the growing attention paid to his personal affairs. "I am under no moral or other obligation to publish to the world," he wrote, "how much my expenses or my incomes amount to yearly. There are times when, and persons to whom, I am not obliged to tell what are my principles and opinions in politicks or religion."[29] Similarly, in 1803, Thomas Jefferson had declared that "licentiousness" and "lying" had become so prevalent that "nothing in a newspaper is to be believed," and he even suggested that a few prosecutions of publishers would "place the whole band more on their guard."[30] Jefferson's unease was common among the Founding Fathers. Once the cadre of former revolutionaries found themselves in positions of power and under public scrutiny, Benjamin Franklin, Alexander Hamilton, and James Madison all sought to rebalance the right of free expression against the suppression of libelous and embarrassing content, including content about themselves.[31] Their attempts to curb the freedom of the press were part of an elite strategy aimed at suppressing information that could become a personal, political, or economic liability.

But tensions between privacy and the freedom of the press continued to expand with the growing media saturation of American society during the second half of the nineteenth century, and the focus broadened from traditional concerns about the publication of libelous content (a form of defamation that involves making a false and damaging statement about someone in public) to a more general concern about the inviolability of private thoughts and letters. This was particularly true for persons of public prominence. As the *Chicago Daily Tribune* noted in 1902, those who had risen "into the scope of the public eye by reason of [their] wealth or business or philanthropy or interest in politics" had, in the modern United States, become the focus of attention to such a degree that their personal lives turned into a kind of "public property," open to examination and judgment by legions of pundits and readers.[32] The gap that separated social elites from those "who do not seek office, who are not so rich that they cannot be ignored, and who are not engaged in occupations that bring them conspicuously into view" was seemingly defined not just by inequalities of wealth or influence but also by the possibility of escaping the gaze of an inquisitive public.[33] Commenting on Warren G. Harding's presidential campaign in the summer of 1920, a satirical poem in the *Richmond Times-Dispatch* from Virginia later noted:

And this shall be his great endeavor
To start in shaking hands at dawn;
His privacy is gone forever
Where visitors track up his lawn;
And where he once knew easy picking
Where life was placid and serene,
Ten thousand cameras stark clicking
Each time his features grace the scene.[34]

The nation's growing interest in the lives of political and economic elites was a distant precursor to the celebrity culture of the twenty-first century, and it meant that individuals of exalted status could not easily "retreat within the privacy of the average citizen" and could seldom venture into public spaces "without becoming subject to the criticism of the press."[35] This was eavesdropping on steroids, backed by the institutional power of publishers like Pulitzer and Hearst and facilitated by modern photographic and printing technologies.

In the summer of 1905, the journalist St. Clair McKelway, editor of the *Brooklyn Eagle*, appeared before an audience in New Haven, Connecticut, to address these tensions head-on. "The press has invaded the right of privacy," he conceded at the outset.[36] But journalists had reason to think that this invasion was often necessary and sometimes invited. Persons of some social standing—but particularly those keen on further increasing their notoriety and prominence—regularly sent handwritten notes to local papers and tabloid publications "with the polite wish that they may be prominently and promptly published" or requested that their weddings, christenings, and dinner receptions be attended by reporters.[37] As McKelway noted, "advance lists of guests, descriptions of gowns, ornaments, decorations and programmes are kindly included." American elites at the turn of the twentieth century chose to relinquish their privacy with some regularity for "a more desirable equivalent," especially when it served their personal ambitions and telegraphed their upward social mobility.[38]

Invasions of privacy were also justified by the demands of public safety and "by a public interest." Magazine articles that documented "how the other half lives" (a phrase made famous by the journalist Jacob Riis) used the power of photography and the written word to focus public attention on the social question by exposing the archetypes, or sometimes stereotypes, of people whom roving reporters and photographers encountered during their forays into poor neighborhoods: the hard worker, the idler, the gambler, the drinker, the despairing wife, or the abandoned child.[39] Especially at a time when politics were dominated by powerful party machines and often subservient to the interests of industrial elites, the American press grew also into its self-assigned role as the fourth estate. McKelway was quick to remind his audience of this, arguing that it was up to journalists to hold the nation's political and economic leaders accountable by exposing their backroom machinations. To him, the press was nothing less than "a moral avenger" and "a public benefactor" of the American people. It promised to contain "the great evil among men . . . secrecy and deceit."[40] As one commentator writing in *The Atlanta Georgian* thus noted: "The cry of life is 'Light! More Light! More light everywhere!"[41] Supreme Court Justice Louis Brandeis later provided the most famous articulation of this view in a 1913 article in *Harper's Weekly*. "Publicity is justly commended for social and industrial diseases," Brandeis wrote beneath the caricature of a banker towering over an American city in his upholstered chair. "Sunlight is said to be the best of disinfectants, electric light the most efficient policeman."[42] "The privacy [the press] invades is a public property," McKelway therefore concluded. "Till wrong abandons secrecy, journalism will invade privacy."

Photographic and journalistic invasions of privacy may have been at the center of many debates, but they were far from the only sources of dispute. Technological innovations in long-distance communication spawned a related set of concerns and claims. Invented in 1876, the telephone removed some of the intermediaries—like telegraph operators or postal delivery workers—that had historically been required for long-distance communication. The number of telephone lines in the United States doubled between 1884 and 1893 to 266,000, with rural regions outpacing cities in early adoption. The number then increased sevenfold during the next decade. By the late 1920s, almost half of American households had acquired a telephone and the American Telephone and Telegraph Company (AT&T) had established itself as a powerful monopolist and one of the first modern corporations in the United States.[43] The telephone in particular became "the electric symbol of the new age".[44]

Telephony changed how people thought about time and space, facilitated the spread of news, and aided the dissemination of stock and commodity prices. But it also elevated concerns about governmental or corporate interference during the transmission of telephone signals that traveled dozens or—in some cases—thousands of miles before arriving at their destination. Such disputes framed privacy violations as problems of *distance* rather than *proximity*. Tapping a telephone (or telegraph) line was, technically speaking, not a difficult undertaking. The farther afield personal data could travel through the wires, the greater the potential for serious and institutional invasions of privacy appeared to be.

In an illustrated full-page article from 1899, *The San Francisco Call* thus warned its readers that the widespread adoption of the telephone had introduced "purchasable spies" into many American households as telephone operators implemented a "gigantic system of espionage" and threatened to share private conversations with state prosecutors (figure 4.2).[45] American society had—in the eyes of the *Call's* editors—become "so dependent upon modern methods of inter-communication, the mail, the telegraph, and the telephone" and so accustomed to sharing personal information and business data over the wire that any violation of telecommunications privacy carried a special significance. As the article continued, "so general is the public confidence in the privacy of [the telephone] that it is safe to say that violation of that privacy is a more serious offense than the opening of letters unlawfully." In 1907, *The New York Times* similarly declared that a person's apartment "is his castle and the telephone a part of his castle" and suggested that invasions of telephone privacy were "worse than eavesdropping, more vicious than scandal, and more detrimental to the welfare of the home-dweller than any other ordinary abuse."[46] And in 1911, the *Hawaiian Star* found even more dramatic words: "Many of life's dramas are enacted . . . through the medium of the automatic telephone. Its psychology is unique, intimate, and intricate. It defies the staunchest ethics of privacy and delicacy. . . . It tears off the disguise of hypocrisy and brazenly bares to public view the sacred secrets of the soul! It reverts like a boomerang into that privacy for the assurance of which it was instituted and approved!"[47]

Even the inventor Nikola Tesla opined on the matter, declaring that engineers first had to "perfect methods for securing complete privacy and non-interference of messages" to make "transmission to great distances a practical success."[48] As personal information and interpersonal communications

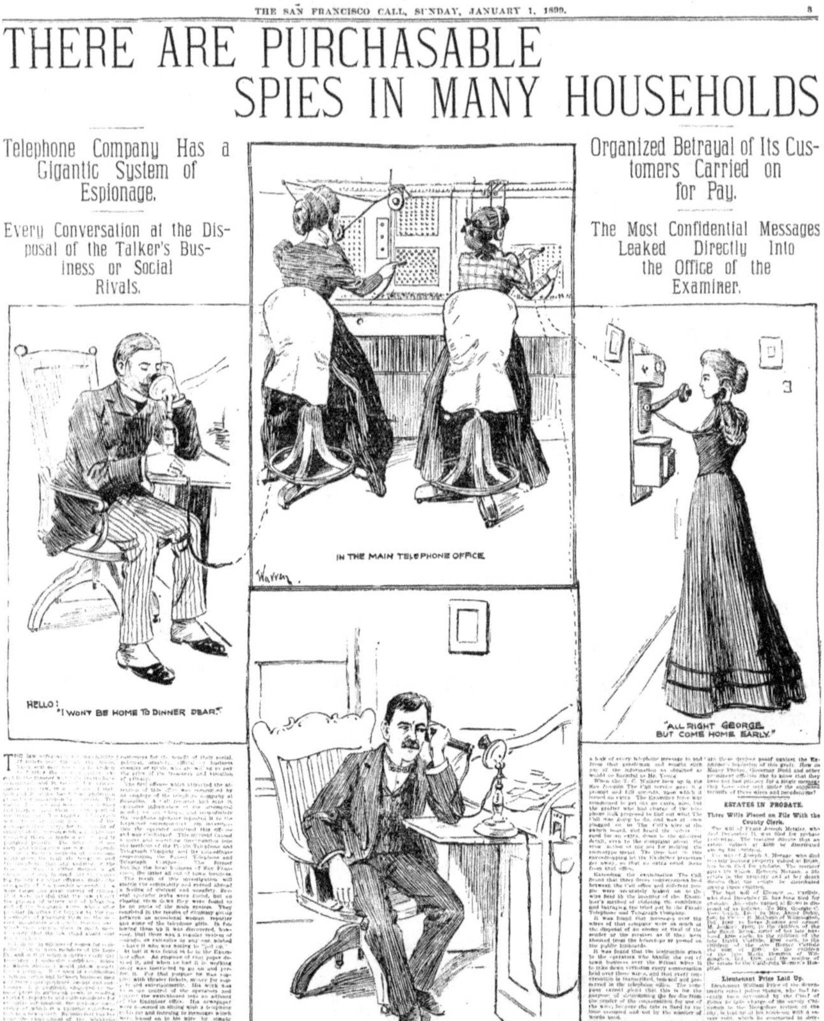

THE SAN FRANCISCO CALL, SUNDAY, JANUARY 1, 1899. 3

THERE ARE PURCHASABLE SPIES IN MANY HOUSEHOLDS

Telephone Company Has a Gigantic System of Espionage.

Every Conversation at the Disposal of the Talker's Business or Social Rivals.

Organized Betrayal of Its Customers Carried on for Pay.

The Most Confidential Messages Leaked Directly Into the Office of the Examiner.

ESTATES IN PROBATE.

Lieutenant Price Laid Up.

The Insane Cause Litigation.

FIGURE 4.2 "There are purchasable spies in many households."
Source: *The San Francisco Call*, January 1, 1899.

traveled farther afield and as technological systems became ever more integral to social exchange and the functioning of American society, old images of eavesdroppers and gossipmongers who hid around corners and pressed their ears against a closed door or a window blind seemed increasingly out of step with the concerns and technological realities of the times.

THE AGE OF PUBLICITY

There is, however, one noteworthy exception to the argument that technological innovation and the trafficking of personal information by institutional actors generated significant opposition: The institution of commercial and consumer credit scoring was primarily regarded as a beneficent technology of financial inclusion. So-called "commercial agencies" had developed since the middle of the nineteenth century and aimed to furnish the "commercial standing of every businessman in the community" in collections of financial reports.[49] These agencies sought information about a person's home and income, "the standing in society of their parents or of [their] friends," "if he is married," "if he goes to saloons or concert rooms or theaters," and "the tradesmen he deals with." In one case, a New York commercial agency dutifully reported on the price of new carpets that a businessman's wife had purchased the previous year, the "occasional" deliveries of fresh cider by the man's father, and his industrious schedule. Approvingly, the report noted that the man began his business dealings already at "about nine in the morning."[50]

One of the earliest agencies, Tappan's Mercantile Agency, had been founded in the wake of the economic panic of 1837. Another agency, John M. Bradstreet Company, emerged in Chicago in 1849 and pioneered the use of typewritten and printed credit reports in 1851. (One newspaper speculated that the true business model of these commercial agencies was closer to extortion: subscribers paid not primarily for the right to consume commercial reports, but for the right to edit their own reports prior to publication.)[51] These early agencies filled a gap that had been created by the federalized structure of the American banking system and the lack of information flows from East Coast banks to the western frontier, which had made it relatively easy for overleveraged businessmen to avoid credit obligations by moving across state borders or applying for new lines of credit under a fictitious name. By the 1870s, Tappan's had been renamed as R.G. Dun & Company, had recruited more than ten thousand local correspondents, and had also begun to hire professionally trained traveling investigators.[52] By 1880, its reports covered more than seven hundred thousand businesses.[53]

Starting in the 1870s, commercial credit ratings were additionally supplemented with what Lendol Calder has called the "stepchild of consumer culture": creditworthiness assessments about individual consumers.[54] The reliance on credit-based purchases increased steadily in the late nineteenth and early twentieth centuries. According to a survey from the National Monetary Commission, the average retail and wholesale business in the United States relied on various credit instruments, including personal checks, for approximately 86 percent of all retail transactions in the first decade of the twentieth century.[55] This necessitated some mechanism that would allow for the sharing of credit data between businesses and across the United States.[56] As one analyst later noted, "In small and stable communities . . . the financial worth, earning capacity, family history, and personal qualities of applicants were matters of common knowledge. In metropolitan cities, on the other hand, the difficulty of appraising credit worth on any basis other than the ownership of readily negotiable collateral led to the denial of credit to classes of consumers whose credit needs were supplied by banks in intimate communities."[57]

This was the time when consumer credit bureaus fully came into their own. Early ventures were sometimes set up as ad hoc cooperatives by chambers of commerce or local merchants, pooling data about customers and overdue payments. But by 1906, thirty specialized retail credit bureaus reported on individual customers and formed the National Association of Retail Credit Agencies in Rochester, New York. The organization eventually evolved, through mergers, into the Associated Credit Bureaus of America (ACB), which proceeded to establish the first uniform system for reporting credit data in the aftermath of World War I.[58] ACB membership soon spiked from fewer than one hundred credit bureaus in 1916 to around eight hundred in 1927. Two of today's major consumer credit bureaus were also founded at this time: Experian's organizational life began in 1897 as the Merchant's Credit Association, and Equifax evolved from the Retail Credit Company founded in 1899.[59]

Such structural changes to American consumer capitalism increased the collection and circulation of personal data more rapidly than any governmental attempt to collect business income data through the Internal Revenue Service or any attempt by penny press newspapers to expose individual misconduct. Yet, perhaps surprisingly, these agencies elicited little resistance. To be clear, journalists occasionally castigated commercial credit agencies for establishing an "organized system of espionage" from which "no possible means of escaping" seemed to exist.[60] For example, *The Brooklyn Daily Eagle* pulled no punches when describing the collection of financial data in New York City in 1873. Credit agencies employed "private detectives," convinced postmasters to "act as their spies," sent "spies around the house and in the kitchen," and made "the family history of business men and their wives . . . a subject of daily record."[61] But unlike during disputes about tabloid journalism, telecommunications, and the "modern inquisition" of the American state, opposition to consumer credit ratings remained a relatively rare phenomenon. The most vocal opponents were generally those who had suffered professional misfortune and social ostracization from poor credit ratings.[62] The lawsuits they filed—again, primarily against commercial credit agencies—challenged the veracity of credit reports that insinuated business owners' marital problems or extramarital affairs (a nontrivial accusation because credit assessments were as much about financial liquidity as about assumed character). But those lawsuits stayed firmly within the bounds of libel and defamation law and focused on the financial harm that had accrued as a result of factually inaccurate reporting.

To many Americans, the sharing of personal financial records with credit bureaus during the late nineteenth and early twentieth centuries was primarily experienced as a pathway toward financial inclusion, and it sparked comparatively little resistance—and almost no resistance that was rooted in arguments about privacy.[63] Credit reports made it possible for a wider swath of the American populace to access monetary resources at a time when such access was also becoming more important for professional success and social mobility and when localized systems of providing credit (based on interpersonal trust and reputation) were falling out of fashion. As *The Washington Times* suggested in 1902, "Society is now an organism and all the atoms composing it are interdependent. The position that any atom or individual shall occupy in the social mass or community depends not only upon his own abilities and worth but upon the appreciation that the rest of the mass or community has of that worth and these abilities."[64] Credit reports allowed for such appreciation across great physical distances and based on standardized metrics of financial risk.

Credit agencies also took active steps to preempt opposition. They specifically began to emphasize the confidentiality of credit reports, just as officials from the U.S. Census Bureau had done during debates about financial censuses and intragovernmental data sharing, and thereby aimed to shift attention from the collection of personal information to its proper handling and storage. For example, at one commercial agency, subscribers who requested business credit reports had to appear in person to have information read to them by a clerk but could not peruse the financial reports themselves. This clerk was additionally instructed to place reports on a lectern at such an angle that the subscriber could not steal an illicit glance.[65]

Overall, the rise of credit ratings remains an instructive negative case. During the Early Information Age, Americans stoutly defended privacy in some areas of life even as they consented to, desired, or at least tolerated the sharing of other types of personal information, contingent not just on prevalent cultural norms but on the expected burdens and benefits.[66] The "era of publicity" was welcomed as well as condemned, buoyed by hopes of inclusion and prosperity even when it was also weighed down by deep anxieties about rapid change.[67]

DEFENDING THE INVIOLATE PERSONALITY

To some observers, the embrace of exposure seemed like a distinctly American phenomenon. Foreign correspondents and travel writers who reported on the cultural sensibilities of the French or the British repeatedly explained to their U.S.-based audiences that a European "love for privacy" was difficult to grasp for the average American.[68] In one such essay, published in the *Atlantic Monthly*, the author suggested that Americans had come to "regard publicity as a sort of duty. We take delight in the reflection of ourselves in the public mirror. Self-exposure seems to us to be a matter of pride. . . . Our sentiment of privacy is symbolized by the open wire fence."[69] Yet disputes about privacy—and especially about institutional invasions of privacy— nonetheless proliferated in this wire-fence society. For much of American history, privacy norms had functioned as tools for the management of everyday social relations because they endowed people with a modicum of control over their presentation of self. Hosts of social gatherings could ask their guests to depart; wives and husbands could retreat into bedrooms and close window blinds; relatives could be kept at bay. When the front stage of social life appeared overwhelming and the back stage beckoned, the decision to move from one realm to the other was a decision that people could (and did) conceivably make. However, those who found themselves in the crosshairs of the press and concerned about the privacy of their telecommunications often had much less agency. The "ruthless publicity" of the media and the infrastructure of long-distance communications had birthed a society where established means of securing privacy were increasingly inadequate and the degree of individual control over access to, and the distribution of, personal information appeared to diminish with each passing decade.[70]

This critique was at the heart of Godkin's writings about tabloid media and the commodification of personal information. It also informed an essay that appeared six months later—in December 1890—in the *Harvard Law Review*. The essay's authors, Samuel Warren and Louis Brandeis, picked up where Godkin had left off (we know that they were aware of each other's writings because they cited them). "The press is overstepping in every direction the obvious bounds of propriety and of decency," Warren and Brandeis claimed. "Gossip is no longer the resource of the idle and of the vicious, but has become a trade, which is pursued with industry as well as effrontery. To satisfy a prurient taste the details of sexual relations are spread broadcast in the columns of the daily papers, to occupy the indolent, column upon column is filled with idle gossip, which can only be procured by intrusion upon the domestic circle."[71]

The specific doctrinal aim of their essay was to protect "the sacred precincts of private and domestic life" and thereby shield the individual against an increasingly inquisitive society in a way that neither libel law nor property rights and copyright could. As Warren and Brandeis argued, "instantaneous photographs and newspaper enterprise" and "numerous mechanical devices" had created a situation where "what is whispered in the closet shall be proclaimed from the house-top." They proposed that privacy had to be guarded against advertisers and the tabloid press through new legal remedies and a new conception of the inviolate self.[72]

Some of their concerns were narrowly focused on the privacy of social elites. Both authors were integrated into the upper strata of New England society and aware of the public interest that social status or ostentatious displays of privilege could generate. In 1883, at age thirty-one, Samuel Warren had experienced this firsthand during his wedding to Miss Mabel Bayard, which was simultaneously an introduction into one of the most influential political families in the United States. The Bayard family had sent its sons to governors' mansions and the U.S. Senate since the late seventeenth century, while its daughters had maintained the family's social station by marrying lawyers, politicians, and financiers. At the time of the wedding, Thomas F. Bayard, Mabel's father, was exploring a possible run for the presidency. Newspaper journalists shadowed the couple's wedding reception, speculated about the newlyweds' expensive art purchases, and dutifully reported on Mabel Bayard's travel schedules and Bayard family burial rites.[73] By 1890, Warren had developed what he later described as a "deep-seated abhorrence of the invasions of social privacy" and approached his former Harvard Law School classmate Louis Brandeis with the idea for an essay that would break new conceptual ground while promising tangible relief from the involuntary publicity he had experienced.[74]

The *Harvard Law Review* essay was therefore part of a "broader legal strategy employed by late nineteenth-century elites to protect family reputations from the masses in the face of disruptive social and technological change."[75] But while Warren and Brandeis voiced repeated concerns about the state of their "social privacy" (in a letter) and the privacy of "social and domestic relations" and "the domestic circle" (in the *Harvard Law Review* essay), their main argument was couched as a more general commitment to the dignity and rights of the individual. They argued that "the intensity and complexity of life, attendant upon advancing civilization, have rendered necessary some retreat from the world, and man, under the refining influence of culture, has become more sensitive to publicity, so that solitude and privacy have become more essential to the individual."[76]

The challenge, as they put it, was to reempower individuals to "be let alone" by defining "anew the exact nature and extent" of protections in a society that too often treated personal lives as a kind of collective property.[77] To do so, they drew on older traditions of legal thinking, including common law principles that protected "personal writings and all other personal productions, not against theft and physical appropriation, but against publication in any form."[78] Yet they added a twist. Common law about libel and defamation was frequently understood as an extension of "the principle of private property," which also covered the contents of personal letters.[79] Warren and Brandeis considered this logic inadequate. As they suggested, the protection of personal writings and other personal information necessitated a pivot from property rights toward the judicial recognition of an "inviolate personality."[80] It did not matter whether the collection and publication of personal communications had resulted in some kind of demonstrable harm, such as a loss of income or embarrassment, and it did not need to be analogized to theft. What mattered was simply the act itself because each individual contained within themselves a sphere of inviolability that could only be breached with the consent of the person concerned.

The two authors strategically framed their intervention as an argument for continuity—privacy protections were "merely an instance of the enforcement of the more general right of the individual to be let alone" that was "as old as the common law." Yet this assertion masked a rather profound triple shift. First, in a society of informational persons, the enjoyment of privacy was no longer a personal choice but depended directly on the actions of publishing houses and advertising agencies. Second, violations of privacy did not need to result in financial or reputational damage, and protecting against such violations necessitated legally codified sanctions rather than physical seclusion and the social stigmatization of habitual eavesdropping. Third, the ultimate aim of such protections was not to restore conditions from a prior historical period but to guard inviolate "thoughts, sentiments, and emotions" in a modernizing society. The first of these interventions framed privacy as a problem of scale. The second emphasized the need for novel judicial frameworks, beyond those offered by existing libel law. And the third betrayed a shift from valuing privacy primarily as a feature of domestic relations toward thinking about privacy as a basic right of citizens and consumers. Warren and Brandeis's essay retained the established language of domesticity and common law but also hinted at a preoccupation with the privacy of the individual and the power of institutions in modern America.

PRIVACY AND THE CULT OF THE INDIVIDUAL

Warren and Brandeis were not the first to articulate a connection between privacy and individualism. As chapter 1 has already shown, calls for privacy during the eighteenth and nineteenth centuries often involved concerns about personal moral rejuvenation. After the Civil War, abolitionist religious communities and a new generation of spiritualist and transcendentalist thinkers also distanced themselves from religious orthodoxy by preaching about the preexistence of the individual soul, the value of individual moral refinement, and the quest for personal salvation.[81] In 1879, Charles Beecher—a minister who is mostly known today as the brother of the author Harriet Beecher Stowe—dove headfirst into these debates with a book titled *Spiritual Manifestations.* In the book, Beecher argued that "the very existence of society seems to demand some power of privacy on the part of the individual" because "the body is not the tower or tent of the soul. It is its castle from which all other minds may be excluded."[82] Others focused less on specific religious teachings than on the general principle of religious liberty. The Unitarian minister Sidney Morse, publisher of the short-lived transcendentalist newspaper *The Radical* between 1865 and 1872, preached that freedom of religion was ultimately rooted in "the privacy of the individual," which forbade "any public enactment requiring observance of the forms of any creed whatsoever."[83] During the 1870s—and at a time when new religious movements were challenging ecclesiastical doctrine in the United States—the case for individual privacy was in part a case for noninterference in matters of personal faith and religious practice.

But by the 1890s, similar arguments about the privacy of individuals had become more widespread and had spilled beyond the realm of theological debates. To E.L. Godkin, privacy expressed nothing less than "respect for a man's personality as an individual" because it protected "that kingdom of the mind, that inner world of thought and feeling."[84]

Looming behind such statements was a continued fascination with the duality of the self, which was widely understood as having a public-facing side as well as a hidden inner personality.[85] Yet, increasingly, the inner aspects of this self were specifically understood as an inviolate domain freed from observation but filled with possibilities. To be an individual was to have the potential of becoming one kind of person or another as one marched forward on the ever-winding "road to selfdom."[86] It is no coincidence that psychoanalysis and psychotherapy became popular at roughly the same time: If the process of individuation unfolded deep inside the self (in other words, if people were not simply products of their environments), excavating repressed feelings from the subconscious promised to reveal a person's true nature and the true source of their psychological ailments.

This was also a period when the cultural, legal, and political valuation of the individual was increasing on both sides of the Atlantic. As Emile Durkheim concurrently argued in France, "from being limited and of small regard, the scope of the individual life expands and becomes the exalted object of moral respect. The individual comes to acquire even wider rights over his own person and over the possessions to which he has title."[87] The solitary self of prior decades was reimagined as an inviolate person deserving of specific rights. Individuals—rather than families—were affirmed

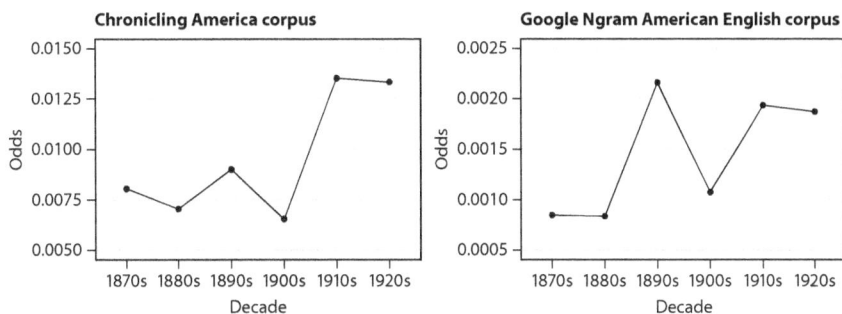

FIGURE 4.3 Discussions of the "privacy of the individual." *Sources: Chronicling America; Google Ngram Corpus of American English.*

as the elementary units of social organization who required a protective shield "against an increasingly intrusive world."[88] Figure 4.3 plots two associations that illustrate the timing and scope of this shift: the co-occurrence odds of "privacy" and "individual" from the *Chronicling America* collection of historical newspapers, and the proportion of books about privacy published in the United States that included specific references to the "privacy of the individual," based on Google Books' American English corpus. The two patterns evince remarkably close agreement despite drawing on very different types of printed materials. In both cases, associations of privacy with individualism rose during the 1890s. They then peaked again during the 1910s and 1920s. As the *Atlantic Monthly* noted, public opinion had "[stooped] to concern itself with the privacy of the individual" to an unprecedented degree.[89]

The bump during the 1890s was in part due to the reception of Warren and Brandeis's essay within American journalistic and legal circles. In the years after its publication, it sparked a lively debate about the merits of legal arguments rooted in "inviolate personalities" and the alleged inadequacies of libel law, which took place in leading newspapers but also in the more specialized pages of academic law reviews. In signed and unsigned essays, the *American Law Register* (published by the University of Pennsylvania), the *Central Law Journal* (published in St. Louis, Missouri), the *Columbia Law Review* (from New York City), and the *Kentucky Law Journal* each wrestled with the implications of individual privacy for the canon of American jurisprudence.[90] But, notably, a commentary on privacy by the editorial board of the *Yale Law Journal* from 1902 had nothing to say about Warren and Brandeis's essay. In many ways, this was still a more accurate reflection of prevailing judicial currents. The young lawyers' contribution in the *Harvard Law Review* essay excited America's legal intelligentsia in 1890, yet the widespread recognition of privacy in American courtrooms came later and was shaped to a much greater degree by lower court jurisprudence and state-level privacy statutes (see chapter 5).[91]

Perhaps the best illustration of the growing association of privacy with liberal individualism appears in the work of Thomas M. Cooley, a contemporary of Godkin, Warren, and Brandeis. Cooley served as Chief Justice of the Michigan Supreme Court from 1864 to 1885 and as Dean of the University of Michigan Law School from 1871 to 1883. His reputation stems in part from his authorship of the most comprehensive analysis of American tort law. The *Treatise on Torts*, first published in 1879, helped to organize an evolving body of law. It also included some of the first explicit references in American legal texts to a "right to be let alone"—the same phrase that was later picked up by Warren and Brandeis. But Cooley's understanding of privacy and "being let alone" during the 1870s and 1880s differed significantly from later restatements. About privacy, he had this to say in the original 1879 edition: "The eavesdropper might with impunity invade the privacy of one's home, by listening at key-holes and playing the spy at windows," since such actions do not "impoverish the family, or deprive them of drink, or food, or clothing, or diminish their current revenue." Therefore, these actions remained outside the scope of common law and libel jurisprudence. Privacy, in the 1870s, was still fundamentally about the spatial integrity of the home and the social integrity of the family, and legal remedies were scarce.

Individuals still had property claims for letters that were "valuable only as a curiosity or as an autograph," and they could always sue based on "pecuniary injury." Legal redress also existed for those who suffered financial or other reputational harm from the publication of slanderous statements. But those statements had to be "malicious" and "false" to fit into the existing repertoire of tort claims. (Cooley added, "A dishonest man is not wronged when his good repute is destroyed by exposure.") The mere fact that someone's personal life was discussed in public did not constitute an actionable offense. "Words never constitute an assault," Cooley concluded, and "it is safer to allow too much liberty [in the publication of intimate details] than to interpose too much restraint."[92] Cooley's writings from this period already pioneered the idea of a right "to be let alone," yet in the same paragraph also clarified that this right was to be understood through the lens of assault. It implied the possibility of physical injury or "an insult, a putting in fear, a sudden call upon the energies for prompt and effectual resistance." It did not yet extend to other types of interference in private life, such as the unauthorized publication of details about a person's character or professional life.

The second edition of Cooley's *Treatise on Torts*, published in 1888, remained largely unchanged. This was the last edition edited entirely by Cooley himself, who died from heart failure in 1898. However, the treatises were considered sufficiently important in the American legal field that revised editions were published after his death. The third edition appeared in 1906, edited by the Chicago lawyer John Lewis. This posthumous publication included Cooley's original text as well as "new matter" that discussed recent developments. One such insertion was an entire section dedicated to privacy. It included a fundamental restatement of how the law thought, or ought to think, about this issue. American courts had not yet reached consensus—more on this in chapter 5—but the prevailing judicial winds were already blowing in the direction of judicial recognition. The third edition of the *Treatise on Torts* confidently assumed that such a recognition was forthcoming and then laid out a view that differed significantly from Cooley's original writings. It now explained that the right to privacy "is a purely personal one" and continued: "It is a right of each individual to be let alone or not to be dragged into publicity. One has no right of privacy with respect to his relatives living or dead. Thus a parent may not enjoin the publication of the picture of his infant child. And the widow children or other relatives of a deceased person cannot enjoin the use of such person's likeness for advertising purposes, the erection of a statute of such deceased, or the publication of a memoir of his life."[93] In texts such as this one, and among an influential segment of the American legal and political intelligentsia, privacy was increasingly "portrayed as an individual good that one enjoys or is deprived of on an individual basis" and that deals "with us as private individuals protecting our own rather than as a collective subject."[94]

The shifting winds that propelled new legal (and individualistic) interpretations of privacy also blew through other domains of public administration. At the federal level, the National Board of Trade asserted, for the first time, that "the right of privacy of the individual should be recognized," which meant, among other things, that "the consent of the individual" had to be obtained before using a person's name or portrait for commercial purposes.[95] And in Kansas, the State Board of Health emphasized that governing agencies had a responsibility not to "intrude upon the privacy of the individual or to assume supervision and control of him as a mere man." Yet the report also continued, "When one becomes inseparably linked with others and takes his place as a component part of the populace . . ., he must compromise with his natural desires and eliminate from his voluntary action whatever is hurtful to this greater whole."[96] There existed situations when the privacy of individuals needed to be made subservient to "those larger and more general interests of the many" and balanced against competing state objectives, such as the policing of public health nuisances. As one public health reformer argued, "to the public good, private respects must yield."[97] Chapter 6 will examine those tradeoffs in greater detail, highlighting the importance of legally codified exceptions and showing that different governing agencies responded in idiosyncratic ways to demands for privacy against the American state. Yet the responses of these agencies converged in one specific sense: by the turn of the twentieth century, privacy was regularly framed through the lens of liberal individualism.

PRIVACY AND LIBERAL INDIVIDUALISM IN THE TWENTIETH CENTURY

The developments of the 1890s were an imperfect prelude to those of the early decades of the twentieth century. They proselytized an explicitly individualistic interpretation of privacy, yet they still focused most explicitly on the actions of journalists and advertisers. Discussions of citizens' privacy against the American state existed, as shown by the intervention from the Kansas State Board of Health, but they were comparatively rare. In contrast, in the 1910s and 1920s, arguments about the privacy of U.S. citizens came to dominate debates about state power and newly sensitized American progressives (who had for years beaten the drum of statism to advance ambitious social reforms) to the threat of executive overreach.

In 1914, Congress had drafted a bill that would have required the New York Stock Exchange (NYSE) to disclose the content of telegrams and other messages during investigations into financial speculation. These investigations were to be performed by the Postal Inspection Service—the investigative arm of the U.S. Post Office—because financial fraud was included within the legal umbrella category of mail fraud. In response, the lawyers hired by the NYSE juxtaposed such fraud prevention against a more basic right of privacy. Their argument hinged on the claim that the forcible disclosure of personal communications from "the books and papers of members" amounted to an "arbitrary" exercise of executive power because the mere possibility of fraud provided "no sufficient reason for the invasion of the privacy of the individual." They continued: "If the power cannot be effectively exercised without the invasion of that privacy, it may be a good reason for not conferring it."[98] Reviving arguments that had first appeared during Congressional debates about the privacy of telegraphic messages during the 1870s and 1880s, the NYSE's lawyers suggested that, in the pursuit of commendable or necessary goals (such as the prevention and punishment of financial fraud), governing agencies could find themselves in the untenable position of violating the basic privacy rights of American citizens. During the late 1880s, similar arguments had been minority views. By 1914, they held sufficient sway to stall the congressional bill.

The prospect of war further heightened concerns about the proper scope of state power. In Massachusetts, labor and materiel shortages during initial military armament campaigns prompted local telephone providers to deny applications for new landlines unless they were clearly "in the public interest" and beneficial to the war effort. Spurred by accusations that telephone operators would thus subject applicants to invasive screenings "for the purpose of determining whether or not reasonable necessity exists for the application," the state's Public Service Commission concluded that the policy "involves such an invasion of the privacy of the individual that it ought not to be permitted."[99] But in most instances, and salient concerns about citizens' privacy notwithstanding, the wartime environment was characterized by an expansive interpretation of the state's power to collect and analyze personal information. The passage of the Espionage Act of 1917 provided the clearest example of this, establishing broad powers to investigate "treasonous" actions, censor postal communications, and prosecute dissent. It was immediately followed by the Sedition Act of 1918, which extended these restrictions by criminalizing criticism of the government, flag, or armed forces.

The passage of both laws alerted many social reformers (who had previously embraced the assertive exercise of federal power to address the social dislocations of the late 1800s) to the repressive capacities of the American state. Those concerns were further fanned by the ratification of the Eighteenth Amendment in 1919 (which instituted Prohibition), when newspapers published myriad stories of wiretapped phone lines and police raids of private cars and residences that painted a dark picture of the state's hunt for illicit liquor.[100] Such concerns were not without precedent. So-called "radical libertarians"—like the lawyer Theodore Schroeder and the women's rights campaigner Ida Craddock—had organized resistance to the governmental censure of "obscene" mail during the 1880s and 1890s, when a series of moral panics swept the nation and sparked a wave of repressive antiobscenity legislation (see chapter 6). But until the experience of World War I, many American progressives had remained skeptical of, as the influential philosopher John Dewey put it, "all the early Victorian political platitudes" about individual rights, and they had largely dismissed the idea that "liberty of thought and speech" could be permanently damaged by an overbearing state.[101] As Dewey still asserted in an article published in 1917 in *The New Republic*, "I cannot arouse any genuine distress on this score." To many progressives, the establishment of powerful governing agencies still appeared as a necessary counterweight to industrial monopolists and as the most promising avenue through which social change could be effected.[102] But in the shadow of World War I and Prohibition, progressives like John Dewey began to reassess their relatively benevolent view of governing institutions and their skepticism about "the sanctity of individual rights and constitutional guaranties."[103] Increasingly, those rights and guarantees seemed like viable remedies against a state apparatus that was not just significantly larger than during the late nineteenth century but also significantly more capable of collecting, analyzing, and utilizing personal and statistical data.

Out of this historical cauldron emerged a complicated patchwork of rules and regulations that firmly anchored commitments to citizens' privacy within American jurisprudence and governance but also made room for the assertive exercise of state power across all levels of government. The governance of privacy during the twentieth century—and the defense of privacy in a society where personal data circulated more widely and was of greater administrative significance than in the past—centrally involved the defense of the inviolable self against inquisitive institutions. The unifying factor behind these various initiatives and developments was a widespread recognition of privacy as an individual right rather than a prerequisite for familial harmony or a social good more generally.

The successful codification of this interpretation partly explains why, in the twenty-first century, the entanglement of privacy and liberal individualism is often regarded as a conceptual necessity—an essential and constitutive feature—rather than an outgrowth of historical circumstance.[104] Even privacy's most zealous contemporary critics—those who treat liberal individualism as an impediment to far-reaching social change and then dismiss privacy rights as a consolation prize that leaves the power structures of politics and surveillance capitalism intact—often direct their analytic fusillade toward a conceptual edifice that was first erected by the likes of Godkin, Beecher, Warren, and Brandeis. Perhaps the time has indeed come to update our conceptual priors and explore, as Priscilla Regan has suggested, "a path that has been largely uncharted" and "acknowledges the social importance of privacy."[105] This requires neither a renunciation of privacy, nor an abandonment of liberal principles. But it necessitates a more thorough assessment of the limitations that come with the now-common operationalization of individual privacy as consent over data sharing, of the relationship between surveillance, the imposition of social control, and social stratification, and of the selectivity of privacy protections that seem universal only at first glance. It is toward the codification of such selectivity and its consequences—in jurisprudence and public administration—that we now turn.[106]

5

A Modern Legal Fact

How Privacy Gained a Foothold in American Jurisprudence

isputes over privacy can easily turn into rearguard actions: attempts to mitigate the consequences of new technologies or an unsettled social order after the fact. Yet the impact of such struggles still propagates forward through time, potentially affecting individuals and organizations for years or decades to come, especially once privacy claims have been institutionalized in one way or another and have thereby become partially insulated against recurring challenges and gradual erosion. This longer-term impact of privacy on the organization and functioning of American society is occasioned through the built environment (i.e., the organization of physical space), through legislative action (i.e., statutes like the 1901 and 1902 laws in New York), and through corporate and governmental routines (i.e., organizational practice). It also, and perhaps most obviously, manifests through the judicial system. When the legal scholar Laurence Tribe referred to privacy as the "limiting principle" of American society, he specifically meant the set of constraints imposed on the exercise of power by a constitutionally derived right to privacy and the affirmation of those constraints through the courts.[1]

In the twentieth and twenty-first centuries, this right has been a fixture of the legal imagination and a touchstone of myriad legal disputes about the ability of government officials to collect personal information and to regulate the intimate spheres of personal and marital life. The right to privacy now appears in court cases that adjudicate anything from phone wiretapping by police departments to the dragnet collection of geolocated data, access to contraception, abortion rights, and same-sex marriage. Rooted in an expansive reading of constitutional safeguards against unreasonable searches and seizures (the Fourth Amendment) and self-incrimination (the Fifth Amendment), as well as the liberty clause of the Fourteenth Amendment, it circumscribes a multifaceted realm of "private life" and also gestures at what Helen Nissenbaum has called "privacy in public": "hiding places" and "protected crannies for the soul" in domains that are otherwise considered legitimate targets of governmental action.[2]

However, that was not always the case. The origins of the judicial recognition of a right to privacy are once again found around the turn of the twentieth century, when it was most frequently derived from common law precedent or natural law and was primarily invoked during legal disputes about the unauthorized use of photographs by yellow press journalists and the use of a person's name by advertising agencies and playwrights. But subsequent jurisprudence preserved few traces of this initial experimentation. Instead, the growth of privacy jurisprudence during the twentieth century has involved the circumscription of privacy as a state-centric right and the pressing of an expanding set of issues—from policing powers to sexual self-determination—into a constitutional corset. This contrasts with "a more lenient regulation of the private sector" that has often left privacy torts conceptually defanged or, in the judgment of the legal historian Lawrence Friedman, "effectively dead."[3] Surveying privacy jurisprudence during the first half of the twentieth century, Neil Richards and Daniel Solove conclude that privacy tort claims against private entities became "relatively unusual" and increasingly functioned as a "residual category" that was populated with whatever disputes did not readily fit under libel or defamation.[4]

How did this happen? Compared to topics covered in the previous chapters, the legal history of privacy is relatively well-trodden terrain. Two perspectives dominate, each drawing attention to inflection points and periods of intense juridical activity that reshaped and canonized privacy in the eyes of the law. *What* types of knowledge are shielded against *whom* and with *which* justifications? Those are the moveable cornerstones of privacy jurisprudence in the United States. But the two perspectives advance competing arguments to explain the "domain formation" and the "settling" of meaning that are commonly regarded as key elements of legal institutionalization.[5] The first view emphasizes the formative impact of prominent legal experts and thus treats legal institutionalization as the consequence of elite interventions that shape the interpretation and canonization of abstract principles from the top down.[6] It foregrounds the publication of Samuel Warren and Louis Brandeis's *Harvard Law Review* in 1890, Brandeis's dissenting opinion in the Supreme Court's 1928 decision in *Olmstead v. United States,* and a later series of legal handbooks written by William Prosser, the dean of the University of California Berkeley Law School, as "milestones" that channeled legal discourse and cemented a distinction between comparatively narrow privacy torts on the one hand and expansive constitutional readings of the right to privacy on the other.[7] The second view focuses on the 1960s and 1970s, when broader shifts in sexual norms, women's rights and gay rights movements, and concerns about electronic data processing by the American government cemented the recognition of privacy as a constitutional right against an invasive state.[8] This view still places considerable emphasis on important milestones of legal development—for example, the Supreme Court's 1965 decision in *Griswold v. Connecticut,* which invoked arguments about marital privacy to invalidate governmental restrictions on contraceptive access—but generally regards those milestones as lagging indicators of shifting public opinion during a period of societal realignment and social movement activism.[9]

Yet neither perspective fully captures the process through which the right to privacy achieved judicial recognition and was integrated into the constitutional tradition. The first approach misconstrues the contributions of elite scholars to the early evolution of privacy jurisprudence.[10] Any single essay paled in significance compared to piecemeal meaning-making and world-building in the American legal field and may be a poor guide to "what was happening to privacy" in American jurisprudence in the Early Information Age.[11] Much of the initial judicial labor to derive and define the right to privacy happened in lower courts, not in the *Harvard Law Review* or before the U.S. Supreme Court. The second approach focuses on a period too close to the present, when judicial discussions of privacy had already become linked to the U.S. Constitution. The debates of the 1960s focused primarily on the various domains of life that were to be protected against governmental intrusion by constitutional provisions and on the legal justifications for doing so.[12] For example, the Supreme Court generally treated privacy in a procedural and place-based manner until its 1965 decision in *Griswold v. Connecticut* (which shifted the justificatory basis from procedural protections to substantive rights and folded contraceptive access into discussions of privacy by prohibiting police searches of "the sacred precincts of marital bedrooms") and the 1967 decision in *Katz v. United States* (which additionally affirmed privacy protections against governmental phone surveillance by declaring that privacy protects "people, not places").[13]

More generally, the focus on landmark contributions in each of the two approaches also risks obscuring developments that galvanized legal thought and judicial practice even if they were ultimately abandoned and written out of the canon of legal precedent. The history of the victors is not the history of the vanquished. Yet it is only by recognizing the full range of possible futures at any given time—only one of which becomes realized—that we can fully grasp jurisprudence as "an arena of conflict within which alternative social visions contended, bargained, and survived."[14]

Chapter 3 has already made clear where I see the chips falling: the gradual and uneven incorporation of privacy into the institutional fabric of American society involved processes of coalition-building, domain formation, and meaning-making that played out over prolonged periods and in specific institutional settings. The conditions needed to be ripe in order for change to become manifest, but people also had to exercise their collective or institutional power to make it so.

This chapter demonstrates that, having been tied more closely than ever before to the tenets of individualism, the right to privacy became a recognized legal fact (and became wedded to the constitutional tradition) across three periods of legal institutionalization. Before the turn of the twentieth century, during a period of *initial judicialization*, the leading exponents were not judges and legal scholars but journalists, who highlighted the intrusive potential of mass media, articulated concerns about the privacy of personal communications, and began to demand new legal remedies. When judges referenced a right to privacy before the turn of the twentieth century, it was frequently with reference to such extrajudicial debates. Between 1900 and 1920, during a period of *intralegal competition*, the logic of privacy began to diffuse across the American judicial system as judges drew on a multitude of traditions to discuss, deny, and defend privacy as an enforceable legal right but without establishing the primacy of any single approach. And after 1920, during a period of *judicial consolidation*, constitutional interpretations of the right to privacy became dominant as lower court judges and the Supreme Court selectively mobilized the power of law to confront the growing reach of the American state. The "modern legal fact" of privacy still bears the marks of this disjointed legal history and the judicial and interpretive struggles it sparked.[15]

HOW THE LEGAL HISTORY OF PRIVACY IS COMMONLY TOLD

The most common starting point for the legal history of privacy is the 1890 essay in the *Harvard Law Review* by Samuel Warren and Louis Brandeis, which has already made an appearance in chapter 4. It is widely regarded as a landmark contribution that "gave birth to" American privacy jurisprudence, added "nothing less than . . . a chapter to our law," laid "the foundation of American privacy law," and marked the "inception" of the right to privacy.[16] By the 1920s, Brandeis had ascended to the U.S. Supreme Court and applied the logic of inviolate personalities to disputes over the exercise of state power. In his dissent to the Supreme Court's 1928 decision in *Olmstead v. United States* (which sanctioned the use of courtroom evidence collected without a warrant from phone wiretaps, as long as police officers did not physically trespass on a suspect's home) he advocated for an expansive reading of constitutional amendments and the subsumption of the right to privacy under their enlarged umbrella. Brandeis suggested that the passage of time had "[brought] into existence new conditions and purposes" that required a reassessment of legal doctrine and argued that "the makers of our Constitution conferred, as against the Government, the right to be let alone."[17] The argument failed in 1928. Yet in the eyes of many legal historians, the *Olmstead* dissent marks the advent of federal privacy claims against the American state.[18]

This reading of sociolegal history foregrounds prominent legal experts, who asserted their "monopoly of the right to determine the law," displaced local forms of legal reasoning, and decisively shaped the content of legal doctrine.[19] Leveraging their academic credentials and prominent positions within the American legal field, they determined the evolution of jurisprudence from the top down. They also anchored emerging communities of legal thought, which could disseminate their ideas to a wider audience, elevate their influence, and build their reputation as canonical figures.[20]

A second perspective focuses specifically on the 1960s and 1970s, when (according to Mary Ziegler) the right to privacy "became a political preoccupation."[21] It treats privacy law as an indicator of prevalent cultural and political values and as a resource that can be strategically deployed by social movements.[22] Proponents of this view are less concerned with the contributions of any single individual than with the macrosocial "conditions of possibility" into which schools of legal reasoning are embedded, including the proliferation of electronic databases and the sexual revolution.[23] Caught in these shifting currents, the Supreme Court used decisions like *Griswold v. Connecticut* in 1965 (about contraceptive access) and *Katz v. United States* in 1967 (about phone wiretaps) to affirm the privacy claims of citizens against the state, thereby adding "a new facet of constitutional meaning" after decades of relative juridical stagnation and bringing privacy jurisprudence into line with growing anxieties about the misuse of electronic surveillance and pervasive concerns about the policing of sexual activities and reproductive decision-making.[24]

This second perspective draws particular attention to the connection between privacy claims, cultural circumstance, and the expanding reach of the American state.[25] It also highlights the importance of extrajudicial actors. Because many social movements exhibit a rights consciousness— an understanding of formal rights as key ingredients and resources in the restructuring of social relations and power dynamics—activists may decide to pursue change through the courts and articulate grievances in explicitly legal terms.[26] The flurry of Supreme Court decisions during the postwar decades was directly linked to political mobilization in a changing society.

So goes the conventional story about early American privacy jurisprudence. But it is a story in need of some revision. The narrow focus on a small number of contributions by legal elites misses a dense forest for its most splendid trees. Much of the judicial labor during the first decades of the twentieth century happened in lower courts as judges wrestled with each other and with common law precedent to derive, define, defend, or dethrone a right to privacy in American courtrooms. The process of legal institutionalization was a collective endeavor, directly tied to the dynamics and shifting currents within the legal field. It also drew on older and well-established precedent and rooted new judicial claims in English common law, natural law, and American libel and defamation case law.[27]

A focus on the 1960s and 1970s gets the collective part right—the reframing of abortion rights and contraceptive decision-making as matters of privacy was the work of many—but gets the period wrong. Constitutional and state-centric approaches to privacy were already woven into the Supreme Court's 1914 decision in *Weeks v. United States* (which held that U.S. marshals could not "invade the house and privacy" of a suspected mail fraudster without a court warrant), Brandeis's 1928 dissent in the *Olmstead* case, and the court's 1932 acknowledgment in *United States v. Lefkowitz et al.* (which also considered the use of evidence obtained through warrantless searches) that courts may "safeguard the right of privacy" through a liberal interpretation of the Fourth Amendment.[28] The debates of the 1960s were predominantly about the scope of privacy claims within the constitutional tradition and the legal justification of those claims, not about an initial pivot toward the constitutional privacy of citizens against the American state. A crucial phase of legal development occurred well before the rise of computational data processing and the sexual revolution.

So how did the logic of privacy evolve from a contested and relatively capacious idea into a clearly defined and tightly bounded "modern legal fact"?[29] The rest of this chapter documents the emergence of two staggered schools of legal thought—one focused on privacy violations by private entities and rooted in the common law and natural law traditions, and the other focused on privacy violations by government agents and rooted in the U.S. Constitution—and traces the shifting dominance of these two schools across several phases of legal institutionalization.

I build my argument in part by constructing a time-series network of legal citations. Such citations matter for legal reasoning because judges who affirmed or dismissed alleged privacy violations as viable legal grievances did not push into a conceptual void. The *stare decisis* principle of American jurisprudence means that judges generally situated their decisions in relation to the existing body of case law.[30] Lower-court judges, in particular, are generally oriented toward the "casuistry of concrete situations": they focus on the articulation of retrospective genealogies that connect disputes to prior decisions and thereby present the piecemeal articulation of justice as the "principled interpretation of unanimously accepted texts."[31] Through the citation of precedent, and within a federalized judicial system, state judges were the first to link the right to privacy to an existing repertoire of legal concepts and cases and thereby began to render it intelligible in the specialized language of the law. Mapping those citation links across many cases and statutes makes it possible to examine the institutionalization of the right to privacy within a larger body of case law and a longer genealogy of judicial decision-making.[32]

TWO STAGGERED SCHOOLS OF LEGAL THOUGHT

Let us begin with a visual aid. Figure 5.1 shows the complete network of legal citations, using data from 1870 to 1930. Each individual case, statute, constitutional amendment, or legal document appears as a network node, and each citation link between two nodes appears as a network tie. The network includes 677 nodes—146 cases that directly discussed the right to privacy between 1870 and 1930 ("egos," in the parlance of social network analysis) and 531 additional nodes that were linked to those 146 cases through their citations ("alters")—and 1,099 ties. The visual representation additionally subsets three period networks, respectively showing citation links for cases that were adjudicated before 1900, from 1900 to 1920, and after 1920. The structure of each network can be measured using a modularity score, which expresses how strongly the network is partitioned into distinct clusters. The overall citation network has a modularity scores of $Q = 0.7$, which is toward the upper bound of modularity scores for empirically observed social networks (i.e., the network has relatively distinct clusters).[33] However, modularity scores for specific period networks are lower, showing that legal discourse *within* each period was less fragmented than legal discourse *across* multiple periods. One exception is the period between 1900 and 1920, which has a modularity score similar to the overall network ($Q = 0.69$) and indicates that legal discourses during this interim period were more fragmented than they were before 1900 (when legal discussions of privacy were still scarce) and during the 1920s (when legal meaning had started to settle).

Two clusters stand out in this network visualization. They represent two distinct schools of legal reasoning and differ along several axes. First, the two clusters capture different thematic foci. Cases in the cluster shown at the bottom of the networks in figure 5.1 predominantly adjudicated disputes about film photography, advertising, and media organizations. *Roberson v. Rochester Folding Co.*, *Schuyler v. Curtis*, and *Pavesich v. New England Life Insurance Co.*—the three cases in the bottom cluster with the highest eigenvector centrality, which is a commonly used measure of structural importance in social networks—all dealt with the unauthorized publication of portrait photographs.[34] Each of these cases also attracted considerable public attention beyond the legal profession. As *The New York Tribune* declared in the wake of the *Roberson* decision in 1902, "it is intolerable that a woman . . . should be at the mercy of every advertiser

(A) 1870–1930

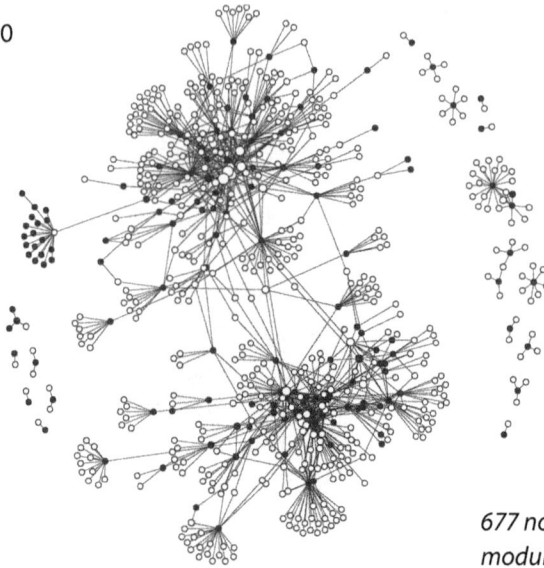

677 nodes; 1,099 ties;
modularity Q=0.70

(B) 1870–1900

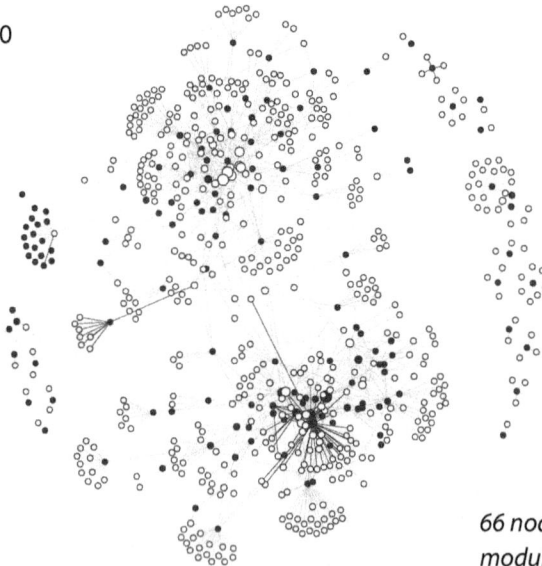

66 nodes; 80 ties;
modularity Q=0.50

FIGURE 5.1 Legal citation networks for "right to privacy" cases. The total network (1870–1930) is shown in panel A. Period-specific networks are shown in panels B, C, and D. *Source*: Nexis Uni.

(C) 1900–1920

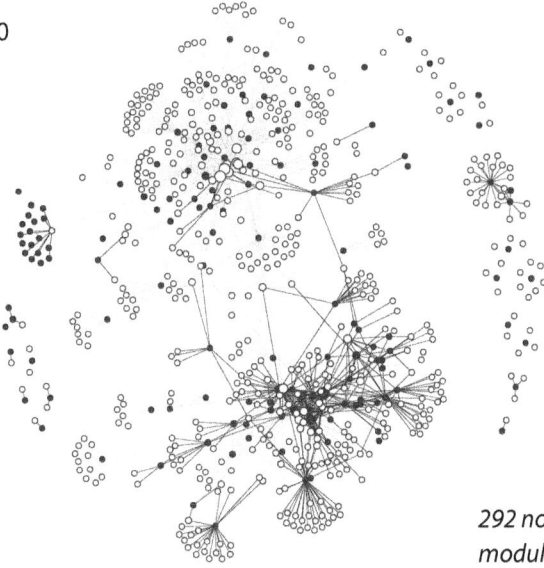

292 nodes; 435 ties;
modularity Q=0.69

(D) 1920–1930

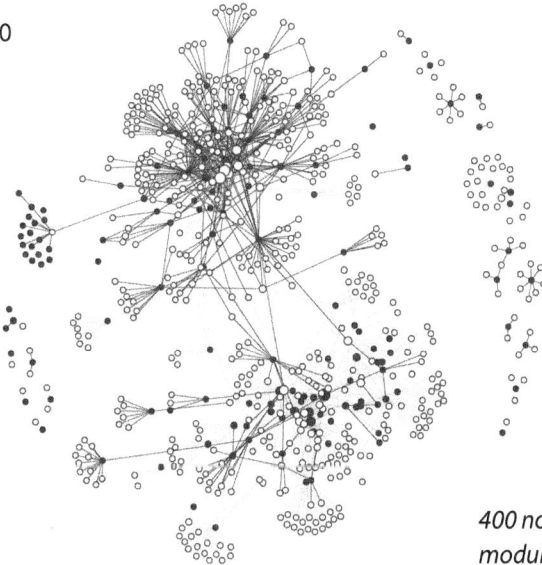

400 nodes; 584 ties;
modularity Q=0.50

FIGURE 5.1 *(continued)*

who can beg, borrow or steal her photograph. This is a great evil and is not the less real because it has only recently been discovered."[35] The paper continued: "New conditions have prepared the way for it, and new remedies are needed." (The same cluster also includes Warren and Brandeis's 1890 essay—one of the first essays to discuss such "new remedies"—, which was occasionally cited during legal disputes about photography and newspaper publishing.) In contrast, cases in the top cluster primarily addressed the privacy of the home and personal information. These cases include *United States v. Kaplan*, *State v. Owens*, and *State ex rel. King v. District Court*, which dealt with police searches for illicit liquor during the Prohibition era, as well as the Supreme Court's 1886 decision in *Boyd v. United States*, which held that unreasonable searches and the compulsory production of personal documents were prohibited by the Fourth Amendment.[36]

Second, the two clusters identify different venues and targets of privacy disputes. Privacy disputes in the bottom cluster were almost always adjudicated in state courts, whereas disputes in the top cluster were more likely to be adjudicated by the federal judiciary. Six percent of cases in the bottom cluster were federal, compared to 15 percent in the top cluster. Crucially, all cases that were decided by the U.S. Supreme Court appear in the top cluster. Cases in the top cluster also focused on privacy violations by agents and agencies of the American state, including local police forces, federal law enforcement, the Internal Revenue Service, the Bureau of Prohibition, and the Census Bureau. In contrast, the disputes shown in the bottom cluster almost always involved privacy claims against private entities, including advertising agencies and newspaper publishers. One exception are several cases about so-called "rogue gallery" photographs that were compiled by local police agencies, which appear in the bottom cluster because they tended to cite prior cases about the illicit use of photographs by advertisers and publishers rather than cases that addressed privacy violations by the police. Overall, only 19 percent of privacy cases against private entities appear in the top cluster, and only 16 percent of privacy cases against state organizations appear in the bottom cluster.

Third, the two clusters capture staggered periods of legal evolution. The bottom cluster is mainly populated by privacy disputes from the 1900s and 1910s, which often cited English common law and American jurisprudence from the 1870s and 1880s as precedents. The most central nodes in this cluster are cases like *Schuyler v. Curtis* and *Roberson v. Rochester Folding Co.* Each case was controversial within American jurisprudence—*Schuyler* because it endorsed a limited right to privacy until death and *Roberson* because it denied the existence of such a right—and each became an important reference point for other judges.[37] In contrast, the top cluster includes privacy jurisprudence from the 1910s and 1920s that referenced more recent case law and constitutional amendments rather than nineteenth-century common law or natural law doctrine. The most central nodes in this cluster, again measured by their eigenvector centrality scores, are cases about searches for illicit liquor by local law enforcement and the Bureau of Prohibition (like *State v. Aime*), police raids on private apartments (like *Weeks v. United States*), and searches for drugs and weapons (like *People v. Jakira*).[38] Such cases rooted privacy claims in the Bill of Rights and hint at a gradual pivot of legal reasoning from common law and natural law toward constitutional law.

Different claims were made, using different arguments, in different courts, vis-à-vis different entities, and at different historical moments. Already in the 1900s and 1910s—decades before William Prosser's treatises on torts and the privacy-related decisions of the U.S. Supreme Court drew a bright line between comparatively expansive constitutional arguments and comparatively narrow and rigid tort law—state and federal judges integrated disputes about state power and corporate practice into different genealogies of American case law.

In addition to plotting network structures, we can map this evolution of legal meaning-making along a time continuum. Figure 5.2 shows the thematic focus of the dispute ("issue"); the origin from which judges derived the right to privacy, if explicitly mentioned ("origin"); and the entity that was alleged to have violated this right ("target") for each of the 146 privacy disputes from the networks above. The results are arranged by median year of adjudication, so that more recent schools of legal reasoning are located toward the bottom of each panel.

Privacy jurisprudence was scarce until the end of the nineteenth century: only seven cases discussed the right to privacy in the decades prior to 1900, followed by sixty-four cases in the twenty years between 1900 and 1919 and another seventy-five cases in the decade between 1920 and 1929. As the number of cases increased, new kinds of disputes were framed through the lens of privacy and new schools of legal reasoning appeared in American courtrooms. During the first two decades of the twentieth century, the right to privacy was most commonly discussed in cases that focused on the use of photographs and the publication of personal information in newspapers and advertisements—the same issues that had also preoccupied

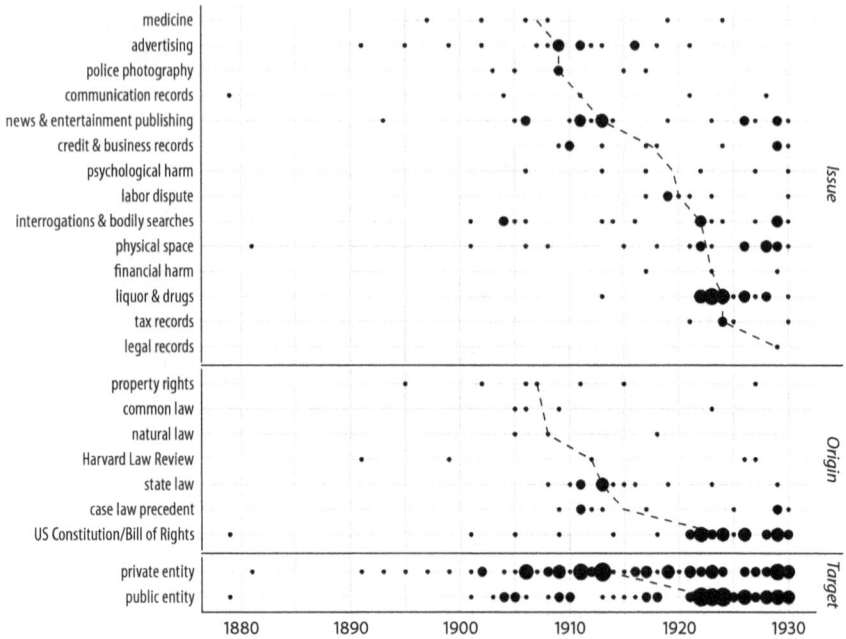

FIGURE 5.2 "Right to privacy" cases by thematic contexts ("Issue"), justifications ("Origin"), and defendant ("Target"). Dot sizes indicate number of cases per year; dashed lines indicate median year of adjudication for each category. *Source*: Nexis Uni.

Samuel Warren and Louis Brandeis. Such cases drew on established legal doctrines like natural law, common law, and property rights to determine whether a distinct right to privacy could be found in the annals of American jurisprudence and whether, if it was found to exist, it had been violated.

But after 1920, the balance shifted from such violations toward the conduct of state officials, and the legality of governmental searches of private residences, luggage, and cars—often conducted to enforce Prohibition laws after the passage of the Eighteenth Amendment in 1919—emerged as a salient topic of legal disputes. These two approaches were separated in time by a decade of juridical development. The median date of cases that alleged privacy violations by private entities occurred in 1913, whereas the median year of cases that alleged violations by the state occurred in 1923. Cases about the use of personal data without consent by publishers and advertising agencies were concentrated in the 1910s, whereas cases about police interrogations, antiliquor raids, and apartment searches occurred primarily in the 1920s.

The growing emphasis on governmental action went hand in hand with constitutional interpretations of privacy. Instead of deriving a right to privacy from common law, natural law, or property rights—or, in New York, by rooting this right in the state's 1902 privacy statute—judges began to place greater weight on the Fourth, Fifth, and Fourteenth Amendments, and thereby folded privacy into an existing set of constitutional principles and the legal precedents that had already developed around them. The median date of such constitutional justifications occurred seventeen years after the median date of the property-based justifications. By 1930, constitutionalism had come to dominate over alternative legal doctrines, and grievances about governmental action had become more prominent than cases against publishers, ad agencies, landlords, or even funeral home operators.

INITIAL JUDICIALIZATION

Early American privacy jurisprudence thus had a distinct structure and temporality. New ideas entered into the specialized discourse of the law and unsettled established modes of legal reasoning, were contested, and became integrated into the judicial canon and affirmed through the federal judiciary.[39] Yet these latent patterns are impossible to detect when we focus merely on a handful of landmark cases, and they illustrate the complex processes of meaning-making that tied novel claims about privacy and state power into a tapestry of legal arguments and case law precedent. Three distinct periods of legal institutionalization stand out. Before 1900, during the period of *initial judicialization*, the language of privacy entered American jurisprudence sporadically and without significant effects on case law decisions, pushed in part by concurrent discussions in the media about the social impact of emerging technologies. Between 1900 and 1920, during a period of *intralegal competition*, judges relied on a multitude of legal doctrines and applied the right to privacy to a wide variety of legal disputes but without agreeing on the existence of such a right, its proper scope, or its legal foundations. After 1920, during a period of *judicial consolidation*, the right to privacy became more deeply anchored in American jurisprudence, closely tied to constitutional law, and increasingly applied to the actions of state officials. Let us examine each period in turn.

The origins of privacy as a legal right coincided with the emergence of large media empires and long-distance communication, which vastly increased the quantities of daily information that the average American could consume, the size of audiences that consumed such information, and the importance of intimate details about a person's life to the business models of the tabloid press. As chapter 4 has already shown, privacy in the Early Information Age was not just negotiated within the family but was decisively affected by the actions of roving photographers, intrepid journalists, and zealous advertising executives. Writing in the *Atlantic Monthly*, the writer Benjamin Sanborn thus criticized the "slanderous character of the modern newspaper" and "its entire disregard of privacy and the right of individuals."[40] Sanborn conceded that "error and slander" were not unique to the late nineteenth century—after all, newspapers had long published stories about the lives of prominent persons, and those persons had likewise tried to shield themselves from observation and public scrutiny—yet he suggested that "we have made error and slander more public by our inventions." What had changed, according to Sanborn, was not the journalistic desire for scoops (or even some basic human interest in gossip) but the technologies involved in the production, collection, and dissemination of portrait photographs and personally identifiable information.

Such concerns—about the precarious state of privacy in an increasingly interconnected and information-rich society—were still conspicuously absent from American jurisprudence in the 1890s, despite the publication of Warren and Brandeis' essay in the 1890 issue of the *Harvard Law Review*. It is true that around 250 opinions from district and state courts had already mentioned the term privacy, as the legal scholar Amy Gajda has pointed out, but almost all of them did so merely in passing.[41] Highlighting the privacy "of the home" and of "quiet occupancy" was certainly in line with the cultural customs and social norms of nineteenth-century America. But judges almost never linked such norms to any legal precedent, nor did they frame privacy as a concept that held specific *legal* meaning and significance.

However, observers outside the legal profession were quickly becoming sensitized to a perceived lack of legal remedies that could meet the challenges of the Early Information Age and resolve disputes that fit poorly into existing legal categories. One such person, writing to the editors of the special interest publication *Photographic Times and American Photographer*, lamented the insufficiency of legal protections against the "demoralizing and degrading habits of some of the amateur photographers" and suggested that a few determined police raids could put an end to their meddlesome activities.[42] Those activities appeared even more corrosive when they were not simply the work of hobbyists but backed by the power of corporate publishers. In the words of E. L. Godkin, the editor of *The Nation*, "the [tabloid] press has no longer anything to fear from legal restriction of any kind" even as "the community has a good deal to fear . . . from the loss by individuals of the right of privacy."[43] This attitude was perhaps best summed up in 1892 by the *Irish Standard*, which wrote: "It is scarcely possible to take up a newspaper without finding in it invasions of the sacred right to privacy. . . . Not only the private affairs of persons holding public relations are pried into and falsely published forth, but those of persons who have no public functions whatever. This tendency is a most deplorable one, and unless it is checked it will bring about a deterioration of public sentiment, and cause deserving persons to shun public relations of every sort."[44] In this context, it seemed increasingly obvious that the American legal profession had to "concern itself with the privacy of the individual" in a much more direct manner than in the past.[45] To a growing number of concerned observers, and in light of sweeping social and technological changes, the gap between established social norms and emerging social realities had become difficult to ignore.[46]

Judges warmed slowly and cautiously to such demands, and early opinions hardly mentioned legal doctrine and judicial precedent at all. When the Michigan Supreme Court affirmed a woman's "legal right to the privacy of her apartment" in 1881—likely the first explicit recognition of such a right in American jurisprudence—they drew on cultural arguments about womanhood and moral innocence rather than specific schools of legal reasoning.[47] The same gendered logic also reappeared nine years later in New York, when the Broadway dancer Marion Manola was surreptitiously photographed during a gender-bending stage performance of the libretto "Castles in the Air." The photograph had been commissioned without Manola's knowledge by the dance company's manager, who correctly surmised that it would stir public sentiment (which it did, including in the *New York Times*) and possibly revive the fortunes of his struggling show. Manola quickly sought an injunction, in part because she was concerned that her young daughter would "see pictures of her mother in shop windows in such costumes as I am now wearing."[48] The injunction (which recognized Marion Manola's proprietary claims in her likeness) was quickly granted *ex parte*. Despite this injunction, however, the company manager arguably achieved his goal of generating newspaper coverage. Rumors *about* the photograph were sufficient to spark and sustain public attention.

Perhaps the gender dimensions of these early legal disputes are no surprise given the close association of privacy and womanhood during the nineteenth century. In the absence of a specialized judicial discourse on privacy, judges resorted to what they knew: prevalent cultural and moral norms that informally cleaved the social world into public and private spaces, male and female domains, and sanctioned and stigmatized ways of being. But invoking privacy additionally gave lower-court judges a language through which they could capture emerging social anxieties that were not specifically concerned with domesticity and were fanned by the winds of technological innovation and mediatization. The photograph of Marion Manola was but one drop in a growing flood of classified ads that used portrait photographs and endorsement quotes to sell all varieties of products and services (see chapter 2), while instant photography and new media ecosystems created additional possibilities for exposure and sparked moral panics about privacy in an age of publicity (see chapter 4). In the words of P.T. Barnum, the prominent American showman and circus director, commercial success in this growing consumer economy hinged directly on a business's ability "to extort attention" from an audience that was exposed to more published content than ever before.[49]

Before the right to privacy gained a firm foothold in the nation's courtrooms, extralegal debates had already embraced privacy as a logic for comprehending social relations within the home and nascent concerns about modern life beyond the home, launched debates about the proper relationship between self and society, and thus spawned both a set of arguments about the significance of privacy and a public audience that was attuned to them. There was not yet a developed judicial discourse about the legal justification of a right to privacy or about the scope of disputes to which it could be applied. But there was an opening for such debates and a constituency of scholars and judges who would soon contest them. As one judge later acknowledged, the increasing salience of privacy claims was therefore a direct reflection of the times rather than the product of deliberate legal reasoning: privacy was forced to the fore of public consciousness to such a degree that jurisprudence could hardly avoid engaging. "The present age . . . may be said to be marked with a characteristic of publicity," another legal scholar wrote in the journal *Green Bag*, "yet this very condition holds within itself the germs of a right of privacy, the returning swing for balance."[50] This right was "unmentioned in the legal tomes" and "based upon no ancient or modern statute." It was instead pushed into the legal field as Americans began to wrestle with the social realities and the "new conditions of life."[51]

INTRALEGAL COMPETITION

Judicial discussions of privacy remained rare until 1900 despite increasing journalistic attention and the publication of Warren and Brandeis's *Harvard Law Review* essay in 1890. When judges mentioned the right to privacy before the turn of the century, it was often to dismiss it as a figment of the legal imagination or to curtail its proposed application.[52] This changed between 1900 and 1920. As one lawyer noted in 1909, the right to privacy "has of late years grown out of the unredressed residue of the law into a recognized right."[53] Yet the growth of privacy jurisprudence did not follow a singular path. Instead, the first two decades of the twentieth century saw a blossoming of competing approaches that aimed to establish a more solid legal footing for the right to privacy by grounding it in natural law, common law, evolving precedent, and state-level legislation and by applying it to the actions of advertising agencies and newspaper publishers as well as the conduct of state officials. Without a federal intervention that could consecrate particular legal genealogies as "correct," lower court judges sought to seize control over the legal meaning of privacy in a series of prolonged interpretive struggles in which the common denominator was often a conflict of opinion about the scope and substance of the right to privacy.[54]

It was not unusual for judges during this period to frame privacy as yet another form of property claims (as had already been the case during the Manola injunction hearing in 1890): in addition to controlling material possessions, a person could also exercise control over immaterial properties like one's speech or image. Thus, one Missouri court opined in 1911 that "if it can be established that a person has a property right in his picture," those who "now deny the existence of a legal right of privacy would freely concede a remedy to restrain its invasion, for all agree that equity will forbid an interference with one's right of property."[55] Indeed, as the Wisconsin Supreme Court argued in *Klug v. Sheriffs*, "many [recent decisions] turn upon property rights or breach of trust, contract, or confidence" to carve out space for a right to privacy.[56] Linking privacy and property allowed judges to establish grounds for legal recognition by way of analogy at a time when the judicial foothold of the right to privacy was still tenuous.[57]

The same analogous reasoning also connected the right to privacy to libel law. Invasions of privacy by journalists, photographers, and advertisers were repeatedly framed by state courts as matters of libel, which provided remedies for material and reputational damage as a result of slanderous publicity. In general, it was the case that "truth is a complete defense in an action for slander, and in an action for libel it is a complete defense if published with good intent and for justifiable ends" (those rules had also been written into various state constitutions, such as the Illinois Constitution of 1870 and the Wyoming Constitution of 1890).[58] But in some cases, conduct could even be ruled actionable when published information contained no demonstrable lies but nonetheless proved ruinous for the affected individual under a concept called "truthful libel," which instead turned instead on the ill intent of those who published this information.[59]

Strictly speaking, libel and defamation law remained focused on the publication of intimate details rather than the collection of personal information. But the conceptual crevasse was sufficiently narrow that judges sometimes attempted to throw their hooks across and anchor a defense of privacy to whatever conceptual holds existed on the other side. Before arguments about basic rights and inviolate personalities severed the link between privacy jurisprudence and libel law, state courts bootstrapped the rhetoric of privacy to those earlier case law traditions. As the Michigan Supreme Court put it in 1899, it was through such bootstrapping in lower courts—not through any single intervention from above—that "this law of privacy seems to have gained a foothold" in American jurisprudence.[60]

Yet case law precedent had long coexisted in the reasoning of American judges with an interest in legal doctrine. The natural law tradition was particularly strong in the nineteenth-century and also became a common doctrinal reference point for privacy discussions in the early twentieth century.[61] Tasked with adjudicating a dispute over yet another unauthorized use of a person's image in an advertisement (this time, for life insurance), the Georgia Supreme Court argued in *Pavesich v. New England* that "each individual as instinctively resents any encroachment by the public upon his rights which are of a private nature as he does the withdrawal of those of his rights which are of a public nature." A right to privacy "is therefore derived from natural law."[62] While the social and technological conditions of modern society had rendered concerns about privacy more acute, the judges ruled that an affirmative reading of the right to privacy did not hinge on any such changes. As the Kentucky Court of Appeals also found in *Brents v. Morgan*, "the doctrine of the right of privacy, while modern in every sense, is older than generally recognized in the opinions of the courts which we have read."[63] In 1908, judges of the Indiana Court of Appeals even drew on treatises about ancient law to highlight the long history of the right to privacy. They argued that such a right was "well recognized," "derived from natural law," and already "embraced in the Roman conception of justice."[64] By 1918, this approach had become sufficiently common to warrant the assertion, in volume 21 of the comprehensive legal guide *Ruling Case Law*, that the right to privacy "is considered as a natural and an absolute or pure right springing from the instincts of nature."[65]

In other rulings, the right to privacy was derived from, and also folded into, an expansive common law tradition. The Supreme Court of Rhode Island noted that the right of privacy had long ago been carried "into the common law, where it appears in various places."[66] And while the majority opinion in *Schuyler v. Curtis*—one of the most widely cited precedents during the 1910s, about the unauthorized construction of a bust that bore the likeness of a recently deceased philanthropist—only embraced a narrow conception of privacy, one judge pushed for a more expansive interpretation of privacy based on the common law tradition. Encouraging his colleagues to move beyond the tight constraints of precedent, he argued that "it would be a reproach to equitable jurisprudence, if equity were powerless to extend the application of the principles of common law, or of natural justice, in remedying a wrong, which, in the progress of civilization, has been made possible as the result of new social, or commercial conditions."[67]

Even without any clear precedent, the twin traditions of natural law and common law provided alternative anchors for the right to privacy. As one legal scholar noted in response to *Schuyler v. Curtis*, bringing those older doctrines to bear on "public convenience or necessity" and the "demands of individual freedom" in a rapidly changing society provided sufficient justification for a right that had previously been "so little defined by judicial decision."[68]

The American press took note of this judicial recognition. In the 1900s, newspapers across the United States reported extensively on court cases that had played out before the New York Court of Appeals and the Georgia Supreme Court. The two courts had reached opposite conclusions in two

cases that otherwise bore striking similarities. The first case, decided in
New York in 1902 and previously discussed at the end of chapter 3, concerned a teenager whose portrait had been sold without her knowledge to
an advertising agency, which had then printed it onto twenty-five thousand poster advertisements for a flour company. The second case, from
1905 and already mentioned above, concerned the unauthorized use of a
person's image in advertisements for an insurance company. In the New
York case, *Roberson v. Rochester*, the court held that no justiciable right
to privacy existed in American case law. In the Georgia case, *Pavesich v.
New England Life Insurance Co.*, judges derived such a right from natural
law and common law precedent. The American press was firmly on the
side of the judges from Georgia, roundly condemning the reasoning of the
New York court and forcing one judge to issue an extended defense of
the ruling.[69] As *The New York Tribune* declared, "it is intolerable that a
woman . . . should be at the mercy of every advertiser who can beg, borrow
or steal her photograph. This is a great evil and is not the less real because
it has only recently been discovered. New conditions have prepared the
way for it, and new remedies are needed."[70]

But the challenge, as many contemporary observers saw it, was to guard
against the unauthorized appropriation of a person's likeness while also
carving out exceptions to privacy that could be defended as matters of
personal choice or public interest. Revisiting its endorsement of the right
to privacy in the wake of the *Roberson* case, *The New York Tribune* declared
years later that "there is no right of privacy in matters which concern all
the people": crime and corruption were matters of such overriding public
interest that those involved "lose to some degree the right to privacy" that
was otherwise afforded to American citizens.[71] In the decades that followed (discussed in chapter 6), the governance of privacy would often turn
out to be the governance of legitimate exceptions.

However, the public outcry that followed in the wake of the 1902 decision
in New York also led to one of the first state statutes that explicitly protected
the privacy of individuals against newspapers and advertising agencies and
forbade the use of "the name, portrait or picture of any living person" without prior consent. As one legal observer noted at the time, "the legislature
is now the only resort for citizens whose modesty and privacy may at any
time be intruded upon or who may awake any morning to discover that their
physical attractiveness or mental superiority has brought their face before
the great world of buyers as an advertising medium."[72] The legal codification

of privacy in state-level statutes opened up an alternative legal genealogy. For the first time, courts could not only refer to general legal principles or case law precedent but also treat the right to privacy as "solely the creation of statute" with "no existence independent of the statute."[73]

Outright rejections of the right to privacy largely disappeared from the reasoning of American judges after the criticism of *Roberson v. Rochester* and the passage of the New York law; and the scope of privacy disputes widened during the 1900s and 1910s.[74] More than two-thirds of privacy cases between 1900 and 1920 dealt with alleged violations by nonstate actors as judges adjudicated disputes over the use of photographs in advertising, the unauthorized publication of personal information in newspapers and in reviews of theater plays, eavesdropping into telephone and telegraph communications, the sharing of medical and business records, access to inheritance and divorce documents, burial practices, and access by landlords to private apartments. But also scattered in their midst were disputes about the power of the state, in which the government commonly prevailed. In Washington State, for example, prison authorities had circulated photographs of recently released inmates to local police departments to facilitate the arrest of potential recidivists. But when an inmate sued and alleged that such "rogue gallery" photographs violated his right to privacy, the state's supreme court sided with the government.[75] In Michigan, courts likewise held that state agencies had considerable authority to determine which types of personal information the government could legitimately collect to protect law and order.[76] And in Massachusetts, the supreme court ruled that business owners could be compelled to report employee wages to the state's labor administration because wage information should not be considered a private matter.[77] While some courts questioned an excessive deference to the executive just after the turn of the twentieth century, the successful application of privacy claims to the problem of state power still remained a relatively rare phenomenon.[78]

By 1920, judicial interpretations of privacy had been deformed by the weight of two decades of intralegal contestation. Moving beyond the "restricted beginnings" of privacy in domestic life and toward "a general right of protection from others," American judges had bestowed growing recognition on the right to privacy in disputes about the powers of advertisers and publishers.[79] Yet it was still far from certain at this historical moment that the right to privacy would eventually be consecrated as a state-centric constitutional right.

JUDICIAL CONSOLIDATION

During the 1920s, the collective gaze of the American legal field shifted. Technologies like the telephone, which had triggered the initial debates about the privacy of personal communications during the 1890s and 1900s, were becoming well established and less controversial.[80] One in eight Americans already had a personal telephone landline, and there would soon be one in almost every household. Newspaper circulation continued to increase, but the media landscape of the United States became more settled.[81] Yet society had begun to change (and had been unsettled) in other ways, and the attention of judges shifted toward the inquisitive tendencies of the American state. The bureaucratic apparatus of the United States had continued to expand; and the passage of the Espionage Act in 1917 and the prohibition of "intoxicating liquors" through the Eighteenth Amendment in 1919 had lifted questions about warrantless searches of luggage, cars, and apartments to the top of the political agenda.[82] Partially in response to the government's growing capacity to survey and surveil and partially in reaction to the expansion of executive authority during World War I, progressives' "prewar faith in a benevolent state" had also began to wane (see chapter 4).[83] As the *Chicago Daily Tribune* opined in 1925, the most significant threats to privacy now stemmed from the overreach of zealous officials. If a police officer "sees you in an automobile," the paper argued,

> All he needs is the license number to find out if you are the owner. He can learn, too, if you have given a mortgage on it. He can search the records and see what real estate you own and how much the mortgages on it are. He can find out how much real estate and personal taxes you pay and what you claim your personal property is worth. He can ascertain where and when you were born, what schools you attended, to whom and by whom you were married, when and why you were divorced, the time, place and cause of your death, the name of the doctor who attended you, the undertaker who buried you and the cemetery that received you. He can learn if there are any suits or judgments for or against you. He can learn what licenses you have taken out and what they cost you. And now he can find out how much income tax you pay.[84]

Some of the first signs of this shifting emphasis appeared in state constitutions.[85] Washington and Arizona became the first states to write privacy protections into their respective constitutions, emphasizing that the "private affairs" of citizens were to be secure against government interference "without authority of law."[86] Such protections did not simply expand the range of protections that already existed in statutory form elsewhere—such as New York's 1902 Civil Rights Law, which had focused on the actions of journalists and advertisers—but specifically moved the focus of privacy claims from any "firm or corporation" toward government officials, and from the publication of "the name, portrait or picture of any living person" without prior consent to the collection of personal data without prior court authorization. In a society that was becoming increasingly bureaucratized, privacy was tied up in larger cultural and political debates about the proper relationship between the American state and its citizenry.[87]

The American legal field had also evolved since the turn of the century. The strong doctrinal emphasis on natural law and common law was replaced in the 1920s by a greater interest in constitutional arguments.[88] In the wake of World War I and during the Prohibition era, scholars began to consider constitutional guardrails that would prevent undue interference of public officials in the "private spheres" of citizens' lives.[89] While federal judges had previously struggled to coalesce around a distinct right to privacy "on the ground of the lack of precedents," as one observer noted in the *Yale Law Journal*, the constitutional revolution within American jurisprudence and the increasing focus on intrusions by government officials provided those judges with a new language through which the "right to be let alone" could be apprehended, and also with a justification for doing so.[90]

Amid such changes, privacy jurisprudence began to shift away from cases against private-sector organizations like advertisers and from disputes over the use of photographs and the publication of intimate personal details. It shifted towards cases against government agencies and disputes over the collection of financial records and the searching of homes, cars, or luggage. Fewer than one-third of court cases about the right to privacy had addressed potential violations by the state in the period between 1900 and 1920, but two-thirds of cases between 1920 and 1930 dealt with the use and abuse of state power. Such disputes were increasingly framed by constitutional arguments rather than natural law or case law precedent. Searches that resulted from the enforcement of Prohibition era liquor laws were found to be a potential "invasion of the right of privacy which the constitutional provision against unreasonable search . . . protects," an "offense against the constitution," and "contrary to the principles of a free government."[91] As the Mississippi Court of Appeals argued in 1925, "enforcement of the law against the liquor evil is highly desirable, but in doing so we must not . . . permit unlawful searches of private premises, and thereby destroy the sacred constitutional right of privacy of the home."[92]

Still, this increased focus on the American state did not necessarily imply tighter restrictions on the power of the executive branch. Some judges certainly warned that search warrants were "executed in a manner that showed complete disregard of defendant's right to privacy."[93] They also observed a "startling increase in illegal searches and seizures" and issued a reminder of "the constitutional provision against unreasonable search and exemption of an accused from being a witness against himself."[94] But in many cases, the state-centric turn of privacy jurisprudence proved eminently compatible with the continued exercise of state power. Judges suggested that officials were not "attempting an entrance which will in any way affect the right of privacy" when they enforced the disclosure of tax and business records, and they argued that the probable cause requirements, narrowly written warrants, and the state's duty to ensure the protection of law and order provided sufficient justification for assertive interventions by government officials.[95] In those cases, private rights were rebalanced against public authority even as privacy jurisprudence became closely tied to constitutional protections.

Yet this should not detract from the significance of the underlying juridical shift. When Louis Brandeis penned his 1928 dissent to the Supreme Court's *Olmstead* decision, state-centric approaches to privacy had already crowded out claims against nonstate entities, and constitutional arguments had already begun to dominate intralegal discussions of privacy as a fundamental legal right. This was not due to any single Supreme Court precedent, as we would expect if the legal institutionalization of novel claims was a strictly top-down process wherein the nation's highest justices imposed their vision on unsuspecting lower courts. The primary reference points of privacy jurisprudence were earlier state court decisions and the constitutional tradition itself, rather than any single landmark decision by federal judges. When the Supreme Court explicitly considered the question of privacy vis-à-vis the American state—in the 1928 *Olmstead* decision or the court's 1932 *Lefkowitz et al.* ruling that invoked the Fourth Amendment as a means of safeguarding the right to privacy—state courts had already initiated a constitutional pivot in the absence of clear federal precedent. The Supreme Court's involvement in privacy disputes during the 1920s then helped to reaffirm and reify this state-centric and consti-tutional interpretation of privacy.[96] By 1930, the constitutional tradition had not only crowded out earlier schools of legal reasoning but also been consecrated by federal courts. The legal meaning of the right to privacy had become settled, and alternative genealogies had started to recede from judicial discourse and the American legal imagination.

THE LONG ARC OF JURISPRUDENCE

The translation of public-facing arguments *about* privacy into a judicially recognized right *to* privacy was a key vector of institutionalization because the law has long been one of the most powerful instruments for the pro-duction and reproduction of social order in the United States. When ideas and ideologies are codified in law and folded into judicial routines, their symbolic power is considerable, and their impact is felt at scale. Also con-tained within the law are the residues of prior struggles, the prejudices and preoccupations of a given society, and the fingerprints of those who interpreted and consecrated legal doctrine.[97] U.S. Supreme Court Justice Oliver Wendell Holmes Jr. put it thusly: the law discloses to the discerning eye "every painful step and every world-shaking contest by which man-kind has worked and fought its way from savage isolation to organic social life."[98] The settling of legal meaning and the production of legal genealogies can bestow legitimacy and impose permanence on a historically contin-gent and initially contested set of norms and practices. American privacy jurisprudence is no exception. It, too, contains "dim figures of an ever-lengthening past," as Holmes put it, that reflect distant struggles over the power or institutional actors and the appropriate relationship between seemingly inviolate selves and society writ large.

In the twenty-first century, constitutional arguments about privacy are interwoven with so many different kinds of disputes that they bear a considerable social and political weight. They helped to support abortion rights prior to the Supreme Court's undoing of *Roe v. Wade*; they underpin rights of sexual self-determination and same-sex marriage; they influence the governmental collection of personal data through electronic surveil-lance; and they safeguard certain physical spaces against wanton intru-sions. But the prodigious growth of constitutional privacy jurisprudence during the last one hundred years (and especially since the 1960s) also overshadows what was initially the dominant approach: an understanding of privacy as an extension of common law and natural law, thrust to the fore by the social problems of the late nineteenth century, and negotiated in disputes about commerce and advertising. The legal history of privacy in the United States is the history of conceptual expansion as well as abandoned alternatives and selective genealogizing. Studying this history from the ground up—from the perspective of lower courts within a federalized judicial system—makes it possible to uncover interpretive struggles and patterns of judicial reasoning that are obscured by a focus on landmark interventions from by the nation's highest court.

Such struggles were necessarily embedded within macrosocial environments and larger debates about technological change and corporate and governmental power. They were also wedded to precedent and prior schools of legal argument. Courts make their own decisions, but they do not make them just as they please.[99] Yet the contributions of legal elites (writing in the *Harvard Law Review*, or sitting on the bench at the Supreme Court) during moments of rupture and realignment should often be understood as consecrations rather than inventions: they impose conceptual order by inscribing retrospective coherence into disjointed juridical traditions and by writing competing schools of thought out of legal genealogies.[100] A processual and networked account of legal institutionalization can shed light on these varied foundations upon which American jurisprudence has historically been based but that are partially obscured by a narrow focus on landmark decisions.[101] Privacy first gained an institutional foothold at lower levels—in state legislatures through statutes like New York's 1901 Tenement House Act and 1902 Civil Rights Law and in state courts through the piecemeal articulation of legal genealogies—before becoming recognized at the federal level. However grand a conceptual edifice may ultimately appear, its construction begins not with the roof but with the laying of a foundation upon which the more visible architecture can rest.

The state-centric and constitutional turn of privacy jurisprudence also exemplified two larger juridico-political trends of the twentieth century. First, American political culture and jurisprudence became more strongly oriented toward the Constitution as an "American creed" that organizes social and political relations on the basis of fundamental rights and through the careful balancing of private, state, and federal interests.[102] The constitutional turn of privacy jurisprudence appears as an early chapter in "a long historical process of constitutional elevation that began during World War I" and reshaped the legal and political landscape of the United States.[103]

Second, the ascendancy of state-centric privacy claims (which were rooted in arguments about individual rights and inviolate personalities, not in claims about financial or reputational damage) fed into a growing categorical distinction in American law and politics between a regulated domain of public administration and a self-regulating economy.[104] As the right to privacy became divorced from property law and closely tethered to constitutional law, questions about the informational autonomy of market participants receded into the background. From the perspective of the law, markets were often understood through the logic of reciprocal exchange rather than the logic of rights, and perturbations to these exchanges could then be addressed through damages and redistributive payments.[105]

The scope of privacy jurisprudence now extends from historical legal disputes about police searches (like *Olmstead v. United States*, in 1928) through landmark cases from the 1960s and 1970s—like *Griswold v. Connecticut* (in 1965, about marital privacy in relation to the use of con-traceptives) and, most prominently, *Roe v. Wade* (in 1973, about abor-tion rights)—to more recent decisions about sexual self-determination (*Planned Parenthood v. Casey*, in 1992), same-sex relationships (*Lawrence v. Texas*, in 2003), and access to digital communications by law enforce-ment agencies (*Riley v. California*, in 2014). Across a large set of domains, such cases have affirmed—as the Supreme Court already declared in its 1957 ruling in *Watkins v. United States*—that "ruthless exposure of private lives" to state officials could place "constitutional freedoms in jeopardy."[106] Tellingly, one of the first official statements after the U.S. Supreme Court's decision to overturn *Roe v. Wade* came from Vice President Kamala Har-ris, who declared that "if the right to privacy is weakened, every person could face a future in which the government can potentially interfere in the personal decisions you make about your life."[107] The piecemeal articu-lation of privacy claims in different domains of life has thus been embed-ded throughout the twentieth century into a more general recognition of privacy as a "limiting principle" of the state against society.[108]

Only in in recent decades have questions about consumer data risen back to the forefront of judicial debates about "surveillance capitalism," bridging across a century of comparative neglect.[109] The collection of con-sumer credit data was first regulated in 1970, and the collection and use of medical information by private-sector insurers and providers of medi-cal services have been regulated since 1996. But a stronger pivot toward privacy in a consumer capitalist economy occurred more recently, during the 2010s and 2020s. From Virginia to California, U.S. states have now adopted dedicated consumer privacy laws that are partly inspired by the European General Data Protection Regulation (GDPR) and regulate how online platforms and data brokers can collect, use, and share personal data. In 2024, the language of privacy appeared in at least thirty bills pending before the U.S. Congress—more than during any prior period of American history—and many of these bills were more concerned with the digital economy than with the dataist state (although comprehensive privacy bills have yet to clear congressional hurdles).[110] We find ourselves once more in a phase of competition and contestation, where new visions of privacy are carried into politics and jurisprudence, aiming to bring the power of law to bear on the problems of the present and thereby shape the space of future possibility.

6

Governance by Exception
Bureaucratic Rule and the Limits of Privacy

ifty years before the experiences of World War I and Prohibition focused judicial attention on governmental invasions of privacy, the American state was something of a paper tiger: more impressive in constitutional theory than in administrative practice. As late as 1861, the federal government employed just 5,837 people, excluding the U.S. Postal Service, and had annual inflation-adjusted per capita expenditures of less than $170.[1] Even the federal government's most daring administrative undertaking—the decennial census—was a relatively ad hoc endeavor, and the Census Bureau did not become a permanent part of the federal bureaucracy until 1902. It was only in the final decades of the nineteenth century that the old "state of courts and parties" was replaced by a patchwork of large bureaucratic agencies, the exercise of governmental power became "ever more defined by statistics," and the United States began to experience "surveillance as a means of bureaucratic power."[2] "Call it socialism, if you choose," the U.S. Commissioner of Labor Carroll D. Wright declared in an 1887 address to a conference of social scientists, but the tendency to "exercise greater and greater supervision over the affairs of the people" appeared "as inevitable as it [was] strong."[3]

Alongside sensitive diplomatic information—the so-called "secrets of state"—statistical and personal data emerged as categories of privileged governmental knowledge that promised to introduce a rational science of "social physics" into the domain of public administration.[4] As one newspaper declared, "the first necessity is to know what we have and where it is."[5] Across different domains of public administration and in service of vastly different political agendas, the "taming of chance" through comprehensive enumeration and probabilistic reasoning held the promise of increasing the state's ability to penetrate and rule over a large territory and a growing population, thereby turning this population from a poorly understood mass into an entity that was legible to the bureaucratic eye. The ability to measure trends and track individuals became more central to the policing of crime, public health, and political order.[6] Means of producing state knowledge were also tools "to construct and constitute the groups they ostensibly describe."[7] The collection and analysis of large troves of data imposed cognitive as well as political and moral order, especially when those initiatives allowed a wide range of social problems to be cast as explicitly *gendered* or *racialized* problems on the basis of governmental statistics.

But while the modern American state is usually referred to in the singular and wrapped into the common cloth of officialdom, the production of state knowledge has historically been accomplished by a great number of administrative agencies that were oriented toward different constituencies and tasked with different things.[8] Figure 6.1 tracks the expansion of state-level infrastructures and databases within this fragmented bureaucratic state, which turned the monitoring of populations across considerable distances into a practical reality of American governance.

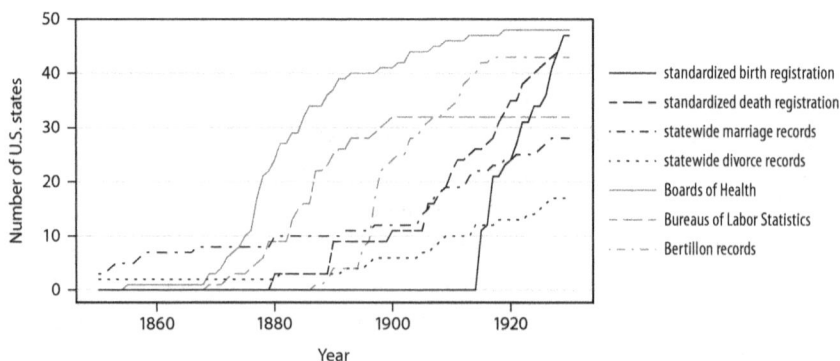

FIGURE 6.1 U.S. state-level data collection initiatives and administrative expansion. *Sources*: State boards of health; U.S. Marine Hospital Service; U.S. Public Health Service; U.S. Department of Health and Human Services; U.S. Department of Labor.

Early data collection outside the decennial census focused on counting (and then keeping count of) recipients of Civil War pensions, especially once the Arrears of Pension Act of 1879 and the Dependent Pension Act of 1890 relaxed eligibility constraints and led to hundreds of thousands of new pension applications.[9] (Several decades later, similar attempts to track public benefits recipients during the Great Depression resulted in the introduction of Social Security numbers.) Boards of health were also established in many U.S. states and cities, bureaus of labor statistics proliferated, and police departments began to rely on photographic evidence, fingerprints, and physiological measurements known as "Bertillon records" to track arrestees, convicted criminals, and (predominantly Black) sex workers.[10] Parts of the white establishment specifically ushered in what Khalil Gibran Muhammad has called a "racial data revolution" and leveraged newly tabulated government data to allege rampant deviance among newly emancipated African Americans, while scholars like W. E. B. Du Bois used similar information to draw attention to persistent discrimination and racial inequality during the Reconstruction era.[11]

From the vantage point of the twenty-first century, these early data collection efforts seem haphazard and almost humble despite their historical novelty. In contrast, attempts to track specific persons and to assemble an ongoing "stock tally of the nation" in the present day often appear as all-encompassing endeavors, with limits imposed only by the technological and institutional capacity to analyze incredible amounts of data in real time or to store them for later retrieval.[12] According to this view, surveillance has become a akin to a way of life as Americans have experienced its "extension and intensification . . . across all sectors of society" and the monitoring of "groups which were previously exempt from routine surveillance."[13] And indeed, when the introduction of telephones (in the 1900s), electronic records (in the 1970s), digital communications (in the 2000s), and biometric and genetic identifiers (in the 2010s) enlarged the space of technological possibility, state-sponsored data collection has tended to ratchet up accordingly.[14] The history of the Information Age is partially a history of "surveillance creep" as more and more domains became targets of deliberate governmental and corporate action.[15] In the modern world, it is often exceedingly difficult to make oneself invisible.[16] Data infrastructures have also become more interwoven than in the past. The informational detritus produced in one specific domain can have cascading effects across multiple domains when discrete data points are merged into comprehensive behavioral profiles and used to sort people into categories and rankings, thereby shaping the distribution of (dis)advantage in the informational society and even our sense of self.[17]

In this context, personal data not only reveal new facts about individual lives or societal patterns but also underpin the reproduction of the social order. They "can be used to make important decisions about people's lives" when such data are fed into algorithmic risk scoring models that appear particularly objective while also being difficult to scrutinize.[18] Thus, it comes as no surprise that two of the most widely cited allegories for governmental data collection are George Orwell's novel *Nineteen Eighty-Four*, in which the fictional government of Oceania has implemented a totalitarian surveillance system, and Foucault's model of the panoptic prison, in which the docility of inmates is ensured through the constant threat of indiscriminate observation.[19] The technosocial realities of the last fifty years raise "the ominous possibility of total surveillance."[20]

But claims about ubiquitous monitoring obscure as much as they reveal, substituting rhetorical oomph for analytic precision. They are especially misleading in one specific sense: surveillance systems are never as absolute and indiscriminate as they could be, given the state of technology, the level of administrative capacity (including the capacity to extract, store, retrieve, and analyze personal data), and the amount of information that can readily be collected. The governmental and corporate collection of personal data tends to remain behind the frontier of technological and administrative possibility, even if officials regularly stretch toward this frontier. Gary Marx refers to this as "surveillance slack"—a measure of the selectivity of state efforts to render populations legible, below the level that is technologically or organizationally feasible.[21]

That is why, in a very practical sense, the answer to the question "Do people still have a reasonable expectation of privacy?" is usually "it depends."[22] Political and financial considerations elevate an organization's interest in *specific* kinds of data about *specific* social facts and populations, directing the official gaze during data-driven monitoring and often increasing the focus on minority populations and the poor. Reasonable expectations of privacy are most consequentially undermined by targeted "encroachments" rather than by the indiscriminate vacuuming of personal data as policymakers, corporate executives, and street-level officials respond to specific problems, demands, moral panics, and exigencies.[23] State forbearance and formal privacy laws also still impose constraints on data collection, either by placing some types of personal data completely out of reach or (more commonly) by making the collection of these data conditional on court authorization and the demonstration of legitimate interest.[24] (As chapter 5 has shown, privacy jurisprudence has historically focused on constraining governmental action rather than corporate practice.)

In this chapter, I leverage data from several administrative agencies that routinely collected, processed, or transported personal data and interpersonal communications—the Public Health Service and the Post Office Department in particular—to argue that such selectivity is a core characteristic of American privacy governance, dating back to the early twentieth century. The privacy architecture that took root during the Early Information Age was marked above all else by the routine use of exceptions. In the eyes of the administrative state, privacy was not so much defined by what it *was* than by what it *was not*. It did not protect basic demographic and socioeconomic information, such as racial identifiers, literacy status, births, deaths, marriages, and divorces. It was sacrosanct—but not during public health emergencies, when it could be overridden by concerns for the public good. It protected the confidentiality of doctor-patient interactions—but not if your doctor diagnosed you with an infectious disease. It applied to sealed letters—but not to postcards and foreign mail. It protected interpersonal communications—but not those communications that were considered treasonous during wartime. The result was a decidedly uneven landscape of legibility that shielded some types of information against unauthorized or warrantless state interference while rendering other information and some populations uniquely accessible to governing agencies and thereby made formal adherence to privacy rules compatible with the real and imagined predicaments of statecraft and the bureaucratic will to know.

This focus on exceptions evokes an intellectual lineage that runs from Carl Schmitt through Walter Benjamin to, more recently, Giorgio Agamben.[25] Writing against the backdrop of political turmoil in the Weimar Republic, Schmitt took issue with what he regarded as an "onslaught against the political," rejecting the view that order could rest on a system of legal rules and bureaucratic procedures that were applied (and had to be adhered to) regardless of circumstance.[26] It fell instead to the sovereign to determine the boundaries and juridical structure of a political community by deciding "on the exceptional case" and thus to suspend normal legal regimes if such a step was required to protect the "concrete existence" of the state during moments of crisis.[27] All law was "situational" to Schmitt: it needed to contend with the ruthlessness of the world and the vulnerability of the state apparatus, including through the assertion of sovereign power over the juridical order.[28]

Such assertions of sovereign power dot American history—and American military history in particular—from Abraham Lincoln's suspension of *habeas corpus* rights along the military front line during the Civil War to changes induced by the Patriot Act after the 9/11 terror attacks.[29] But I am not primarily concerned with this particular type of wartime exceptions, the study of which tends to be predicated on a highly formalistic separation of law, bureaucratic administration, and politics and which correspondingly regards the introduction of strictly political considerations (i.e., considerations born from sovereign power) into a relatively autonomous juridical domain and the transformation of "provisional and exceptional [measures]" into a permanent feature of governance as crucial steps on the road toward authoritarianism.[30] However, sovereign power and legal regimes are no "strange bedfellows" of republican governance—conceptually separate and perpetually in tension—but "frequent fellow travelers in the history of American law and statecraft."[31] We must not draw too bright a line between constitutional rights and sovereign power and only search for exceptions outside the prevailing structure of law. The residues of prior political struggles and the prerogatives of sovereign power are already encoded within the structure of legal and juridical regimes.[32]

Indeed, reckoning with the governance of privacy in the modern United States requires us to recognize exceptions as central elements of juridical regimes and to reinscribe moral values and political ideologies as key determinants of those exceptions. These exceptions modify rather than suspend existing rules. Their routine (i.e., predictably recurring) invocation thus occurs within the confines of the law, which makes them functionally central to the practice of statecraft but also logically central to the structure of juridical regimes in the modern United States. The routine reliance on exceptions allows governing agencies to put legally mandated privacy protections up against a plethora of competing political considerations (such as considerations about public morals, public health, or national security) and thereby manage conflicting demands that are placed upon the state and inherent in democratic societies.[33] Exceptions thus constitute a juridico-political fine print of sorts, helping to bridge the zone of ambiguity that inevitably exists when the logic of law comes into contact with the exigencies of administrative practice. As important elements of legal casuistry, they aid the mapping of general legal principles onto the complexities of public administration and the social world.[34]

In short, exceptions function as "one of the most common ways that democratic states exercise power every day."[35] We shall now search for these exceptions "at the lowest extremities of the social body" and among "officials in action" who staffed some of agencies that dealt most directly with personal data and interpersonal communication around the turn of the twentieth century.[36] It was often among frontline bureaucrats and in the capillaries of state power that the principles of actuarialism were first put into practice and the routine use of exceptions came to define the governance of privacy as the United States entered the Early Information Age.[37]

THE POLITICS OF PUBLIC INFORMATION

The American state has collected basic data for the purposes of taxation, apportionment, and military recruitment since the founding of the republic. The paradigmatic example of such data collection is the U.S. Census, which first took place in 1790. But toward the end of the nineteenth century, the list of data points that were explicitly considered public records and thereby considered as legitimate targets of governmental enumeration broadened considerably. Collecting information about employment, literacy, business activity, criminal offenses, births, deaths, marriages, and divorces became a central focus.

Information relevant to public health attracted particular attention with the spread of municipal and state boards of health. Early health initiatives during the eighteenth and early nineteenth centuries had focused almost exclusively on coastal inspections of incoming ships and sailors for infections like yellow fever and smallpox.[38] But—beginning in the 1870s and informed by the success of preventative health campaigns during the Civil War and advances in medical knowledge (including the gradual acceptance of the "germ theory of disease," which posited that infectious diseases were caused by microscopic pathogens rather than mysterious "miasmas")—cities increasingly policed such "health nuisances" not just aboard seafaring vessels but also in the inns and brothels that sprung up in the vicinity of ports and in the American interior. By the early twentieth century, most states and big cities had established dedicated boards of health.[39] At the federal level, the National Quarantine Act of 1878 established a short-lived

National Board of Health, which was soon superseded by the Public Health and Marine Hospital Service (in 1902) and the Public Health Service (in 1912) as the emphasis shifted from health screenings at ports of entry toward nationwide public health administration.

The collection of standardized vital statistics improved as well, and the bookends of life and key biographical events—when someone was born and to whom, whom they married and divorced, when they had children, when and why they died—were folded into a list of records that were generally considered "public."[40] Government officials reasoned that the standardized collection of such records could help to determine the right "to enter certain occupations, to vote, to marry, to hold or to dispose of property, to employment by the state or country in military of civil service; responsibility for crime or misdemeanor; exemption from military or jury duty; [and] qualifications or disqualifications for certain public offices."[41] Education officials also sought to use birth records to establish public school eligibility, and the Children's Bureau proposed to use the same records to enforce prohibitions against child labor and sort suspected criminal offenders into the juvenile and adult criminal justice systems.[42] Some government officials were interested in vital records from Black Americans for overtly racist reasons, especially in states that had begun to pass antimiscegenation and racial purity laws during the Jim Crow era. For example, Virginia's head statistician Walter A. Plecker pushed for the addition of racial identifiers to birth certificates to enforce the state's Racial Integrity Act, which had outlawed interracial marriage. Municipalities were ordered to collect racial identities at birth to prevent subsequent violations of the color line by mixed-race and indigenous Virginians, whom Plecker suspected of hiding their racial identity later in life.[43]

By 1900, eleven U.S. states reported at least 90 percent of their deaths to the federal bureaucracy through standardized death certificates. By 1920, thirty-four states did. Standardized birth registration also increased, albeit at a slower pace, when public health authorities organized local audits in collaboration with the Census Bureau and the newly established Children's Bureau.[44] By 1928, an estimated 94.4 percent of Americans lived in the so-called Birth Registration Area, that is, in states where at least 90 percent of births were recorded in a standardized manner.[45] In practice—and despite the interest in data about racial minorities—this collection of vital records included significantly more comprehensive data for white Americans than for Black Americans until the 1930s. In 1910, for example, the U.S.

government obtained death statistics for 58 percent of the country's white population but only 18 percent of the Black population. This was largely due to the geographic distribution and concentration of different racialized populations. Especially before the northward Great Migration of the 1920s and 1930s, Black Americans were more likely than whites to reside in the rural South, which lagged behind urban communities in ensuring the completeness and standardized collection of vital records.[46] Black Americans thus faced the unique experience of being overexposed as well as undercounted: more likely than white Americans by an order of magnitude to enter the prison system in the postbellum South but also less visible to statisticians and policymakers through databases that aggregated individual public records into statistical portraits of the United States.[47] When W. E. B. Du Bois published *The Philadelphia Negro*, a groundbreaking 1899 study of the Black community in Philadelphia's Seventh Ward, it was in part to correct the correspondingly "faulty" and "crude" picture of Black life that had been painted by incomplete or nonexistent government statistics.[48]

The classification of vital statistics and other basic data as public records meant that those records were never included under the umbrella of privacy protections. They were personal information—or, in today's parlance, personally identifiable information (PII)—but, technically speaking, not private information. Conflicts occasionally arose over the expansiveness of this category, for example, during attempts by the Census Bureau and the Internal Revenue Service to add questions about business incomes to census schedules in the 1880s (see chapter 2). But such episodes of contention remained relatively rare. For the most part, disputes about the collection of such records were kept off the policy agenda.[49] The classification of a wide range of personal information as public records thus remains the large and often overlooked hole at the center of the governance of privacy in American public administration. (It can be instructive, in recognizing the particularity of the U.S. case, to briefly glance across the Atlantic. In Germany, even the *idea* of authorizing a nationwide census with the *Volkszählungsgesetz* sparked widespread protests and prompted an intervention by the constitutional court as late as 1983—although Germans think nothing of registering with local authorities whenever they change their place of residence. In France, racial identifiers are rarely collected even today. Memories of totalitarian rule and racial purity laws, as well as principled commitments to universalism, mean that the umbrella category of public records has historically differed in those countries, and continues to do so today.)

PRIVATE CITIZENS AND PUBLIC GOODS

While a large array of ostensibly public records was unquestionably at the heart of many governmental data collection efforts, bureaucratic agencies also endeavored to collect information that was not considered public by default, including personal medical information. During the late nineteenth century, boards of health aimed to prevent infectious disease outbreaks by collecting data on the number and type of infections, as well as the identities of infected patients. Tuberculosis ranked among the most common causes of death in the United States at that time, and about one in forty urban residents died from infectious diseases.[50] By 1901, every U.S. state had adopted formal reporting requirements for smallpox and cholera, and several states required that reports be made about outbreaks of diphtheria, scarlet fever, typhoid fever, yellow fever, and venereal diseases.

In some cities, physicians could meet their legal reporting obligations by collating local case counts before forwarding summary tables to the authorities. But in other jurisdictions, primary care doctors were asked to mark the type of disease on government-issued forms; add the patient's name, address, and employer; and forward the information to the nearest board of health (figure 6.2).[51] These so-called "sentinel surveillance" regimes imposed a relatively small organizational burden on nascent public health agencies—because much of the work was outsourced to local doctors, who acted as deputized sentinels for government agencies—but still provided the American state with an increasingly comprehensive tally of infectious disease outbreaks and with the ability to track and monitor specific patients.[52]

Municipal officials also policed infectious disease outbreaks more directly by embracing their mandate as a "sanitary police." In Boston, public health initiatives during the second half of the nineteenth century were run directly out of the city's police department, which was tasked with conducting "a thorough and systematic examination of the whole city," quarantining infectious disease patients, and instituting a public warning system by placing red flags on their homes.[53] Similar developments played out across the United States.[54] In New York City, a municipal sanitary committee recommended "the establishment of a thoroughly organized medical police" as a matter of urgent necessity.[55] Public health work by civic associations was to be supplemented with the "systematic sanitary inquiry and inspection in every street, block, [and] tenant-house."[56] Health officials

No. 1.

Boston,_____189

The Board of Health is hereby notified that_____

age, _____years, living at No._____Ward_____

is ill with_____. The first symptoms occurred

on_____. ___he attends_____school.
　　[DATE.]

_____M.D.

Is patient going to Hospital?_____

Note. — Physicians are expected, under the law, to report EACH case of diphtheria, membranous croup, scarlet fever, cholera, small-pox, measles, chicken-pox, typhus fever, and typhoid fever to which they may be called.

Note. — In unnumbered streets a favor will be conferred by stating, in addition to the name of the street, the nearest cross street.

REPORT OF VENEREAL DISEASE.

(To be treated as confidential so far as is consistent with public safety and the Rules for the Control of Venereal Diseases.)

(1) ....191..
　　　　　　　　　(City.)　　　　　　　　　(Date.)

The undersigned hereby reports a

(2) Case of.................................; (3) Laboratory findings. ....;
　　　　　　　(Name of disease.)　　　　　　　　　(Pos. Neg. None.)

(4) Name of patient...;
　　(Case or key number may be given instead of correct name under certain circum-
　　stances. See rule 1, Rules for Control of Venereal Diseases in Illinois.)

(5) Sex.................; (6) Color.................; (7) Age.............years;
(8) Single, married, widowed, divorced..............................;
(9) Address of patient...;
　　Street and house number may be omitted under certain circumstances, but name of
　　city, town, or village must be given in accordance with rule 1.)

(10) Is living at home, in boarding house, hotel, hospital, or elsewhere?.........
....
　　　　　　　　　　　　(Specify which.)

(11) Occupation ....;
(12) Employer.................................; (13) Address.................;
....
　　(Name and address of employer may be omitted under certain circumstances, in
　　accordance with rule 1.)

(14) Does patient handle milk, milk products, or foodstuffs?....................;
(15) Has patient discontinued employment?..............................;
(16) Probable source of infection....................................;
　　(Where a prostitute is the probable source of infection, give name and address in full.)

(17) Probable date of infection.....................................;
(18) Other known cases contracted from same source...................;
　　　　　　　　　　　　(State number of cases.)

(19) Is patient regularly under treatment with you?.....................;

Signed...........................M. D.
　　　　　　(Attendant.)

Address...........................
　　　　　(Of attendant.)

FIGURE 6.2 Infectious disease reporting forms issued by the Massachusetts Board of Health (*top*) and the U.S. Public Health Service (*bottom*). *Sources*: Massachusetts Historical Society; U.S. National Archives.

made periodic visits to tenement buildings and more than two thousand sworn officers of the city's law enforcement apparatus were tasked with enforcing health statutes through inspection, quarantine, fines, and forcible removal.[57] By 1900, the New York City Board of Health conducted close to two hundred thousand inspections per year, took executive action in tens of thousands of cases, and forcibly vacated hundreds of tenements for health-related reasons.[58]

But when public health agencies focused local surveillance campaigns on populations that were seen as likely carriers of disease, their assessment of epidemiological facts—and their defense of a disproportionate focus on minority communities during public health emergencies—was often infused with scientifically dubious or overtly racist logic and placed immigrant and minority communities at the center of the state's quest for medical information.[59] Health inspectors and physicians repeatedly described immigrant and nonwhite neighborhoods as a "moral purgatory," a "stagnant pool of human immorality and crime," a "laboratory of infection," and a breeding ground for disease that had to be closely surveilled and managed.[60] As one Los Angeles official noted in response to an outbreak of typhoid fever, "every individual hailing from Mexico should be regarded as potentially pathogenic."[61] This fear of foreign-born diseases led Los Angeles officials to focus their enforcement of health ordinances on Mexican workers who resided in nearby railroad camps. And in Baltimore, health authorities singled out predominantly Black neighborhoods for tuberculosis inspections in specifically designated "lung blocks," arguing that Black maids employed by affluent white families were key vectors of disease transmission across racial lines.[62]

This infusion of sentinel surveillance campaigns with racist and xenophobic imaginaries played out across the United States, but it is exemplified in the policing of disease outbreaks in San Francisco, which had an especially large Chinese-born population (72,472 individuals in a total population of 300,000, according to the 1890 census). When the city was struck by an outbreak of the bubonic plague just after the turn of the century, the board of health asserted that the disease had likely originated in the densely populated Chinatown district. Officials demanded that the Chinese community be placed under surveillance because it was "defiled by Mongolian filth or disease" and spread "contaminating vapors just like swamps poisoned the air."[63] Police officers set up perimeter checkpoints around Chinatown, and the board of health sent inspectors to local pharmacies to identify potentially infected patients through their medicine purchases, combed through 14,117 rooms in a matter of weeks, and put around 14,000 Chinese immigrants under strict quarantine.[64] As one board member later declared: "[Chinatown] should be depopulated, its buildings leveled by fire and its tunnels and cellars laid bare. Its occupants should be colonized on some distant portion of the peninsula, where every building should be constructed under strict municipal regulation and where every violation of the sanitary laws could be at once detected. The day has passed when a progressive city like San Francisco should feel compelled to tolerate in its midst a foreign community, perpetuated in filth."[65]

Unlike the collection of distinctly public records, however, the sentinel surveillance campaign of San Francisco officials was met with immediate opposition from Chinese American community leaders and the judiciary. The surveillance powers of San Francisco officials were eventually reined in by a series of decisions from the Court of Appeals of the Ninth Circuit, which found that municipal health authorities had presented no evidence to support the targeting of Chinese immigrants and ruled that their health surveillance campaign without probable cause was unconstitutional.[66]

Similar opposition to expanding public health powers and targeted sentinel surveillance campaigns also germinated outside the judicial system. Immigrant leaders in other cities spoke up against campaigns that targeted foreign-born populations.[67] Citizen initiatives in Ohio and Iowa opposed close cooperation between boards of health and police departments as an infringement of privacy and personal liberty.[68] And newspaper editors regularly condemned the disclosure of medical information as an "invasion of the confidential relation of the physician to his patients," "the most tyrannical thing that the government has undertaken," and a violation of "the right of privacy guaranteed by the common law from time immemorial."[69] In those instances, and in many others, contestation over the limits of state power was the constant companion of administrative growth.

When faced with such contestation, public health authorities responded by emphasizing the high prevalence of infectious diseases and the need to place the fight against such diseases on a more scientific footing. According to U.S. Surgeon General Walter Wyman, reducing infectious disease deaths required "modern methods of sanitation" that utilized the full repertoire of medical knowledge and the full capacity of the state.[70] Arguments about the scientific necessity and beneficial impact of public health initiatives also went hand in hand with an emphasis on their legality. Central to such arguments was the so-called *salus populi* doctrine, which states that the health of the population is the supreme guiding principle of governance. (In its full Latin form, which is still the official state motto of Missouri, the doctrine states: *salus populi suprema lex esto.* The health of the people is the supreme law.) State officials—as well as social reformers sympathetic to the growth of the state apparatus during the 1880s and 1980s—routinely couched their defenses of health policing and sentinel surveillance in the language of *salus populi*, arguing that the state's "sacred" responsibility to protect the well-being of its population legitimated a resolute fight against germs and filth, even if it resulted in the seizure of private property, forced entry into private homes, the mandatory reporting of personal medical data, and the establishment of boards of health that were "clothed with extraordinary power."[71]

This focus on *salus populi* anchored defenses of sentinel surveillance and public health policing not just in the language of immunological science but in an emerging theory of the American state as the guarantor of the public's well-being and (as Philip Abrams has written) in a defense of the common good "as the device in terms of which subjection is legitimated."[72] Especially during outbreaks of infectious disease epidemics, but also in the routine course of disease prevention, boards of health claimed the authority to prioritize public health and the defense of the common good over the privacy rights and Fourth Amendment protections of individuals. Although the resulting sanitary measures were "sometimes autocratic," as the prominent physician and public health campaigner Hermann Biggs conceded, the significance of infectious diseases as a leading cause of death superseded concerns about medical privacy and justified measures that may have seemed excessive and arbitrary "if they were not plainly designed for the public good, and evidently beneficent in their effects."[73]

Arguments about this so-called "reason of state"—and correlate defenses of the "common good" as the guiding principle of governance—had been enshrined in American caselaw and constitutional thought since the founding of the republic.[74] And while *specific* initiatives (such as the disproportionate surveillance of Chinatown residents by the San Francisco Board of Health) did not meet the legal bar, American courts remained *generally* receptive to arguments about the primacy of the reason of state.[75] A broad interpretation of the *salus populi* doctrine had already been affirmed by the Supreme Court in *Gibbons v. Ogden* in 1824, which had turned on the question of interstate commerce and given the federal government the authority to implement health inspections and mandatory quarantine. But in the late nineteenth and early twentieth centuries, the same logic was more directly applied to disputes about privacy and individual rights. Medical information had long been considered a private matter, especially when it involved socially stigmatized venereal diseases.[76] Homes and apartments were also categorized as private spaces into which police officials and health bureaucrats could not ordinarily intrude.[77] But as one New York court ruled, *salus populi* precedent implied that local health authorities still retained "absolute control over persons and property, so far as the public health was concerned," even if this required the temporary curtailment of other rights.[78] For example, expectations of personal privacy and doctor-patient confidentiality could, during outbreaks of infectious disease epidemics, be subordinated to the defense of public health, and doctors could be compelled by local authorities to report on their patients.[79]

When judges objected to the scope and targeting of public health interventions, as they had done in San Francisco in 1900, it was usually on relatively narrow procedural grounds. Probable cause and court-ordered warrants became common prerequisites for large health surveillance campaigns and medical data collection, but state and federal courts nonetheless affirmed that health officials had "full power to isolate individuals suspected of having the disease and should otherwise be shown great deference" during public health emergencies.[80]

By the 1920s, the expanding powers of the Public Health Service were thus embedded into a legal regime that affirmed the constitutional right of Americans to be (as the Fourth Amendment states) "secure in their persons, houses, papers, and effects, against unreasonable searches and seizures" but also carved out considerable space for the policing of individuals and entire communities in the name of public health. Some types of information, like vital records, were never brought under the umbrella of privacy protections. Greater protections existed for medical information. Yet the administrative and judicial embrace of the *salus populi* doctrine still meant that such information could be collected when it was considered necessary to the policing of public health. Defining this necessity was largely left to the administrative state, since boards of health determined not just *what* measures were required but also *whether* the necessary circumstances existed in the first place. Public health officials often found themselves in the dual role of judge and executioner: those who defined the exceptional circumstance also determined the scope of the intervention.[81]

INTERPERSONAL COMMUNICATIONS AND
THE DEFENSE OF PUBLIC MORALS

Public health was one domain in which surveillance emerged as a central means of bureaucratic power. Postal administration was another. By the mid-1800s, postal delivery routes already functioned as the central nervous system of an emerging nation, helping to connect millions of Americans across great distances and providing the necessary infrastructure for the dissemination of personal correspondence, commercial data, news, advertisements, and mail-order catalogues.[82] The sanctity of the sealed letter had been anchored in the logic of this system since its inception, and postal officials had the duty to carry and deliver the mail without knowing the contents of sealed letters and packages and without endeavoring to find out (see chapter 1). When the Continental Congress established the precursor to the U.S. Postal Service in 1782, it already included a provision against any attempts to "open, detain, delay, secrete, embezzle, or destroy" mailed matter.[83] As the postmaster general therefore reminded his clerks in several circulars throughout the late nineteenth and early twentieth centuries, they were "expected to use extraordinary vigilance in guarding the mails under their charge"[84] and had no legal authority "to open under any pretext a sealed letter while in the mails."[85]

Yet the Post Office's institutional commitment to the privacy of written communications existed alongside persistent efforts to "suppress public nuisances" and defend "public morals" through the inspection of mailed matter.[86] For some postal officials, building a national community depended not only on open avenues of communication and commerce but also on the state's ability to contain the spread of moral and ideological threats. (Here, too, public health and postal administration were more tightly linked than may be apparent at first glance: One agency was tasked with containing the spread of physical illness. The other agency claimed responsibility for containing the spread of moral disease.)

Such efforts were particularly encouraged amid the moral panics of the 1870s and 1880s, when conservative activists from the Young Men's Christian Association or the New York Society for the Suppression of Vice took to the streets and the bully pulpit to condemn the perceived moral ills of modern life, including prostitution and premarital sex, gambling, female voting rights, and widespread liquor consumption. Anthony Comstock was a central figure in campaigns to enforce reactionary social and sexual norms in American society. He had arrived in New York City after being decommissioned from the Union Army in 1865 and soon allied himself with religious campaigns against intemperance and sexual indecency. Life on the front lines of the Civil War had already exposed a twenty-year-old Comstock to prevalent drinking and swearing among the enlisted men, and his exposure to New York City streets only strengthened his perception that public morals and family values were in a state of great decay.[87] Styling himself as a proudly reactionary "weeder in God's garden," Comstock cofounded the New York Society for the Suppression of Vice with the dual aim of organizing local campaigns and of building a political coalition that could support so-called "antivice legislation" at the state and federal level.

The efforts soon bore fruit. Starting with the passage of the Act for the Suppression of Trade in, and Circulation of, Obscene Literature and Articles of Immoral Use in 1873 and continuing until the early twentieth century, Congress and fifty percent of all state legislatures passed new laws that criminalized the distribution of "obscene" and "indecent" materials through the U.S. postal system—a deliberately ambiguous category that included references to gambling and lottery tickets, medical quackery, information about contraception, sexually explicit content, and discussions of extramarital sexual relations. Collectively, these laws became known (and infamous) as "Comstock laws."[88]

But Comstock also envisioned a more direct prosecutorial role for himself. Using his political clout, he managed to secure an appointment as the lead investigator of obscenity cases within the Post Office Department. His new professional home was known as the Postal Inspection Service, which was staffed by sworn officers and tasked with investigating suspected cases of mail fraud. It had historically been something of an administrative backwater, employing less than fifty inspectors when the first Comstock law came into force in 1873. Anthony Comstock endeavored to change this. Within a year, he had increased the number of inspectors, opened hundreds of investigations, and ordered fifty-five arrests for the illicit distribution of pornographic pictures.[89] By the time Comstock contracted pneumonia and died in September 1915 (leaving behind, among other things, an extensive personal collection of sexually explicit magazines and postcards), close to four hundred inspectors pursued investigations for pornography and financial fraud, often in collaboration with local law enforcement agencies. Comstock had personally supervised more than thirty-five hundred of these investigations and claimed to have overseen four thousand arrests and the seizure of 160 tons of "obscene" literature. His advocacy of postal censorship had even been sufficiently influential to occasion the introduction of a new term into the American vernacular, coined by *New York Times* editors in 1895: to practice "Comstockery" was to use censorship as a means of suppressing immorality.[90]

Yet in order to police mailed matter, postal inspectors needed to know its contents. They initially focused on mail that was not protected by the seal. Postcards and other unsealed mail and merchandise could be visually inspected without breaking a letter's seal. In cases where such visual screenings uncovered compromising direct or circumstantial evidence, suspected offenders were then reported by the Postal Inspection Service to the police for additional investigations. In Philadelphia, for example, postal inspectors stopped the recipient of sexually explicit postcards when he arrived to retrieve his sealed mail from the local post office. Forced to open it on site, he was found to be running a matchmaking service that connected unmarried women to potential suitors.[91] The man was handed over to the local police and charged with violating antiobscenity laws. This was no isolated incident. Sworn officers from the Postal Inspection Service regularly pursued indictments for "sending obscene matters through the mail" and assisted police officers in investigating and arresting people who had sent or received "filthy pictures and circulars."[92] When police raids uncovered sexually explicit photographs in New York and New Jersey, postal officials additionally took it upon themselves to track mail that was addressed to, or sent by, the suspected offenders.[93] In other cases, reported by inspectors from Colorado and Kansas, the Postal Inspection Service even approached local schools to ask for archived handwriting samples of former students, hoping to compare such samples to the writing on unsigned postcards to track down their senders.[94]

By 1910, officials estimated that the fight against pornography and sexual promiscuity resulted in hundreds of mail tracing requests and investigations per year.[95] Postal inspectors additionally investigated several thousand annual cases of mail fraud by people who "[preyed] on the gullible" by promising imaginary profits from oil wells; by selling dubious medical cures, weight-loss potions, and false teeth; and by circulating forged lottery tickets.[96] And they expanded their screening efforts beyond postcards. The privacy of the mail was waived for some categories of merchandise, including packages sent from abroad. Once a foreign sender or recipient of such packages had been added to the Postal Inspection Service's list of suspicious addresses, future shipments of international mail then could be intercepted and examined before they cleared U.S. customs.[97]

Postal censorship reached its apex during World War I, when the Post Office acted on orders from a newly established Censorship Board and the War Department to implement mass screenings of foreign mail for seditious materials. President Theodore Roosevelt (the same politician who had been instrumental to the passage of New York's 1901 Tenement House Act) and his attorney general, Charles Bonaparte, had approached Congress as early as 1908 with requests for legislation that would criminalize the sending of radical political letters and magazines through the mail. These early requests were unsuccessful, but the authority to impound letters and packages that undermined the military readiness of the United States (for example, by advocating for pacifism or socialism) was ultimately granted to the postmaster general by the Espionage Act of 1917. The official response was swift. A day after the law's passage, the Post Office informed all local postmasters to maintain "close watch" on any mail that could weaken the American war effort.[98] Postal officials also began to build out a system of screening points at major ports capable of handling large volumes of foreign mail, maintained a database of suspicious foreign addresses against which all incoming mail could be compared, and began to open letters and packages that were sent to and from wartime enemies of the United States. In 1918, the fifty officials at the Censorship Office in San Francisco opened 37,095 pieces of mail in a span of two weeks.[99]

Censorship offices were decommissioned at the end of the war, but postal officials continued to screen large financial and securities transfers to and from Germany during subsequent years in accordance with prohibitions imposed by the Treaty of Versailles. Publications with anarchist or socialist tendencies—as well as packages thought to contain such publications—also continued to be seized as American officials grew concerned about socialist agitation in Germany and Italy and the success of the Bolshevik revolution in Russia.[100] Mail censorship was one lever they had to interrupt the transmission of such radical ideas and to nip fermenting political discontent at home in the bud. Just as the system of antiobscenity screenings had outlasted the antivice campaigns of the 1870s and 1880s to become a permanent element of postal administration—and just as the governmental seizure of telegrams during the Civil War had become a precedent for subsequent attempts to seize personal communications—censorship efforts that had been born out of a wartime emergency partially carried over into peacetime routines.

This expansive system of postal surveillance and censorship was established even as popular concerns about mail privacy became more salient and formal protections of mailed matter increased during the late 1800s and early 1900s. When postcards were first adopted in the United States in the 1870s, newspapers had been quick to point out that they carried a price tag that wasn't covered by the postage itself: they did "not secure that privacy to mail communications to which we have been accustomed," which seemed to limit their use to matters "where such publicity as they occasion will not be a matter of much concern."[101] While earlier generations had worried primarily about mail theft (see chapter 1), invasions of privacy became a growing concern in the late 1800s and elicited strong responses from the American press. As the editorial board of the *Detroit Free Press* opined, "the right of the people to secrecy and privacy in intercommunication is one of the most cherished rights," yet it had come under growing threat in a society that relied more heavily than ever before on long-distance communications.[102] Other newspapers echoed this view, demanding protections against "all espionage" and proposing that "the privacy of the mails should be guarded as sacredly as the freedom of the press, the habeas corpus act, or trial by jury."[103] Political turmoil in Russia during the anti-czarist revolution of 1905 also put the American valuation of mail privacy into stark relief. One newspaper compared the United States favorably against revolutionary Russia by summarizing the revolution in three sentences: "Personal Liberty dead. Censorship of the Press. Privacy of Mails Unknown."[104]

Of course this juxtaposition overstated the difference between the American republic and the czarist empire. On the eve of World War I, when the signs of wartime surveillance were already appearing on the horizon, *The Evening World* was justifiably less sanguine about the state of civil liberties in the United States, arguing in a front-page editorial: "Censorship of mails in this country has already been carried too far. Yet year by year, here a little and there a little, it is being extended upon one pretense or another. Sometimes the extension is by law, sometimes it is by order of the Postmaster-General; sometimes by presumption of local postmasters. All of it is wrong. . . . We have censorship that is none the less despotic because petty and puritanical."[105] Such concerns were rendered particularly acute by the passage of the 1917 Espionage Act, yet they already existed during the United States' previous military campaigns. Popular concerns about violations of mail privacy were sufficiently widespread at the beginning of the Spanish-American War in 1898 that Charles Emory Smith, postmaster general of the United States, contacted newspaper editors across the country to convey a straightforward message: "All reports indicating that post office inspectors or other officials have been detailed or authorized to open letters within the mails are untrue and misleading. The privacy of the mails at no time nor under any condition or circumstances will be invaded during the war. All mail properly addressed and upon which sufficient postage is paid will be delivered to the addresses as expeditiously and scrupulously as it ever has been."[106]

Partly in response to such concerns, the Post Office adapted internally to ensure "the inviolability of the contents from all eyes but those for which they were intended."[107] Locked mailbags were introduced to discourage crimes of opportunity, including violations of mail privacy. Postal officials also changed the design of government mailboxes to prevent tampering with the mail, introduced glue-sealed and lined envelopes that did not expose their contents even when they were held up against the light, and levied increasing fines for violations of the seal by postal officials.[108] These organizational and design changes were mirrored in regulatory updates. Starting in the early 1900s, the U.S. Postal Rules and Regulations included a section specifically on mail privacy, which outlawed the opening of letters without legal warrants "not even though [they] may contain improper or criminal matter."[109]

Even relatively inconsequential violations of mail privacy could spark public criticism and occasion administrative change. Around Christmastime, the Post Office Department ordinarily received several dozen children's letters addressed to Santa Claus each day. In the nineteenth century, some of these letters had routinely been handed to local newspapers that would reprint them for added seasonal entertainment. But postal officials put a stop to this practice after 1900, fearing that "laxity in observing the privacy of the mails" would eventually lead to public outrage and that people would erroneously infer that "letters of a more personal character might be treated in a similar manner."[110]

How was this institutionalized commitment to postal privacy balanced against the demands of the Postal Inspection Service and the concern—prevalent among postal officials who wrote internal memos or testified in congressional hearings—that dangerous content could "reach many a noble boy and girl, and utterly degrade them" under "the sanctity of the seal, and the secrecy of the mails"?[111] The answer lies, once again, in governance by exception. To facilitate the fight against obscenities and other illicit materials, the postmaster general's office proposed that certain classes of mailed matter should be exempt from standard mail handling procedures. Breaking the seal would remain strictly forbidden—"except for the most urgent official cause."[112] Drawing on older legal precedents that had already established a distinction between "letters and sealed packages" and matter that "is open to inspection, such as newspapers, magazines, pamphlets, and other printed matter, purposely left in condition to lie examined," postal leadership pushed for regulatory authorization to screen the content of magazines and postcards, which accounted for a growing percentage of postal deliveries.[113] Backed by influential antivice campaigners, postal officials also lobbied successfully for legislative changes that affirmed the legality of postcard monitoring and grouped the circulation of "indecent, filthy, and disgusting" materials under the general category of mail fraud.[114] And during World War I, Postmaster General Albert S. Burleson formally approached Congress and the White House to request the wartime exceptions that legalized the screening of incoming and outgoing international mail.[115] Burleson's postal service was committed to the privacy of the mails but also to doing its part for the war effort.[116]

The net result was a tiered system of postal surveillance that distinguished between acceptable (protected) and dangerous (unprotected) mailed matter, a distinction that was infused with moral and political value judgments about sexual and ideological deviance. This two-tiered approach turned the general principle of postal privacy into an increasingly negative space: it was defined as much by what it *was* as by what it *was not*. Far from being anomalies in an otherwise integrated regulatory landscape, the unexceptional use of exceptions began to constitute one of the Post Office Department's most "quotidian ways of exercising power" and established the policing of the mail in the name of national security and moral decency as a legitimate technique of bureaucratic rule.[117] The governance of postal privacy was embedded within a moralized hierarchy of acceptable communication in the United States.

THE SELECTIVE GAZE OF THE MODERN STATE

The elevation of personal information into a central technology of governance was characterized not just by the *amount* of data that flowed into governmental databases but by the *dispersion* of such data across, and *concentration* within, governing agencies, the *integration* of new types of information into processes of bureaucratic decision-making, and the targeted *utilization* of the knowledge thus obtained.[118] Populations and individuals became unevenly *legible* to the bureaucratic eye rather than merely *measurable* through quantitative data when large caches of data were brought to bear on specific problems of governance. After the 1870s, and within a bureaucratic system that therefore depended directly on access to statistical and personal information, the governance of citizens' privacy involved the routine reliance on exceptions and the codification of such exceptions through administrative regulations, legislative action, and judicial affirmation.

The fallout from World War I and the Prohibition era temporarily threatened to destabilize this system. During the 1920s, disputes about the privacy of space, information, and communication became more prominent and American judges turned their focus toward citizens' constitutional right of privacy against a potentially overbearing state (see chapter 5). But what actually happened when concerns about the scope of executive power collided with institutionalized exceptions? At first glance, privacy won out. The right to privacy was recast as a constitutional right, became more firmly ensconced in American jurisprudence, and was written into the complex web of regulations that govern the work of administrative agencies. Supreme Court Justice Louis Brandeis still found himself on the side of a dissenting minority in the 1928 *Olmstead* case, yet the idea that anchored his spirited dissent—the need for privacy "as against the Government"—was already embedded in political discourse, congressional debates, administrative rules and regulations, and increasingly the judicial canon as well. The tides were clearly turning and also seemed to turn the ship of state.

Yet this simple story—about the course corrections of a constitutional republic in uncertain times and the deliberate rebalancing of personal rights, public interests, and executive power—is immediately complicated by events that took place a mere two years after the end of World War I. On July 1, 1920, the nation's first cipher bureau—the predecessor to the National Security Agency (NSA)—flexed its institutional muscles for the first time when:

> . . . a slim balding man in his early thirties moved into a four-story townhouse at 141 East 37th Street in Manhattan. This was the birth of the

Black Chamber, the NSA's earliest predecessor, and it would be hidden in the nondescript brownstone. But its chief, Herbert O. Yardley, had a problem. To gather intelligence for Woodrow Wilson's government, he needed access to the telegrams entering, leaving, and passing through the country, but because of an early version of the Radio Communications Act, such access was illegal. With the shake of a hand, however, Yardley convinced Newcomb Carlton, the president of Western Union, to grant the Black Chamber secret access on a daily basis to the private messages passing over his wires—the Internet of the day.[119]

A simple handshake between a state official and a business leader established the peacetime continuity of a framework of exceptions in the governance of interpersonal communications that had originated amid the moral panics of the late nineteenth century and had been turbocharged during World War I. In other instances, stronger lobbying efforts and judicial interventions were needed. But the result was, broadly speaking, the same: growing constitutional protections still existed alongside a patchwork of institutionally specific exceptions that created considerable space for the exercise of informational power.

The unexceptional use of such exceptions helped to resolve the apparent tension between the governmental will to know and the rising valuation of privacy vis-à-vis the state. Privacy was meaningfully defined by what it was *not*, that is, by the types of information or the specific contexts of data collection that were permanently or temporarily outside the juridical umbrella of privacy protections. Crucially, such exceptions did not suspend or annul the existing legal order. They were essential to the structure of that order and key aspects of the uneven development of American governing institutions during the twentieth century.[120] Such exceptions were also not simply imposed by Congress or the White House on the vast network of agencies that collectively form the bureaucratic infrastructure of the modern American state. There was no central war room where heads of departments got together to circumscribe the scope of privacy claims as if they were drawing colonial borders across the continents of the non-Western world. The selective institutionalization of privacy often took shape close to the front lines of administrative administration and through the courts.

Samuel Warren and Louis Brandeis had foreseen some of this in their 1890 article in the *Harvard Law Review*, warning that the right to privacy could become "uncertain in its operation and easily rendered abortive."[121]

However, to them, the primary difficulty lay in differentiating between matters "which concern the private life, habits, acts, and relations of an individual" without any "legitimate relation to or bearing upon any act done by him in a public or quasi public capacity" and matters that were fundamentally relevant to public administration and democratic governance.[122] If only a line could be so easily drawn that the benefits of privacy accrued to all private matters and the benefits of publicity to all public acts. As this chapter has shown, the choice to extend privacy protections to specific people, spaces, or types of information (or, alternatively, to exempt them from such protections) was itself a deeply political act that involved the balancing of potentially competing rights and objections. It also remained tightly coupled to moral and ideological agendas. The power to shape the social order was in part a power to designate specific issues as matters of public concern—or, alternatively, to claim privacy in ostensibly public settings—to determine the people, spaces, and data that were considered as legitimate targets for governmental intervention, and to tip the scales in favor of any number of potentially conflicting political and social goods.

Basic privacy protections thus appear ironclad only at first glance. They are threatened not only by an "autocratic legalism" that aims at deliberately manipulating existing legal structures until the rule of law becomes functionally meaningless but also by a more routine reliance on exceptions as essential components of regulatory frameworks and bureaucratic administration.[123] Existing legal and juridical regimes already contain features (often essential to their functioning) that can undermine the spirit of the law and the substantive impact of privacy protections if wielded poorly or toward dubious ends by (in Louis Brandeis's words) "men of zeal" who manipulate the levers of bureaucratic power.[124]

Some exceptions remained germane to the late 1800s and early 1900s. Wartime legislation was partially repealed in the early 1920s, and improvements in sanitation and medical care reduced the bureaucratic imperative to conduct aggressive health surveillance campaigns. But other aspects of the American privacy architecture have survived into more recent times, illustrating the path dependencies that can emerge when legal protections and their attendant exceptions are permanently encoded into the law and into administrative rules and regulations.[125] The settled struggles of prior periods can still enable or prohibit techniques of governance in the present. For example, remnants of the Comstock laws have survived until today, contained in Title 18, Chapter 71, Sections 1460–1470 of the U.S. Code.

The *salus populi* doctrine has survived as well and continues to shape the governance of infectious diseases during public health emergencies. Even sentinel surveillance campaigns that were directed against immigrant populations during the early 1900s have a contemporary expression. Since 1944, Section 42 of the Public Service Act has granted health authorities the power to close the US border to prevent migrants from carrying foreign diseases into the country (this law has repeatedly been used to restrict the inflow of immigrants from Central and South America). Within the United States, nonwhite and poor communities also tend to feel the breath of the surveillance state more directly than other populations and often have to accept targeted surveillance as the consequence of living in stigmatized inner-city neighborhoods or as the price that has to be paid for access to welfare services.[126] Even in an age of (allegedly) ubiquitous data collection, the distribution of legibility across populations tends to mirror the distribution of social status and symbolic capital in society.

More generally, the routine use of exceptions has remained a characteristic feature of the American privacy architecture throughout the twentieth century and into the twenty-first. When marital and reproductive issues were first brought under the umbrella of privacy during the 1960s and 1970s—and thus shielded from the regulatory ambitions of the American state—such efforts focused specifically on the protection of heterosexual couples and sexual relations within the nuclear family, excluding many homosexual and nonmarital relationships.[127] More recently, and reflecting a very different set of political aims, the Virginia legislature passed a bill that would have explicitly excluded menstrual histories from police search warrants to prevent law enforcement from using smartphone data to prosecute antiabortion law violations after the Supreme Court overturned *Roe v. Wade*. (The bill was swiftly vetoed by the governor.) Other twenty-first-century initiatives, such as the expansion of dragnet surveillance after the passage of the 2001 Patriot Act or the collection of geo-coded infection data during the COVID-19 pandemic, have similarly relied on the logic of exceptions, partly by enforcing a categorical distinction between the rights of citizens and foreigners and partly by balancing the privacy rights of those citizens against national security and public health during national or global emergencies. Challenges to post-9/11 data collection are also adjudicated not through the regular court system but—another exception!—through the Foreign Intelligence Surveillance Court (FISC), which has existed as a parallel judicial institution since 1978 and is tasked with overseeing surveillance activities against noncitizens within the United States, although "overseeing" might be a generous term. According to an investigation by *The Wall Street Journal*, FISC has historically rejected only 0.03 percent of warrant requests.[128]

The same reliance on exceptions also characterizes consumer-focused legislation. The California Consumer Privacy Act (CCPA) of 2018, often considered a template for other privacy legislation in the United States, spelled out (1) the right to know what personal information is collected, used, and shared; (2) the right to delete personal information from corporate databases; (3) the right to opt out of the sale or sharing of personal information; and (4) the right to nondiscrimination for exercising CCPA rights. Yet the law also included several exceptions that protected governmental access to consumer data by law enforcement, legalized the collection of data that are essential to the operation of some e-commerce systems, and facilitated the collection of medical data and consumer credit data.[129] A subsequent "delete me" law from 2023 empowered California residents to request the deletion of all personal data with one single request, instead of filing requests with individual companies that may or may not hold such data. Arguably, this closed a key loophole because consumers often do not know who holds their personal data and because such data are actively shared and sold on secondary markets. But the law also came with a major caveat: it applied only to roughly five hundred businesses that met new definitional standards for "data brokers"—defined to include any business that "knowingly collects and sells to third parties the personal information of a consumer with whom the business does not have a direct relationship"—and were recognized as such by the state's Privacy Protection Agency.[130]

A key question today is how this inherited architecture of sectoral protections and exceptions will evolve as personal information flows more easily across administrative boundaries and between public and private entities. Notably, privacy has been one of the few policy domains that attracts interests from both major parties, and several new privacy bills are introduced in state legislatures across the United States each year. But if the legislative momentum of the last few years should stall or the apparatuses of the American state should come under the control of those who profess a calculated disregard toward the institutions and principles of liberal democracy, the contemporary American privacy architecture is unlikely to form an effective bulwark that could fetter the ratcheting up of surveillance efforts. It has always been, and remains, potentially compatible with an expansive interpretation of state (and corporate) power and a wide range of political ideologies.

When privacy becomes closely wedded to such ideologies—about limited governance, the sanctity of the family, the war on terror, and so forth—they can journey jointly onward through legislatures and courtrooms like barnacles on a vessel and render a formal commitment to the privacy of citizens and consumers eminently compatible with assertive exercises of institutional power. To recognize privacy as a limiting principle in the modern United States is to recognize these exceptions and entanglements alongside any promises of spatial integrity and informational self-determination: the logic of privacy is closely tied to the power structures, preferences, and prejudices of time and place. It carries many hopes and visions, but it can offer no strong assurances that they shall be meaningfully realized or prove resilient in turbulent times.

Conclusion

Privacy in an Age of Surveillance

F or well over a century, privacy has now defied attempts to confine it to one narrow category or another while also becoming tied into an ever-expanding set of debates about individual rights and informational power. It generally refers to those aspects of our lives and ourselves that we seek to shield—sometimes temporarily, sometimes permanently—against an inquisitive society. But this inventory of privacy is ever-shifting, and there is not a single correct approach to defining the term with any degree of specificity. It usually requires only a little tugging before even the strongest seams begin to burst.[1] Instead of asking what the essence of privacy *is* (as if such an essence could be discovered if we only peeled back a sufficient number of layers and thus discovered a strong core beneath the variegated outer skin), I have therefore been interested in how the logic of privacy *became* widely diffused and increasingly institutionalized. Far from being a self-evident historical fact, the breadth, prominence, and durability of privacy claims in public life demand our attention.

My foray into the Early Information Age has been guided by several analytic imperatives: focus less on collective sensibilities than on contextually specific rules of access and disclosure; aim to understand those rules not as the necessary consequence of technological circumstance but as the outcome of ongoing political struggles over social organization; recognize the moral imaginaries and political ideologies that are inherent in those struggles and encoded into the language of spatial and informational access; and thereby also pay close attention to the effects of privacy and surveillance for the imposition of social control and the distribution of (dis)advantage in society.

My central argument has been this: between the 1880s and the 1920s, conceptions of privacy that were reactive to modernization and the attendant moral panics diffused into different domains of public discourse and were embedded into law, jurisprudence, and urban space, often for the first time in American history. Privacy assumed public significance and was increasingly deemed worthy of political and judicial attention. It still structured how individuals or families moved between the front stage and back stage of everyday life but also left an indelible mark on the institutional fabric of American society.[2]

This was a time when the United States was experiencing far-reaching social and technological changes. Privacy became *broad* amid the moral anxieties and political struggles that arose in a nation searching for a new social and institutional order.[3] It attracted large public audiences and subsumed a vast array of discussions about emerging social problems under one conceptual roof, and in doing so, it merged disparate conceptions of the social and moral order of the United States into the language of spatial and informational access. This growing salience in politics and public life reflected the fact that privacy was often won and lost at scale in the Early Information Age because the greatest threats to privacy increasingly seemed to come from governing institutions.[4]

Privacy also became *sticky*.[5] Traditional moral imaginaries and emerging conceptions of the inviolate self anchored political coalitions, motivated legislative action, and supported the gradual recognition of privacy as a constitutional right. To a much greater extent than before, the management of privacy began to involve codified rules and regulations rather than locked doors and social custom.[6] The privacy architecture that first took shape during this period in American politics and public life exhibited several defining characteristics: the sheer breadth of privacy debates that played out before various audiences, the tight coupling of privacy and public morals, the sectoral fragmentation of privacy protections, and the reconciliation of those protections with an assertive exercise of informational power through the routinized use of exceptions.

Many struggles over privacy arose in response to the real or perceived consequences of rapid social change and social dislocation. The case for privacy was made most forcefully after new social, institutional, or technological realities had already begun to emerge and the integrity of private spaces and personal data had already begun to degrade. But this does not mean that the fight for privacy was necessarily a rearguard action. To the contrary. While some campaigns sought to shield traditional (and sometimes reactionary) gender norms and family structures against the forces of social progressivism, many were decisively oriented toward the future, aiming to shape relations among individuals, families, governing agencies, and society writ large in a changing society. The logic of spatial and informational privacy became a salient way of addressing the tensions, social problems, and pathologies of the Early Information Age. The politics of the present are still linked to these distant historical antecedents because the contours of privacy at any given moment are partly contingent on the problems thrown up during prior periods and on the settling of prior struggles.[7]

These developments were fanned but not foreordained by the winds of modernization. In periods of rapid societal change, new ideas and conceptions of the social order can spread widely without ever becoming durably anchored in laws, regulations, and institutional practices; or alternatively, they can become institutionalized from the top down without previously appealing to a large and diverse public audience.[8] For example, it is unlikely that the logic of privacy would have attracted such varied public audiences (and would have also attracted attention from legislators) without the collective labor of social reformers and journalists during the 1880s and 1890s; that it would have been tied as closely to the tenets of liberal individualism in a society with collectivist traditions and rigid class structures; or that so many experimental claims about a new "modern legal fact" would have successfully percolated in highly centralized judicial and bureaucratic systems.[9] In fact, the events of the Early Information Age set the United States on a path that differed meaningfully from those taken by several European countries, despite broadly comparable technological contexts and concurrent buildups of bureaucratic apparatuses. Americans borrowed freely from European precedent during the late nineteenth century but moved quickly beyond it in the 1900s. For example, in France—whence the American Founding Fathers had imported some of their revolutionary rhetoric and liberal-democratic ideas and which was the center of nineteenth-century European privacy discourse—the Napoleonic Code of 1804 and a flurry of civil cases during the 1850s already discussed a protected "private sphere" and imposed fines for publishing "a fact of private life."[10] It was the same for English common law, which provided a basis for early American privacy jurisprudence before it was cast aside during the 1920s in favor of constitutional arguments. But English judges then continued to treat the unauthorized distribution of personal communications as a violation of property rights rather than privacy well into the twentieth century, and jurisprudence that explicitly covered privacy violations by state and nonstate entities did not take hold in France until the postwar era, several decades *after* American judges had begun to adjudicate such cases. Even stronger differences existed between the United States and the strictly hierarchical society of Prussia.[11] Prussian law remedied grievances about the publication of personal photographs as a matter of libel rather than privacy and imposed few restrictions on bureaucratic administration and the secret police. To the contrary, the so-called "secrecy of letters" was only recognized as a civil right after the abdication of the German emperor and the proclamation of the Weimar Republic in 1919, and fully fledged privacy laws did not emerge until after World War II.[12]

While the American privacy architecture had its roots in a sprawling set of moral panics, social reform campaigns, and political disputes about the social ills of the late nineteenth century, European discussions of privacy have been disproportionately shaped by more recent political debates and (especially in Germany and France) by memories of authoritarianism and genocidal violence in the twentieth century. In 1950, Article 8 of the European Convention on Human Rights first codified protections for private life, the home, and correspondence as part of a larger effort to build a liberal-democratic order atop the ruins of World War II (which later also morphed into a Cold War effort to differentiate Western European governance structures from those adopted by the nations of the Warsaw Pact).[13] In the 1970s, similar protections were written into national legislation like the German *Bundesdatenschutzgesetz* (in 1977) and the French *Loi informatique et libertés* (in 1978), which each spelled out basic principles for the processing of personal data and emphasized the necessity of obtaining individual consent.

Compared to the United States, where the privacy architecture has continued to evolve through sectoral legislation that often arose in response to specific political pressure campaigns and regulated the collection and use of personal data and the sanctity of personal spaces in very specific settings, these European omnibus bills (which have additionally been harmonized through the European Union's Data Protection Directive in 1995 and the General Data Protection Regulation in 2018) reflected a greater emphasis on general principles that could be applied across a wide set of contexts and covered the rights of consumers as well as citizens. Some issues that are firmly tied to the logic of privacy in the United States also barely feature in these debates—like access to abortion or contraception—although European privacy law has been extended to disputes that remain wholly separate from privacy in the United States, such as freedom from environmental pollution.[14]

Several features of the early American privacy architecture have outlived the particularities of their birth and continue to affect privacy discourse and privacy regulation in the twenty-first century.[15] This is why a historical sociology of privacy is not simply a quest to discover archaeological facts that can be excavated from the archives but an attempt to reconstruct genealogies that can illuminate more proximate events. One particularly enduring feature is the reliance on sectoral regulation. New York's 1901 tenement law and 1902 civil rights law are early examples, as are the rules and regulations that govern how the U.S. Postal Service processes sealed letters and postcards. But since the early 1900s, many other sectoral provisions have appeared. Constitutional protections against unreasonable searches and seizures (the Fourth Amendment), self-incrimination (the Fifth Amendment), and violations of due process (the Fourteenth Amendment) are now enmeshed with a large corpus of laws that regulate how specific governmental or corporate actors can access specific types of personal space or personal information. For example, less than six months before the Watergate scandal in 1974, President Nixon declared that "the time has come for a major initiative to define the nature and extent of the basic rights of privacy." This initiative took the form of the Privacy Act of 1974, which governs the collection, maintenance, use, and dissemination of personally identifiable information by federal agencies.[16] The privacy of health-related data is additionally regulated through the Health Insurance Portability and Accountability Act (HIPAA); children's educational records are protected by the Family Educational Rights and Privacy Act (FERPA); online records for some children fall within the scope of the Children's Online Privacy Protection Act (COPPA); consumer credit data are covered by the Fair Credit Reporting Act (FCRA) and the Gramm-Leach-Bliley Act (GLBA); unauthorized disclosure of personal communications is covered by the Electronic Communications Privacy Act (ECPA); video rental records are protected by the Video Privacy Protection Act (VPPA) and motor vehicle records by the Driver's Privacy Protection Act (DPPA); and so forth. The governance of privacy in the contemporary United States has set off an avalanche of acronyms.

The second enduring feature of this privacy architecture is the routine use on exceptions. Sectoral privacy protections often cover only those scenarios and actions that remain once political ideologies and value judgments have already been baked into the structure of legal regimes and the interests of the American state and the corporate sector have already been taken into account.[17] The net long-term result is a legal landscape that offers uneven protections against varying sets of stakeholders and that additionally continues to evolve as individual states pass their own privacy laws, layering additional protections and exceptions on top of an already fragmented system. In many settings, legislation is therefore most successful at encoding what Ari Ezra Waldman has called "symbols of compliance," while offering much more limited substantive protections.[18]

Other features of the American privacy architecture have evolved since the Early Information Age, especially during the 1960s and 1970s. This was another uniquely transformative period, which is why many political histories of privacy choose these decades as their point of departure.[19] Social movements for gender equality and civil rights unsettled an entrenched social order, and the introduction of electronic databases unleashed a new torrent of concerns about governmental and (to a lesser degree) corporate surveillance.[20] A powerful set of "electronic eyes" was trained on "some of the most important junctures between private individuals and the major institutions" of American society.[21]

Today, this postwar era is largely remembered for landmark Supreme Court decisions such as *Griswold v. Connecticut*, *Katz v. United States*, and *Roe v. Wade*, which reaffirmed the constitutional basis of the right to privacy and also brought access to abortion and contraception under its protective umbrella.[22] But those landmark cases may once again be poor indicators of what was actually happening to privacy at this time. The Supreme Court's "rights revolution" obscures a more general trend of the postwar era: Overall, the governance of privacy became less focused on offering categorical protections for specific types of information or spaces. It was instead reorganized around procedural fairness in data collection, consent over data sharing, and the secure storage of personal records.[23] At a time when the logic of information politics fully came into its own as a defining feature of modern administration, the inviolate personality of the 1900s gradually gave way to the procedural guardrailing of data collection and the self-management of informational persons. On the one hand, courts were tasked with overseeing a growing array of procedural requirements (such as court-ordered warrants for emerging forms of electronic surveillance) and confidentiality mandates (such as the anonymized or time-limited storage of personal data in electronic databases) within an already-institutionalized "culture of surveillance."[24] On the other hand, consumers and citizens were increasingly tasked with deciding how to "weigh the costs and benefits" of exposure for themselves—a perspective summarized in 1967 by Alan Westin's description of privacy as "the claim of individuals, groups, or institutions to determine for themselves when, how, and to what extent information about them is communicated to others."[25] This operationalization of privacy as consent has now become one of the defining features of privacy governance. But it is a double-edged sword: what appears at first glance as the restitution of individual agency can all too easily turn into a false sense of security, consent fatigue, and the illusion of true choice.

These historical twists and turns lend credence to the claim that burdening privacy with grand hopes can easily lead it to buckle under the load.[26] Exceptions that are already baked into the internal structure of legal regimes as well as external pressures on those regimes are powerful impediments to a transformative politics of privacy governance. But those hopes can seem particularly misplaced in light of the technopolitical realities of the twenty-first century, when institutional surveillance has fully evolved into one of the central political problematics of our time. Broadly speaking, this evolution has been characterized by the following: (1) the precipitous expansion of surveillance initiatives during wartime, from the seizure of telegrams during the Civil War through the expansion of military surveillance during the Philippine-American War of 1899 and World War I, to the Cold War–era COINTELPRO program and beyond (which also serve as a reminder that surveillance jumps as much as it "creeps")[27]; (2) the incorporation of technologies and procedures that were first trialed overseas or in explicitly military contexts into the more routine realities of domestic policing[28]; (3) the elevation of aggregate and personalized data into important tools of bureaucratic rule, which have both incited and supported the growth of the administrative apparatuses of the modern state[29]; (4) periodic reconceptions of the informational imperative within those apparatuses as the focus shifted from the analysis of aggregate patterns toward the ranking and scoring of specific individuals[30]; (5) an extension of surveillance apparatuses into new spheres of social life and growing focus on emergent behavioral patterns, made possible by new technologies of data transmission, data collection, and data analysis[31]; (6) a gradual shift toward monitoring at a distance, up to the point where the subjects of surveillance are unaware of their visibility and of the forces that act upon them[32]; (7) an increasingly fluid circulation of information within administrative apparatuses and across institutional and national boundaries[33]; (8) a growing reliance on computationally derived profiles and scores in the governance of risk, the management of populations, and the sorting of people[34]; (9) an interpenetration of state-sponsored and nonstate data collection efforts that frequently blur the divisions among social control, socioeconomic inclusion, and commodification[35]; and (10), a growing embrace of automated systems of evaluation as engines of self-actualization, and of algorithmic scores as measures of true merit.[36]

One could thus be forgiven for concluding—despite the proliferation of privacy statutes since the middle of the twentieth century—that we now find ourselves before "a giant ledger where privacy is slipping ever more swiftly into the deficit column" as ubiquitous surveillance systems threaten to catch people in tightly woven and inescapable dragnets.[37] The new-fangled forces of technology that facilitate global information flows have turned into tools of perpetual examination and algorithmic judgment.[38] While the proverbial nineteenth-century flaneur could still observe metropolitan life from a position of relative anonymity, such anonymity now appears to be in short supply.

The tyranny of the present all too often lurks behind such totalizing claims, and the degree of visibility at any moment has predictably been assessed to be lower than during a distant (and often imaginary) past. *The Washington Times* already proclaimed an "era of publicity" in 1902, and the *Chicago Tribune* asserted that there was "no privacy in city life" in the same year. In 1970, *Newsweek* provocatively asked its readers, "Is Privacy Dead?," while *Time Magazine* concluded more confidently in 1993 that America had just witnessed the "Death of Privacy." More recently still, *Science* declared to its readers in 2015 that "privacy as we have known it is ending," while the *New Statesman* warned that we have now "sleepwalk[ed] into a world without privacy."[39] Consumers trade it away for added convenience; companies find it incompatible with their business models; states subordinate it to the prerogatives of efficient governance and national security. The "golden age" of privacy is never in the here and now.[40]

But perhaps the technopolitical realities of the twenty-first century have finally caught up with those dire predictions, as strategies of intense tracking and observations that were previously "only feasible in village-scale settings" have evolved into "routine means of mass surveillance by modern states."[41] Resistance to such surveillance is often relegated to the political margins as mass data collection has evolved into an almost natural fact of the world, a central technology of governance, and a key ingredient in the maintenance of social and political order.[42] As the privacy scholar Spiros Simitis has observed, the computational processing of personal data "increasingly appears as the ideal means to adapt an individual to a predetermined, standardized behavior that aims at the highest possible degree of compliance with the model patient, consumer, taxpayer, employee, or citizen."[43] As I write this, in the spring of 2025, a newly institutionalized Department of Government Efficiency (DOGE) has sought blanket access to taxpayer and social security data while a landmark achievement of the 1970s—the judicial embrace of abortion and contraception as basic rights, initially couched in the language of privacy—has been eroded. While the language of privacy still surrounds us, the uncomfortable reality might be that, as a practical matter, privacy barely exists.[44]

Such is the argument of many contemporary texts that lean heavily on the language of panopticism and its many derivatives: the "electronic panopticon" (porting disciplinary power from the physical site of the prison to delocalized digital networks), the "participatory panopticon" (in which people become agents of their own commodification), or the "synopticon" (when the many are watching the few).[45] A Google Scholar search currently returns close to fifty thousand hits for each of the search term combinations "surveillance + panopticon" and "privacy + panopticon." Based on the eighteenth-century writings of Jeremy Bentham (who envisioned a circular prison architecture where each incarcerated person found themselves exposed to "a sort of invisible omnipresence" of control emanating from a central watchtower) and popularized for a modern audience by Michel Foucault, the panopticon has become the unrivaled descriptive shorthand for surveillance and social control.[46] Insofar as its disparate conceptualizations and extensions share a common conceptual root, it is this: surveillance operates in modern societies in a manner that is ubiquitous, discreet, asymmetrical, and productive. It extends rather than subverts the Enlightenment concern with rationalization and measurement; it permanently encases individuals without requiring spectacular displays of authority (and thereby also decenters individual actors, while centering the tools and technologies that can produce such encasements); it is characterized by great inequalities between observers and the observed; and it aids the subjugation of people and populations through the self-disciplining of the subjects of power.[47]

When scholars have parted ways with the panoptic metaphor, the reason has usually been that it did not go far enough in capturing the novelties of twenty-first-century surveillance. For example, Gilles Deleuze suggests that the "disciplinary societies" that were defined by technologies of deliberate monitoring and confinement have been replaced by "societies of control," marked by continuous visibility and the universal modulation of behaviors and desires.[48] The collection of personal data now underpins a vast ecosystem of governance that is arguably more expansive and less contained within specialized institutions than in the past. While invasions of privacy may have previously meant that "someone had somehow gotten at some personal secret of yours and had revealed it to some third party or to the world at large," such invasions now involve behavioral data that are both more trivial when viewed in isolation but potentially more consequential when aggregated to a sufficient degree.[49] For Kevin Haggerty and Richard Ericson, surveillance structures of the twentieth century—the Orwellian state; the Foucauldian prison and factory—have therefore given way to rhizomatic "assemblages" that spread more widely and penetrate society more deeply than ever before.[50] And for Giorgio Agamben, clearly bounded monitoring regimes have been replaced by "zones of indistinction," that is, domains where traditional distinctions between law and power become blurred and individuals find themselves in a condition of suspended legality.[51] Whatever vestiges of structured twentieth-century surveillance systems still exist, they are being overtaken by techniques of "hypercontrol" (the universal extension of control across the social body so that differences in the kind of surveillance experienced by different groups are reduced to mere differences in degree), "dataveillance" (the highly discreet monitoring of individuals through their behavioral and communications data), or "überveillance" (the surveillance of bodies through embedded devices).[52] This world of total diffusion and absolute control may be "almost enough to make one nostalgic for the old systems of discipline and surveillance."[53]

The shift from panopticism to hypercontrol—and from enclosures to assemblages—thus adds a third act to the Foucauldian history of modernity: the exercise of disciplinary power within the confines of the prison and the factory was superseded by the governance of populations through the regulation of life processes and market mechanisms, which was in turn superseded by the deinstitutionalization of surveillance and its infusion into the totality of social relations.[54] Tellingly, two possible avenues of resistance that are readily conceivable within this framework—"sousveillance" (watching the watchers) and "countervailance" (quotidian resistance against data collection)—posit the impossibility of *evading* surveillant assemblages and instead aim to *invert* the surveillant gaze or *impede* the exercise of informational power.[55] There is thus an intuitive appeal to the argument that we have reached the end of a "great pause between the semipublic life of the villager and the semipublic life of the netizen, during which culturally contingent values such as privacy and exclusivity came to seem like natural social rights."[56] According to this view, privacy was a phenomenon of an interregnum period of industrial and technological development, book-ended on both sides by a dominance of the public or the semipublic over the private. As social complexity and the social valuation of the individual increased, privacy became recognized as a social good. But when subsequent technological innovations birthed new techniques of data extraction and social control, privacy once again withered. Our grandparents still dwelled within this "privacy parenthesis."[57] We may have already outlived it.

But just because a mode of social organization is pervasive does not mean that it is "totalizing" in the sense, as Marion Fourcade and Kieran Healy write, "of relentlessly subordinating every last shred of action and experience to a single template."[58] References to ubiquitous surveillant assemblages offer a clear descriptive vision but also risk overestimating the newness of new surveillance infrastructures and risk underestimating the hierarchical nature of those infrastructures and the selectivity of the surveillant gaze; misrecognize the nature of this gaze in modern nation-states; and ultimately offer few tools to conceptualize the connections between informational exposure, individuation, and social inclusion. I have already alluded to these criticisms at various points throughout the book. However, claims about the novelty and totalizing characteristics of surveillance in the twenty-first century are so prevalent that I should justify my position more fully.

Contemporary surveillance systems are often less unprecedented than they appear at first glance because they are layered on top of older systems of social control and integrated into established bureaucratic processes and governing institutions that have strong institutional cultures of their own.[59] It is undeniably true that the exercise of informational power and social control is now less confined to dedicated sites than in the past, and information circulates more freely and through a denser network of conduits. Large data collection programs like the recording of cellphone location data by telephone service providers can also be deliberately indiscriminate. Indeed, the central condition of contemporary data subjects is often their embeddedness into—rather than their enclosure by—systems of surveillance. But the layering and integration of new surveillance systems with established systems of governance still engender clear hierarchies that channel, dam, concentrate, and direct data flows and administrative attention. Decisions about the focus and scope of surveillance initiatives emanate outward from *centers of executive power*, for example, when political and corporate leaders approve new data collections programs or micromanage the targeted tracking and assassination of so-called "enemies of the state."[60] Data are collected and processed in dedicated and highly technical *centers of calculation* even when data flows are global, which is one reason why the European General Data Protection Regulation is specifically concerned with the geography of data processing and mandates that some types of information must not be transferred beyond the territory over which European courts have jurisdictional power.[61] The administrative deployment of such data and their application to specific problems of biopolitical governance or corporate practice require *centers of administration* that are in turn embedded into bureaucratic hierarchies. And challenges over privacy and the limits of informational power still play out in *centers of jurisprudence*, all the way to the U.S. Supreme Court. Not all that was solid has melted into air.

References to rhizomes and "liquid societies" are not particularly suited to capture the combination of dispersed data flows and concentrated data governance that often characterize contemporary surveillance infrastructures. They instead foreground "the extent to which we are known to others, the extent to which others have physical access to us, and the extent to which we are the subject of others' attention" and compel us to ask: How much privacy is still possible?[62] When our environment is saturated with surveillance systems that operate more opaquely but also more completely than in the past, the stated answer is often: very little. But it is hardly obvious that the *degree* of visibility is higher today than in communal settings during the preindustrial age, in small villages, or in the densely populated tenements of late-nineteenth-century New York City. The difference is rather a difference in *kind* because the technologies and primary agents of surveillance of the present day are vastly different from those of prior periods, the consequences of visibility are different when the collection of personal information and the invasion of personal space involves powerful institutions rather than close relatives, and the balance of informational power between individuals and those institutions has greatly shifted. It is also a difference in *distribution*. While it is generally the case that "individuals at every level of the social hierarchy are now scrutinized"—especially when scrutinization is simply defined as the totality of data collection efforts through which seemingly insignificant observations from everyday life are fed into corporate and governmental databases—the types and volumes of information that are ingested by surveillance apparatuses still vary considerably across a diverse population of differently situated individuals. The same is true for the techniques through which these data are collected, the institutions tasked with such data collection, and (perhaps most significantly) the application of personal data to specific problems of governance.[63]

While the targeting of the surveillant gaze has historically been conditioned by outwardly visible signs of privilege and stigma—skin color, place of residence, and so forth—the increased reliance on behavioral profiles and ordinal ranks now means that suspicions can be triggered (and administrative attention can be directed) by longitudinal and dynamically emergent patterns and computational indices of (dis)honor that are less readily apparent to outside observers. Prior attention begets future analysis; mathematical precision can replace crude proxies and approximations.[64] Yet in practice, the contours of an uneven landscape of legibility still tend to follow familiar lines of demarcation. They disproportionately break down by race, class, and citizenship because innovations in the techniques of governments are inevitably linked to "other modes of social ordering" and integrated with the decision-making—which is "human, all too human," as Friedrich Nietzsche famously wrote—of frontline bureaucratic officials.[65] Immigrants and foreigners are often subject to stricter and more targeted data collection efforts than citizens, and populations in heavily policed neighborhoods find themselves under special scrutiny and are subjected to enhanced surveillance regimes through a combination of CCTV cameras, license plate scanners, police patrols, and other initiatives that tightly couple the collection of personally identifiable data to the governance of risk and deviance.[66] The persistent tendency to associate race with (urban) crime—what Khalil Gibran Muhammad has called the "condemnation of Blackness"—also means that the burdens of overpolicing in the inner city still fall disproportionately on racial minorities.[67] Likewise, the relative privacy to which middle-class families are accustomed remains more elusive for the American poor because the price of access to social services is often paid in informational currency and because state interventions in family life are uniquely common among poorer families.[68] Khiara Bridges has referred to this as the "poverty of privacy rights": the exposure of individuals and families to persistent monitoring and periodic examinations is generally correlated with low socioeconomic status and specifically correlated with the use of public assistance.[69] The differential experience of privacy and surveillance is often a proxy for "one's status and power in any given situation," and it can concentrate relative advantage and disadvantage at opposing ends of the social spectrum.[70]

Many surveillance technologies of the present are seen as quasi-mysterious black boxes, ubiquitous in their presence, indiscriminate in their targeting, opaque in their operations, and totalizing in their effects. Yet they are better understood as technologies of the governmental frontier: they aim to extend the terrain of data collection and impose order on administrative decision-making through algorithmic judgment, and they are directly tied into existing webs of institutions, procedures, and prejudice at the bureaucratic front line. Their effects are disparate: discerning in the types and volumes of information that are considered pertinent to the governance of risk, selective in the individuals and populations on whom the surveillant gaze is focused, and uneven in the subsequent utilization of personal data by the corporate sector and by the welfarist "left hand" and the punitive "right hand" of the state. Claims about total surveillance pay scant attention to such characteristics and, in doing so, also risk misrecognizing governing agencies as quintessentially nefarious entities that will indiscriminately "infringe our privacy at every possible turn and will keep such infringements as secret as [they] can."[71] Yet "dystopian gestures" toward the administrative state as a *diabolus in machina*—a diabolical state apparatus that operates in a relatively unified manner—are difficult to square with the highly racialized nature of state interventions and governmental surveillance, the demonstrably uneven development of American political institutions, the devolution of administrative power to lower levels of government, and the complex field of penal and welfarist initiatives that rely on the collection and administrative deployment of personal data.[72]

The act of "[enumerating] someone or something by an institution that commands authority or legitimacy" is, within the context of modern nation-states and consumer capitalism, also essential to legal personhood, political recognition, and socioeconomic inclusion.[73] This is partly why the social valuation of privacy exists alongside desires for exposure and pursuits of publicity.[74] The balancing of these competing goals is con-textually specific and perennially evolving, but *some* balancing always occurs.[75] Already in the late nineteenth century, the ability to participate in an increasingly credit-based consumer economy became contingent on remote assessments of financial risk, which helped to turn consumers into "informational persons" who were defined by and treated in accordance with personalized and quantified measures of worthiness, responsibility, and long-term value.[76] The *valued* consumer has long been a *visible* consumer. For example, a contributor to *Hunt's Merchant Magazine* wrote as early as 1853 about such credit ratings by observing that "[go] where you may to purchase goods, a character has preceded you, either for your benefit or your destruction."[77] Since their inception, credit scores have functioned as sources of stigma and exclusion but also as tools of financial inclusion that facilitate access to mortgages and other forms of credit.[78] Social Security numbers have a similarly complex history and also illustrate the delicate dance between visibility-as-deprivation and visibility-as-privilege. As a "beneficent technology of citizenship," they first became instrumental to the administration of welfare support during the Great Depression and exemplified a vision of government as a solver of large-scale social problems.[79]

As the writer Franny Choi has put it, "truth is, I wanted to be known, cracked open by gentle hands."[80] The "inexhaustible eagerness of people to tell their life stories" and the quest for socioeconomic inclusion are often-neglected drivers of voluntary exposure in the Information Age.[81] But given the tight coupling of exposure to social inclusion and the individuation of the modern self, it is too easy a response to dismiss demands for greater visibility as expressions of a false consciousness, as if the informational persons of the twentieth and twenty-first centuries were bereft of agency and unsuspecting participants in their own subjugation and com-modification. The centrality of personal data to public administration and private commerce means that, when viewed from the perspective of the informational person, the costs of privacy routinely outweigh the costs of surveillance. There is rarely an obvious material benefit to privacy, which has repeatedly made its defense "the most difficult of tasks," according to an article already published in 1918 in *Harper's Magazine*.[82] Privacy-as-invisibility and privacy-as-seclusion can easily become unappealing rather than impossible as people recalibrate their need and desire for exposure in the Information Age.

In many ways, we are now living through another inflection point—a period when decades happen in a matter of weeks, months, or years. The rapid spread of general artificial intelligence (GAI) has made data-sharing through proprietary application programming interfaces (API) seem almost quaint by comparison. It marks a sea change in the ability to extract and consolidate information from a wide range of (structured and unstructured) sources. At the same time, the expansion of executive power in the United States tests many of the formal checks and balances and informal norms of democratic governance that have historically prevented state institutions from exploiting the full range of their technological and administrative capacities. It used to be said that those who controlled the security forces controlled political power. Now that power seems to lie disproportionately with those who control data, as sysadmins—those who manage the vast troves of data that are under corporate or governmental control—have emerged as newly empowered operatives at the frontier of informational power.

But what happens when unbound power meets consolidated data? If history can serve as a guide, we ought to expect the hierarchization of exposure rather than the leveling of difference. Even if the collection of personal data is indiscriminate, the deployment of such data is often targeted and oriented towards specific commercial or ideological ends—and resistance also breaks down along familiar partisan lines. In this changing world, privacy often dwells in the uncanny valley of information politics. On the one hand, privacy has completed the proverbial march through the institutions and has become integral to the organization and functioning of modern society.[83] On the other hand, it often remains a comforting fiction that the existence of formal privacy rights offers substantive protection against the exercise of informational power, that the perceived benefits of privacy necessarily outweigh the perceived benefits of exposure, or that substantive agreement exists about the nature and scope of legitimate data collection.[84] There is a real risk of tasking privacy "with doing work beyond its capabilities" and, in so doing, to erect political platforms on a brittle foundation.[85]

One thing appears certain: The winds of change are blowing, and we will not simply return to the technosocial or technopolitical realities of prior decades.[86] Yet, in the long succession of conflicts over the structure of society, privacy has been a constant struggle not just for the preservation of the old but for the reconfiguration of inherited concepts.[87] It has also been a balancing act, as the relative benefits of "being let alone" were weighed (and weighed differently in different contexts) against the appeal of visibility and the pursuit of "selfdom."[88] The fatalism of the present notwithstanding, privacy has not been extinguished during those struggles.[89] But it has been deformed and reimagined, throwing up new questions even as it settles prior conflicts: What grievances, values, or ideologies now motivate public demands for privacy or defenses of surveillance? How is the scope of privacy protections affected by balances of power and the political process? And who benefits? Here, as elsewhere, the task of social science is neither the task of acolytes nor of undertakers. But social science can provide us with the tools to examine a notoriously elusive concept with a grasp of history and thus also to grasp the challenges that now present themselves before us.

Methodological Coda

T here is more to be said about data and methodology, and there are at least two reasons to say it. First, I ought to be transparent as a matter of principle about what I have done and how I have done it. Second, I hope that this coda can serve other historical social scientists even if they ultimately decide that things can be done better by being done differently.

Throughout my research, I have embraced the role of the "sociologist as historian," as Damon Mayrl and Nicholas Hoover Wilson have called it, and I have rooted my work in the tradition of analytical sociology.[1] This means that I have relied extensively on primary source materials; I have endeavored to find evidence of macrosocial change (or stasis) in specific mezzo-social settings; and I have explained such change with reference to dynamics of collective action, shifting network structures, and sequences of events.[2] As Norbert Elias once wrote, the social world does not merely go through a process, it is a process, because social reality is continuously and dynamically emerging.[3]

It is a truism that such processes are highly contingent—most things are, if we look closely enough. The social world is structurally complex, causally overdetermined, and probabilistic.[4] No single theory can fully capture this. In fact, simplification is the entire point of theory: explanatory models are often useful when they rely on a small number of propositions or

208 | METHODOLOGICAL CODA

identify specific mechanisms to explain stasis or change. The challenge is to deploy those models within an analytic framework that can nonetheless capture the complex facets and unexpected twists of history, instead of treating historical processes as self-explanatory or inevitable. We must give ourselves the luxury of explanatory choice: of being able to accept or reject competing claims about historical trends by measuring them against empirical data.

My solution has been to pay particular attention to the "boundedness, continuity, plasticity, and complexity" of diffusion and institutionalization.[5] In doing so, I have largely followed the advice of Jeannette Colyvas and Stefan Jonsson, who urge a triple focus on "objects (that spread or stick), subjects (who influence or adopt), and settings (within which each process takes place)."[6] (Their work also includes thirteen propositions about dynamics of diffusion and institutionalization. Many of these propositions are reflected in the arguments of the preceding chapters.) Instead of identifying global paradigm shifts that dislodge formerly hegemonic ideas or epistemes that provide overarching structure to knowledge and power during a given period, I have thus endeavored to build a coherent argument by studying highly varied and clearly bounded cases. I have looked for these cases in multiple sites of "world-making" where conceptions of society and the social order are challenged and reproduced, including politics, jurisprudence, and bureaucratic administration.[7] Some of them may appear idiosyncratic at first glance. Others have already been discussed elsewhere in the literature on privacy, and I have included them here because existing accounts struck me as empirically incomplete or theoretically misleading. I have left out many facets of history that could rightfully have been included. I ask the reader to judge this book not by whether it is exhaustive but by whether it is persuasive.

ARCHIVES AND COLLECTIONS

The research for this book took me from coast to coast and involved several extended stints in the Library of Congress and the National Archives in Washington, DC, and College Park, MD, as well as shorter research visits to the Massachusetts Historical Society in Boston, the San Francisco History Center, the New York Public Library, and the University of California (UC), Berkeley Bioscience, Natural Resources, and Public Health Library. When possible, I additionally relied on digital collections. For example, data about the National Conference on Social Welfare come from collections that have been digitized at the University of Michigan. Publications from successive New York tenement commissions and annual reports from the Department of Tenements are available in situ at the New York Public Library (NYPL) and also partly accessible through the NYPL's growing digital collection. I accessed data from the *Congressional Globe* (which contains congressional debates from 1833 to 1873) and the *Congressional Record* (which contains more recent debates) at the Library of Congress in Washington, DC, and through online repositories that are maintained by the U.S. Congress, the Library of Congress, and the Social Science Data Collection at Stanford University. Historical public health reports (which were published annually by the Marine Hospital Service and, later, by the Public Health Service) are partially available as digital files through the Google Books American English corpus and fully accessible in print at the UC Berkeley Bioscience, Natural Resources, and Public Health Library. Historical legal texts dating back to 1790 can be accessed through the Nexis Uni database, and digital archives for fifteen law review journals were specifically made available for this project by Hein Online as a bulk dataset. All data from historical newspapers, magazines, and novels also come from digital collections (like the *Chronicling America* collection from the National Digital Newspaper Program) and curated digital datasets (like the Corpus of Historical American English). Table M.1 provides an overview of my main data sources. All sources are fully cited in the notes; major datasets and archival collections are additionally listed in the bibliography and described below.

Unless otherwise noted, all analyses that involve population counts or other population-level estimates (such as literacy rates or percentages of foreign-born residents) are based on historical full-count census records from the U.S. Bureau of the Census, available through IPUMS USA.[8] Counts for intercensal years are interpolated. Some additional data come from summary statistics published by the Census Bureau and the National Center for Education Statistics.[9]

COMPUTATIONAL TEXT ANALYSIS

The computational analyses in this book treat discourses as social phenomena that have micro-level foundations but macro-level significance. Any individual mention of a term matters less than the aggregate because a

Table M.1 Primary datasets and data sources

Analysis	Data Source
Computational text analysis	*Chronicling America* collection (via Library of Congress)
	Corpus of Historical American English (via Brigham Young University)
	American English 2019 Corpus (via Google Ngram)
Citation network analysis	Historical legal opinions (via Nexis Uni)
Geospatial analysis	Historical statistics of the United States (via U.S. Census Bureau, IPUMS USA)
	New York (NY) Department of Tenements reports (online and via NY Public Library [NYPL])
	Tenement floor plans (via NYPL)
	NY shapefiles and demographic data (via National Historical Geographic Information System/IPUMS)
Trend-line graphs	Historical statistics of the United States (via U.S. Census Bureau, IPUMS USA)
	Secondary sources on print media and telegraph/telephone history
	Congressional Record (via Library of Congress and Stanford University)
	Proceedings of the National Conference on Social Welfare (via University of Michigan)
Qualitative analysis	Archives of U.S. law reviews/journals (via Hein Online)
	NY reports of legislative commissions (online and via NYPL)
	(Auto)biographies of key protagonists
	Chronicling America collection (via Library of Congress)
	Corpus of Historical American English (via Brigham Young University)
	Archives of *The New York Times* and the *Real Estate Record and Builders Guide*
	Records from Public Health Service and Post Office Department (via U.S. National Archives)
	State/municipal public health records (via city/state historical societies and Berkeley Public Health Library)
	U.S. Postal Bulletins (via U.S. Postal Bulletin Consortium)

discourse is composed of thousands of idiosyncratic speech acts that might individually seduce us into one interpretation or another, yet there is no guarantee that any single utterance captures something meaningful about the larger phenomenon under study. But viewed from a distance, signals begin to appear: accumulations around certain topics or shifts over time, or rising and ebbing tides of prominence or ruptures in the meaning of a word. These were the patterns I aimed to identify.

I relied on two primary corpora of digitized historical texts: the *Chronicling America* (CA) collection produced by the National Digital Newspaper Program and maintained by the Library of Congress and the Corpus of Historical American English (COHA) at Brigham Young University.[10] CA is a large database of historical newspaper content published between 1777 and 1963, with the bulk of the digitized content published between 1840 and 1925. At the time of this writing, the CA collection includes more than 21 million total pages of text, of which around 15.5 million come from the years between 1870 and 1920. COHA is a genre-balanced dataset that includes content from historical newspapers but additionally includes magazine articles, nonfiction books, and literary fiction. It totals more than 475 million words of text, of which around 130 million come from the period between 1870 and 1920. Unlike CA data, COHA data are already preprocessed and cleaned; the quality of the resulting dataset is excellent. I additionally used data from Google Books' American English corpus in chapter 4.[11]

One challenge of working with CA data is the uneven quality of machine-readable files that were produced through optical character recognition (OCR). Decay of the original newspaper copies due to age and poor paper quality can confuse image recognition software and result in misspellings and produce random ASCII sequences in the digitized text. Global text accuracy is highly sensitive to such errors: a character-level misrecognition rate of 2 percent can result in 10–20 percent of words being misspelled.[12] This is a perennial challenge when working with digitized historical data.

I addressed this in two ways. First, I manually corrected common misspellings of 289 relevant terms in the CA corpus—"rrivacy" becomes "privacy," "privato" becomes "private," "intrud" becomes "intrude," "cvre" becomes "cure," and so forth. I developed this list of terms iteratively over many runs of the text analysis models discussed below, each time checking model outputs against the original image files to identify the correct spellings for commonly misspelled words. Second, I fed digitized text files through a spellchecker and a word prediction algorithm. The spellchecker identifies words not included in standard English dictionaries. The word prediction algorithm—based on a pretrained Bayesian additive regression trees (BART) model—then takes the spellchecker's output as input and replaces all words that have been marked as misspelled with most-likely substitutes, using the surrounding context words to make those predictions. This approach resulted in a small increase in the size of the useful vocabulary, between 2 percent and 5 percent depending on the decade. (Newer models would likely achieve better results, especially since the development of large-scale artificial intelligence [AI] transformer models has given researchers vastly more powerful tools to process, clean, and analyze unstructured text.)

I followed standard data cleaning and preprocessing practices, removing stop words and certain parts of speech like modal verbs (would, could), auxiliary verbs (may, must), adverbs (even, apart, away, first, also, strictly, thereby), conjunctions (though, until, yet, either), prepositions (without, upon, per, like), pronouns (hers, his, theirs), and numbers. I also ran a bigram detection program; lemmatized all words in the dataset using the Python WordNet lemmatizer; and tokenized the text so that each word in a sentence is contained in a separate token.

I then selected for my analysis all texts that contain the term "privacy" and were originally published between 1870 and 1920, which resulted in decadal datasets that vary between 6,159 pages of newspaper content for the 1870s and 32,707 pages for the 1910s. These pages came from local, regional, and national publications in forty-six U.S. states. I did not include newspaper content from the 1920s in any computational models because, at the time that these analyses were performed, the number of digitized and relevant pages from that decade was still too small. This was largely due to copyright constraints: newspapers published in the United States enter the public domain after ninety-five years, which means that the National Digital Newspaper Program's newspaper digitization program did not yet extend to 1930 when these data were collected.

I relied on two primary models to analyze these corpora of historical text: a Word2Vec model that can be used to identify most similar words and embedding biases (e.g., gender bias) and an n-gram-based word co-occurrence model that can shed light on the thematic contexts in which a given term appears on the printed page.[13] Word2Vec models have a relatively straightforward architecture: the embeddings they produce are vectors of coefficients—calculated by reducing the loss function of a neu-tral network model—that allow each word in a corpus to be located in a high-dimensional vector space in relation to all other words. The usage and meaning of different words can then be compared by comparing their respective vector representations. In effect, this so-called "shallow" approach retains the first bag-of-words layer and the second vector layer of common natural language processing models but does not include a final prediction layer. (Since I performed these analyses, generative AI models have become widely available. These are conceptually similar but addition-ally include so-called "transformer layers," which implement a self-attention mechanism that allows the model to weigh the importance of different words in the input sequence when making predictions.)

Word2Vec models facilitate the inductive discovery of distributional similarities, which can be then proxied for semantic similarity between words.[14] For example, a Word2Vec model would be able to identify "king" and "monarch" as similar terms if their embedding spaces resemble each other, even if these terms never occur alongside each other on the printed page. In fact, we would not expect similar terms to appear in proximity. To write about a "monarch king" is as redundant as it is to speak about "chai tea." Two distributionally similar terms are not always exact synonyms—although this is true in many instances—but at least share membership in the same family of terms and concepts.

I implemented a continuous bag-of-words (CBOW) model to calculate embedding vectors. Two advantages of this model—compared to an alter-native skip-gram model—are that it is computationally less demanding and more reliable with frequently occurring words (which were my focus). I identified similar words by comparing their vector representations, using cosine similarity scores. These scores are pervasive in computational text analysis and plagiarism detection because they establish a quantitative measure of similarity by measuring the angle between two vectors in a multidimensional space: diametrically opposed vectors have a cosine simi-larity of −1; orthogonal vectors have a similarity of 0; and similar vectors have a cosine similarity approaching 1.[15] The same approach can also shed light on latent discursive biases. For example, it is possible to estimate the extent of a word's gender bias by comparing its embedding space to the embedding spaces of explicitly gendered words like wife, husband, father, mother, masculine, feminine, and so forth. The embedding bias is then equal to the dissimilarity between the term of interest and the average of all female-coded words, minus the dissimilarity between the term of interest and the average of all male-coded words.[16]

Word embedding models are sometimes presented as "unsupervised" methodologies because they do not require prelabeled datasets or prespecified dictionaries.[17] But researchers must still set several model parameters, including the vector size (What is the dimensionality of the model?), the window size (How large is the context window from which the CBOW model makes its predictions?), the minimum word count (How often does a word have to appear in the dataset to be considered by the model?), and the number of modeling epochs (How many iterations of the model are run?). Appropriate thresholds and the general sensitivity of embedding distances to parameter specifications are still an active area of research—often using simulation exercises—but certain parameter ranges have been found to strike an appropriate balance between model robustness and computational demands.[18] For example, Word2Vec outputs have been found to stabilize for window sizes greater than 8 and vector size greater than 50.[19] The results presented here are based on models with vector size 100, window size 10, minimum word count 20, and 50 epochs. I arrived at these specifications after systematically testing model specifications across a wide parameter space, summarized in table M.2.

My second set of models identified word co-occurrence odds. Instead of generating word-specific embedding vectors (the "second layer" in the description above), these models analyze first-layer patterns directly by extracting all relevant n-grams, which are text sequences of length n that

Table M.2 Examined Word2Vec/n-gram parameter space

Model Parameter	Results	Comments
Continuous bag-of-words (CBOW) model dimensions (50/100/150/200)	Stable for n ≥ 100	Longer vectors become computationally demanding
CBOW window size (5/10/15/20)	Stable for sizes 10–15	
Minimum number of CBOW word occurrences (10/20/30/40)	Misspelled words too frequent for n < 10	n > 20 significantly reduces vocabulary size
CBOW model epochs (10/20/30/40/50/75/100)	Stable for n ≥ 20	
N-gram window size (11/15/21)	Stable	

contain the term "privacy." A challenge implicit in this approach is to bound the window of relevant text. Just because a term appears in one paragraph does not mean that it retains a meaningful connection to whatever else appears several paragraphs down the page. Generally speaking, terms that occur in the same small fragment of text are more likely to have such a connection than words that appear on opposite ends of a page. The boundaries of context are inevitably fuzzy, but they do exist. I report results from the analysis of 21-grams, i.e., text fragments centered on "privacy" that also include the ten words immediately to the left and the right (excluding stop words, adverbs, etc.). But the exact length of the n-gram does not matter: analyses using more tightly bounded 15-grams or 11-grams yielded very similar results. I grouped 21-grams by decade and calculated the co-occurrence odds for each word in the resulting reduced dataset, which measured the probability of an event occurring—which, in this case, is the co-occurrence of privacy with term X—divided by the probability of the event not occurring.

I additionally validated core findings with probabilistic topic models (not reported in the main text) that infer the most likely theme of any given text or document by analyzing local and global word distributions.[20] In technical terms, each "topic" refers to the specialized probability distribution over a given set of words. It is possible to estimate the prevalence of topics within documents by comparing the distribution of words within each document to the distribution of words across the entire dataset. Similarly, it is possible to chart the prevalence of topics over time. This latter approach builds on so-called latent Dirichlet allocation (LDA) models but specifically models time alongside word distributions in a "topics over time" model. Such topic modeling generally requires documents to have a certain minimum length. One possible approach is to consider each newspaper article or page as a single document, but this is misleading. Just because an article mentions privacy does not mean that it is meaningfully *about* privacy. Often, analyzing the nuances of public discourse requires a focus on the immediate embedding of a word rather than the much wider text in which it appears.[21] Therefore, I adopted an alternative approach in these supplemental models and treated each *year* as a document. This document contains all words that appeared in the privacy n-grams of that year. Results from these topic models showed close agreement with the co-occurrence analyses presented in chapter 2.

CITATION NETWORK ANALYSIS

I analyzed the legal institutionalization of the right to privacy by constructing and analyzing a time series network of legal citations. Citation network analysis has previously been used to examine the emergence of scientific schools of thought, the diffusion of new and innovative ideas across scientific subfields, and the formation of scientific communities.[22] But this approach is new to the historical study of privacy and legal institutionalization. It has allowed me to study the right to privacy as part of a genealogy of case law, and it has enabled me to identify commonalities in juridical interpretation through shared precedents.

I began with a dataset of 1,025 state and federal cases that discussed privacy in majority opinions, concurring opinions, or dissenting opinions from the U.S. Supreme Court, circuit courts, state supreme courts, and state courts of appeal between 1870 and 1930, aggregated from the Nexis Uni database. This dataset includes cases that were substantively *about* privacy but also includes a plethora of cases that mention privacy in passing without framing it as a topic of judicial concern. I manually coded each case and then restricted my analysis to 146 cases that directly engaged with the right to privacy (sometimes also called the "right of privacy"). Judges occasionally copied extended passages from existing opinions instead of providing their own formulations. I included these in the dataset if quoted passages directly contributed to judges' legal reasoning. Replicating the analyses without these borderline cases resulted in networks that were smaller and less dense, but it had no impact on the network's overall structure.

I then mapped out a citation network that included all 146 cases ("egos") as well as any other case, constitutional amendment, statute, legislative act, or law review essay that was cited as precedent for the right to privacy ("alters"). In the parlance of social network analysis, "ego" refers to focal nodes in a network, and "alters" refers to any additional nodes that are directly connected to such egos. I excluded cases that were cited only for procedural reasons, for example, to establish rules of evidence, legal standing, or jurisdiction. The resulting network was composed of 677 nodes— 146 egos and 531 alters—and 1,099 citation ties.

I calculated two network parameters, modularity and eigenvector centrality. Modularity Q is a commonly used measure of global network clustering, defined as the ratio of the total number of ties within a cluster to the total number of ties in the entire network. I obtained modularity scores through a two-step process that uses a random walk algorithm to identify multiple clusters within a larger network and then takes the assigned cluster membership of each node to calculate Q.[23] Eigenvector centrality scores are calculated for each node within a network, with higher scores indicating that a node is connected to other influential nodes. (The logic of eigenvector centrality also underlies Google's PageRank search algorithm.) Simply put, eigenvalue centrality allows researchers to identify the most important nodes in any given network.[24]

For each of the 146 egos in the network, I also recorded several additional data points: the year of adjudication, the thematic context (e.g., advertising or police searches), the target of privacy disputes (e.g., government agencies or private companies), and the legal justification for privacy claims (e.g., natural law, common law, or the U.S. Constitution). I developed the thematic coding scheme through an iterative process. First, I coded all 146 egos as well as 100 additional alters to obtain an initial list of 34 thematic categories. After merging categories that closely resembled each other—like "advertising" and "marketing"—I recoded each case and all additional alters based on a final eighteen-category coding scheme. I also replicated my analysis using the granular initial coding scheme and found no substantive differences. However, it was sometimes impossible to determine a legal justification. Judges may have omitted references to the origins of the right to privacy because they were hesitant to commit to any particular school of thought, because they considered the question of ultimate origins to be insignificant to their legal reasoning, or because they assumed such origins to be self-evident. I was able to identify a stated origin in 78 of the 146 cases. In a supplementary analysis, I restricted the citation network's egos to this subset of 78 cases. This truncated network was necessarily smaller but retained the same two-cluster structure and the same distribution of state-centric and business-centric cases across clusters as the primary (146-case) network.

GEOSPATIAL ANALYSIS

To test whether the legislative codification of privacy norms had a measurable impact on urban space, I performed two spatial analyses. First, I calculated ward-level population density at different points in time. Second, I estimated the annual average floor area per person (FAPP) for each New York City borough.

Density calculations are based on full-count census microdata and area shapefiles that I obtained through IPUMS USA and the National Historical Geographic Information System (NHGIS).[25] Knowing the number of persons living in each census ward and the total area of that ward allowed me to compute persons per area unit. However, this measure is easily polluted by uncertainty about the total amount of livable space per area unit and about changes in the amount of livable space over time (e.g., due to an increase/decrease in the average number of floors per building or an increase/decrease in the total built-up area due to road construction and other large-scale infrastructure and park projects).[26] FAPP provides an alternative measure of the residential use of urban space and is subject to a very different set of assumptions. It is influenced by five major variables: L, the average size of the building lot; B, the average percentage of the lot occupied by a building; H, the average percentage of the building given to walls and hallways rather than private apartments; A, the average number of one-family apartments per floor within a building; and P, the average number of persons per family. Given these variables, FAPP is then calculated as:

$$\frac{L * B * H}{A * P}$$

Floor areas for many current buildings in New York City are available from the Primary Land Use Tax Lot Output (PLUTO) database. However, I found that this database does not accurately capture tenements built before the 1920s, which were often torn down during subsequent decades. Instead, I relied on annual reports from the Department of Tenements to approximate FAPP for different New York City boroughs. This approach required several steps. First, the annual reports listed the number of building permits for post-1901 tenements by lot width and borough. Because lot depths were widely standardized to 100 feet in New York, lot area in square feet can be approximated by multiplying lot width by 100. This yields a distribution of lot sizes for each New York City borough. Second, tenement officials did not keep detailed statistics on the percentage of each lot that was occupied by a building or the total rentable floor area per lot. But we can roughly approximate these quantities by taking advantage of well-established facts about New York tenement construction, as well as occasional government surveys. Tenement officials repeatedly sampled buildings from each borough to estimate B. Their data indicate that buildings on average covered 73 percent of lots in Manhattan and around 65 percent in the outer boroughs.

Developers were also constrained by the 1901 law, which prohibited buildings from occupying more than 75 percent of any given lot. Lot coverage should lie close to 75 percent as developers attempted to maximize floorspace without violating state law. In my calculations, I used Department of Tenement estimates of lot size coverage. Third, data on the expected percentage of building space lost to public hallways, staircases, and static elements can be derived from tenement floor plans published by the New York City Public Library. I used image processing software to calculate the total area of rentable floor space in each floor plan and then averaged the results. I also estimated rentable floor space independently by comparing 1903 Department of Tenements statistics on "rentable areas per floor" for different buildings against the total square footage of those buildings. Both methods of calculation indicate that walls, hallways, and other nonrentable spaces in tenements built after the passage of New York's 1901 tenement law account for 20 percent of a building's footprint. Fourth, data on the number of apartments per floor per year per borough are also available from Department of Tenement annual reports. Fifth, data on average family size can be computed from full-count census microdata for each New York City borough, interpolated for intercensal years.

QUALITATIVE ANALYSES

In addition to these computational analyses, I relied on the close reading of newspapers, magazine articles, and novels because staying close to the printed page can aid the detection of nuances and subtleties that are not necessarily detectable across an entire corpus of text.[27] To do this, I first collected 752 privacy-related magazine articles and passages from novels, drawing on the COHA corpus. For each text, I recorded basic publication details (year of publication, author, venue), the sentence(s) including the term "privacy," and a brief characterization of the substantive nature of the discussion. I then built a similar dataset by sampling 3,001 newspaper articles from the CA corpus for the period between 1870 and 1920 (I resampled 100 articles per decade for in-depth analysis). I also analyzed 87 essays about privacy jurisprudence, collected from 395 issues of 15 prominent law reviews and law journals. Included in this dataset of law reviews were the *American Law Review, American Lawyer, Central Law Journal, Columbia Law Review, Green Bag, Harvard Law Review, Kentucky Law Journal, Medico-Legal Journal, Michigan Law Journal, Minnesota Law Review,*

Northwestern Law Review, The American Law Register and Review, The American Law Register, Virginia Law Register, Western Reserve Law Journal, and *Yale Law Journal.* The selection of legal periodicals was negotiated with the data provider Hein Online, which usually prohibits bulk downloads of historical text but agreed to provide a customized dataset consisting of the archives of fifteen legal periodicals for this project.

My analyses of tenement reform campaigns relied on conference proceedings from the National Conference on Social Welfare, made available by the University of Michigan.[28] Proceedings run between 200 and 600 pages per year; I surveyed all proceedings published between 1874 and 1930 and selected 86 thematically relevant speeches and plenary discussions for a detailed analysis. For each of these, I recorded (1) why a speaker considered privacy to be relevant to discussions of social reform, (2) whether they considered privacy to be under threat, (3) reasons for the precarious state of urban privacy, if stated, and (4) proposed remedies, if stated. I supplemented these data with information obtained from the writings of tenement reform protagonists and politicians like Jacob Riis, Lawrence Veiller, Theodore Roosevelt, and Ernest Flagg, with reports produced by the 1884 Legislative Commission on Tenement Housing, the 1894 Tenement House Committee of the Charity Organization Society of New York City, and the 1900 New York State Tenement House Commission, and with 126 newspaper articles about privacy and tenement reform published between 1867 and 1923 in *The New York Times*—the city's paper of record—and the trade publication *Real Estate Record and Builders Guide*, which was one of the primary specialist venues for urban planners, developers, architects, and housing advocates interested in construction and housing policy in New York.

To study the incorporation of privacy claims into bureaucratic administration, I used archival records (housed in the U.S. National Archives, the Library of Congress in Washington, DC, the California Historical Society in San Francisco, the Massachusetts Historical Society in Boston, the New York Public Library, and the Public Health Library at UC Berkeley) from the Public Health Service and the Post Office Department. Both agencies exemplified the "infrastructural power" of the American state to penetrate society, often through the collection and dissemination of personal data or interpersonal communication.[29] But they also differed in their developmental histories, in their substantive areas of focus and expertise, and in their techniques of bureaucratic administration. These differences provided comparative analytical leverage, and they allowed me to build a "positive empirical case" and study the institutionalization of privacy in two distinct settings.[30] For each organization, I identified and examined materials relating to the period between 1870 and 1930, including daily reports from the Postal Inspection Service and weekly bulletins from the Public Health Service (compiled in annually published Public Health Reports), regulatory missives like the Postal Laws and Regulations, internal pamphlets like the Post Office Bulletin, internal memos, and summaries of regulatory changes from the *Federal Register*. I also analyzed 379 passages pertaining to privacy from the *Congressional Record*, spanning the period from the Forty-Second Congress (1871–1872) to the Seventy-First Congress (1929–1930) and obtained both from the Library of Congress and from Stanford University's Social Science Data Collection.[31]

My qualitative analyses made extensive use of spreadsheets and memos. I built a spreadsheet for each dataset/case and then translated information from these spreadsheets into memos to identify common themes and case-specific differences.[32] This allowed me to study specific organizations, schools of legal reasoning, and political struggles in their concrete environments and thereby connect macro-level patterns to mezzo-level institutions, organizational practices, and collective action. In several of the preceding chapters, I combined this qualitative archival research with one or more computational analyses.

Acknowledgments

When I first conceived this project in 2016, privacy seemed moribund. An earlier generation of scholars had written eloquently about the complicated politics of personal data—people like Alan Westin, James Rule, and Gary Marx—but the "surveillance studies" of the 2010s were most concerned with demonstrating that the scope of informational power, properly understood, was nearly total. There was nothing really worth explaining about privacy, since the concept had seemingly been reduced to a charade. This situation has changed dramatically in the interim, thanks to scholars whose work often sits at the intersection of sociology, technology studies, legal studies, and social history: Khiara Bridges, Danielle Citron, Julie E. Cohen, Sarah Igo, Helen Nissenbaum, Sarah Seo, Scott Skinner-Thompson, Ari Ezra Waldman, Rebecca Wexler, and others. First and foremost, I am grateful for the path they have already charted.

My work has also benefitted tremendously from feedback and encouragement by an early group of mentors at the University of California (UC), Berkeley. They include Marion Fourcade, Christopher Muller, Dennis Feehan, and—above all else—Mara Loveman. Mara also brought together a group of junior scholars who are now spread far and wide but whose invisible fingerprints remain all over this book: Elizabeth McKenna, Robert Pickett, Michaeljit Sandhu, and Mary Shi.

I owe additional gratitude to Andrés Argüello, Garrett Baker, Alexander Barnard, Paul Chung, Isaac Dalke, Nora Eiermann, Claude Fischer, Neil Fligstein, Cybelle Fox, Heather Haveman, Christopher Herring, Jocelyn Huang, Andrew Jaeger, Matty Lichtenstein, Samuel Lucas, Jon Marshall, Santiago Molina, Yascha Mounk, Dylan Riley, Christopher Ruiz Chiu, Maria-Fátima Santos, Caleb Scoville, David Showalter, Phung Su, Ann Swidler, Jay Varellas, Dexter Walcott, Jakob Weissinger, Nicholas Hoover Wilson, Steven Wolfe, the members of the Berkeley Empirical Legal Studies Fellowship community (especially Jonathan Simon, our fearless and gentle leader), the Computational Text Analysis Working Group and the Computational Social Science Workshop at UC Berkeley (especially Tim Thomas and David Harding), and various discussants and interlocutors at the annual conferences of the American Sociological Association and the Social Science History Association. Laura Nelson, Rochelle Terman, and the staff at the D-Lab deserve a special mention for training an entire generation of UC Berkeley graduate students in computational research methods.

In collecting data for this project, I relied on many experts in academic and governmental libraries and archives across the United States: Cody Hennesy, Stacy Reardon, Dean Rowan, and Jim Ronningen at the UC Berkeley library; Shane Marmion (who helped to negotiate bulk data access at Hein Online); Mark Davies (compiler of the Corpus of Historical American English); and researchers and staff members at Nexis Uni, the Minnesota Population Center, the University of Michigan library system, the Library of Congress, the National Archives in Washington, DC, and College Park, Maryland, the New York Public Library, the Massachusetts Historical Society, and the San Francisco History Center. Special thanks also go to the Research Division of the Bureau of the Census (where staff agreed to share internal reports and working papers on data privacy) and the volunteer corps of enthusiasts who sustain the U.S. Postal Bulletin project. Stephen Jay Gould once wrote that good science is a product of fruitful doing rather than clever thinking.[1] The people listed above helped me to do the doing by making historical data much more readily accessible.

My research was generously supported by the UC Berkeley graduate fellowship program, the UC Berkeley Department of Sociology, the Allan Sharlin Memorial Fellowship of the UC Berkeley Institute of International Studies, and the Berkeley Empirical Legal Studies Fellowship. Christopher Wildeman then took me under his wing as a postdoctoral scholar at Duke and provided me with the flexibility and financial resources to complete this book manuscript. At Columbia University Press, I am especially grateful to Eric Schwartz for his early enthusiasm and competent editorial hand, to the outstanding editorial team of the "Middle Range" series—Peter Bearman, Emily Erikson, Christopher Muller, and Catherine Turco—and to Alyssa Napier and Ben Kolstad for editorial assistance.

I am hopeful that this book will make it easier to explain to concerned family members what exactly an academic does all day. Yet it would not exist, or exist only in lesser form, without steadfast encouragement from my partner Devon Youngblood. She is her ancestors' wildest dream and my most passionate cheerleader, although I would love her just the same if she enforced a strict moratorium on dinner table sociology.

Notes

EPIGRAPH

The epigraph to the book comes from Georg Simmel, *Soziologie: Untersuchungen über die Formen der Vergesellschaftung* (Duncker & Humblot, 1908), 361. Translated by the author.

PREFACE

1. "The Era of Publicity—the Twentieth Century," *Washington Times*, July 31, 1902.
2. Malcolm Bradbury, *The History Man* (Picador, 2017), 78.
3. Bradbury, *The History Man*, 78.

INTRODUCTION: PRIVACY FOR A NEW AGE

1. Thurman B. Rice, *The Hoosier Health Officer: A Biography of Dr. John N. Hurty* (Indiana State Board of Health, 1946).
2. Theda Skocpol, *Protecting Soldiers and Mothers: The Political Origins of Social Policy in the United States* (Harvard University Press, 1995); James H. Madison, "The Evolution of Commercial Credit Reporting Agencies in Nineteenth-Century America," *Business History Review* 48, no. 2 (1974): 164–86; Margo J. Anderson, *The American Census: A Social History* (Yale University Press, 1988).
3. Ian Hacking, *The Taming of Chance* (Cambridge University Press, 1990), 34.
4. For a similar periodization, see Josh Lauer, "Surveillance History and the History of New Media: An Evidential Paradigm," *New Media and Society* 14, no. 4 (2012): 566–82; Sharon Hayes and Laura Miller, "Informed Control: Dun & Bradstreet and the Information Society," *Media, Culture and Society* 16, no. 1 (1994): 117–40. Gilman M. Ostrander refers to roughly the same period as the "first machine age"; see Gilman M. Ostrander, *American Civilization in the First Machine Age, 1890–1940* (Harper Collins, 1970). Readers may disagree about when exactly the Early Information Age began: With the invention of the printing press in 1448? With the completion of ENIAC, the world's first

electronic general-purpose computer, in 1945? With the birth of the internet in 1983? My historical periodization directs attention, but my argument does not hinge on where exactly the continuous flow of history is dammed.

5. Rice, *The Hoosier Health Officer*, 17–19.
6. Rice, *The Hoosier Health Officer*, 53–56.
7. Gregory L. Armstrong et al., "Trends in Infectious Disease Mortality in the United States During the 20th Century," *Journal of the American Medical Association* 281, no. 1 (1999): 61–66.
8. Rice, *The Hoosier Health Officer*, 97.
9. Rice, *The Hoosier Health Officer*, 191.
10. John N. Hurty, "The Bookkeeping of Humanity," *Journal of the American Medical Association* 55, no. 14 (1910): 1157–60.
11. Campbell Gibson and Kay Jung, "Historical Census Statistics on the Foreign-Born Population of the United States: 1850–2000," Working Paper 81 (U.S. Bureau of the Census Population Division, Washington, DC, 2006); Stephen Skowronek, *Building a New American State: The Expansion of National Administrative Capacities, 1877–1920* (Cambridge University Press, 1982).
12. Thomas Byrnes, *Professional Criminals of America: New and Revised Edition* (G.W. Dillingham, 1895); Charles Brackett, "The Early Criminal Record on the Boundary of Entertainment: Thomas F. Byrnes' Professional Criminals of America and the Spectacle of Criminal Identification," *Surveillance and Society* 20, no. 2 (2022): 157–71.
13. Joseph Stromberg, "Herman Hollerith's Tabulating Machine," Accessed January 24, 2023, https://www.smithsonianmag.com/smithsonian-institution/herman-holleriths-tabulating-machine-2504989/.
14. Milton Mueller, "Universal Service in Telephone History: A Reconstruction," *Telecommunications Policy* 17, no. 5 (1993): 352–69; William A. Dill, *Growth of Newspapers in the U.S.: A Study of the Number of Newspapers, of the Number of Subscribers, and of the Total Annual Output of the Periodical Press, from 1704 to 1925, with Comment on Coincident Social and Economic Conditions* (Bulletin of the Department of Journalism of the University of Kansas, 1928); Claude S. Fischer, "The Revolution in Rural Telephony, 1900–1920," *Journal of Social History* 21, no. 1 (1987): 5–26.
15. Hayes and Miller, "Informed Control"; Jonathan Levy, *Freaks of Fortune: The Emerging World of Capitalism and Risk in America* (Harvard University Press, 2012); Bruce G. Carruthers, "From Uncertainty Toward Risk: The Case of Credit Ratings," *Socio-Economic Review* 11, no. 3 (2013): 525–51; Lendol Calder, *Financing the American Dream: A Cultural History of Consumer Credit* (Princeton University Press, 1999); Dan Bouk, *How Our Days Became Numbered: Risk and the Rise of the Statistical Individual* (University of Chicago Press, 2015); Josh Lauer, "From Rumor to Written Record: Credit Reporting and the Invention of Financial Identity in Nineteenth-Century America," *Technology and Culture* 49, no. 2 (2008): 301–24.

16. Colin Koopman, *How We Became Our Data: A Genealogy of the Informational Person* (University of Chicago Press, 2019), 156; James Gleick, *The Information: A History, a Theory, a Flood* (Pantheon, 2011); James W. Cortada, *All the Facts: A History of Information in the United States Since 1870* (Oxford University Press, 2016).

17. Robert H. Wiebe, *The Search for Order, 1877–1920* (Hill and Wang, 1967), xiii.

18. Charles Hirschman and Elizabeth Mogford, "Immigration and the American Industrial Revolution from 1880 to 1920," *Social Science Research* 38, no. 4 (2009): 897–920; Louise Payson Latimer, *Your Washington and Mine* (Charles Scribner's Sons, 1924), 166; Monica Prasad, *The Land of Too Much American Abundance and the Paradox of Poverty* (Harvard University Press, 2012). Unless otherwise noted, population-level statistics in this book are based on historical full-count census microdata, accessed via IPUMS USA. Area and population density estimates use New York City shapefiles with historical census ward boundaries, accessed through the Urban Transition Historical GIS Project at Brown University and IPUMS NHGIS.

19. Guy H. Thompson, "The Right of Privacy as Recognized and Protected in Law and in Equity," *Central Law Journal* 47, no. 8 (1898): 150.

20. Anthony Giddens, "The 'Individual' in the Writings of Emile Durkheim," *European Journal of Sociology/Archives Européennes de Sociologie* 12, no. 2 (1971): 210–28.

21. Emile Durkheim, *The Division of Labor in Society* (Free Press, 1964), 172; G. Edward White, *Tort Law in America: An Intellectual History* (Oxford University Press, 2003), 3.

22. "No Privacy in City Life," *Los Angeles Times*, August 10, 1902. Reprinted from the *Chicago Daily Tribune*.

23. Thompson, "The Right of Privacy as Recognized and Protected in Law and in Equity," 150; Michel Foucault, *A History of Sexuality: Volume 1* (Vintage Books, 1990), 26–27; Sarah E. Igo, *The Known Citizen: A History of Privacy in Modern America* (Harvard University Press, 2018), 3 and 16.

24. By "logic," I refer to the totality of beliefs, claims, and rules about privacy, as well as the practices (e.g., of spatial access or data collection) that were thence informed and legitimated.

25. Nathaniel Hawthorne, *The Scarlett Letter* (James R. Osgood, 1850), 223; Charles Dickens, *Barnaby Rudge: A Tale of the Riots of Eighty* (T.B. Peterson, 1841), 294–95.

26. "Letter of Mr. T. M. Randolph to His Constituents," *The Enquirer*, April 24, 1806.

27. The focus on breadth and durability (i.e., diffusion and institutionalization) is adapted from Jeannette A. Colyvas and Stefan Jonsson, "Ubiquity and Legitimacy: Disentangling Diffusion and Institutionalization," *Sociological Theory* 29, no. 1 (2011): 27–53. The authors focus on three aspects, which are mirrored in the empirical chapters of this book: "The objects that flow or stick;

the subjects who adopt or influence; and the social settings through which an innovation travels." See the Methodological Coda for a discussion.

28. Foucault, *A History of Sexuality*, 26.

29. John Durand, "French Domestic Life and Its Lessons," *Atlantic Monthly*, August 1881, 164–79.

30. David Lyon, *The Electronic Eye: The Rise of Surveillance Society* (University of Minnesota Press, 1994); Robert Ellis Smith, *Ben Franklin's Web Site: Privacy and Curiosity from Plymouth Rock to the Internet* (Privacy Journal, 2000), 9; Reg Whitaker, *The End of Privacy: How Total Surveillance Is Becoming a Reality* (New Press, 2000); Jeffrey Rosen, *The Unwanted Gaze: The Destruction of Privacy in America* (Vintage, 2011).

31. Oscar H. Gandy Jr., *The Panoptic Sort: A Political Economy of Personal Information*, 2nd ed. (Oxford University Press, 2021), 29.

32. Kevin D. Haggerty and Richard V. Ericson, "The Surveillant Assemblage," *British Journal of Sociology* 51, no. 4 (2000): 62.

33. Myron Brenton, *The Privacy Invaders* (Coward-McCann, 1964), 163.

34. Mary Madden et al., "Teens, Social Media, and Privacy," *Pew Research Center* 21, no. 1055 (2013): 2–86; Alice E. Marwick and danah boyd, "Networked Privacy: How Teenagers Negotiate Context in Social Media," *New Media and Society* 16, no. 7 (2014): 1051–67; Ralf De Wolf, "Contextualizing How Teens Manage Personal and Interpersonal Privacy on Social Media," *New Media and Society* 22, no. 6 (2020): 1058–75.

35. Igo, *The Known Citizen*, especially 307ff.

36. Ian Bogost, "Welcome to the Age of Privacy Nihilism," *The Atlantic*, August 23, 2018, https://www.theatlantic.com/technology/archive/2018/08/the-age-of -privacy-nihilism-is-here/568198.

37. Edward Shils, "Privacy: Its Constitution and Vicissitudes," *Law and Contemporary Problems* 31, no. 2 (1966): 292.

38. Smith, *Ben Franklin's Web Site*, 73. For a related argument in public discourse, also see Richard V. Denenberg, "Privacy: Wanted but Vague," *New York Times*, February 3, 1974.

39. Tobias Dienlin and Sabine Trepte, "Is the Privacy Paradox a Relic of the Past? An In-Depth Analysis of Privacy Attitudes and Privacy Behaviors," *European Journal of Social Psychology* 45, no. 3 (2015): 285–97.

40. Louis Harris and Alan F. Westin, *The Dimensions of Privacy: A National Opinion Research Survey of Attitudes Toward Privacy* (Garland Publishing, 1981); Neil Vidmar and David H. Flaherty, "Concern for Personal Privacy in an Electronic Age," *Journal of Communication* 35, no. 2 (1985): 91–103; Oscar H. Gandy Jr., "The Preference for Privacy: In Search of the Social Locations of Privacy Orientations" (presentation, Annual Meeting of the Speech Communication Association, San Francisco, CA, November 18–21, 1989); James E. Katz and Annette R. Tassone, "Public Opinion Trends: Privacy and Information Technology," *The Public Opinion Quarterly* 54, no. 1 (1990): 125–43; Steven L. Nock, *The Costs of Privacy: Surveillance and Reputation in America*

(De Gruyter, 1993); Bernhard Debatin et al., "Facebook and Online Privacy: Attitudes, Behaviors, and Unintended Consequences," *Journal of Computer-Mediated Communication* 15, no. 1 (2009): 83–108; Gandy, *The Panoptic Sort*, 163–204.

41. Igo, *The Known Citizen*, 307ff.
42. See, for example, legal notices from Tesla (https://www.tesla.com/en_eu/legal/privacy) and Apple (https://www.apple.com/legal/privacy/data/en/apple-maps), accessed April 7, 2023.
43. Geoffrey Fowler, "I Tried to Read All My App Privacy Policies. It Was 1 Million Words," *The Washington Post*, May 31, 2022; Brooke Auxier et al., "Americans and Privacy: Concerned, Confused and Feeling Lack of Control Over Their Personal Information" (Washington, DC: Pew Research Center, 2019).
44. Steven L. Nock, "Too Much Privacy?," *Journal of Family Issues* 19, no. 1 (1998): 107. For a philosophical statement of this view (and a defense of "oblivion" as a prerequisite for a good life), see Lowry Pressly, *The Right to Oblivion: Privacy and the Good Life* (Harvard University Press, 2024).
45. Haggerty and Ericson, "The Surveillant Assemblage," 61; Shoshana Zuboff, *The Age of Surveillance Capitalism: The Fight for a Human Future at the New Frontier of Power* (Public Affairs, 2019).
46. Helen Nissenbaum, "Toward an Approach to Privacy in Public: Challenges of Information Technology," *Ethics and Behavior* 7, no. 3 (1997): 207–19.
47. Laurence H. Tribe, *American Constitutional Law*, 2nd ed. (Foundation Press, 1988), 1302ff. Also quoted in Amy L. Fairchild et al., *Searching Eyes: Privacy, the State, and Disease Surveillance in America* (University of California Press, 2007), xvi.
48. *Olmstead v. United States*, 277 U.S. 438 (1928) (Brandeis, J., dissenting).
49. Mary Ziegler, *Beyond Abortion: Roe v. Wade and the Battle for Privacy* (Harvard University Press, 2018); Zuboff, *The Age of Surveillance Capitalism*.
50. For a similar typology (but a different set of conclusions), see Nock, "Too Much Privacy."
51. Mark Neocleous, "Privacy, Secrecy, Idiocy," *Social Research* 69, no. 1 (2002): 85–110. For a Marxist perspective on surveillance (which situates different types of surveillance within different phases of the cycle of accumulation), see Christian Fuchs, "Political Economy and Surveillance Theory," *Critical Sociology* 39, no. 5 (2013): 671–87.
52. Barrington Moore, *Privacy: Studies in Social and Cultural History* (Routledge, 1984), 12 and 268; Peter Berger and Thomas Luckmann. *The Social Construction of Reality* (Anchor Books, 1966), 67–72; Denise Anthony et al., "Toward a Sociology of Privacy," *Annual Review of Sociology* 43 (2017): 263; Debbie V. S. Kasper, "Privacy as a Social Good," *Social Thought and Research* 28 (2007): 165–89.
53. For a related discussion of positive liberties, see David Nicholls, "Positive Liberty, 1880–1914," *American Political Science Review* 56, no. 1 (1962): 114–28. For a more recent restatement of the idea that privacy has social impacts that

need to be realized through active interventions, see Kasper, "Privacy as a Social Good."

54. Ruth Gavison, "Privacy and the Limits of Law," *Yale Law Journal* 89, no. 3 (1980): 421–71; Rose Laub Coser, "Insulation from Observability and Types of Social Conformity," *American Sociological Review* 26, no. 1 (1961): 9.

55. Arthur L. Stinchcombe, "Institutions of Privacy in the Determination of Police Administrative Practice," *American Journal of Sociology* 69, no. 2 (1963): 150–60; Sarah A. Seo, "The New Public," *Yale Law Journal* 125 (2016): 1616–71.

56. Barry Schwartz, "The Social Psychology of Privacy," *American Journal of Sociology* 73, no. 6 (1968): 741–52; David Popenoe, *Private Pleasure, Public Plight: Urban Development, Suburban Sprawl, and the Decline of Community* (Routledge, 2001).

57. Georg Simmel, "The Sociology of Secrecy and of Secret Societies," *American Journal of Sociology* 11, no. 4 (1906): 441–98; Spiros Simitis, "Reviewing Privacy in an Information Society," *University of Pennsylvania Law Review* 135, no. 3 (1987): 707.

58. Schwartz, "The Social Psychology of Privacy," 742; Erving Goffman, *The Presentation of Self in Everyday Life* (Allen Lane, 1959).

59. Tribe, *American Constitutional Law*, 1302.

60. The analogy to desert islands paraphrases Daniel Solove: Daniel J. Solove, "Conceptualizing Privacy," *California Law Review* 90, no. 4 (2002), 1104. The quote is taken from Moore, *Privacy*, 73.

61. Moore, *Privacy*, 8ff; Lidia Sciama, "The Problem of Privacy in Mediterranean Anthropology," in *Women and Space: Ground Rules and Social Maps*, ed. Shirley Ardener (Routledge, 1993), 87–111. For non-Western perspectives, see Payal Arora, "Decolonizing Privacy Studies," *Television and New Media* 20, no. 4 (2019): 366–78; Divya Dwivedi and Viswanathan Sanil, *The Public Sphere from Outside the West* (Bloomsbury Publishing, 2015); Vladimir Shlapentokh, *Public and Private Life of the Soviet People: Changing Values in Post-Stalin Russia* (Oxford University Press, 1989); Yan Yunxiang, *Private Life Under Socialism: Love, Intimacy, and Family Change in a Chinese Village, 1949–1999* (Stanford University Press, 2003).

62. Richard Sennett, *The Fall of Public Man* (Norton, 1974); Bruce Redford, *The Converse of the Pen: Acts of Intimacy in the Eighteenth-Century Familiar Letter* (University of Chicago Press, 1986); Cecile M. Jagodzinski, *Privacy and Print: Reading and Writing in Seventeenth-Century England* (University of Virginia Press, 1999); Diana Webb, *Privacy and Solitude in the Middle Ages* (Hambledon Continuum, 2007); Jessica Martin and Alec Ryrie, eds., *Private and Domestic Devotion in Early Modern Britain* (Ashgate, 2012); Patricia M. Spacks, *Privacy: Concealing the Eighteenth-Century Self* (University of Chicago Press, 2003); Jill Lepore, "The Prism: Privacy in an Age of Publicity," *The New Yorker*, June 24, 2013.

63. David H. Flaherty, *Privacy in Colonial New England, 1630–1776* (University of Virginia Press, 1972), 20.

64. Amy Gajda, *Seek and Hide: The Tangled History of the Right to Privacy* (Penguin, 2022), xi.
65. Norberto Bobbio, *Democracy and Dictatorship: The Nature and Limits of State Power* (Polity Press, 1989), xxx.
66. Moore, *Privacy*, 122ff.
67. Karl Marx, "On the Jewish Question," in *The Marx-Engels Reader*, ed. Robert C. Tucker (Norton, 1978), 25–52.
68. Benjamin Constant, *Constant: Political Writings*, ed. Biancamaria Fontana (Cambridge University Press, 1988). Also see Simitis, "Reviewing Privacy in an Information Society," 730–31: "The citoyen's access to information ends where the bourgeois' claim for privacy begins."
69. Philip Abrams, "Notes on the Difficulty of Studying the State (1977)," *Journal of Historical Sociology* 1, no. 1 (1988): 58–89; Karl Marx, "The German Ideology," in *The Marx-Engels Reader*, ed. Robert C. Tucker (Norton, 1978), 160.
70. John Stuart Mill, *On Liberty and Other Essays* (Oxford University Press, 1998), 18; Norbert Elias, *The Civilizing Process: Sociogenetic and Psychogenetic Investigations* (Blackwell Publishing, 2000), 472.
71. Hannah Arendt, *On Revolution* (Penguin Books, 1963), 269; Alexis de Tocqueville, *Democracy in America* (Penguin Books, 2003), 701 and 604.
72. For a contemporary version of this argument, see Amitai Etzioni, *The Limits of Privacy* (Basic Books, 1999).
73. As Robert Ellis Smith has argued—wrongly, I think—Americans seemed to pursue physical privacy "for the first half" of the nation's history and informational privacy "after the Civil War," largely as a reaction to newly invented technologies. See Smith, *Ben Franklin's Web Site*, 9.
74. Solove, "Conceptualizing Privacy," 1093. Also see Stinchcombe, "Institutions of Privacy in the Determination of Police Administrative Practice."
75. Gajda, *Seek and Hide*, xvii.
76. Seo, "The New Public." For a general discussion of boundary-drawing and world-making, see Thomas F. Gieryn, "Boundary-Work and the Demarcation of Science From Non-Science," *American Sociological Review* 48, no. 6 (1983): 781–95; Eviatar Zerubavel, "Lumping and Splitting: Notes on Social Classification," *Sociological Forum* 11, no. 3 (1996): 421–33; Ian Hacking, *The Social Construction of What?* (Harvard University Press, 1999), 4; Geoffrey C. Bowker and Susan Leigh Star, *Sorting Things Out: Classification and Its Consequences* (MIT Press, 2000); Sheila Jasanoff, "Ordering Knowledge, Ordering Society," in *States of Knowledge: The Co-Production of Science and Social Order* (Routledge, 2004), 13–45.
77. Charles A. Reich, "Police Questioning of Law Abiding Citizens," *Yale Law Journal* 75 (1966): 1170; Jason W. Patton, "Protecting Privacy in Public? Surveillance Technologies and the Value of Public Places," *Ethics and Information Technology* 2 (2000): 181; Nicole A. Moreham, "Privacy in Public Places," *The Cambridge Law Journal* 65, no. 3 (2006): 606–35.
78. Joel R. Reidenberg, "Privacy in Public," *University of Miami Law Review* 69 (2014): 141 and 143.

79. Nissenbaum, "Toward an Approach to Privacy in Public," 207; Helen Nissenbaum, "Protecting Privacy in an Information Age: The Problem of Privacy in Public," *Law and Philosophy* 17 (1998): 559–96.

80. Reinhart Koselleck, *The Practice of Conceptual History* (Stanford University Press, 2002); Reinhart Koselleck, *Futures Past: On the Semantics of Historical Time* (Columbia University Press, 2004); Andrew Abbott, "Things of Boundaries," *Social Research* 62, no. 4 (1995): 857–82.

81. Ludwig Wittgenstein, *Philosophical Investigations*, 4th ed., ed. Joachim Schulte (Wiley-Blackwell, 2009), 66; Paul Patton, "MetamorphoLogic: Bodies and Powers in A Thousand Plateaus," *Journal of the British Society for Phenomenology* 25, no. 2 (1994): 157–69. Also quoted in Haggerty and Ericson, "The Surveillant Assemblage," 608. For a longer discussion of privacy as a Wittgensteinian concept, see Solove, "Conceptualizing Privacy."

82. Abbott, "Things of Boundaries," 877–78. For a different view, see Pressly, *The Right to Oblivion*, 30: Starting in the late 1800s, privacy may have emerged as "something in which everyone had an interest solely by virtue of being human."

83. Schwartz, "The Social Psychology of Privacy"; Moore, *Privacy*; Leon A. Pastalan, "Privacy as a Behavioral Concept," *Social Science* 45, no. 2 (1970): 93–97; Barbara Laslett, "The Family as a Public and Private Institution: An Historical Perspective," *Journal of Marriage and Family* 35, no. 3 (1973): 480–92. But see James B. Rule, *Private Lives and Public Surveillance: Social Control in the Computer Age* (Schocken Books, 1974); James B. Rule et al., *The Politics of Privacy: Planning for Personal Data Systems as Powerful Technologies* (Elsevier, 1980).

84. Helen Nissenbaum, "Privacy as Contextual Integrity," *Washington Law Review* 79 (2004): 119–58; Daniel J. Solove, *Understanding Privacy* (Harvard University Press, 2010); Chris Jay Hoofnagle and Jennifer M. Urban, "Alan Westin's Privacy Homo Economicus," *Wake Forest Law Review* 49 (2014): 261–317; Bouk, *How Our Days Became Numbered*; Simone Browne, *Dark Matters: On the Surveillance of Blackness* (Duke University Press, 2015); Rebecca Wexler, "Privacy as Privilege: The Stored Communications Act and Internet Evidence," *Harvard Law Review* 134 (2020): 2721–92; Khiara M. Bridges, *The Poverty of Privacy Rights* (Stanford University Press, 2017); Ari Ezra Waldman, "Privacy Law's False Promise," *Washington University Law Review* 97 (2019): 773–834; Ari Ezra Waldman, *Industry Unbound: The Inside Story of Privacy, Data, and Corporate Power* (Cambridge University Press, 2021).

85. Igo, *The Known Citizen*, 7.

86. Judith Jarvis Thomson, "The Right to Privacy," *Philosophy and Public Affairs* 4, no. 4 (1975): 295–314.

87. Christena E. Nippert-Eng, *Islands of Privacy* (University of Chicago Press, 2010).

88. In this book, I sidestep discussions of privacy that are rooted in philosophical arguments, e.g., in arguments about human dignity and normative conceptions of the good life (although I discuss how privacy became linked to theories of individualism and the inviolate personality in chapter 4). Relevant

philosophical works include Milton R. Konvitz, "Privacy and the Law: A Philosophical Prelude," *Law and Contemporary Problems* 31, no. 2 (1966): 272–80; Glenn Negley, "Philosophical Views on the Value of Privacy," *Law and Contemporary Problems* 31, no. 1 (1966): 319–25; Thomson, "The Right to Privacy"; Robert S. Gerstein, "Intimacy and Privacy," *Ethics* 89, no. 1 (1978): 76–81; Gavison, "Privacy and the Limits of Law"; Ferdinand D. Shoeman, ed., *Philosophical Dimensions of Privacy: An Anthology* (Cambridge University Press, 1984); Sissela Bok, *Secrets: On the Ethics of Concealment and Revelation* (Pantheon Books, 1985); Jed Rubenfeld, "The Right of Privacy," *Harvard Law Review* 102, no. 4 (1989): 737–807; Ralph F. Gaebler, "Is There a Natural Law Right to Privacy?," *American Journal of Jurisprudence* 37 (1992): 319–36; Etzioni, *The Limits of Privacy*; Pressly, *The Right to Oblivion*.

89. Fernand Braudel, "History and the Social Sciences: The Longue Durée," in *On History*, trans. Sarah Matthews (University of Chicago Press, 1980), 31. Also see Andrew Abbott, *Department and Discipline: Chicago Sociology at One Hundred* (University of Chicago Press, 1999), 203 and 232.

90. Nissenbaum, "Privacy as Contextual Integrity," 119; Helen Nissenbaum, "A Contextual Approach to Privacy Online," *Daedalus* 140, no. 4 (2011): 32–48. For a recent application of this perspective to privacy practices and systems design, see Louise Barkhuus, "The Mismeasurement of Privacy: Using Contextual Integrity to Reconsider Privacy in HCI," in *Proceedings of the SIGCHI Conference on Human Factors in Computing Systems* (2012), 367–76.

91. Georg Simmel, *The Sociology of Georg Simmel*, ed. Kurt H. Wolff (Free Press, 1967), 326.

92. Anthony et al., "Toward a Sociology of Privacy," 259. Also see Christian Parenti, *The Soft Cage: Surveillance in America, from Slavery to the War on Terror* (Basic Books, 2007); James B. Rule, *Privacy in Peril* (Oxford University Press, 2009); Gandy, *The Panoptic Sort*; Frank Pasquale, *The Black Box Society* (Harvard University Press, 2015); Julie E. Cohen, *Between Truth and Power: The Legal Constructions of Informational Capitalism* (Oxford University Press, 2019); Spiros Simitis, "Privacy—An Endless Debate?," *California Law Review* 98, no. 6 (2010): 1989–2005.

93. Nippert-Eng, *Islands of Privacy*, 4; Simitis, "Reviewing Privacy in an Information Society," 709.

94. Stanley Lieberson and Freda B. Lynn, "Barking Up the Wrong Branch: Scientific Alternatives to the Current Model of Sociological Science," *Annual Review of Sociology* 28, no. 1 (2002): 1–19.

95. Smith, *Ben Franklin's Web Site*, 9; Igo, *The Known Citizen*.

96. Guy B. Peters et al., "The Politics of Path Dependency: Political Conflict in Historical Institutionalism," *The Journal of Politics* 67, no. 4 (2005): 1289.

97. Priscilla M. Regan, *Legislating Privacy: Technology, Social Values, and Public Policy* (University of North Carolina Press, 1995), xiv.

98. Donna Haraway, "Situated Knowledges: The Science Question in Feminism and the Privilege of Partial Perspective," *Feminist Studies* 14, no. 3 (1988):

575–99; Patricia Hill Collins, *Black Feminist Thought: Knowledge, Consciousness, and the Politics of Empowerment* (Routledge, 2002).

99. Flaherty, *Privacy in Colonial New England*; Karen V. Hansen, "Rediscovering the Social: Visiting Practices in Antebellum New England and the Limits of the Public/Private Dichotomy," in *Public and Private in Thought and Practice*, ed. Jeff A. Weintraub and Krishan Kumar (University of Chicago Press, 1997), 268–302; Jagodzinski, *Privacy and Print*; Spacks, *Privacy.*

100. Margaret D. Jacobs, *White Mother to a Dark Race: Settler Colonialism, Maternalism, and the Removal of Indigenous Children in the American West and Australia, 1880–1940* (University of Nebraska Press, 2009).

101. See pp. 31–62 in Browne, *Dark Matters*, for a discussion of the "panoptic" vision of slave traders and southern plantation owners. Also see Parenti, *The Soft Cage.*

102. Michael Freeden, *Ideologies and Political Theory: A Conceptual Approach* (Clarendon, 1996). For a treatment of privacy as a "racialized" idea, see Jessica Vasquez-Tokos and Priscilla Yamin, "The Racialization of Privacy: Racial Formation as a Family Affair," *Theory and Society* 50, no. 5 (2021): 717–40; Browne, *Dark Matters*; Bridges, *The Poverty of Privacy Rights.*

103. Michael C. Behrent, "Foucault and Technology," *History and Technology* 29, no. 1 (2013): 54–104.

104. James Scott, *Seeing Like a State: How Certain Schemes to Improve the Human Condition Have Failed* (Yale University Press, 1998); Marion Fourcade and Kieran Healy, "Seeing Like a Market," *Socio-Economic Review* 15, no. 1 (2017): 9–29.

105. Simitis, "Reviewing Privacy in an Information Society," 709 and 735.

106. For a related discussion of the "conduct of conduct," see Michel Foucault, "The Subject and Power," *Critical Inquiry* 8, no. 4 (1982): 790. Also see James Waldo et al., eds., *Engaging Privacy and Information Technology in a Digital Age* (National Academies Press, 2007); Browne, *Dark Matters*; Bridges, *The Poverty of Privacy Rights*; Solove, "Conceptualizing Privacy," 1091 and 1127–29; Simitis, "Reviewing Privacy in an Information Society," 707–9. For a more general discussion of the link between information technologies and the governance of social vulnerability and risk, see Virginia Eubanks, *Automating Inequality: How High-Tech Tools Profile, Police, and Punish the Poor* (St. Martin's Press, 2018).

107. Anthony et al., "Toward a Sociology of Privacy," 269; Stephen T. Margulis, "Privacy as a Social Issue and Behavioral Concept," *Journal of Social Issues* 59, no. 2 (2003): 243–61; Marwick and boyd, ""Networked Privacy"; De Wolf, "Contextualizing How Teens Manage Personal and Interpersonal Privacy"; Goffman, *The Presentation of Self*; Schwartz, "The Social Psychology of Privacy"; Jagodzinski, *Privacy and Print*, 1.

108. Parenti, *The Soft Cage*; Gandy, *The Panoptic Sort*; Haggerty and Ericson, "The Surveillant Assemblage"; William Bogard, *The Simulation of Surveillance: Hypercontrol in Telematic Societies* (Cambridge University Press, 1996); Rita

Raley, "Dataveillance and Countervailance," in *Raw Data Is an Oxymoron*, ed. Lisa Gitelman (MIT Press, 2013), 121–46. But see Jordan Brensinger, "Identity Theft, Trust Breaches, and the Production of Economic Insecurity," *American Sociological Review*, 88, no. 5 (2023): 844–71.

109. Igo, *The Known Citizen*, especially chapter 4. For a discussion of privacy and gender in early American privacy jurisprudence, also see Dorothy Glancy, "Privacy and the Other Miss M," *Northern Illinois University Law Review* 10 (1989): 401–40.

110. Gary T. Marx, "What's New About the 'New Surveillance'? Classifying for Change and Continuity," *Surveillance and Society* 1, no. 1 (2002): 17 and 22.

111. Abbott, *Department and Discipline*, 3.

112. Joseph Schumpeter, *The Economics and Sociology of Capitalism*, ed. Richard Swedberg (Princeton University Press, 1991), 101.

113. Koopman, *How We Became Our Data*. For discussions of the "rights revolution," also see Cass Sunstein, *After the Rights Revolution: Reconceiving the Regulatory State* (Harvard University Press, 1993); Charles R. Epp, *The Rights Revolution: Lawyers, Activists, and Supreme Courts in Comparative Perspective* (University of Chicago Press, 1998).

114. Andrew Abbott, "History and Sociology: The Lost Synthesis," *Social Science History* 15, no. 2 (1991): 230.

115. For a lengthier discussion of this approach, see Niek Veldhuis, "Exploring Ancient Networks," *H2D Revista de Humanidades Digitais* 3, no. 1 (2021).

116. Abbott, "History and Sociology," 225. Also see William H. Sewell, "Three Temporalities: Toward an Eventful Sociology," in *The Historic Turn in the Human Sciences*, ed. Terrence McDonald (University of Michigan Press, 1996), 245–80; Morgan Jouvenet, "Contexts and Temporalities in Andrew Abbott's Processual Sociology," *Annales. Histoire, Sciences Sociales-English Edition* 71, no. 3 (2016): 361–92.

117. Karen Barkey, "Historical Sociology," in *The Oxford Handbook of Analytical Sociology*, ed. Peter Bearman and Peter Hedström (Oxford University Press, 2011), 712–32.

118. Andrew Abbott, *The System of Professions: An Essay on the Division of Expert Labor* (University of Chicago Press, 1988), xi–xiii.

1. UNDER THE EAVES OF THE HOME: DOMESTIC PRIVACY AND THE CULTIVATION OF SELF

1. Robert Louis Stevenson, *The Amateur Immigrant* (Association for Scottish Literary Studies, 2014), 12 and 23; Robert Louis Stevenson, "An Inland Voyage," in *Travels with a Donkey in the Cévennes and Selected Travel Writings*, ed. Emma Letley (Oxford University Press, 1992), 222. I list books, newspapers, magazines, and other historical publications in the chapter notes when I consulted them as primary sources but only list secondary sources in the

bibliography at the end of the book. Primary data sources are additionally listed and discussed in the Methodological Coda.

2. Robert Louis Stevenson, *The Silverado Squatters. Sketches from a California Mountain* (Chatto & Windus, 1883).

3. Stevenson, *The Silverado Squatters*, 273.

4. For a summary (and critique) of the individualistic interpretation of privacy, see Kasper, "Privacy as a Social Good" and Etzioni, *The Limits of Privacy*. For an additional Marxist critique, see Neocleous, "Privacy, Secrecy, Idiocy."

5. See, for example, Alan F. Westin, *Privacy and Freedom* (Athenum, 1967); Schwartz, "The Social Psychology of Privacy"; Pastalan, "Privacy as a Behavioral Concept"; Eric Sundstrom et al., "Privacy at Work: Architectural Correlates of Job Satisfaction and Job Performance," *The Academy of Management Journal* 23 (1980): 101–17; Darhl M. Pedersen, "Psychological Functions of Privacy," *Journal of Environmental Psychology* 17, no. 2 (1997): 147–56; Margulis, "Privacy as a Social Issue and Behavioral Concept"; Anthony et al., "Toward a Sociology of Privacy."

6. Moore, *Privacy*, 45.

7. Edward Shils, "Privacy," 281; Schwartz, "The Social Psychology of Privacy"; Pastalan, "Privacy as a Behavioral Concept"; Charles Fried, "Privacy," *Yale Law Journal* 77, no. 3 (1968): 482–83; Gerstein, "Intimacy and Privacy," 81; Zick Rubin et al., "Self-Disclosure in Dating Couples: Sex Roles and the Ethic of Openness," *Journal of Marriage and the Family* 42, no. 2 (1980): 305–17; Kasper, "Privacy as a Social Good." Also see Janna Malamud Smith, "Privacy and Private States," in *The Private I: Privacy in a Public World*, ed. Molly Peacock (Graywolf Press, 2001), 3–22.

8. Goffman, *The Presentation of Self*, 24.

9. Goffman, *The Presentation of Self*, 112.

10. Moore, *Privacy*, 76.

11. Schwartz, "The Social Psychology of Privacy," 742; Shani Pindek et al., "Finally, Some 'Me Time': A New Theoretical Perspective on the Benefits of Commuting," *Organizational Psychology Review* 13, no. 1 (2023): 44–66.

12. Etzioni, *The Limits of Privacy*; Nock, *The Costs of Privacy*.

13. Georg Simmel, "The Secret and the Secret Society," in *The Sociology of Georg Simmel*, ed. Kurt H. Wolff (Free Press, 1950), 311–12.

14. Alan P. Bates, "Privacy—A Useful Concept?," *Social Forces* 42, no. 4 (1964): 429–34; Daniel J. Solove, "Why Privacy Matters Even if You Have 'Nothing to Hide,'" *Chronicle of Higher Education* 15 (2011), https://www.chronicle.com/article/why-privacy-matters-even-if-you-have-nothing-to-hide. For a literary treatment of seeking to hide from the "front stage" in the Soviet Union, see Aleksandr Solzhenitsyn, *Cancer Ward* (Penguin Books, 1974).

15. Moore, *Privacy*, 276; Jeff Weintraub and Krishan Kumar, eds., *Public and Private in Thought and Practice: Perspectives on a Grand Dichotomy* (University of Chicago Press, 1997); Bates, "Privacy—A Useful Concept?," 429; Alan F.

Westin, *Whistleblowing! Loyalty and Dissent in the Corporation* (McGraw-Hill, 1981).

16. Robert K. Merton, *Social Theory and Social Structure* (Free Press, 1968), 399.

17. Moore, *Privacy*; Simmel, "The Secret and the Secret Society," especially 307–29.

18. Charles Taylor, *Philosophical Papers: Volume 2, Philosophy and the Human Sciences* (Cambridge University Press, 1985), 261–62. Also see Nock, "Too Much Privacy?"

19. Elias, *The Civilizing Process*, 365 and 406.

20. Haggerty and Ericson, "The Surveillant Assemblage," 619. Also see Sennett, *The Fall of Public Man*; Webb, *Privacy and Solitude in the Middle Ages*; Redford, *The Converse of the Pen*; Jagodzinski, *Privacy and Print*; Martin and Ryrie, *Private and Domestic Devotion in Early Modern Britain*.

21. Schwartz, "The Social Psychology of Privacy"; Pastalan, "Privacy as a Behavioral Concept"; Laslett, "The Family as a Public and Private Institution," 481; Nock, "Too Much Privacy?"; Smith, *Ben Franklin's Web Site*; Frederick S. Lane, *American Privacy: The 400-Year History of Our Most Contested Right* (Beacon, 2009); Webb, *Privacy and Solitude in the Middle Ages*; Martin and Ryrie, *Private and Domestic Devotion in Early Modern Britain*; Nippert-Eng, *Islands of Privacy*.

22. Zuboff, *The Age of Surveillance Capitalism*; Sarah Brayne, "Big Data Surveillance: The Case of Policing," *American Sociological Review* 82, no. 5 (2017): 977–1008; Parenti, *The Soft Cage*; Westin, *Privacy and Freedom*; Harris and Westin, *The Dimensions of Privacy*; Ponnurangam Kumaraguru and Lorrie Faith Cranor, "Privacy Indexes: A Survey of Westin's Studies," Carnegie Mellon University Institute for Software Research Working Paper, 2005; Dienlin and Trepte, "Is the Privacy Paradox a Relic of the Past?"; Madden et al., "Teens, Social Media, and Privacy"; Marwick and boyd, "Networked Privacy"; De Wolf, "Contextualizing How Teens Manage Personal and Interpersonal Privacy"; Debatin et al., "Facebook and Online Privacy"; Vidmar and Flaherty, "Concern for Personal Privacy in an Electronic Age."

23. See Instagram's privacy tools page at https://help.instagram.com/196883487377501, accessed July 17, 2024.

24. V. S. Naipaul, *The Enigma of Arrival* (Vintage, 1988); Siegfried Giedion, *Mechanization Takes Command: A Contribution to Anonymous History* (Oxford University Press, 1970), 2.

25. Smith, *Ben Franklin's Web Site*, 30–31.

26. Gajda, *Seek and Hide*, xi.

27. Georg Simmel, "The Stranger," in *Georg Simmel on Individuality and Social Forms*, ed. Donald N. Levine (University of Chicago Press, 1971), 143–49.

28. Homer L. Calkin, "Pamphlets and Public Opinion During the American Revolution," *The Pennsylvania Magazine of History and Biography* 64, no. 1 (1940): 22–42; John R. Howe, *Language and Political Meaning in Revolutionary America* (University of Massachusetts Press, 2004); Michael Warner, *The*

Letters of the Republic: Publication and the Public Sphere in Eighteenth-Century America (Harvard University Press, 2009).

29. Rodger Streitmatter, *Mightier than the Sword: How the News Media Have Shaped American History* (Routledge, 2018).

30. Newspaper readership remained stratified by race, In 1870, up to 80 percent of the Black population aged fourteen and older were illiterate due to their being denied access to a basic education. See National Center for Education Statistics, *120 Years of American Education: A Statistical Portrait*, ed. Tom Snyder (U.S. Department of Education, 1993).

31. Historical newspapers cited in this chapter come from the Chronicling America corpus. Quotes from historical magazines and literary fiction are based on digitized text available through the Corpus of Historical American English. See the Methodological Coda for a list of primary sources.

32. Maria Susanna Cummins, *Mabel Vaughan* (John P. Jewett and Co., 1857); Theodore Sedgwick, "Political Portraits No. XVII," *U.S. Democratic Review* 2 (1840): 129–53; Charles Fenno Hoffman, *Wild Scenes in the Forest and Prairie: With Sketches of American Life* (William H. Colyer, 1843); Effie Afton, *Eventide: A Series of Tales and Poems* (Fetridge and Co., 1854); Maturin Murray Ballou, *The Heart's Secret; Or, the Fortunes of a Soldier: A Story of Love and the Low Latitudes* (1852); Mary Ashley Townsend, *The Brother Clerks: A Tale of New-Orleans* (Derby and Jackson, 1857); Edgar Allan Poe, *The Works of Edgar Allan Poe*, vol. 2 (Benediction Classics, 2011).

33. Robert Montgomery Bird, *The Hawks of Hawk-Hollow, Volume 2: A Tradition of Pennsylvania* (Carey, Lea & Blanchard, 1835); Catharine Maria Sedgwick, *Clarence; or, a Tale of Our Own Times* (J.C. Derby, 1853); Theodore S. Fay, ed., *Crayon Sketches, by an Amateur*, vol. 1 (New York, 1833); James D. Knowles, "Memoir of Roger Williams, the Founder of the State of Rhode Island," *New England Magazine*, March 1834.

34. Nathaniel Hawthorne, *The Blithedale Romance* (Ticknor, Reed, and Fields, 1852); Emerson Bennett, *Viola; or, Adventures in the Far South-West* (T. B. Peterson and Brothers, 1852); John Turvill Adams, *The Knight of the Golden Melice: A Historical Romance* (Derby and Jackson, 1857).

35. F. B. Head, "Life of Theobald Wolfe Tone, and the Condition of Ireland," *North American Review* (April 1827): 321–45; Albert Brisbane, *A Concise Exposition of the Doctrine of Association, or Plan for a Re-Organization of Society: Which Will Secure to the Human Race, Individually and Collectively, Their Happiness and Elevation* (J. S. Redfield, 1843); Cornelius Mathews, *The Various Writings of Cornelius Mathews* (Harper & Brothers, 1863).

36. W. J. Cash, *The Mind of the South* (Alfred A. Knopf, 1941), 57; Franny Trollope, *Domestic Manners of the Americans* (Penguin Books, 1832), 43. Quoted in Smith, *Ben Franklin's Web Site*, 78–79. Also see Nock, *The Costs of Privacy*.

37. Virginia Woolf, *The Waves* (Harcourt, 1931), 128.

38. Lydia Maria Child, *Philothea: A Grecian Romance* (C. S. Francis & Co.), 1851.

39. Quoted in Flaherty, *Privacy in Colonial New England*, 4–5.

40. Smith, *Ben Franklin's Web Site*, 31.
41. Oliver Wendell Holmes, "The Professor at the Breakfast-Table," *Atlantic Monthly* (December 1859): 751–70; Henry T. Tuckerman, "New England Philosophy," *U.S. Democratic Review*, January 1845. For a discussion of privacy as a tool of relationship management, see Moore, *Privacy*, and Schwartz, "The Social Psychology of Privacy."
42. For a discussion of the wider social function of privacy, also see Priscilla M. Regan, "Privacy as a Common Good in the Digital World," *Information, Communication and Society* 5, no. 3 (2002): 382–405; Kasper, "Privacy as a Social Good"; Westin, *Privacy and Freedom*, 24–65.
43. Georg Simmel, "Bridge and Door," *Theory, Culture and Society* 11 (1994): 5–10. For an in-depth discussion of privacy and domestic space in Victorian England, see Robin Evans, "Figures, Doors, and Passages," in *Translations from Drawing to Building and Other Essays* (Architectural Association Publications, 1997), 55–92.
44. Stephanie Coontz, *The Social Origins of Private Life: A History of American Families, 1600–1900* (Verso Books, 1988). For a corresponding account of bourgeois domestic privacy in Europe, see Sennett, *The Fall of Public Man*.
45. Richard Grant White, "London Streets," *Atlantic Monthly* (February 1879): 230–42. In the middle of the nineteenth century, conceptions of domesticity and domestic space were more closely aligned on both sides of the Atlantic than during the eighteenth century. See Evans, "Figures, Doors, and Passages," for a discussion of the influence of Victorian social norms.
46. See Zelizer, *Pricing the Priceless Child*, e.g., Chapter 1, for a discussion of children's leisure and moral valuation.
47. Coontz, *The Social Origins of Private Life*; Francis M. L. Thompson, *The Rise of Respectable Society: A Social History of Victorian Britain, 1830–1900* (Harvard University Press, 1990); Talcott Parsons, "Age and Sex in the Social Structure of the United States," *American Sociological Review* 7, no. 5 (1942): 604–16.
48. Evans, "Figures, Doors, and Passages," 88; Henri Lefebvre, *The Production of Space* (Blackwell, 1991), 315. For a contemporary discussion of privacy and sexuality, see James Ford, "Bad Housing and Ill Health," in *National Conference on Social Welfare: Official Proceedings of the Annual Meeting 1919* (George H. Ellis, 1919), 240.
49. Hansen, "Rediscovering the Social."
50. Coontz, *The Social Origins of Private Life*, 308.
51. Coontz, *The Social Origins of Private Life*, 35.
52. Dawn Peterson, *Indians in the Family: Adoption and the Politics of Antebellum Expansion* (Harvard University Press, 2017), 12. Also see Vasquez-Tokos and Yamin, "The Racialization of Privacy."
53. Tsianina Lomawaima, "Domesticity in the Federal Indian Schools: The Power of Authority Over Mind and Body," *American Ethnologist* 20, no. 2 (1993): 227–40.
54. Barbara J. Fields and Karen E. Fields, *Racecraft: The Soul of Inequality in American Life* (Verso Books, 2012).

55. Anita L. Allen, "Surrogacy, Slavery, and the Ownership of Life," *Harvard Journal of Law and Public Policy* 13 (1990): 141.
56. Wilma A. Dunaway, "Diaspora, Death, and Sexual Exploitation: Slave Families at Risk in the Mountain South," *Appalachian Journal* 26, no. 2 (1999): 128.
57. Smith, *Ben Franklin's Web Site*, 86–87.
58. Browne, *Dark Matters*. In particular, see pp. 45–55 for a discussion of surveillance during the slave trade and on southern plantations.
59. Karen Lystra, *Searching the Heart: Women, Men, and Romantic Love in Nineteenth-Century America* (Oxford University Press, 1992).
60. Coontz, *The Social Origins of Private Life*, 332.
61. For discussions of public discourse as an indicator of culture, see: Robert Wuthnow, *Meaning and Moral Order: Explorations in Cultural Analysis* (University of California Press, 1987); Orlando Patterson, "Making Sense of Culture," *Annual Review of Sociology* 40 (2014): 1–30.
62. For an account of semantic similarities among families of terms, see: Ludwig Wittgenstein, *The Blue and Brown Books* (Basil Blackwell, 1958), 16–17; Wittgenstein, *Philosophical Investigations*, 66–67.
63. For two restatements of this thesis, see Igo, *The Known Citizen*; and Richard F. Hixson, *Privacy in a Public Society: Human Rights in Conflict* (Oxford University Press, 1987). See Etzioni, *The Limits of Privacy*, for a normative argument in favor of publicity.
64. Coontz, *The Social Origins of Private Life*, 306.
65. James Payn, *The Eavesdropper: An Unparalleled Experience* (Harper & Brothers, 1888), 3 and 97.
66. Flaherty, *Privacy in Colonial New England*, 89.
67. Joel Bishop, *Commentaries on the Criminal Law*, vol. 2 (Little, Brown and Company, 1866), 1122. For a discussion of American case law, see David J. Seipp, "The Right to Privacy in American History," Harvard University Program on Information Resources Policy Publication P-78-3 (1978).
68. Elizabeth J. Clapp, "A Virago-Errant in Enchanted Armor? Anne Royall's 1829 Trial as a Common Scold," *Journal of the Early Republic* 23 (2): 207–32. Also discussed in Seipp, "The Right to Privacy in American History," 7.
69. Seipp, "The Right to Privacy in American History," 5, quoting from *State v. Pennington* (14 Tenn. 119, 1859).
70. Arthur R. Miller, *The Assault on Privacy: Computers, Data Banks, and Dossiers* (University of Michigan Press, 1971). Also see Edward J. Bloustein, "Privacy as an Aspect of Human Dignity," *New York University Law Review* 39 (1964): 984.
71. Ann Swidler, "Culture in Action: Symbols and Strategies," *American Sociological Review* 51, no. 2 (1986): 273–86. Also see Charles Tilly, "Contentious Repertoires in Great Britain, 1758–1834," *Social Science History* 17, no. 2 (1993): 253–80; Eviatar Zerubavel, *Social Mindscapes: An Invitation to Cognitive Sociology* (Harvard University Press, 1999).
72. Paul DiMaggio, "Culture and Cognition," *Annual Review of Sociology* 23 (1997): 263–87; Stephen Vaisey, "Motivation and Justification: A Dual-Process Model of Culture in Action," *American Journal of Sociology* 114, no. 6 (2009): 1675–715.

73. Nock, "Too Much Privacy?," 107; Flaherty, *Privacy in Colonial New England.*
74. David H. Fischer, *Albion's Seed: Four British Folkways in America* (Oxford University Press, 1989), 660.
75. Robert S. Lynd and Helen M. Lynd, *Middletown* (Harcourt Brace, 1929); Flaherty, *Privacy in Colonial New England*, 40.
76. Coontz, *The Social Origins of Private Life*, 85.
77. Smith, *Ben Franklin's Web Site.* 20.
78. Flaherty, *Privacy in Colonial New England*, 77; Coontz, *The Social Origins of Private Life.*
79. John Demos, *Past, Present, and Personal: The Family and the Life Course in American History* (Oxford University Press, 1986); Zelizer, *Pricing the Priceless Child.*
80. Nock, "Too Much Privacy?"
81. Max Weber, *The Protestant Ethic and the Spirit of Capitalism* (Routledge Classics, 2005), 75; Edmund S. Morgan, *The Puritan Family: Religion and Domestic Relations in Seventeenth-Century New England* (Harper, 1944).
82. Smith, *Ben Franklin's Web Site*, 9–10.
83. Smith, *Ben Franklin's Web Site*, 10.
84. Flaherty, *Privacy in Colonial New England*, 169; John Demos, *A Little Commonwealth: Family Life in Plymouth Colony* (Oxford University Press, 2000).
85. Coontz, *The Social Origins of Private Life*, 4; Laslett, "The Family as a Public and Private Institution."
86. Charlotte Perkins Gilman, *The Home: Its Work and Influence* (Charlton, 1910).
87. Bernard Farber, *Guardians of Virtue: Salem Families in 1800* (Basic Books, 1972), 49; Laslett, "The Family as a Public and Private Institution," 485.
88. David D. Hall, *Worlds of Wonder, Days of Judgment: Popular Religious Belief in Early New England* (Harvard University Press, 1990).
89. Donald G. Mathews, "The Second Great Awakening as an Organizing Process, 1780–1830: An Hypothesis," *American Quarterly* 21, no. 1 (1969): 23–43; Timothy L. Smith, *Revivalism and Social Reform in Mid-Nineteenth Century America* (Abingdon, 1957).
90. Lepore, "The Prism."
91. Coontz, *The Social Origins of Private Life*, 269ff. Also see John Higham, *Hanging Together: Unity and Diversity in American Culture* (Yale University Press, 2001).
92. Smith, *Ben Franklin's Web Site*, 93.
93. Hansen, "Rediscovering the Social."
94. Barbara Welter, "The Cult of True Womanhood," *American Quarterly* 18, no. 2 (1956): 151–74; Laslett, "The Family as a Public and Private Institution," 488–89.
95. Nancy F. Cott, "Eighteenth-Century Family and Social Life Revealed in Massachusetts Divorce Records," *Journal of Social History* 10, no. 1 (1976): 20–43.
96. Octave Thanet, "Under Five Shillings," *Scribner's Magazine* (July 1890): 68–80.
97. Zelizer, *Pricing the Priceless Child.* For historical studies of this transition in different social environments, see Sennett, *The Fall of Public Man*; Spacks,

Privacy; Flaherty, *Privacy in Colonial New England*; Hansen, "Rediscovering the Social."

98. Michael McKeon, *The Secret History of Domesticity: Public, Private, and the Division of Knowledge* (Johns Hopkins University Press, 2006); Lepore, "The Prism"; Durkheim, *The Division of Labor in Society*. For an alternative history that traces conceptions of privacy in premodern Jewish law, see Kenneth A. Bamberger and Ariel Evan Mayse, "Pre-Modern Insights for Post-Modern Privacy: Jewish Law Lessons for the Big Data Age," *Journal of Law and Religion* 36, no. 3 (2021): 495–532.

99. Quoted in Smith, *Ben Franklin's Web Site*, 99.

100. See Henry David Thoreau, *The Portable Thoreau*, ed. Jeffrey S. Cramer (Penguin, 2012), 303.

101. David Rosen and Aaron Santesso, "Inviolate Personality and the Literary Roots of the Right to Privacy," *Law and Literature* 23, no. 1 (2011): 1–25.

102. William Penn, *Fruits of Solitude, in Reflections and Maxims Relating to the Conduct of Human Life* (Benjamin Johnson, 1792), x and 50. Also quoted in Smith, *Ben Franklin's Web Site*, 17.

103. William Wordsworth, "Prospectus to the Recluse," in *The Poems*, vol. 2, ed. John O. Hayden (Penguin Books, 1977), 38. Also quoted in Rosen and Santesso, "Inviolate Personality and the Literary Roots of the Right to Privacy," 15. Wordsworth began working on *The Recluse* in 1798 and continued to do so until his death in 1850. The passage quoted here was likely written between 1798 and 1800 and appears in early published editions of the poem.

104. Sue Halpern, *Migrations to Solitude* (Vintage, 2011).

105. Samuel Bazzi et al., "Frontier Culture: The Roots and Persistence of 'Rugged Individualism' in the United States," *Econometrica* 88, no. 6 (2020): 2239–369.

106. Seipp, "The Right to Privacy in American History," 2.

107. Seipp, "The Right to Privacy in American History," 2.

108. "Privacy," *M'Arthur Democrat*, November 17, 1859.

109. Mitchell Dawson, "Paul Pry and Privacy," *The Atlantic Monthly* 150, no. 4 (October 1932), accessed November 14, 2024, https://www.theatlantic.com /magazine/archive/1932/10/paul-pry-and-privacy/650335. Also see Seipp, "The Right to Privacy in American History," 3–4.

110. Clarence Chatham Cook, "Beds and Tables, Stools and Candlesticks," *Scribners Magazine* (January 1876): 342–57.

111. Benjamin Franklin, "The Busy-Body, No. 4," *The American Weekly Mercury*, February 25, 1729, accessed February 2, 2024, https://founders.archives.gov /documents/Franklin/01-01-02-0038.

112. Neocleous, "Privacy, Secrecy, Idiocy," 89.

113. Philip Abrams, "Notes on the Difficulty of Studying the State (1977)," *Journal of Historical Sociology* 1, no. 1 (1988): 61.

114. Samuel Johnson, *A Dictionary of the English Language* (Times Books, 1979). Also quoted in Neocleus, "Privacy, Secrecy, Idiocy," 103.

115. William Gilmore Simms, *Beauchampe*, vol. 2 (Lea and Blanchard, 1842).

116. Dawson, "Paul Pry and Privacy"; Edwin L. Godkin, "Privacy," *Scribner's Magazine*, August 1980.
117. Colin Bell and Howard Newby, eds., *The Sociology of Community: A Selection of Readings* (Frank Cass and Co., 1974).
118. Richard R. John, *Spreading the News: The American Postal System from Franklin to Morse* (Harvard University Press, 1998); Winifred Gallagher, *How the Post Office Created America: A History* (Penguin, 2016); Devin Leonard, *Neither Snow nor Rain: A History of the United States Postal Service* (Grove Press, 2016). Also see Seipp, "The Right to Privacy in American History," 7ff. Also see "Scrapbook of Circulars, Notices, Instructions, Regulations, and Newspaper Clippings, 1823–1871," USNA Record PI-168, 27
119. Quoted in Smith, *Ben Franklin's Web Site*, 56–57. Also see Solove, "Conceptualizing Privacy," 1143.
120. Solove, "Conceptualizing Privacy," 1142–43.
121. James Holbrook, *Ten Years Among the Mail Bags* (H. Cowperthwait and Co., 1855), 394.
122. Seipp, "The Right to Privacy in American History," 16.
123. For one clear statement of this view, see Smith, *Ben Franklin's Web Site*, 9. Also see Lane, *American Privacy*.
124. Maria Antoniak and David Mimno, "Evaluating the Stability of Embedding-Based Word Similarities," *Transactions of the Association for Computational Linguistics* 6 (2018): 107–19.
125. Brian Martin, *Information Liberation: Challenging the Corruptions of Information Power* (Freedom Press, 1998), 65. Quoted in Laura Huey, "A Social Movement for Privacy/Against Surveillance: Some Difficulties in Engendering Mass Resistance in a Land of Twitter and Tweets," *Case Western Reserve Journal of International Law* 42 (2009): 699–709.

2. IN THE GLARE OF THE CALCIUM:
PRIVACY IN THE EARLY INFORMATION AGE

1. Montgomery B. Pickett, "Opening of the Great Fair," *Harper's Weekly*, May 13, 1893, 442; "Near A Half-Million," *Chicago Tribune*, May 2, 1893, 3.
2. Joint Committee on Ceremonies of the World's Columbian Commission, *Dedication and Opening Ceremonies of the World's Columbian Exhibition* (Stone, Kastler, and Painter, 1893).
3. "Springs Into Being," *Chicago Tribune*, May 2, 1893, 3.
4. Khalil Gibran Muhammad, *The Condemnation of Blackness: Race, Crime, and the Making of Modern Urban America* (Harvard University Press, 2010), 15; Ostrander, *American Civilization in the First Machine Age*; Durkheim, *The Division of Labor in Society*, 119–44; Igo, *The Known Citizen*, 16.
5. "No Such Thing as Private Citizen," *Chicago Daily Tribune*, July 27, 1902.
6. "No Such Thing as Private Citizen," *Chicago Daily Tribune*.

7. Dawson, "Paul Pry and Privacy."

8. Denenberg, "Privacy: Wanted but Vague."

9. Solove, "Conceptualizing Privacy," 1087; Robert C. Post, "Three Concepts of Privacy," *Georgetown Law Journal* 89 (2001): 2087–98.

10. Harriet F. Pilpel, "The Challenge of Privacy," in *The Price of Liberty*, ed. Alan Reitman (Norton, 1969), 44; Westin, *Privacy and Freedom*, 7.

11. Neil Smelser, *Social Change in the Industrial Revolution* (University of Chicago Press, 1959), 2; Miller, *The Assault on Privacy*, 190; Daniel J. Solove, "Introduction: Privacy Self-Management and the Consent Dilemma," *Harvard Law Review* 126, no. 1 (2012): 1880–903; Sjoerd Keulen and Ronald Kroeze, "Privacy from a Historical Perspective," in *The Handbook of Privacy Studies: An Interdisciplinary Introduction*, ed. Bart van der Sloot and Aviva de Groot (Amsterdam University Press, 2018), 21–56; William A. Parent, "Recent Work on the Concept of Privacy," *American Philosophical Quarterly* 20, no. 4 (1983): 341–55; Gerald Dworkin, "The Younger Committee Report on Privacy," *The Modern Law Review* 36, no. 4 (1973): 399–406.

12. Tom Gerety, "Redefining Privacy," *Harvard Civil Rights-Civil Liberties Law Review* 12, no. 2 (1977): 233–96; Katherine J. Day, "Perspectives on Privacy: A Sociological Analysis" (PhD diss., University of Edinburgh, 1985).

13. Deborah Nelson, *Pursuing Privacy in Cold War America* (Columbia University Press, 2001), xii.

14. Sue Halpern, "Private Eyes," *New York Review of Books*, March 9, 2023, accessed March 10, 2024, https://www.nybooks.com/articles/2023/03/09/private-eyes-the-fight-for-privacy-citron; Stephen T. Margulis, "Conceptions of Privacy: Current Status and Next Steps," *Journal of Social Issues* 33, no. 3 (1977): 5–21; Solove, "Conceptualizing Privacy"; Christian Fuchs, "Towards an Alternative Concept of Privacy," *Journal of Information, Communication and Ethics in Society* 9, no. 4 (2011): 220–37; David Hollinger, *In the American Province: Studies in the History and Historiography of Ideas* (Indiana University Press, 1985), 130–51.

15. Vincent Dubois, *The Bureaucrat and the Poor: Encounters in French Welfare Offices* (Routledge, 2016), vii; Karl Mannheim, *Ideology and Utopia* (Routledge, 1964), 245; Haraway, "Situated Knowledges."

16. Solove, "Conceptualizing Privacy," 1091–92.

17. Helen Nissenbaum, *Privacy in Context: Technology, Policy, and the Integrity of Social Life* (Stanford University Press, 2010).

18. For various theoretical discussions of the link between present and past, see Friedrich Nietzsche, "On the Uses and Disadvantages of History for Life," in *Untimely Meditations*, ed. Daniel Breazeale (Cambridge University Press, 1997), 57–125; Deborah Poole, *Vision, Race, and Modernity: A Visual Economy of the Andean Image World* (Princeton University Press, 1997), 18; Jan-Werner Müller, "On Conceptual History," in *Rethinking Modern European Intellectual History*, ed. Darrin M. McMahon and Samuel Moyn (Oxford University Press, 2014), 80.

19. Danielle Keats Citron, *The Fight for Privacy: Protecting Dignity, Identity, and Love in the Digital Age* (Norton, 2022); Halpern, *Migrations to Solitude*, vii.

20. Wiebe, *The Search for Order*.

21. Thompson, "The Right of Privacy as Recognized and Protected in Law and in Equity," 156.

22. Jack Shafer, "Who Said It First? Journalism is the 'First Rough Draft of History,'" *Slate*, August 30, 2010.

23. 65th Cong., 2nd sess., Cong. Rec. 56, pt. 9: 8716; 67th Cong., 1st sess., Cong. Rec. 61, pt. 5: 4726.

24. Claude Lévi-Strauss, *Structural Anthropology* (Basic, 1963); Alix Rule et al., "Lexical Shifts, Substantive Changes, and Continuity in State of the Union Discourse, 1790–2014," *Proceedings of the National Academy of Sciences of the United States of America* 112, no. 35 (2015): 10837–44. For conceptual discussions, see Charles Sanders Peirce, *Collected Papers of Charles Sanders Peirce, Volumes I and II: Principles of Philosophy and Elements of Logic*, ed. Charles Hartshorne et al. (Harvard University Press, 1932), 302ff; Pierre Bourdieu, "Social Space and Symbolic Power," *Sociological Theory* 7, no. 1 (1989): 14–25; Ian Hacking, "Kinds of People: Moving Targets," *Proceedings of the British Academy* 151, no. 1 (2007): 285–317.

25. Jean-Baptiste Michel et al., "Quantitative Analysis of Culture Using Millions of Digitized Books," *Science* 331, no. 6014 (2011): 176–82.

26. Lorraine Daston, "Calculation and the Division of Labor, 1750–1950," *Bulletin of the German Historical Institute* 62 (2017): 9–30.

27. William L. Hamilton et al., "Cultural Shift or Linguistic Drift? Comparing Two Computational Measures of Semantic Change," in *Proceedings of the 2016 Conference on Empirical Methods in Natural Language Processing* (Association for Computational Linguistics, 2016), 2116–21; Derry Tanti Wijaya and Reyyan Yeniterzi, "Understanding Semantic Change of Words Over Centuries," in *Proceedings of the 2011 International Workshop on DETecting and Exploiting Cultural DiversiTy on the Social Web—DETECT* (ACM, 2011), 34–40.

28. See, for example, John Shute Duncan, *Collections Relative to Systematic Relief of the Poor, at Different Periods, and in Different Countries: With Observations on Charity, Its Proper Objects and Conduct, and Its Influence on the Welfare of Nations* (R. Cruttwell, 1815); *The Soul's Welfare: A Magazine for the People* (Houlston and Stoneman, 1850).

29. John Haiman, *Natural Syntax: Iconicity and Erosion* (Cambridge University Press, 1985); Bodo Winter et al., "Cognitive Factors Motivating the Evolution of Word Meanings: Evidence from Corpora, Behavioral Data and Encyclopedic Network Structure," in *Evolution of Language: Proceedings of the 10th International Conference (EVOLANG10)*, 353–60 (2014); William L. Hamilton et al., "Diachronic Word Embeddings Reveal Statistical Laws of Semantic Change," arXiv preprint, arXiv:1605.09096 (2016).

30. Paul J. Hopper and Elizabeth Closs Traugott, *Grammaticalization* (Cambridge University Press, 2003), 78, quoting from Dwight Bolinger, *Meaning and Form*

(Longman, 1977). For a discussion of *polysemy*, i.e., the coexistence of multiple meanings, see Ann Copestake and Ted Briscoe, "Semi-Productive Polysemy and Sense Extension," *Journal of Semantics* 12 (1995): 15–67.

31. For a discussion of the argument that semantic change precedes polysemy, see Hopper and Traugott, *Grammaticalization*, and Winter et al., "Cognitive Factors Motivating the Evolution of Word Meaning."

32. Rule et al., "Lexical Shifts, Substantive Changes, and Continuity," 10839.

33. Copestake and Briscoe, "Semi-Productive Polysemy and Sense Extension."

34. Heather A. Haveman, *Magazines and the Making of America: Modernization, Community, and Print Culture, 1741–1860* (Princeton University Press, 2015), 1.

35. Karin Becker, "Photo-Journalism and the Tabloid Press," in *Journalism and Popular Culture*, ed. Peter Dahlgren and Colin Sparks (SAGE, 1992), 132.

36. *The San Francisco Call*, September 27, 1903; *New York Tribune*, February 27, 1910; *The Conservative*, November 22, 1900; *New York Tribune*, January 13, 1903.

37. Jürgen Habermas, *The Structural Transformation of the Public Sphere* (MIT Press, 1991), 39.

38. Patterson, "Making Sense of Culture," 7.

39. On the topic of "meaning maintenance," see David Heise, "Understanding Social Interaction with Affect Control Theory," in *New Directions in Sociological Theory*, ed. J. Berger and M. Zelditch (Rowman & Littlefield, 2002), 17–40.

40. Richard B. Du Boff, "Business Demand and the Development of the Telegraph in the United States, 1844–1860," *Business History Review* 54, no. 4 (1980): 459–79.

41. U.S. Bureau of the Census, *Historical Statistics of the United States: Colonial Times to 1970, Bicentennial Edition* (Government Printing Office, 1976); David Hochfelder, *The Telegraph in America, 1832–1920* (Johns Hopkins University Press, 2012).

42. 45th Cong., 2nd sess., Cong. Rec. 7, pt. 3: 2104.

43. "The Explanation About the French Cable," *New York Times*, February 2, 1870.

44. "Congress and the Western Union Telegraph Company," *Telegrapher* January 6, 1877, 13.

45. Smith, *Ben Franklin's Web Site*. See Igo, *The Known Citizen*, for a more nuanced version of this argument.

46. "Census data" generally refers to full-count microdata files made available through IPUMS-USA. Counts for intercensal years are interpolated. Also see James G. Gimpel et al., "The Urban–Rural Gulf in American Political Behavior," *Political Behavior* 42, no. 4 (2020): 1343–68.

47. Robert DeForest and Lawrence Veiller, eds., *The Tenement House Problem: Including the Report of the New York State Tenement House Commission of 1900*, vol. 1 (MacMillan, 1903); Edward Marshall, "New York Tenements," *The North American Review* 157, no. 445 (1893): 753–56.

48. Albert Rhodes, "Woman's Occupations," *Galaxy*, January 1876, 45–56.

49. *Washington Times*, July 31, 1902; "Etiquette on Privacy in Life," *Washington Herald*, June 21, 1914.

50. "The Era of Publicity—The Twentieth Century," *Washington Times*, July 31, 1902.

51. Edward Everett Hale, "The Congestion of Cities," *Forum* 4 (January 1880), 530; Nock, *The Costs of Privacy*, 1.

52. "Privacy in the Home Is Scarcely Possible," *Pierre Weekly Free Press*, May 8, 1913.

53. W. A. Linn, "Building and Loan Associations," *Scribner's Magazine*, June 1889, 700–712.

54. *Kenosha Telegraph*, September 15, 1882.

55. *Bossier Banner*, May 15, 1884.

56. *Bossier Banner*, May 15, 1884.

57. *Bossier Banner*, May 15, 1884.

58. Daphne Spain, "Gender and Urban Space," *Annual Review of Sociology* 40 (2014): 195–205.

59. David A. Cotter et al., "Women's Work and Women Working: The Demand for Female Labor," *Gender and Society* 15, no. 3 (2001): 429–52; Mignon Duffy, "Doing the Dirty Work: Gender, Race, and Reproductive Labor in Historical Perspective," *Gender and Society* 21, no. 3 (2007): 313–36.

60. Thomas Wentworth Higginson, *Women and the Alphabet* (Houghton Mifflin, 1881).

61. Frances Marshall, "Work and Play in the Household," *Washington Herald*, June 21, 1914.

62. William Conant Church, "The Right Not to Vote," *Scribner's Magazine*, November 1871, 73–85.

63. All quotes from congressional delegates are taken from the *Congressional Globe/Congressional Record*. See specific notes for page numbers.

64. 43rd Cong., special sess., Cong. Rec. 1, pt. 1: 166; 43rd Cong., 1st sess., Cong. Rec. 2, pt. 2: 1208; 43rd Cong., 2nd sess., Cong. Rec. 3, pt. 2: 972; 43rd Cong., 2nd sess., Cong. Rec. 3, pt. 2: 973; 43rd Cong., 2nd sess., Cong. Rec. 3, pt. 1: 1875.

65. Alvin F. Harlow, *Old Wires and New Waves: The History of the Telegraph, Telephone, and Wireless* (D. Appleton-Century, 1936). See pp. 264–65 for wartime censorship and surveillance of the telegraph system. Also see David Homer Bates, *Lincoln in the Telegraph Office: Recollections of the United States Military Telegraph Corps During the Civil War* (University of Nebraska Press, 1995).

66. Reprinted in *Arkansas True Democrat*, August 8, 1861.

67. "Administration of the Telegraph," *New York Times*, December 31, 1866.

68. Seipp, "The Right to Privacy in American History," 31.

69. 40th cong., 2nd sess., part 2: 2579.

70. 40th cong., 2nd sess., part 2: 2579.

71. See Seipp, "The Right to Privacy in American History," 31–32, for a discussion of Western Union regulations.

72. 40th cong., 2nd sess., May 25, 1868. 2579; 40th Cong., 2nd sess.: 89–92; 44th cong., 2nd sess: 356–358. For additional comments by Representative Knott on telegraphic privacy, see the debate of January 12, 1877.
73. 44th Cong., 2nd sess., Cong. Rec. 5, pt. 1: 356, 440, and 442.
74. "Telegrams in Court," *New York Tribune*, January 8, 1877; "The Investigating Committees," *New York Times*, December 13, 1876; *New York Sun*, December 13, 1876; *Detroit Free Press*, December 13, 1876.
75. *Baltimore Sun*, December 13, 1876.
76. "Secrets of the Telegraph," *New York Times*, June 24, 1876.
77. 46th Cong., 2nd sess., Cong. Rec. 10, pt. 4: 3169.
78. 46th Cong., 2nd sess., Cong. Rec. 10, pt. 4: 3173.
79. 46th Cong., 2nd sess., Cong. Rec. 10, pt. 4: 3174.
80. 50th Cong., 1st sess., Cong. Rec. 19, pt. 7: 6422.
81. 53rd Cong., 2nd sess., Cong. Rec. 26, pt. 2: 1651.
82. 57th Cong., 1st sess., Cong. Rec. 35, pt. 2: 1616; 57th Cong., 1st sess., Cong. Rec. 35, pt. 4: 3609.
83. "Trials of the Census-Taker," *New York Times*, July 19, 1875.
84. *New Orleans Daily Picayune*, June 6, 1890; *New York Times*, May 26, 1890.
85. 21 Cong. Rec. 5158, May 22, 1890.
86. "The New Inquisition," *Boston Globe*, May 27, 1890; "The Census—A Questionable Feature," *Los Angeles Times*, June 2, 1890. Also see *New York Times*, June 1, 1890; *Chicago Tribune*, June 4, 1890.
87. 61st Cong., 1st sess., Cong. Rec. 44, pt. 2: 1331.
88. 41st Cong., 2nd sess.: 2937.
89. Brian Sawers, "The Poll Tax Before Jim Crow," *American Journal of Legal History* 57, no. 2 (1997): 166–97.
90. Census Advisory Committee on Privacy and Confidentiality, U.S. National Archives (USNA) A1 417; Scrapbook Concerning Legislation for the 14th Census, 1917–1919, USNA P 128; Census Advisory Committee on Privacy and Confidentiality, USNA A1 417; Scrapbook Concerning Legislation for the 14th Census, 1917–1919, USNA P 128; Letter from Chief Statistician Hill to Walter F. Wilcox, March 27, 1922; Correspondence of Joseph A. Hill, Box 2, USNA PI-161 202; Office Files of Robert H. Holley, 1942–1944, Box 56, USNA PI-161 274. Also see Frederick G. Bohme and David M. Pemberton, "Privacy and Confidentiality in the U.S. Censuses—A History," Paper Presented at the Annual Meeting of the American Statistical Association, Atlanta, GA, August 18–22, 1971; Margo Anderson and William Seltzer, "Challenges to the Confidentiality of U.S. Federal Statistics, 1910–1965," *Journal of Official Statistics* 23, no. 1 (2007): 1–34; "Appendix: Requests from Federal Agencies and Elected Officials to Access Statistical Information Collected Under a Pledge of Confidentiality," U.S. Bureau of the Census; Vincent Barabba, "The Right of Privacy and the Need to Know," in *The Census Bureau: A Numerator and Denominator for Measuring Change*, Technical Paper 37, U.S. Bureau of the Census (Government Printing Office, 1975); Attorney General, September 29,

1930; Census Legislation, 1930 and 1940, Box 29, USNA PI-161 160. Also see *Congressional Record*, vol. 56, 9, 8659, and 2359–60.

91. 60th Cong., 1st sess., Cong. Rec. 42, pt. 6: 5496.
92. 61st Cong., 1st sess., Cong. Rec. 44, pt. 2: 1680.
93. John Tipple, "Big Businessmen and a New Economy," in *The Gilded Age: A Reappraisal*, ed. H. Wayne Morgan (Syracuse University Press, 1970), 26; Seipp, "The Right to Privacy in American History"; Carly R. Knight, "Classifying the Corporation: The Role of Naturalizing Analogies in American Corporate Development, 1870–1930," *Socio-Economic Review* 21, no. 3 (2023): 1630.
94. Smith, *Ben Franklin's Web Site*, 9.

3. THE CHIEF CURSE OF THE TENEMENT: MORAL ANXIETIES AND THE CODIFICATION OF PRIVACY IN URBAN LIFE

1. Karl Marx, "Speech at the Anniversary of the People's Paper," in *The Marx-Engels Reader*, ed. Robert C. Tucker (Norton, 1978), 577.
2. Thomas Piketty and Emmanuel Saez, "Inequality in the Long Run," *Science* 344, no. 6186 (2014): 838–43; W. E. B. Du Bois, *The Philadelphia Negro* (Cosimo Classics, 2007).
3. W. E. B. Du Bois, *The Souls of Black Folk* (Oxford World's Classics, 2007), 11
4. Jacob Riis, *How the Other Half Lives: Studies Among the New York Tenements* (Charles Scribner's Sons, 1890), 1–2.
5. Riis, *How the Other Half Lives*, 159.
6. *National Conference on Social Welfare (NCSW): Official Proceedings of the Annual Meeting 1922*, 296.
7. Colyvas and Jonsson, "Ubiquity and Legitimacy."
8. Richard Hofstadter, *The Age of Reform* (Vintage, 1955), 11.
9. William H. Sewell, *Logics of History: Social Theory and Social Transformation* (University of Chicago Press, 2005), 361.
10. Cal. Penal Code § 258 (1899). See *The Statutes of California and Amendments to the Codes, Passed at the Thirty-Third Session of the Legislature, 1899* (A. J. Johnston, 1899).
11. Lefebvre, *The Production of Space*, 317. For theoretical, historical, and contemporary perspectives on the link between architecture, urban planning, and social/moral order, see Evans, "Figures, Doors, and Passages"; Gwendolyn Wright, *Building the Dream: A Social History of Housing in America* (MIT Press, 1983); Gunther Barth, *City People: The Rise of Modern City Culture in Nineteenth-Century America* (Oxford University Press, 1982); Neil Brenner and Nik Theodore, "Cities and the Geographies of 'Actually Existing Neoliberalism,'" *Antipode* 34, no. 3 (2002): 349–79; David Harvey, "The Right to the City," *International Journal of Urban and Regional Research* 27, no. 4 (2003): 939–41; Douglas S. Massey, "American Apartheid: Segregation and the Making of the Underclass," *American Journal of Sociology* 96, no. 2 (1990): 329–57;

Richard Rothstein, *The Color of Law: A Forgotten History of How Our Government Segregated America* (Liveright, 2017); Neil Smith, *The New Urban Frontier: Gentrification and the Revanchist City* (Routledge, 1996); Spain, "Gender and Urban Space," 583; Catharine R. Stimpson et al., eds., *Women and the American City* (University of Chicago Press, 1981); Nathaniel R. Walker, "American Crossroads: General Motors' Midcentury Campaign to Promote Modernist Urban Design in Hometown USA," *Buildings and Landscapes: Journal of the Vernacular Architecture Forum* 23, no. 2 (2016): 89–115; Gwendolyn Wright, *Building the Dream: A Social History of Housing in America* (MIT Press, 1983); Sharon Zukin, *Landscapes of Power: From Detroit to Disney World* (University of California Press, 1991).

12. Roger V. Gould, *Insurgent Identities: Class, Community, and Protest in Paris from 1848 to the Commune* (University of Chicago Press, 1995); Dingxin Zhao, "Ecologies of Social Movements: Student Mobilization During the 1989 Prodemocracy Movement in Beijing," *American Journal of Sociology* 103, no. 6 (1998): 1493–529; Habermas, *The Structural Transformation of the Public Sphere*; Philip Kasinitz, ed., *Metropolis: Centre and Symbol of Our Times* (Macmillan, 1995); Walter Benjamin, *The Arcades Project* (Harvard University Press, 1999); Jane Jacobs, *The Death and Life of Great American Cities* (Vintage, 1992); Mario L. Small and Laura Adler, "The Role of Space in the Formation of Social Ties," *Annual Review of Sociology* 45 (2019): 111–32; Bess Williamson, "The People's Sidewalks: Designing Berkeley's Wheelchair Route, 1970–1974," *Boom: A Journal of California* 2, no. 1 (2012): 49–52.

13. Thomas F. Gieryn, "A Space for Place in Sociology," *Annual Review of Sociology* 26 (2000): 475. For discussions of the link between the social construction of space and the construction of the self, see Michel Foucault, *Discipline and Punish: The Birth of the Prison* (Vintage, 1995); Erving Goffman, *Asylums: Essays on the Social Situation of Mental Patients and Other Inmates* (Anchor, 1961).

14. For related discussions of space and collective action, see Karl Marx, *Capital: Volume 1: A Critique of Political Economy* (Penguin Classics, 1992); Zoe Trodd, "In Possession of Space," in *Representing Segregation: Toward an Aesthetics of Living Jim Crow, and Other Forms of Racial Division*, ed. Brian Norman and Piper Kendrix Williams (SUNY Press, 2012), 223–244; Robert Doyle Bullard et al., eds., *Highway Robbery: Transportation Racism and New Routes to Equity* (South End Press, 2004).

15. Sarah Deutsch, *Women and the City: Gender, Space, and Power in Boston, 1870–1940* (Oxford University Press, 2000), 6. This significance of physical space as an object of cultural and political struggle was not lost on Michel Foucault, who used a 1967 lecture to an audience of architects to characterize the modern era as an epoch defined by spaces of otherness and "relations of propinquity" rather than cycles of revolution and restoration: an "epoch of the near and far, of the side-by-side, of the dispersed." See Michel Foucault, "Of Other Spaces," *Diacritics* 16, no. 1 (1986): 22. Also see Lefebvre, *The Production of Space*, 59, 191, and 386.

16. Martin C. Melosi, *The Sanitary City: Urban Infrastructure in America from Colonial Times to the Present* (Johns Hopkins University Press, 2000); Joanne Abel Goldman, *Building New York's Sewers: Developing Mechanisms of Urban Management* (Purdue University Press, 1997).

17. Warren D. Devine, "From Shafts to Wires: Historical Perspective on Electrification," *The Journal of Economic History* 43, no. 2 (1983): 347–72; Mark Granovetter and Patrick McGuire, "The Making of an Industry: Electricity in the United States," *The Sociological Review* 46, no. 1 (1998): 147–73; Larry R. Ford, *Cities and Buildings: Skyscrapers, Skid Rows and Suburbs* (Johns Hopkins University Press, 2005); Roberta Moudry, *The American Skyscraper: Cultural Histories* (Cambridge University Press, 2005).

18. Nell Irvin Painter, *Standing at Armageddon: A Grassroots History of the Progressive Era* (Norton, 2008), 105–6; Michael McGerr, *A Fierce Discontent: The Rise and Fall of the Progressive Movement in America* (Oxford University Press, 2003), 102; Paul Boyer, *Urban Masses and Moral Order in America, 1820–1920* (Harvard University Press, 1978), 238; William H. Wilson, *The City Beautiful Movement* (Johns Hopkins University Press, 1989).

19. See Section 2 of the 1901 Tenement House Act in "An Act in Relation to Tenements Houses in Cities of the First Class," *Laws of New York* 124, sess. I (1901): 889–923.

20. Ernest Flagg, "The New York Tenement House Evil and Its Cure," *Scriber's Magazine* 16 (1894): 108.

21. DeForest and Veiller, *The Tenement House Problem*; Roy Lubove, *The Progressives and the Slums: Tenement House Reform in New York City, 1890–1917* (University of Pittsburgh Press, 1963).

22. Russ Lopez, *Building American Public Health: Urban Planning, Architecture, and the Quest for Better Health in the United States* (Palgrave Macmillan, 2012), 17; Margaret Garb, "Health, Morality, and Housing: the 'Tenement Problem' in Chicago," *American Journal of Public Health* 93, no. 9 (2003): 1420–30. For a history of tenement reform efforts, see Robert W. DeForest, "A Brief History of the Housing Movement in America," *The Annals of the American Academy of Political and Social Science* 51, no. 1 (1914): 8–16. For data on Lawrence Veiller, see "The Reminiscences of Lawrence Veiller" in *New York Times Oral History Program and Columbia University Oral History Collection, Part IV* (Columbia University, 1979), https://dx.doi.org/10.7916/d8-a82h-x016.

23. "Etiquette on Privacy in Life," *Washington Herald*, June 21, 1914; Marshall, "New York Tenements," 753. Also see Joseph R. Gusfield, "Social Structure and Moral Reform: A Study of the Woman's Christian Temperance Union," *American Journal of Sociology* 61, no. 3 (1955): 221–32.

24. Edwin L. Godkin, "The Rights of the Citizen—IV. To His Own Reputation," *Scribner's Magazine* (June 1890): 65.

25. Riis, *How the Other Half Lives*, 133.

26. Evans, "Figures, Doors, and Passages," 101.

27. John Ihlder, "Extent of the Housing Shortage in the United States," *National Conference on Social Welfare (NCSW): Official Proceedings of the Annual Meeting 1921*, 335; James Ford, "Bad Housing and Ill Health," *NCSW: Official Proceedings of the Annual Meeting 1919*, 240; Lawrence Veiller, "Housing, Health, and Recreation," *NCSW: Official Proceedings of the Annual Meeting 1911*, 316; "The Right to Privacy," *The Forest Republican*, December 5, 1906.

28. "The Tenement Question," *New York Times*, December 30, 1894.

29. Sarah Stage, "The Greening of Suburbia," *American Quarterly* 37, no. 5 (1985): 749–54; Beatriz Colomina, *Privacy and Publicity: Modern Architecture as Mass Media* (MIT Press, 1996); Julie E. Cohen, "Privacy, Visibility, Transparency, and Exposure," *The University of Chicago Law Review* 75, no. 1 (2008): 181; Elaine T. May, *Homeward Bound: American Families in the Cold War Era* (Basic, 2008); David P. Handlin, *The American Home: Architecture and Society, 1815–1915* (Little, Brown, 1979); Evans, "Figures, Doors, and Passages."

30. Haggerty and Ericson, "The Surveillant Assemblage," 619.

31. For a discussion of rural and urban architectures as templates for the regulation of privacy in the digital domain, see Lawrence Lessig, "The Architecture of Privacy," *Vanderbilt Journal of Environmental Law and Practice* 1, no. 1 (1999): 56–65. For a discussion of contemporary rural privacy, see Deborah Warr and Lynne Hillier, "'That's the Problem with Living in a Small Town': Privacy and Sexual Health Issues for Young Rural People," *Australian Journal of Rural Health* 5, no. 3 (1997): 132–39.

32. Nock, *The Costs of Privacy*, 7.

33. Robert Park, *On Social Control and Collective Behavior* (University of Chicago Press, 1997), 3; Gieryn, "A Space for Place in Sociology." For a related discussion of the role of material objects in the constitution of the self, see Colin Jerolmack and Iddo Tavory, "Molds and Totems: Nonhumans and the Constitution of the Social Self," *Sociological Theory* 32, no. 1 (2014): 64–77.

34. Walter Benjamin, *Charles Baudelaire: A Lyric Poet in the Era of High Capitalism* (Verso, 1993); Keith Tester, ed., *The Flâneur* (Routledge, 1994).

35. Georg Simmel, "The Metropolis and Mental Life," in *The Sociology of Georg Simmel*, ed. Kurt H. Wolff (Free Press, 1950), 416.

36. Simmel, "The Metropolis and Mental Life," 411.

37. Haggerty and Ericson, "The Surveillant Assemblage"; Nippert-Eng, *Islands of Privacy*, 273ff; Nock, *The Costs of Privacy*; David Lyon, ed., *Surveillance as Social Sorting: Privacy, Risk, and Digital Discrimination* (Routledge, 2003).

38. "The Effect of the New Tenement House Law on Flats," *Real Estate Record and Builders Guide* 69, February 1, 1902, 202. For a discussion of urban apartment layouts, also see Thomas J. Gorman, *Growing Up Working Class: Hidden Injuries and the Development of Angry White Men and Women* (Palgrave Macmillan, 2017), 48.

39. "The Tenement Question," *New York Times*, December 30, 1894.

40. "Better Tenement Houses," *New York Times*, November 22, 1896.

41. "Contributor's Club," *Atlantic Monthly* (September 1883): 419–30.

42. Wiebe, *The Search for Order*; Painter, *Standing at Armageddon*; Boyer, *Urban Masses and Moral Order*; McGerr, *A Fierce Discontent*; Nicola Beisel, "Class, Culture, and Campaigns Against Vice in Three American Cities, 1872–1892," *American Sociological Review* 55, no. 1 (1990): 44–62. Wiebe's history of the Progressive Era (*The Search for Order*) and widely cited studies of tenement reform make no mention of privacy but focus on "standards for light, ventilation, sanitation, and safety" (McGerr, *A Fierce Discontent*, 101). The most direct engagement with urban space usually comes in discussions of park beautification and "broad open space," focusing on attempts to increase the access of working-class residents to public spaces in the pursuit of leisure and moral uplift (Painter, *Standing at Armageddon*, 105–6; Boyer, *Urban Masses and Moral Order*, 238; McGerr, *A Fierce Discontent*, 102; Wilson, *The City Beautiful Movement*, 1989). Studies that draw attention to the perceived moral hazards of urban life (Sennett, *The Fall of Public Man*; Boyer, *Urban Masses and Moral Order*; Coontz, *The Social Origins of Private Life*; Beisel, "Class, Culture, and Campaigns Against Vice") seldom consider how the organization of residential space reflects or forecloses contemporary moral imaginaries, and they say little about the management of visibility and the restructuring of residential space as proposed remedies to the perceived ills of the modern city.

43. Nippert-Eng, *Islands of Privacy*.

44. The presumptions of morality and good citizenship were never universal. Racist undertones of social reform campaigns are evident in Riis, *How the Other Half Lives*, 131: the term privacy "carries no more meaning" among some immigrants than "would a lecture on social ethics to an audience of Hottentots."

45. Lawrence Veiller, "The Tenement House Problem," *New York Times*, July 1, 1899.

46. Frank J. Bruno, *Trends in Social Work* (Columbia University Press, 1948).

47. For a conceptual discussion of moral entrepreneurs, see Howard Becker, *Outsiders: Studies in the Sociology of Deviance* (Free Press, 1963), 147ff.

48. "Report of Committee on Charity Organization," *NCSW: Official Proceedings of the Annual Meeting 1885*, 371.

49. "Charity from the Standpoint of the Knights of Labor," *NCSW: Official Proceedings of the Annual Meeting 1890*, 60.

50. "Crime," *NCSW: Official Proceedings of the Annual Meeting 1885*, 413; "Health and Profit," *New York Times*, November 29, 1896. Also quoted in *Scientific American* Supplement 1093, December 12, 1896, 17471.

51. James Hayden Tufts, "The Ethics of the Family," *NCSW: Official Proceedings of the Annual Meeting 1915*, 36; Grosvenor Atterbury, "The Phipps Model Tenement Houses," *Charities and the Commons* 17 (1907), 57. Also quoted in Zachary J. Violette, *The Decorated Tenement: How Immigrant Builders and Architects Transformed the Slum in the Gilded Age* (University of Minnesota Press, 2019), 205; Joanna Merwood-Salisbury, "Architecture as Model and Standard: Modern Liberalism and Tenement House Reform in New York City at the Turn of the Twentieth Century," *Architectural Theory Review*, 23, no. 3 (2019): 355.

52. Theodore Roosevelt, "A Judicial Experience," *Outlook*, March 13, 1909, 564; Sophonisba P. Breckinridge and Edith Abbott, "Housing Conditions in Chicago," *American Journal of Sociology* 16, no. 4 (1911): 433–68; Elizabeth C. Cromley, "A History of American Beds and Bedrooms," *Perspectives in Vernacular Architecture* 4 (1991): 177–86.

53. Lawrence Veiller, "The Tenement House Problem," *New York Times*, July 1, 1899. Also see "Housing Reform in Chicago," *NCSW: Official Proceedings of the Annual Meeting 1902*, 358.

54. DeForest and Veiller, *The Tenement House Problem*, 14.

55. Ernest Flagg, "A Profitable Tenement House," *Real Estate Record and Builders Guide* 66 (May 19, 1900): 865.

56. "The House Hunter," *Real Estate Record and Builders Guide* 58 (November 29, 1896): 793.

57. W. Alexander Johnson, "Report of Committee on Charity Organization," *NCSW: Proceedings of the Annual Meeting 1885*, 370.

58. "The Effect of the New Tenement House Law on Flats," *Real Estate Record and Builders Guide* 69 (February 1, 1902): 204; "The Sanitary Reformation," *Real Estate Record and Builders Guide* 75 (February 11, 1905): 301.

59. Mary E. Richmond, "How Social Workers Can Aid Housing Reform," *NCSW: Official Proceedings of the Annual Meeting 1911*, 327. Also see "How to Build Tenements," *New York Times*, October 12, 1900.

60. "Sixth Report of the Tenement House Department of the City of New York, 1910 and 1911," New York: Tenement House Department, 33.

61. Lubove, *The Progressives and the Slums*, 174.

62. Evans, "Figures, Doors, and Passages," 108–9. Also see "Centralizing Tendencies in Administration," *NCSW: Official Proceedings of the Annual Meeting 1900*, 163.

63. Riis, *How the Other Half Lives*, 2.

64. Elgin R. L. Gould, "The Housing Problem in Great Cities," *Quarterly Review of Economics* 14, no. 3 (1900): 381.

65. Gould, "The Housing Problem in Great Cities," 378.

66. "Remedial Work in Behalf of our Youth," *NCSW: Official Proceedings of the Annual Meeting 1890*, 235.

67. Lawrence Veiller, "The Housing Problem in American Cities," *The Annals of the American Academy of Political and Social Science* 25, no. 2 (1905): 50. Also see James Ford, "Bad Housing and Ill Health," *NCSW: Official Proceedings of the Annual Meeting 1919*, 240.

68. "Joseph A. Farley's 108th St Residences," *Real Estate Record and Builders Guide* 64 (September 2, 1899): 336. Also see an untitled article on p. 437 of *Real Estate Record and Builders Guide* 74 (August 27, 1904); "Hurley Heights Goes on the Market," *The Arizona Republican*, May 3, 1914; "Million Dollar Front Yards of New York Mansions," *Sun*, July 12, 1914.

69. Veiller, "The Housing Problem in American Cities," 51–52. For a discussion of suburbanization as a remedy to the "social question," also see Violette, *The Decorated Tenement*, 215ff; Lubove, *The Progressives and the Slums*, 131ff;

Evans, "Figures, Doors, and Passages," 109; Robert H. Bremner, "The Big Flat: History of a New York Tenement House," *The American Historical Review* 64, no. 1 (1958): 54–62; Merwood-Salisbury, "Architecture as Model and Standard"; Richard Plunz, *History of Housing in New York City* (Columbia University Press, 1990), 17.

70. Violette, *The Decorated Tenement*, 9. For classic discussions of the "view from somewhere" in sociology and especially in feminist epistemology, see Haraway, "Situated Knowledges"; Collins, *Black Feminist Thought.*

71. Violette, *The Decorated Tenement*, 67 and 73; Evans, "Figures, Doors, and Passages," 111–12; Lubove, *The Progressives and the Slums*, 97.

72. Lefebvre, *The Production of Space*, 314; Goffman, *The Presentation of Self*, 123; Elias, *The Civilizing Process.*

73. "Second Report of the Tenement House Department of the City of New York, July 1 1903 to December 31 1905" (Tenement House Department, 1905), 77; "Annual Report of the Tenement House Department of the City of New York, 1904" (Tenement House Department, 1904), xvi; DeForest and Veiller, *The Tenement House Problem*, 395.

74. Violette, *The Decorated Tenement*, 8 and 12.

75. Merwood-Salisbury, "Architecture as Model and Standard," 362: "Veblen famously described conspicuous consumption as the social result of the mixture of demographic types bought together in Americans cities." Paraphrasing: Thorstein Veblen, *The Theory of the Leisure Class* (Penguin, 1994).

76. Lawrence Veiller, "Housing, Health, and Recreation," *NCSW: Official Proceedings of the Annual Meeting 1911*, 316; Bleecker Marquette, "The Human Side of Housing," *NCSW: Official Proceedings of the Annual Meeting 1923*, 346.

77. Jane Addams, *The Spirit of Youth and the City Streets* (University of Illinois Press, 1972), xxvi–xxvii.

78. Henry L. Stimson and McGeorge Bundy, *On Active Service in Peace and War* (Harper & Brothers, 1948), 188. Also quoted in Olga Khazan, "Gentlemen Reading Each Others' Mail: A Brief History of Diplomatic Spying," *The Atlantic*, June 13, 2013, accessed March 15, 2024, https://www.theatlantic.com/international/archive/2013/06/gentlemen-reading-each-others-mail-a-brief-history-of-diplomatic-spying/276940/.

79. Violette, *The Decorated Tenement*, 13.

80. Veiller, "Housing, Health, and Recreation," 57; Lubove, *The Progressives and the Slums*, 130 and 137.

81. Lilian Brandt, *The Charity Organization Society of the City of New York, 1882–1907: Twenty-Fifth Annual Report for the Year Ending September Thirtieth, Nineteen Hundred and Seven* (Charity Organization Society, 1907), 45. For developer resistance to tenement reform, see "The Tenement Houses," *New York Times*, April 11, 1901; Adolph Bloch, "History of Tenement House Legislation," *Real Estate Record and Builders Guide*, July 21, 1909, 84; Andrew S. Dolkart, *Biography of a Tenement House in New York City: An Architectural History of 97 Orchard Street* (University of Virginia Press, 2006).

82. Roy Lubove, "Lawrence Veiller and the New York State Tenement House Commission of 1900," *The Mississippi Valley Historical Review* 47, no. 4 (1961): 659–77.

83. "Report of the Special Committee of the Assembly Appointed to Investigate the Public Offices and Departments of the City of New York and of the Counties Therein Included" (James B. Lyon, 1900), 3457. Also see Lubove, "Lawrence Veiller and the New York State Tenement House Commission of 1900," 667; "Building Code Attacked," *New York Times*, September 10, 1899.

84. Lubove, *The Progressives and the Slums*, 125–29.

85. Lawrence Veiller, "The Reminiscences of Lawrence Veiller."

86. Gould, "The Housing Problem in Great Cities."

87. Theodore Roosevelt, *Theodore Roosevelt: An Autobiography* (Macmillan, 1913), 80–81

88. Roosevelt, *Theodore Roosevelt*, 80 and 174. For a discussion of the relationship between Roosevelt and Riis, see Doris Kearns Goodwin, *The Bully Pulpit: Theodore Roosevelt, William Howard Taft, and the Golden Age of Journalism* (Simon and Schuster, 2013), 203–17; Jacob Riis, *The Making of an American* (Macmillan, 1901).

89. Roosevelt (1913), 200–201.

90. For conceptual frameworks, see Peter K. Eisinger, "The Conditions of Protest Behavior in American Cities," *American Political Science Review* 67, no. 1 (1973): 11–28; Doug McAdam, *Political Process and the Development of Black Insurgency, 1930–1970* (University of Chicago Press, 1999); David S. Meyer and Debra C. Minkoff, "Conceptualizing Political Opportunity," *Social Forces* 82, no. 4 (2004): 1457–92.

91. Veiller, "The Reminiscences of Lawrence Veiller," 20.

92. Veiller, "The Reminiscences of Lawrence Veiller," 21–22.

93. Veiller, "The Reminiscences of Lawrence Veiller," 24.

94. Veiller, "The Reminiscences of Lawrence Veiller," 28.

95. Michael Lipsky, *Street-Level Bureaucracy: Dilemmas of the Individual in Public Services* (Russell Sage Foundation, 1980); Dubois, *The Bureaucrat and the Poor*; Robert Baldwin et al., *Understanding Regulation: Theory, Strategy, and Practice* (Oxford University Press, 2011); Bettina Lange, "Sociology of Regulation," in *Research Handbook on the Sociology of Law*, ed. Jiří Přibáň (Edward Elgar, 2020), 93–108. After 1902, inspectors could rely on so-called "I-Cards" to certify compliance—preprinted forms that allowed building inspectors to check off each construction and retrofitting requirement of the 1901 law, starting with an inspection of the roof and ending in the cellar. See Dolkart, *Biography of a Tenement House in New York City*, 84.

96. Lubove, *The Progressives and the Slums*, 92.

97. Gould, "The Housing Problem in Great Cities," 380.

98. "Fourth Report of the Tenement House Department of the City of New York, January 1 1907 to December 31 1908" (Tenement House Department, 1908).

99. Lubove, *The Progressives and the Slums*, 111; Daniel Little, *New Contributions to the Philosophy of History* (Springer Netherlands, 2009), 110; Jason Barr and Teddy Ort, "Population Density Across the City: The Case of 1900 Manhattan," Working Paper (Rutgers University, 2013); Shlomo Angel and Patrick Lamson-Hall, "The Rise and Fall of Manhattan's Densities, 1800–2010," Marron Institute of Urban Management Working Paper 14 (New York University, 2014); Sam B. Warner Jr., *Streetcar Suburbs: The Process of Growth in Boston (1870–1900)* (Harvard University Press, 1962).

100. Lubove, *The Progressives and the Slums*, 143–44.

101. Lubove, *The Progressives and the Slums*, 146.

102. John Ihlder, "Extent of the Housing Shortage in the United States," *NCSW: Official Proceedings of the Annual Meeting 1921*, 335; *Real Estate Record and Builders Guide* 27 (August 27, 1904): 437.

103. Elmer E. Schattschneider, *The Semisovereign People: A Realist's View of Democracy in America* (Holt, Rinehart, and Winston, 1960), 3.

4. INVIOLATE PERSONALITIES: INDIVIDUAL PRIVACY IN AN ERA OF INFORMATIONAL PERSONS

1. Edwin L. Godkin, "Opinion-Moulding," *The Nation*, August 12, 1869. For a discussion of Godkin's writings on tabloid media, see Erin K. Coyle, "E. L. Godkin's Criticism of the Penny Press: Antecedents to a Legal Right to Privacy," *American Journalism* 31, no. 2 (2014): 262–82.

2. Paul Collins, *The Murder of the Century: The Gilded Age Crime That Scandalized a City and Sparked the Tabloid Wars* (Broadway, 2011).

3. Edwin Lawrence Godkin, "The Eclipse of Liberalism," *The Nation*, August 9, 1900, 105–6.

4. Myles Beaupre, "'What Are the Philippines Going to Do to Us?' E. L. Godkin on Democracy, Empire and Anti-imperialism," *Journal of American Studies* 46, no. 3 (2012): 711–27. For a discussion of privacy, trust, and social solidarity, see Nock, *The Costs of Privacy*; Etzioni, *The Limits of Privacy*; Ari Ezra Waldman, *Privacy as Trust: Information Privacy for an Information Age* (Cambridge University Press, 2018).

5. Edwin L. Godkin, "The Rights of the Citizen—IV. To His Own Reputation," *Scribner's Magazine* (June 1890): 58–67.

6. Robert E. Mensel, "'Kodakers Lying in Wait': Amateur Photography and the Right of Privacy in New York, 1885-1915," *American Quarterly* 43, no. 1 (1991): 28–29.

7. Godkin, "The Rights of the Citizen," 61. Also see Richard V. Denenberg, "Privacy: Wanted but Vague," *New York Times*, February 3, 1974; Levy, *Freaks of Fortune*.

8. Koopman, *How We Became Our Data*, 4. Also see Steffen Mau, *The Metric Society: On the Quantification of the Social* (Wiley, 2019).

9. "Millions That Take Flights," *Pacific Commercial Advertiser*, February 2, 1904; "The Right to Privacy," *Daily Gate City*, February 27, 1917; "America and the Right to Privacy," *Herald and News*, November 30, 1909.

10. Samuel D. Warren and Louis D. Brandeis, "The Right to Privacy," *Harvard Law Review* 4, no. 5 (1890): 193–220; Diane L. Zimmerman, "Requiem for a Heavyweight: A Farewell to Warren and Brandeis's Privacy Tort," *Cornell Law Review* 68, no. 3 (1982): 291–367; Amy Gajda, "What if Samuel D. Warren Hadn't Married a Senator's Daughter: Uncovering the Press Coverage That Led to the Right to Privacy," *Michigan State Law Review* (2008): 35–60; Neil M. Richards, "The Puzzle of Brandeis, Privacy, and Speech," *Vanderbilt Law Review* 63, no. 5 (2010): 1295–352; Rosen, *The Unwanted Gaze*; Rosen and Santesso, "Inviolate Personality and the Literary Roots of the Right to Privacy."

11. Natalie H. Snyder, "Women and Home," *Presbyterian Banner*, February 30, 1908.

12. Bloustein, "Privacy as an Aspect of Human Dignity," 971. Also see Jeffrey H. Reiman, "Privacy, Intimacy, and Personhood," in *Privacy*, ed. Eric Barendt (Routledge, 2001), 23–41.

13. Bloustein, "Privacy as an Aspect of Human Dignity," 974.

14. Solove, "Conceptualizing Privacy," 1116ff.

15. Stanley I. Benn, "Privacy, Freedom, and Respect for Persons," in *Privacy and Personality*, ed. Russell L. Ciochon (Routledge, 1971), 1–26.

16. *Planned Parenthood of Southeastern Pennsylvania v. Casey*, 505 U.S. 833 (1992).

17. Rubenfeld, "The Right of Privacy," 794; Constant, *Constant: Political Writings*; Bobbio, *Democracy and Dictatorship*; de Tocqueville, *Democracy in America*.

18. Tribe, *American Constitutional Law*, 1302; Kasper, "Privacy as a Social Good," 166; Neocleous, "Privacy, Secrecy, Idiocy," 110.

19. Robert K. Merton, "Social Structure and Anomie," *American Sociological Review* 3, no. 5 (1938): 672–82; Jouvenet, "Contexts and Temporalities," 375.

20. Dill, *Growth of Newspapers in the U.S.* For example, see pp. 11ff in Dill for total number of newspapers and pp. 35ff for annual newspaper subscriptions. Also see: *Alexander J. Field, "Newspapers and Periodicals: Number and Circulation by Type, 1850–1967," in Historical Statistics of the United States: Earliest Times to the Present, Millennial Edition (Cambridge University Press, 2006), 4:1055.*

21. For a more general discussion of the sociopolitical significance of journalism in U.S. history, see Streitmatter, *Mightier Than the Sword*; Goodwin, *The Bully Pulpit*.

22. "The Right of Privacy," *Scranton Tribune*, July 22, 1902.

23. *New York Tribune*, July 3,1892, 15. Also quoted in Mensel, "Kodakers Lying in Wait," 24 and 29

24. Karen Halttunen, *Confidence Men and Painted Women: A Study of Middle-class Culture in America, 1830-1870* (Yale University Press, 1982), 83.

25. "The Right to Privacy," *Daily Gate City*, February 27, 1917. Also see Henry L. Mencken, *Newspaper Days, 1899–1906* (Johns Hopkins University Press,

1996); David R. Spencer, *The Yellow Journalism: The Press and America's Emergence as a World Power* (Northwestern University Press, 2007).

26. "The Decrease of Privacy," *Martinsburg Daily Gazette*, May 31, 1887

27. "America and the Right of Privacy," *Herald and News*, November 30, 1909.

28. Lane, *American Privacy*.

29. Massachusetts Historical Society, *Diary of John Adams, Vol. 1*, August 20, 1770, accessed January 10, 2021, http://www.masshist.org/publications/adams-papers/view?id=ADMS-01-01-02-0014-0005-0003.

30. "From Thomas Jefferson to Thomas McKean, 19 February 1803," Founders Online, National Archives, accessed January 12, 2021, https://founders.archives.gov/documents/Jefferson/01-39-02-0461. Original source: Barbara B. Oberg, ed., *The Papers of Thomas Jefferson, Vol. 39, 13 November 1802–3 March 1803* (Princeton University Press, 2012), 552–55.

31. Gajda, *Seek and Hide*, 17ff.

32. "No Privacy in City Life," *Chicago Daily Tribune*, July 27, 1902; Also see James L. Crouthamel, *Bennett's New York Herald and the Rise of the Popular Press* (Syracuse University Press, 1989).

33. "No Privacy in City Life," *Chicago Daily Tribune*, July 27, 1902.

34. Grantland Rice, "We Have With Us Today," *Richmond Times-Dispatch*, July 18, 1920.

35. "Vanderbilt's Privacy," *Chicago Daily Tribune*, March 3, 1884; "A Wrong Done and Not Repaired," *New York Times*, November 10, 1870; "Frank James Wins Suit," *Chicago Daily Tribune*, February 13, 1902; "Privacy," *New York Times*, May 9, 1929.

36. "Lecture on Journalism," *Daily Morning Journal and Courier*, March 7, 1905.

37. Also see "The Right to Privacy," *Daily City Gate*, February 27, 1917.

38. "Lecture on Journalism," *Daily Morning Herald*, March 7, 1905.

39. Riis, *How the Other Half Lives*.

40. "The Dictograph," *Atlanta Georgian*, June 23, 1913.

41. "The Dictograph," *Atlanta Georgian*, June 23, 1913.

42. Louis Brandeis, "What Publicity Can Do," *Harper's Weekly*, December 20, 1913, 10–13.

43. Estimates of U.S. telephone landlines come from the 1902 Census of Telephones by the U.S. Census Bureau and from Fischer, "The Revolution in Rural Telephony, 1900–1920," and Mueller, "Universal Service in Telephone History." For an early history of the U.S. telephone industry and the rise of the modern telecommunications corporation, see Nooba R. Danielian, *AT&T: The Story of Industrial Conquest* (Arno Press, 1974).

44. "The Dictograph," *Atlanta Georgian*, June 23, 1913.

45. "There Are Purchasable Spies in Many Households," *San Francisco Call*, January 1, 1899, 1.

46. "Right of Privacy Includes Telephone," *New York Times*, December 7, 1907.

47. "Society," *Hawaiian Star*, October 3, 1911.

48. "Tesla Talks of New Telegraph," *Chicago Daily Tribune*, February 15, 1901.

49. "Agencies," *Brooklyn Daily Eagle*, November 15, 1873.
50. "Agencies," *Brooklyn Daily Eagle*, November 15, 1873.
51. "Agencies," *Brooklyn Daily Eagle*, November 15, 1873.
52. Sarah Jeong, "Credit Bureaus Were the NSA of the 19th Century," *The Atlantic*, April 21, 2016, accessed May 29, 2024, https://www.theatlantic.com/technology /archive/2016/04/mass-surveillance-was-invented-by-credit-bureaus/479226.
53. James D. Norris, *R. G. Dun & Co. 1841–1900: The Development of Credit-Reporting in the Nineteenth Century* (Greenwood Press, 1978).
54. Calder, *Financing the American Dream*, 13; Robert H. Cole and Lon Mishler, *Consumer and Commercial Credit Management*, 11th ed. (McGraw-Hill, 1998), 220; Josh Lauer, *Creditworthy: A History of Consumer Surveillance and Financial Identity in America* (Columbia University Press, 2017).
55. David Kinley, *The Use of Credit Instruments in Payments in the United States (National Monetary Commission)* (Augustus M. Kelley, 1910), 198–99.
56. Marco Pagano and Tullio Jappelli, "Information-Sharing in Credit Markets," *Journal of Finance* 48, no. 5 (1993): 1693–718; Nicola Jentzsch, "The Regulation of Financial Privacy: The United States vs. Europe," ECRI Research Report no. 5 (2003), https://ecri.eu/publications/research-reports/regulation -financial-privacy-united-states-vs-europe.
57. Rolf Nugent, *Consumer Credit and Economic Stability* (Russell Sage Foundation, 1939), 82.
58. Cole and Mishler, *Consumer and Commercial Credit Management*.
59. Jeong, "Credit Bureaus Were the NSA of the 19th Century."
60. Thomas Francis Meagher, *The Commercial Agency "System" of the United States and Canada Exposed. Is The Secret Inquisition a Curse or a Benefit?* (New York: 1876), 18; George G. Foster, *New York Naked* (DeWitt & Davenport, 1852), 119–20. Also quoted in Jeong, "Credit Bureaus Were the NSA of the 19th Century."
61. "Agencies," *Brooklyn Daily Eagle*, November 15, 1873.
62. Seipp, "The Right to Privacy in American History"; Lauer, *Creditworthy*, 23.
63. Fuchs, "Towards an Alternative Concept of Privacy," 221. Also see Lauer, *Creditworthy*, for a similar conclusion.
64. "The Era of Publicity—the Twentieth Century," *Washington Times*, July 31, 1902. Also see pp. 9–21 in Adam Smith, *The Wealth of Nations* (Bantam Classics, 2003) and pp. 149ff in Durkheim, *The Division of Labor in Society*.
65. Jeong, "Credit Bureaus Were the NSA of the 19th Century."
66. "Writing a Novel," *The Sun*, April 27, 1919. Also see "The Era of Publicity—The Twentieth Century," *Washington Times*, July 31, 1902.
67. "The Era of Publicity—The Twentieth Century," *Washington Times*, July 31, 1902.
68. *The Hattiesburg News*, February 4, 1915.
69. John Durand, "French Domestic Life and Its Lessons," *Atlantic Monthly* (August 1881): 164–79. For a similar discussion about the relative valuation of residential privacy in the United States and the United Kingdom, also see E. W.

Baylor, "After London Types," *Washington Post*, January 19, 1896; Frances Marshall, "Work and Play in the Household," *Washington Herald*, June 21, 1914.

70. Warren and Brandeis, "The Right to Privacy," 220.

71. Warren and Brandeis, "The Right to Privacy," 196.

72. Warren and Brandeis, "The Right to Privacy," 214. For a recent study of related laws and jurisprudence, see Samantha Barbas, *Laws of Image: Privacy and Publicity in America* (Stanford Law Books, 2015).

73. "The Washington Society World: Marriage of Senator Bayard's Daughter—A Reception and Two Banquets," *New York Times*, January 26, 1883, 1; William L. Prosser, "Privacy," *California Law Review* 48, no. 3 (1960): 383–423; Gajda, "What if Samuel D. Warren Hadn't Married a Senator's Daughter"; Amy Gajda, *The First Amendment Bubble: How Privacy and Paparazzi Threaten a Free Press* (Harvard University Press, 2015).

74. Dorothy J. Glancy, "The Invention of the Right to Privacy," *Arizona Law Review* 21 (1979): 1–39; Don R. Pember, *Privacy and the Press: The Law, the Mass Media, and the First Amendment* (University of Washington Press, 1972); Ken Gormley, "One Hundred Years of Privacy," *Wisconsin Law Review* (1992): 1335–441.

75. Neil. M. Richards and Daniel J. Solove, "Prosser's Privacy Law: A Mixed Legacy," *California Law Review* 98, no. 6 (2010): 1892.

76. Warren and Brandeis, "The Right to Privacy," 196.

77. Warren and Brandeis, "The Right to Privacy," 193.

78. Warren and Brandeis, "The Right to Privacy," 205.

79. Warren and Brandeis, "The Right to Privacy," 205.

80. Warren and Brandeis, "The Right to Privacy," 205.

81. See, for example, "The Trial of Rev. Charles Beecher: He Is Convicted of Heresy," *New York Times*, June 26, 1863.

82. Charles Beecher, *Spiritual Manifestations* (Lee and Shepard, 1879), 99.

83. Sidney H. Morse, "Notes," *The Radical* 10 (1972): 154.

84. E. L. Godkin, "The Rights of the Citizen," 65. Also quoted in Mensel, "'Kodakers Lying in Wait,'" 27.

85. For a detailed account of late nineteenth-century theories of "personality," see Warren I. Susman, *Culture as History: The Transformation of American Society in the Twentieth Century,* (Pantheon, 1973), 271–85.

86. Fourcade and Healy, *The Ordinal Society*, 187. Also see Pressly, *The Right to Oblivion*, 46ff.

87. Emile Durkheim, *Professional Ethics and Civic Morals* (Free Press, 1958), 58. Also see Durkheim, *The Division of Labor in Society*, 407; Charles E. Marske, "Durkheim's 'Cult of the Individual' and the Moral Reconstitution of Society," *Sociological Theory* 5, no. 1 (1987): 11.

88. Reich, "Police Questioning," 1170.

89. *The Atlantic Monthly*, vol. LXVII (January–June 1891), 428–29.

90. "Notes," *Central Law Journal* 32 (1891): 69–78; "Editorial," *Harvard Law Review* 5, 3 (1892): 146–48; "The Right to Privacy," *Green Bag* 6, no. 11 (1894):

498–501; Augustus N. Hand, "Schuler Against Curtis and the Right to Privacy," *The American Law Register and Review* 45, no. 12 (1897): 745–59; Elbridge L. Adams, "Right to Privacy: Relation to the Law of Libel," *American Law Review* 39 (1901): 41ff; "Notes," *Kentucky Law Journal* 4 (3): 97ff; "The Law of Privacy," *Columbia Law Review* 12 (1911): 716ff.

91. *Yale Law Journal* 12, no. 1 (1902): 35.
92. Thomas M. Cooley, *A Treatise on the Law of Torts or the Wrongs Which Arise Independent of Contract* (Callaghan, 1879), 29–30, 64, and 359.
93. Thomas M. Cooley, *A Treatise on the Law of Torts or the Wrongs Which Arise Independent of Contract*, 3rd ed., vol. 1, ed. John Lewis (Callaghan, 1906), 364.
94. Kasper, "Privacy as a Social Good"; Neocleous, "Privacy, Secrecy, Idiocy," 110.
95. National Board of Trade, *Proceedings of the Thirty-Third Annual Meeting of the National Board of Trade* (McFetrigdge and Sons, 1903), 233.
96. Kansas State Board of Health, *Seventh Annual Report of the State Board of Health of Kansas* (Press of the Hamilton Printing, 1892), 184.
97. Moses C. White, *Proceedings of the Medical Communications of the Connecticut Medical Society, Second Series*, vol. IV (Connecticut Medical Society, 1875), 81.
98. Committee on Banking and Security, *Hearings Before the Committee on Banking and Security* (Government Printing Office, 1914), 561.
99. Frederick J. Macleod, *Department Reports of the Commonwealth of Massachusetts Containing Decrees, Rulings, and Awards of the Executive, Legislative, and Commission Branches of Government*, vol. IV (Bureau of Department Reports, 1917), 454. Also see Adams, "The Right to Privacy and Its Relation to the Law of Libel," 90 and 108.
100. See chapter 5 for a detailed discussion of the link between Prohibition era search and privacy jurisprudence.
101. John Dewey, "Conscription of Thought," *The New Republic*, September 1, 1917. Also quoted in David M. Rabban, *Free Speech in Its Forgotten Years* (Cambridge University Press, 1997), 23 and 246.
102. Wiebe, *The Search for Order*; Robert C. McMath, *American Populism: A Social History, 1877–1898* (Macmillan, 1993).
103. John Dewey, "Conscription of Thought," 128. Also quoted in Rabban, *Free Speech in Its Forgotten Years*, 247. Additionally see Laura Weinrib. "Freedom of Conscience in War Time: World War I and the Limits of Civil Liberties," *Emory Law Journal* 65, no. 4 (2016): 1081ff.
104. See Kasper, "Privacy as a Social Good," for a summary and critique of this perspective. Also see Etzioni, *The Limits of Privacy*, for a communitarian perspective that aims to rebalance individual rights against collective responsibilities.
105. Regan, *Legislating Privacy*, xiv.
106. My basic orientation is similar to the sentiment expressed by the fictional Mr. Keuner in Bertolt Brecht's collection of aphorisms. Mr. Keuner encounters Mr. Wirr, "a fighter against the press" whose critique of mainstream journalism culminates in a demand for "no more newspapers"—to which Mr. Keuner responds: "I am a greater opponent of the press: I want different newspapers." As a political

matter, the aim ought not to be the rejection of privacy as an individual right and a powerful limiting principle of modern society, but an approach that reaches beyond the now-common operationalization of privacy as consent. See Bertolt Brecht, *Geschichten vom Herrn Keuner* (Surhkamp, 2013), 78–79.

5. A MODERN LEGAL FACT: HOW PRIVACY GAINED A FOOTHOLD IN AMERICAN JURISPRUDENCE

1. This chapter is adapted from Martin Eiermann, "The Process of Legal Institutionalization: How Privacy Jurisprudence Turned Towards the U.S. Constitution and the American State," *Law and Social Inquiry* 49, no. 1 (2024): 537–68.
2. Reich, "Police Questioning," 1165 and 1172; Nissenbaum, "Toward an Approach to Privacy in Public: Challenges of Information Technology," 208. For a discussion of the "distinguished career" of the right to privacy as a constitutional principle, see Lawrence M. Friedman, "Name Robbers: Privacy, Blackmail, and Assorted Matters in Legal History," *Hofstra Law Review* 30, no. 4 (2002): 1125.
3. Simitis, "Privacy—An Endless Debate?," 1125; Prosser, "Privacy"; Zimmerman, "Requiem for a Heavyweight"; Friedman, "Name Robbers: Privacy, Blackmail, and Assorted Matters in Legal History"; James Q. Whitman, "The Two Western Cultures of Privacy: Dignity Versus Liberty," *Yale Law Journal* 113 (2004): 1151–221; Danielle K. Citron, "Cyber Civil Rights," *Boston University Law Review* 89 (2009): 61–125; William M. Beaney, "The Right to Privacy and American Law," *Law and Contemporary Problems* 31 (1966): 253–71; Solove, "Conceptualizing Privacy"; David A. Sklansky, "Too Much Information: How Not to Think About Privacy and the Fourth Amendment," *California Law Review* 102, no. 5 (2014): 1069–122. For examples of relevant "landmark" legal decisions, see *Griswold v. Connecticut*, 381 U.S. 479 (1965), *Katz v. United States*, 389 U.S. 347 (1967), *Eisenstadt v. Baird*, 405 U.S. 438 (1971), *Roe v. Wade*, 410 U.S. 113 (1972), *Lawrence v. Texas*, 539 U.S. 558 (2003), *United States v. Jones*, 565 U.S. 400 (2012), and *Carpenter v. United States*, 585 U.S. 296 (2018).
4. Richards and Solove, "Prosser's Privacy Law."
5. Valerie Jenness, "The Emergence, Content, and Institutionalization of Hate Crime Law: How a Diverse Policy Community Produced a Modern Legal Fact," *Annual Review of Law and Social Science* 3 (2007): 141–60; Scott Phillips and Ryken Grattet, "Judicial Rhetoric, Meaning-Making, and the Institutionalization of Hate Crime Law," *Law and Society Review* 34, no. 3 (2000): 567–606.
6. Gerety, "Redefining Privacy"; Glancy, "The Invention of the Right to Privacy"; Zimmerman, "Requiem for a Heavyweight"; Irwin P. Kramer, "The Birth of Privacy Law: A Century Since Warren and Brandeis," *Catholic University Law Review* 39, no. 3 (1990): 703–24; Benjamin Bratman, "Brandeis and Warren's the Right to Privacy and the Birth of the Right to Privacy," *Tennessee Law Review* 69 (2001): 623–52.

7. Richards and Solove, "Prosser's Privacy Law"; Vernon V. Palmer, "Three Mile-stones in the History of Privacy in the United States," *Tulane European and Civil Law Forum* 26 (2011): 67–97. Also see Brandeis' dissent in *Olmstead v. United States*, 277 U.S. 438 (1928).

8. William M. Beaney, "The Right to Privacy and American Law," *Law and Contemporary Problems* 31 (1966): 253–71; Patricia Boling, *Privacy and the Politics of Intimate Life* (Cornell University Press, 1996); David A. Sklansky, "One Train May Hide Another: Katz, Stonewall, and the Secret Subtext of Criminal Procedure," *U.C. Davis Law Review* 41, no. 3 (2008): 875–934; Igo, *The Known Citizen*; Danielle K. Citron, "Sexual Privacy," *Yale Law Journal* 128 (2019): 1870–960.

9. *Griswold v. Connecticut*, 381 U.S. 479 (1965).

10. Harvard Law Review Association, "The Right to Privacy Today," *Harvard Law Review* 43, no. 2 (1929): 297–302; Roy Moreland, "The Right of Privacy To-Day," *Kentucky Law Journal* 19, no. 2 (1931): 101–38.

11. Igo, *The Known Citizen*, 40.

12. Debbie V. S. Kasper, "The Evolution (or Devolution) of Privacy," *Sociological Forum* 20, no. 1 (2005): 69–92.

13. *Katz v. United States*, 389 U.S. 347 (1967); Seo, "The New Public." See *Mapp v. Ohio*, 367 U.S. 643 (1961) for an elaboration of this proceduralist inter-pretation. See Justice Jackson's early draft opinion for *Papachristou v. City of Jacksonville*, 405 U.S. 156 (1972) for an (abandoned) argument that vagrancy ordinances violate privacy rights of citizens.

14. Hendrik Hartog, "Pigs and Positivism," *Wisconsin Law Review* 1985, no. 4 (1985): 934–35; Marian Burchardt et al., "The Judicial Politics of Burqa Bans in Belgium and Spain: Socio-legal Field Dynamics and the Standardization of Justificatory Repertoires," *Law and Social Inquiry* 44, no. 2 (2019): 333–58.

15. Jenness, "The Emergence, Content, and Institutionalization of Hate Crime Law"; Berger and Luckmann, *The Social Construction of Reality*; Mary Doug-las, *How Institutions Think* (Syracuse University Press, 1986); Phillips and Grattet, "Judicial Rhetoric, Meaning-Making, and the Institutionalization of Hate Crime Law."

16. Glancy, "The Invention of the Right to Privacy," 1; Richards, "The Puzzle of Brandeis, Privacy, and Speech"; Palmer, "Three Milestones in the History of Privacy," 70; Kramer, "The Birth of Privacy Law"; Fred R. Shapiro and Michelle Pearse, "The Most-Cited Law Review Articles of All Time," *Michigan Law Review* 110, no. 8 (2012): 1483–520.

17. *Olmstead v. United States*, 277 U.S. 438. (1928) (L. Brandeis, dissenting).

18. Shils, "Privacy"; Daniel J. Solove et al., *Privacy, Information, and Technology* (Aspen, 2006); Richards and Solove, "Prosser's Privacy Law." Also see the rea-soning in *Harris v. United States*, 331 U.S. 145 (1947). For a comprehensive list of congressional acts that regulate the search and seizure of personal papers based on the Fourth Amendment, see the Appendix to *Davis v. United States*, 328 U.S. 582 (1946). Three decades after *Olmstead*, William Prosser (the dean

of the University of California Berkeley School of Law from 1948 to 1961) tried to impose order on the field of privacy jurisprudence by defining four torts that defined invasions of privacy into a person's private affairs, the disclosure of personal information, the depiction of a person in a false or misleading light, and the appropriation of a person's likeness. By constructing a set of relatively narrow and rigid categories—and by treating privacy claims as extensions of property claims rather than protections for an inviolable self—Prosser elevated the stature of privacy torts within the larger body of American tort law but also "stripped [it] of any guiding concept to shape its future development" (Richards, "The Puzzle of Brandeis") and helped to ensure that privacy claims against non-state entities languished in a doctrinal backwater of American jurisprudence for the second half of the twentieth century. See Solove, "Prosser's Privacy Law," 1890 and 1894; Harry Kalven Jr., "Privacy in Tort Law: Were Warren and Brandeis Wrong?," *Law and Contemporary Problems* 31, no. 2 (1966): 326–41.

19. Pierre Bourdieu, "The Force of Law: Toward a Sociology of the Juridical Field," *Hastings Law Journal* 38 (1986): 816–17; Yves Dezalay and Mikael Rask Madsen, "The Force of Law and Lawyers: Pierre Bourdieu and the Reflexive Sociology of Law," *Annual Review of Law and Social Science* 8 (2012): 433–52; Elizabeth Mertz, "A New Social Constructionism for Sociolegal Studies," *Law and Society Review* 28, no. 5 (1994): 1251; Meagan Richardson, *The Right to Privacy: Origins and Influence of a Nineteenth-Century Idea* (Cambridge University Press, 2017).

20. For related discussions of communities of knowledge, see Robert K. Merton, *The Sociology of Science: Theoretical and Empirical Investigations* (University of Chicago Press, 1979); Bruno Latour, *The Pasteurization of France* (Harvard University Press, 1993).

21. Ziegler, *Beyond Abortion*, 21.

22. For discussions of law and jurisprudence as they relate to collective action, see Frances K. Zemans, "Legal Mobilization: The Neglected Role of Law in the Political System," *American Political Science Review* 77, no. 3 (1983): 690–703; Durkheim, *The Division of Labor in Society*; Morton J. Horwitz, *The Transformation of American Law, 1870–1960: The Crisis of Legal Orthodoxy* (Oxford University Press, 1992); Terence C. Halliday and Lucien Karpik, eds., *Lawyers and the Rise of Western Political Liberalism: Europe and North America from the Eighteenth to Twentieth Centuries* (Clarendon Press, 1998); William Wiecek, *The Lost World of Classical Legal Thought* (Oxford University Press, 2001); Michael McCann, "Law and Social Movements: Contemporary Perspectives," *Annual Review of Law and Social Science* 2 (2006): 17–38. For a general discussion of resources (including symbolic resources, like the law) in collective action, see John D. McCarthy and Mayer N. Zald, "Resource Mobilization and Social Movements: A Partial Theory," *American Journal of Sociology* 82, no. 6 (1977): 1212–41.

23. Shils, "Privacy"; Amy Allen, "Foucault and Enlightenment: A Critical Reappraisal," *Constellations* 10, no. 2 (2003): 192; Michel Foucault, *The Order of*

Things (Routledge, 2002); James B. Rule et al., "Documentary Identification and Mass Surveillance in the United States," *Social Problems* 31, no. 2 (1983): 222–34. For a specific discussion of social movements and privacy jurisprudence during the 1960s and 1970s, see Igo, *The Known Citizen*, e.g., 144ff and 157–59 (for a discussion of *Roe v. Wade*).

24. *Griswold v. Connecticut*, 381 U.S. 479 (1965); *Katz v. United States*, 389 U.S. 347 (1967); Sklansky, "One Train May Hide Another," 875; Igo, *The Known Citizen*, 160; Robert G. Dixon, "The Griswold Penumbra: Constitutional Charter for an Expanded Law of Privacy?," *Michigan Law Review* 64, no. 2 (1965): 197.

25. Moore, *Privacy*, 268; Shils, "Privacy," 287; Kasper, "The Evolution (or Devolution) of Privacy"; Julie E. Cohen, "What Privacy Is For," *Harvard Law Review* 126, no. 7 (2012): 1904–33; Igo, *The Known Citizen*; Louise Marie Roth, "The Right to Privacy Is Political: Power, the Boundary Between Public and Private, and Sexual Harassment," *Law and Social Inquiry* 24, no. 1 (1999): 45–71; Browne, *Dark Matters*.

26. Epp, *The Rights Revolution*; McCann, "Law and Social Movements," 22; William N. Eskridge, "Some Effects of Identity-Based Social Movements on Constitutional Law in the Twentieth Century," *Michigan Law Review* 100, no. 8 (2002): 2062–407; Patricia Ewick and Susan S. Silbey, *The Common Place of Law: Stories from Everyday Life* (University of Chicago Press, 1998); Anna-Maria Marshall, "Injustice Frames, Legality, and the Everyday Construction of Sexual Harassment," *Law and Social Inquiry* 28, no. 3 (2003): 659–90; Jack M. Balkin, "How Social Movements Change (or Fail to Change) the Constitution: The Case of the New Departure," *Suffolk University Law Review* 39, no. 1 (2005): 27–66.

27. Gajda, *Seek and Hide*.

28. *Weeks v. United States*, 232 U.S. 383 (1914); *Olmstead v. United States*, 277 U.S. 438. (1928); *United States v. Lefkowitz et al.*, 285 U.S. 452 (1932).

29. Jenness, "The Emergence, Content, and Institutionalization of Hate Crime Law," 141.

30. Bourdieu, "The Force of Law," 832.

31. Bourdieu, "The Force of Law," 824 and 818.

32. I also supplement this network analysis with a qualitative examination of historical legal opinions, law review essays, and newspaper articles, including all articles that discussed the right to privacy from 395 issues of 15 prominent law reviews and law journals and 500 newspaper articles that mentioned the right to privacy (sometimes also called the "right of privacy") drawn from the *Chronicling America* database of historical U.S. newspapers.

33. Mark E. Newman, "Modularity and Community Structure in Networks," *Proceedings of the National Academy of Sciences* 103, no. 23 (2006): 8577–82.

34. *Roberson v. Rochester Folding Co.*, 171 N.Y. 538 (1902); *Schuyler v. Curtis*, 147 N.Y. 434 (1895); *Pavesich v. New England Life Insurance Co.*, 122 Ga. 190 (1905). Also see Phillip Bonacich, "Factoring and Weighting Approaches to Status Scores and Clique Identification," *Journal of Mathematical Sociology* 2 (1972): 113–20.

35. "The Right to Privacy," *New York Tribune*, June 29, 1902.

36. *United States v. Kaplan*, 286 F. 963 (1923); *State v. Owens*, 302 Mo. 348 (1924); *State ex rel. King v. District Court*, 70 Mont. 191 (1924); *Boyd v. United States*, 116 U.S. 616 (1886).

37. *Roberson v. Rochester Folding Co.*, 171 N.Y. 538 (1902); *Schuyler v. Curtis*, 147 N.Y. 434 (1895).

38. *State v. Aime*, 62 Utah 476 (1923); *Weeks v. United States*, 232 U.S. 383 (1914); *People v. Jakira*, 193 Misc. 306 (1922).

39. Neil Fligstein and Doug McAdam, *A Theory of Fields* (Oxford University Press, 2015); Burchardt et al., "The Judicial Politics of Burqa Bans in Belgium and Spain."

40. Franklin Benjamin Sanborn, "Journalism and Journalists," *Atlantic Monthly* (July 1874): 55–66. Also see notes to chapter 4 for additional sources.

41. Gajda, *Seek and Hide*, 7.

42. *Photographic Times and American Photographer* 18 (August 24, 1888): 403.

43. Edwin L. Godkin, "Libel and Its Legal Remedy," *Atlantic Monthly* (December 1880): 729–39.

44. "The Right to Privacy," *Irish Standard*, February 6, 1892.

45. Glancy, "The Invention of the Right to Privacy," 6.

46. For a related argument, see Hollinger, *In the American Province*, 130–51, who argues that public discourse can inform and reshape knowledge production in more specialized domains, like academia or jurisprudence.

47. *De May v. Roberts*, 46 Mich. 160 (1881). Also see Caroline Danielson, "The Gender of Privacy and the Embodied Self: Examining the Origins of the Right to Privacy in U.S. Law," *Feminist Studies* 25, no. 2 (1999): 311–44.

48. Jessica Lake, *The Face That Launched a Thousand Lawsuits: The American Women Who Forged a Right to Privacy* (Yale University Press, 2016), 151; Dorothy Glancy, "Privacy and the Other Miss M," *Northern Illinois University Law Review* 10 (1989): 401–40.

49. Phineas Taylor Barnum, *Life of P. T. Barnum. Written by Himself* (Courier Co. Printers, 1886), 57. Also quoted in Glancy, "Privacy and the Other Miss M," 407.

50. Archibald McClean, "The Right of Privacy," *Green Bag* 15, no. 10 (1903): 494–97. The previous sentence paraphrases the majority opinion in *McSwane v. Foreman*, 78 NE 630 (1906). For an early statement of a similar argument, also see *Ex parte Brown*, 7 Mo.App. 484 (1879).

51. "Editorial," *Harvard Law Review* 7, no. 3 (1894): 177–82. Also see "Inviolability of Telegraphic Correspondence," *American Law Register* 27, no. 2 (1879): 65–78.

52. See, for example, *Atkinson v. John E. Doherty & Co.*, 121 Mich. 372 (1899) and *Schuyler v. Curtis*, 147 N.Y. 434 (1895).

53. *Sanning v. City of Cincinnati*, 81 Ohio St. 142 (1909).

54. Also see a related discussion in "Recent Cases," *Harvard Law Review* 24, no. 8 (1911), 667–82.

55. *Munden v. Harris*, 134 S.W. 1076 (1911).

56. *Klug v. Sheriffs*, 129 Wis. 468 (1906).

57. Recall that this was precisely the kind of argument that Warren and Brandeis had dismissed in 1890 as inadequate. That it survived nonetheless points to the limited short-term impact of their essay on the *practice* of legal meaning-making even as it offered a new legal *theory* of privacy.

58. John F. Lynch, "Truthful Libel and Right of Privacy in Wyoming," *Wyoming Law Journal* 11, no. 3 (2019): 185.

59. Gajda, *Seek and Hide*, xi; Michael J. Polelle, "The Unconstitutionality of the Qualified Truth Defense to Libel Actions," *UIC Law Review* 11, no. 2 (1978): 259–81.

60. *Atkinson v. John E. Doherty & Co.*, 121 Mich. 372 (1899).

61. Roscoe Pound, *Law and Morals* (University of North Carolina Press, 1924); William P. Sternberg, "Natural Law in American Jurisprudence," *Notre Dame Lawyer* 13, no. 2 (1938): 89–100; Brendan F. Brown, "Natural Law and the Law-Making Function in American Jurisprudence," *Notre Dame Law Review* 15, no. 1 (1939): 9–25; Benjamin F. Wright, *American Interpretations of Natural Law: A Study in the History of Political Thought* (Russell and Russell, 1962); Horwitz, *The Transformation of American Law*.

62. *Pavesich v. New England Life Insurance Co.*, 122 Ga. 190 (1905).

63. *Brents v. Morgan*, 221 Ky. 765 (1927).

64. *Pritchett v. Board of Commissioners*, 42 Ind. App. 3 (1908).

65. William M. McKinney, ed., *Ruling Case Law* 21 (Edward Thompson, 1918).

66. *Henry v. Cherry Webb*, 30 R.I. 13 (1909). For a similar argument that traces privacy claims back to Jewish legal traditions, see Samuel H. Hofstadter and George Horowitz, *The Right to Privacy* (Central Book Company, 1964).

67. *Schuyler v. Curtis*, 147 N.Y. 434 (1895).

68. Augustus N. Hand, "Schuyler Against Curtis and the Right to Privacy," *American Law Register and Review* 45, no. 12 (1897): 759.

69. *Roberson v. Rochester Folding Co.*, 171 N.Y. 538 (1902); *Pavesich v. New England Life Insurance Co.*, 122 Ga. 190 (1905).

70. "The Right of Privacy," *New York Tribune*, June 29, 1902.

71. "Right to Privacy," *New York Tribune*, July 13, 1922.

72. "Editorial," *The American Law Register* 50, no. 11 (1902): 669–78.

73. *Wyatt v. Hall's Portrait Studio*, 71 Misc. 199 (1911).

74. For an exception, see *Owen v. Partridge*, 40 Misc. 425 (1903).

75. *Hodgeman v. Olsen*, 86 Wash. 615 (1915).

76. *Miller v. Gillespie*, 196 Mich. 423 (1917).

77. *Holcombe v. Creamer*, 231 Mass. 99 (1918).

78. *State ex rel. Mendenhall v. District Court*, 29 Mont. 363 (1903); *Matter of Davies*, 168 N.Y. 89 (1901).

79. Richardson, *The Right to Privacy*, 10; Koopman, *How We Became Our Data*.

80. Dill, *Growth of Newspapers in the U.S.*; Mueller, "Universal Service in Telephone History"; Field, "Newspapers and Periodicals."

81. Dill, *Growth of Newspapers in the U.S.*; Robert Thompson, *Wiring a Continent* (Princeton University Press, 1947).

82. Wiebe, *The Search for Order*; Skowronek, *Building a New American State*; Daniel Carpenter, *The Forging of Bureaucratic Autonomy: Reputations, Networks, and Policy Innovation in Executive Agencies, 1862–1928* (Princeton University Press, 2002); Brian Balogh, *A Government Out of Sight: The Mystery of National Authority in Nineteenth-Century America* (Cambridge University Press, 2009). For contemporaneous discussions of government searches during the Prohibition era, see (for example) Andrew Alexander Bruce, "Arbitrary Searches and Seizures as Applied to Modern Industry," *The Green Bag* 18, no. 5 1906), 300; "Liquor Purchased Before August 1," *The Ogden Standard*, September 11, 1917; "Drys' Get Hard Jolt in Action by House," *Omaha Daily Bee*, August 17, 1921.

83. Rabban, *Free Speech in Its Forgotten Years*, 4.

84. "Privacy," *Chicago Daily Tribune*, September 27, 1925.

85. Charles W. Johnson and Scott P. Beetham, "The Origin of Article I, Section 7 of the Washington State Constitution," *Seattle University Law Review* 31 (2007): 431–67.

86. See Art. 2, Para. 8 of the Arizona State Constitution. Several other states have since added an explicit recognition of a right to privacy to their respective constitutions, including Alaska (1972), California (1972), Florida (1978), Hawaii (1978), Illinois (1970), Louisiana (1974), Montana (1972), New Hampshire (2018), and South Carolina (1971).

87. Wiebe, *The Search for Order*.

88. Horwitz, *The Transformation of American Law*; Wiecek, *The Lost World of Classical Legal Thought*; Aziz Rana, "Constitutionalism and the Foundations of the Security State," *California Law Review* 103, no. 2 (2015): 335–85; Aziz Rana, *The Constitutional Bind: How Americans Came to Idolize a Document That Fails Them* (University of Chicago Press, 2024).

89. Rabban, *Free Speech in Its Forgotten Years*; Raymond Geuss, *Public Goods, Private Goods* (Princeton University Press, 2001); G. Edward White, *The Constitution and the New Deal* (Harvard University Press, 2002); William J. Novak, "The Myth of the 'Weak' American State," *The American Historical Review* 113, no. 3 (2008): 752–72.

90. Henry T. Terry, "Constitutionality of Statutes Forbidding Advertising Signs on Property," *Yale Law Journal* 24, no. 1 (1915): 1–11. Also see *Brents v. Morgan*, 221 Ky. 765 (1927).

91. See, for example, *People v. Mayen*, 188 Ca. 237 (1922); *State v. Owens*, 259 S.W. 100 (1924); *People v. Wren*, 210 P. 60 (1922); *People v. Jakira*, 118 Misc. 303 (1922); *People v. Bishop*, 225 Ill. App. 610 (1922); *Schwartz v. United States*, 294 Fed. 528 (1924); *State v. Gardner*, 249 P. 574 (1926).

92. *Gardner v. State*, 141 Miss. 192 (1925).

93. *Hessian v. State*, 196 Wis. 435 (1928). For later jurisprudence, also see *State ex rel. King v. District Court*, 70 Mont. 191 (1938).

94. *Knight v. State*, 171 Ark. 882 (1926), and *Jessner v. State*, 202 Wis. 184 (1930).

95. See *Warner v. Gregory*, 203 Wis. 65 (1930), and *Goodman v. State*, 158 Miss. 269 (1930).

96. See, for example, *Harris v. United States*, 331 U.S. 145 (1947); *United States v. Lefkowitz et al.*, 285 U.S. 452 (1932); *Griswold v. Connecticut*, 381 U.S. 479 (1965).

97. Steven Lukes and Andrew Scull, eds., *Durkheim and the Law* (Palgrave Macmillan, 2013), 54–61, 150–63; Max Rheinstein, ed., *Max Weber on Law in Economy and Society* (Simon and Schuster, 1967), 11–20, 322ff, 338ff.

98. Leonard A. Jones, "Oliver Wendell Holmes, the Jurist," *The American Law Review* 36 (1902), 719.

99. Paraphrased from Marx, "The Eighteenth Brumaire of Louis Bonaparte," 595: "Men make their own history, but they do not make it as they please; they do not make it under self-selected circumstances, but under circumstances existing already, given and transmitted from the past." Also see William L. F. Felstiner et al., "The Emergence and Transformation of Disputes: Naming, Blaming, Claiming," in *Theoretical and Empirical Studies of Rights*, ed. Laura Beth Nielson (Routledge, 2017), 633.

100. Walter Benjamin, "Theses on the Philosophy of History," in *Critical Theory and Society: A Reader*, ed. Stephen Eric Bronner and Douglas MacKay Kellner (Routledge, 1989), 255–63; Andrew Abbott, "The Historicality of Individuals," *Social Science History* 29, no. 1 (2005): 1–13; Robert Gordon, *Taming the Past: Law in History and History in Law* (Cambridge University Press, 2017).

101. Hartog, "Pigs and Positivism," 935.

102. Gunnar Myrdal, *An American Dilemma: The Negro Problem and Modern Democracy* (Harper, 1944), xlvi.

103. Rana, "Constitutionalism and the Foundations of the Security State," 380.

104. Clifford Geertz, *The Interpretation of Cultures* (Basic, 1973); Anthony et al., "Toward a Sociology of Privacy," 262.

105. Timothy Mitchell, "Everyday Metaphors of Power," *Theory and Society* 19 (1990): 545–77.

106. *Watkins v. United States*, 354 U.S. 178 (1957).

107. Kamala Harris, Twitter post, May 3, 2022, 1:15 P.M., accessed May 10, 2022, https://twitter.com/VP/status/1521584127568498689.

108. Tribe, *American Constitutional Law*, 1302; Dixon, "The Griswold Penumbra."

109. Cohen, "What Privacy Is For"; Frank Pasquale, "Privacy, Antitrust, and Power," *George Mason Law Review* 20, no. 4 (2012): 1009–24; Sebastian Sevignani, "The Commodification of Privacy on the Internet," *Science and Public Policy* 40, no. 6 (2013): 733–39; Mikella Hurley and Julius Adebayo, "Credit Scoring in the Era of Big Data," *Yale Journal of Law and Technology* 18 (2016): 148–216; Fourcade and Healy, "Seeing Like a Market"; Dan Bouk, "The History and Political Economy of Personal Data Over the Last Two Centuries in Three Acts," *Osiris* 32, no. 1 (2017): 85–106; Nick Srnicek, *Platform Capitalism* (Polity, 2017); Zuboff, *The Age of Surveillance Capitalism*; Jathan Sadowski, "When Data Is Capital: Datafication, Accumulation, and Extraction," *Big Data and Society* 6, no. 1 (2019): 1–12; Jathan Sadowski, *Too Smart: How Digital Capitalism Is Extracting Data, Controlling Our Lives, and Taking Over the World* (MIT Press, 2020); Waldman, *Industry Unbound*.

110. Simitis, "Privacy—An Endless Debate?," 1996.

6. GOVERNANCE BY EXCEPTION:
BUREAUCRATIC RULE AND THE LIMITS OF PRIVACY

1. Daniel A. Farber, "Lincoln, Presidential Power, and the Rule of Law," *Northwestern University Law Review* 113, no. 3 (2018): 667–700; Randall G. Holcombe, "The Growth of the Federal Government in the 1920s," *The Cato Journal* 16 (1996): 175–99.

2. Skowronek, *Building a New American State*; Wendy N. Espeland and Mitchell L. Stevens, "A Sociology of Quantification," *European Journal of Sociology* 49, no. 3 (2008): 424; Christopher Dandeker, *Surveillance, Power and Modernity: Bureaucracy and Discipline from 1700 to the Present Day* (St. Martin's, 1990), vii. More generally, see Koopman, *How We Became Our Data*; Patricia C. Cohen, *A Calculating People: The Spread of Numeracy in Early America* (University of Chicago Press, 1982); Sarah E. Igo, *The Averaged American: Surveys, Citizens, and the Making of a Mass Public* (Harvard University Press, 2007); John Torpey, *The Invention of the Passport: Surveillance, Citizenship and the State* (Cambridge University Press, 2000); Rule et al., "Documentary Identification"; Michael Biggs, "Putting the State on the Map: Cartography, Territory, and European State Formation," *Comparative Studies in Society and History* 41, no. 2 (1999): 374–405. For studies of the production and quantification of governmental knowledge, see Scott, *Seeing Like a State*; Hacking, *The Taming of Chance*; Theodore M. Porter, *Trust in Numbers: The Pursuit of Objectivity in Science and Public Life* (Princeton University Press, 1995); Alain Desrosières, *The Politics of Large Numbers: A History of Statistical Reasoning* (Harvard University Press, 1998); William Alonso and Paul Starr, eds., *The Politics of Numbers* (Russell Sage Foundation, 1987); Adam Tooze, *Statistics and the German State, 1900–1945: The Making of Modern Economic Knowledge* (Cambridge University Press, 2001); Francisca Grommé and Stephan Scheel, "Doing Statistics, Enacting the Nation: The Performative Powers of Categories," *Nations and Nationalism* 26, no. 3 (2020): 576–93; Michel Foucault, *Security, Territory, Population: Lectures at the Collège de France, 1977–78* (Picador, 2007); Michel Foucault, *The Birth of Biopolitics: Lectures at the Collège de France, 1978–1979* (Picador, 2008); Nikolas Rose et al., "Governmentality," *Annual Review of Law and Social Science* 2 (2006): 83–104. For studies of census-taking, see Anderson, *The American Census*; Melissa Nobles, *Shades of Citizenship: Race and the Census in Modern Politics* (Stanford University Press, 2000); David Kertzer and Dominique Arel, eds., *Census and Identity: The Politics of Race, Ethnicity, and Language in National Censuses* (Cambridge University Press, 2002); Mara Loveman, *National Colors: Racial Classification and the State in Latin America* (Oxford University Press, 2014); Rebecca J. Emigh et al., *Antecedents of Censuses from Medieval to Nation States: How Societies and States Count* (Palgrave Macmillan, 2016). For a non-Western perspective, see Timothy Longman, "Identity Cards, Ethnic Self-Perception, and Genocide in Rwanda," in *Documenting Individual Identity: The Development of State Practices in the Modern World*, ed. Jane Caplan and John Torpey (Princeton University Press, 2001), 345–57.

3. Carroll D. Wright, *Problems of the Census: Opening Address Before the American Social Science Association at Saratoga* (Wright & Potter Printing, 1887). Also quoted in David Seipp, "The Right to Privacy in American History," 30.

4. Lawrence Quill, *Secrets and Democracy* (Palgrave Macmillan, 2014), 10; Auguste Comte, *Social Physics: From the Positive Philosophy of Auguste Comte* (Calvin Blanchard, 1856); Kevin Donnelly, *Adolphe Quetelet, Social Physics and the Average Men of Science, 1796–1874* (University of Pittsburgh Press, 2015); Cortada, *All the Facts.*

5. "Scrapbook Concerning Legislation for the 14th Census 1917–1919," USNA Record P-128.

6. Hacking, *The Taming of Chance.*

7. Hacking, "Kinds of People," 294; Timothy Mitchell, "Everyday Metaphors of Power," *Theory and Society* 19, no. 5 (1990): 545–77.

8. Kimberly J. Morgan and Ann Shola Orloff, "The Many Hands of the State," in *The Many Hands of the State: Theorizing Political Authority and Social Control*, ed. Kimberly J. Morgan and Ann Shola Orloff (Cambridge University Press, 2017), 1–32; Karen Orren and Stephen Skowronek, *The Policy State: An American Predicament* (Harvard University Press, 2017), 9.

9. Theda Skocpol, "State Formation and Social Policy in the United States," *American Behavioral Scientist* 35, nos. 4–5 (1992): 559–84; Theda Skocpol, *Protecting Soldiers and Mothers: The Political Origins of Social Policy in the United States* (Harvard University Press, 1995).

10. Howard D. Kramer, "The Beginnings of the Public Health Movement in the United States," *Bulletin of the History of Medicine* 21 (1947): 352–76; Seipp, "The Right to Privacy in American History"; Heather L. Brumberg et al., "History of the Birth Certificate: From Inception to the Future of Electronic Data," *Journal of Perinatology* 32, no. 6 (2012): 407–11; Rule, *Privacy in Peril*; Lyon, *Surveillance as Social Sorting*; Freda L. Fair, "Surveilling Social Difference: Black Women's 'Alley Work' in Industrializing Minneapolis," *Surveillance and Society* 15, no. 5 (2017): 655–75.

11. Muhammad, *The Condemnation of Blackness*, 15; W. E. B. Du Bois, *The Philadelphia Negro: A Social Study* (University of Pennsylvania Press, 2023). Also see Nathaniel S. Shaler, "Science and the African Problem," *Atlantic Monthly* (July 1890), https://www.theatlantic.com/magazine/archive/1890/07/science-and-the-african-problem/523647.

12. "Scrapbook Concerning Legislation for the 14th Census 1917–1919," USNA Record P-128; Kevin D. Haggerty Ericson, "The Surveillant Assemblage"; Bernard E. Harcourt, "Against Prediction: Sentencing, Policing, and Punishing in an Actuarial Age," University of Chicago Public Law Working Paper 94 (2005); David Lyon, *The Culture of Surveillance: Watching as a Way of Life* (Polity, 2018).

13. Haggerty and Ericson, "The Surveillant Assemblage," 606 and 607; Lyon, *The Culture of Surveillance.*

14. Dandeker, *Surveillance, Power and Modernity*; Peter P. Swire, "The System of Foreign Intelligence Surveillance Law," *George Washington Law Review* 72 (2003): 1306–72; Kasper, "Privacy as a Social Good."

15. Dorothy Nelkin and Lori Andrews, "Surveillance Creep in the Genetic Age," in *Surveillance as Social Sorting*, ed. David Lyon (Routledge, 2005), 108–24

16. Janet Vertesi, "My Experiment Opting Out of Big Data Made Me Look Like a Criminal," *TIME Magazine*, May 1, 2014, accessed June 17, 2022, https://time .com/83200/privacy-internet-big-data-opt-out.

17. Espeland and Stevens, "A Sociology of Quantification"; Eubanks, *Automating Inequality*; Mau, *The Metric Society*; Marion Fourcade and Jeffrey Gordon, "Learning Like a State: Statecraft in the Digital Age," *Journal of Law and Political Economy* 1, no. 1 (2020): 78–108; Marion Fourcade and Kieran Healy, *The Ordinal Society* (Harvard University Press, 2024).

18. Solove, "Conceptualizing Privacy," 1154.

19. George Orwell, *Nineteen Eighty-Four* (Signet Classics, 1961); Foucault, *Discipline and Punish*. Notably, Haggerty and Ericson ("The Surveillant Assemblage") argue that Orwell *underestimated* the ubiquity of surveillance by assuming that the lowest social stratum would be partially exempt from it. I return to this point in the conclusion.

20. Richard V. Denenberg, "Privacy: Wanted but Vague," *New York Times*, February 3, 1974.

21. Marx, "What's New About the 'New Surveillance'?," 17 and 22.

22. Seo, "The New Public," 1668. Also see Sklansky, "'One Train May Hide Another,'" 883; John Fiske, "Surveilling the City: Whiteness, the Black Man and Democratic Totalitarianism," *Theory, Culture and Society* 15, no. 2 (1998): 67–88; Browne, *Dark Matters*.

23. Solove, "Conceptualizing Privacy," 1120.

24. Seo, "The New Public," 1665; Shils, "Privacy," 282; Gary G. Hamilton and John R. Sutton, "The Problem of Control in the Weak State: Domination in the United States, 1880–1920," *Theory and Society* 18, no. 1 (1989): 1–46; Kasper, "Privacy as a Social Good." For a discussion of forbearance and American state power, see Steven Levitsky and Daniel Ziblatt, *How Democracies Die* (Broadway, 2018); Bertrand Badie and Pierre Birnbaum, *The Sociology of the State* (University of Chicago Press, 1983); Novak, "The Myth of the 'Weak' American State." For a discussion of legal-rational legitimacy, see Max Weber, *Economy and Society*, vol. 1 (University of California Press, 1978), 212–26.

25. Carl Schmitt, *Die Diktatur* (Duncker & Humblot, 1921); Carl Schmitt, *Political Theology* (MIT Press, 1985); Walter Benjamin, "On the Concept of History," in *Selected Writings, Vol. 4: 1938–1940*, ed. Howard Eiland and Michael W. Jennings (Harvard University Press, 2003); Giorgio Agamben, *State of Exception* (University of Chicago Press, 2005).

26. Schmitt, *Political Theology*, 48 and 65.

27. Schmitt, *Political Theology*, 5.

28. Schmitt, *Political Theology*, 13 and 136.

29. Agamben, *State of Exception*, 20.
30. Agamben, *State of Exception*, 2 and 53. Also see Clinton L. Rossiter, *Constitutional Dictatorship: Crisis Government in the Modern Democracies* (Princeton University Press, 1948).
31. William J. Novak et al., "Democratic States of Unexception: Toward a New Genealogy of the American Political," in *The Many Hands of the State: Theorizing Political Authority and Social Control*, eds. Kimberly J. Morgan and Ann Shola Orloff (Cambridge: Cambridge University Press, 2018), 236.
32. Weber, *Economy and Society*.
33. John Dewey, *The Public and Its Problems* (Holt and Co., 1927).
34. Bourdieu, "The Force of Law," 824.
35. Novak et al., "Democratic States of Unexception," 232.
36. Nancy Fraser, "Foucault on Modern Power: Empirical Insights and Normative Confusions," *Praxis International* 1, no. 3 (1981): 272–87; John R. Commons, *Legal Foundations of Capitalism* (Transaction, 1995), 367; Dandeker, *Surveillance, Power and Modernity*, 13.
37. Gil Rothschild-Elyassi et al., "Actuarial Justice at a Quarter Century," in *The Handbook of Social Control*, ed. Mathieu Deflem (Wiley, 2019), 194–206.
38. George W. Morton, *Laws and Ordinances Relative to the Preservation of Public Health* (Edmund Jones and Co, 1860); Samuel W. Abbott, *Past and Present Condition of Public Hygiene and State Medicine in the United States* (Wright and Potter, 1900).
39. Marine Hospital Service, *Public Health Reports*, vol. XVI, Part II, No. 27 to 52 (Government Printing Office, 1902), 2956. Also see Wilson Smillie, "The Basis of Communicable Disease Control," *Public Health Reports* 67, no. 3 (1952): 289–92; Jason Waterman and William Fowler, *Municipal Ordinances, Rules, and Regulations Pertaining to Public Health, 1917–1919. Supplement No. 40 to the Public Health Reports* (Government Printing Office, 1921).
40. "The Organization of the Civil Registration System of the United States," International Institute for Vital Registration and Statistics Technical Paper 8. Also see Robert D. Leigh, *Federal Health Administration in the United States* (Harper, 1927); Richard H. Shryock, "The Early American Public Health Movement," *American Journal of Public Health* 27, no. 10 (1937): 965–71.
41. Hurty, "The Bookkeeping of Humanity," 1157–58; Central File Box 5, "Interdepartmental Social Hygiene Board," USNA Record NC-34, 30; Central File Box 2, "National Board of Health: Minutes of Meetings," USNA Record PI-141, 1.
42. James J. Davis and Grace Abbott, *Juvenile-Court Standards: Report of the Committee Appointed by the Children's Bureau, August, 1921, to Formulate Juvenile-Court Standards* (Government Printing Office, 1923).
43. Philip Reilly and Margery Shaw, "The Virginia Racial Integrity Act Revisited: The Plecker-Laughlin Correspondence: 1928–1930," *American Journal of Medical Genetics* 16, no. 4 (1983): 483–92; Shane Landrum, "Registering Race, Policing Citizenship: Delayed Birth Registration and the Virginia Racial Integrity Act, 1924–1975," Working Paper (Columbus: Policy History Conference, 2010).

44. Brumberg et al., "History of the Birth Certificate"; Koopman, *How We Became Our Data*, 35–65; Robert E. Chaddock, "Sources of Information Upon the Public Health Movement," *Annals of the American Academy of Political and Social Science* 37, no. 2 (1911): 63–66; U.S. Bureau of the Census, *Legal Importance of Registration of Births and Deaths* (Government Printing Office, 1906); U.S. Bureau of the Census, *Birth Statistics for the Registration Area of the United States, First Annual Report* (Government Printing Office, 1917).
45. U.S. Bureau of the Census, *Birth, Stillbirth, and Infant Mortality Statistics for the Birth Registration Area of the United States, Thirteenth Annual Report, 1927* (Government Printing Office, 1930). Also see Koopman, *How We Became Our Data*, 48–57.
46. Samuel H. Preston and Michael R. Haines, *Fatal Years: Child Mortality in Late Nineteenth-Century America* (Princeton University Press, 2014), 83–84. Estimates of proportional coverage were computed by the author based on IPUMS historical population counts.
47. Christopher Muller, "Freedom and Convict Leasing in the Postbellum South," *American Journal of Sociology* 124, no. 2 (2018): 367–405; Martin Eiermann et al., "Racial Disparities in Mortality During the 1918 Influenza Pandemic in United States Cities," *Demography* 59, no. 5 (2022): 1953–79.
48. Du Bois, *The Philadelphia Negro*, 71 and 149.
49. For a similar conception of politics as agenda-setting, see George A. Gonzalez, *The Politics of Air Pollution: Urban Growth, Ecological Modernization, and Symbolic Inclusion* (SUNY Press, 2005).
50. Armstrong et al., "Trends in Infectious Disease Mortality"; James J. Feigenbaum et al., "Regional and Racial Inequality in Infectious Disease Mortality in U.S. Cities, 1900–1948," *Demography* 56, no. 4 (2019): 1371–88; Mary R. Jackman and Kimberlee A. Shauman, "The Toll of Inequality: Excess African American Deaths in the United States Over the Twentieth Century," *DuBois Review* 16, no. 2 (2019): 291–340.
51. Central File Box 240, "Venereal Diseases," USNA Record NC-34, 10. Also see Interdepartmental Social Hygiene Board, Box 5, USNA Record NC-34, 30.
52. Smillie, "The Basis of Communicable Disease Control"; John W. Kerr and Aristides A. Moll, *Public Health Bulletin 54: Organization, Powers, and Duties of Health Authorities* (Government Printing Office, 1912).
53. Henry G. Clark, "Superiority of Sanitary Measures Over Quarantines: An Address Delivered Before the Suffolk District Medical Society at Its Third Anniversary Meeting, Boston, April 24, 1852," City of Boston: Sanitary Visitation, October 30, 1865.
54. See Kerr and Moll, *Public Health Bulletin 54*, 22, 28, 35–39, 41, and 398–403.
55. Council of Hygiene and Public Health of the Citizens' Association of New York, *Report on Epidemic Cholera* (Sanford, Harroun & Co., 1865), 31.
56. Council of Hygiene and Public Health, *Report on Epidemic Cholera*, 33.
57. Council of Hygiene and Public Health, *Laws and Ordinances Relative to the Preservation of Public Health* (Edmund Jones and Co., 1860); Citizens

Association of New York, *The Public Health: The Basis of Sanitary Reform* (Metropolitan Board of Health, 1866), 13–19.

58. Abbott, *Past and Present Condition of Public Hygiene*, 55–56; Stephen Smith, *The City That Was* (Frank Allaben, 1911); James A. Tobey, *Public Health Law* (Williams & Wilkins, 1926), 31–43.

59. "Indiana Board of Health Records," Central File Box 679, USNA Record NC-34, 10.

60. California State Board of Health, "Report of the California State Board of Health, 1870–1871" (D. W. Gelwicks, 1871), 5; San Francisco Board of Supervisors, "Report of Special Committee on the Condition of the Chinese Quarter" (W. M. Hinton and Co., 1885), 208.

61. Quoted in Natalia Molina, *Fit to Be Citizens? Public Health and Race in Los Angeles, 1879–1939* (University of California Press, 2006), 63. Also see W. Michael Byrd and Linda A. Clayton, "Race, Medicine, and Health Care in the United States: A Historical Survey," *Journal of the National Medical Association* 93, no. 3 (2001): 11S–34S; Susan Craddock, *City of Plagues: Disease, Poverty, and Deviance in San Francisco* (University of Minnesota Press, 2004); Nancy Bristow, *American Pandemic: The Lost Worlds of the 1918 Influenza Epidemic* (Oxford University Press, 2012); Elizabeth Schlabach, "The Influenza Epidemic and Jim Crow Public Health Policies and Practices in Chicago, 1917–1921," *The Journal of African American History* 104, no. 1 (2019): 31–58.

62. Samuel Roberts, *Infectious Fear Politics, Disease, and the Health Effects of Segregation* (University of North Carolina Press, 2009), 110–30 and 148–55.

63. California State Board of Health, "Report of the California State Board of Health, 1870–1871" (D. W. Gelwicks, 1871), 5; San Francisco Board of Supervisors, "Report of Special Committee on the Condition of the Chinese Quarter," 208; Otis Gibson, *The Chinese in America* (Hitcock and Walden, 1877). Also see Craddock, *City of Plagues*, and Guenter Risse, Plague, Fear, and Politics in San Francisco's Chinatown (Johns Hopkins University Press, 2012), 68.

64. *San Francisco Municipal Reports for the Fiscal Year 1901–1902* (Commercial Publishing Co., 1902), 491; *Public Health Reports*, vol. XVI, Part II, 2837 (Government Printing Office, 1902); Vernon Link, "A History of Plague in the United States of America," *Public Health Monograph* 26, Publication 392 (Government Printing Office, 1955), 3–4. Digitized versions of historical public health reports are additionally available at https://stacks.cdc.gov/.

65. Samuel Gompers and Herman Gutstadt, *Meat vs. Rice: American Manhood Against Asiatic Coolieism* (Asiatic Exclusion League, 1908). Also quoted in "Removal of Chinatown Urged," *San Francisco Call*, November 22, 1902.

66. See *Wong Wai v. Williamson*, 103 Fed. Rep. 1 (1900), and *Jew Ho v. Williamson*, 103 Fed. Rep. 10 (1900).

67. Joan Trauner, "The Chinese as Medical Scapegoats in San Francisco, 1870–1905," *California History* 57, no. 1 (1978): 70–87; Charles McClain, "Of Medicine, Race, and American Law: The Bubonic Plague Outbreak of 1900," *Law and Social Inquiry* 13, no. 3 (1988): 447–513; Howard Markel, *Quarantine!*

East European Jewish Immigrants and the New York City Epidemics of 1892 (Johns Hopkins University Press, 1999); Molina, *Fit to Be Citizens?*; Risse, *Plague, Fear, and Politics.*

68. Kramer, "The Beginnings of the Public Health Movement in the United States."

69. "Doctors Will Not Reply," *New York Times*, May 29, 1890; "Debts, Disease and the Census," *Chicago Tribune*, May 28, 1890; "A Vicious Measure," *Montpelier Examiner*, March 20, 1903.

70. "The Scourge of the Century," *Lincoln County Leader*, May 11, 1900. Also see Risse, *Plague, Fear, and Politics*, 118 and 143.

71. Council of Hygiene and Public Health, 44; Abbott, *Past and Present Condition of Public Hygiene*, 19.

72. Philip Abrams, "Notes on the Difficulty of Studying the State (1977)," 68.

73. Quoted in Fairchild et al., *Searching Eyes*, 6. Also see Samuel Osgood, *Health and the Higher Culture: A Discourse Delivered Before the American Public Health Association in Philadelphia by Samuel Osgood* (E.P. Dutton and Company, 1878), 4.

74. For a classic statement, see Niccolo Machiavelli, *The Prince and Other Writings* (Simon and Schuster, 2014).

75. See *Seavey v. Preble*, 64 Me. 120 (1874); *Labrie v. Manchester*, 59 N.H. 120 (1879); *Farmington v. Jones*, 36 N.H. 271 (1858); *Inhabitants of Kennebunk v. Inhabitants of Alfred*, 19 Me. 221 (1841).

76. David J. Seipp, "The Right to Privacy in Nineteenth Century America," *Harvard Law Review* 94, no. 8 (1981): 1892–910.

77. Fairchild et al., *Searching Eyes*; Igo, *The Known Citizen.*

78. *Metropolitan Bd. of Health v. Heister*, 37 N.Y. 661 (1868).

79. *State v. Peirce*, 87 Vt. 144 (1913); *Michigan v. Brady*, 90 Mich. 490 (1892); *Michigan v. Shurly*, 131 Mich. 177 (1902); *Johnson v. District of Columbia*, 27 App. D.C. 259 (1906); *Chicago v. Craig*, 172 Ill. App. 126 (1912); *Pennsylvania v. Evans*, 59 Pa. Super 607 (1915).

80. McClain, "Of Medicine, Race, and American Law," 510; John Fabian Witt, *American Contagions: Epidemics and the Law from Smallpox to COVID-19* (Yale University Press, 2020).

81. Agamben, *State of Exception.*

82. Richard R. John, *Spreading the News: The American Postal System from Franklin to Morse* (Harvard University Press, 1998); Winifred Gallagher, *How the Post Office Created America: A History* (Penguin, 2016); Devin Leonard, *Neither Snow nor Rain: A History of the United States Postal Service* (Grove Press, 2016).

83. Gaillard Hunt, ed., *Journals from the Continental Congress 1774–1789, Volume 23* (Government Printing Office, 1914), 671. Also see Anuj C. Desai, "Wiretapping Before the Wires: The Post Office and the Rebirth of Communications Privacy," *Stanford Law Review* 60 (2007): 553–94.

84. "Scrapbook of Circulars, Notices, Instructions, Regulations, and Newspaper Clippings, 1823–1871," USNA Record PI-168, 27.

85. "U.S. Postal Bulletins, Vol. 37, Issue 11218," December 9, 1916. Digitized versions of historical postal bulletins are also available at http://www.uspostal bulletins.com/.
86. "Records of the Inspection Office at New York, 4/27/1907–10/7/1908," USNA Record PI-168, 240.
87. Leonard, *Neither Snow nor Rain.*
88. "Records of the Inspection Office at New York, 4/27/1907–10/7/1908," Box 2. For an overview of birth control legislation, see Jacob C. Ruppenthal, "Criminal Statutes on Birth Control," *Journal of Criminal Law and Criminology* 10 (1919): 48–61.
89. Anthony Comstock, *Frauds Exposed. Or, How the People Are Deceived and Robbed, and Youth Corrupted* (J. Howard Brown, 1880), 391. Also see Heywood Broun and Margaret Leech, *Anthony Comstock: Roundsman of the Lord* (Literary Guild of America, 1927).
90. Craig L. LaMay, "America's Censor: Anthony Comstock and Free Speech," *Communications and the Law* 19, no. 3 (1997): 1–59.
91. "Records of the Inspection Office at Philadelphia, 1896–1909," Box 13, Document 603, USNA Record PI-168, 239.
92. "Records of the Inspection Office at New York, 4/27/1907–10/7/1908," Box 1, Documents 55–57, 156, 288, and 293, USNA Record PI-168, 239; "Records of the Inspection Office at Philadelphia, 1896–1909," Box 16, Documents 200, 230, 232, 459, 888, and 969, USNA Record PI-168, 239.
93. "Records of the Inspection Office at New York, 4/27/1907–10/7/1908," Box 1, Document 596. Also see Documents 606 and 609.
94. "Records of the Inspection Office at Denver, 12/20/1879–5/8/1907," Box 11, USNA Record PI-168, 238.
95. "Post Office Department. Identification Notices 1899–1910," USNA Record A1 270. Also see James C. N. Paul and Murray L. Schwartz, "Obscenity in the Mails: A Comment on Some Problems of Federal Censorship," *University of Pennsylvania Law Review* 106 (1957): 214–53.
96. "Publicity Materials Concerning Postal Crimes and Mail Frauds, 1931–1945," Box 1, USNA Record UD-173.
97. "Records of the Inspection Office at New York, 4/27/1907–10/7/1908," Box 1, Document 583.
98. Quoted in Christopher Capozzola, *Uncle Sam Wants You: World War I and the Making of the Modern American Citizen* (Oxford University Press, 2008), 151.
99. "Records of the Censorship Board, 1917–1918," Box 3, February 2018, USNA Record PI-168, 17. Because the legal frameworks were relatively vague, local officials had considerable leeway to decide how wartime censorship would be operationalized.
100. "Records of the Censorship Board," Box 2, September 1918. Also see Morris E. Cohn, "The Censorship of Radical Materials by the Post Office," *Washington University Law Review* 17, no. 2 (1932): 95–119.

101. "Notice," *Elk County Advocate*, April 24, 1873.
102. Quoted in Seipp, "The Right to Privacy in American History," 40. Also see "Congress and the Western Union Telegraph Company," *The Telegrapher*, January 6, 1877.
103. "A Serious Charge," *Clinch Valley News*, August 23, 1912; "The Honor of the Post Office," *The Evening World*, March 3, 1913; "Writing—By the Card," *New York Times*, July 10, 1872.
104. "Passing of Autocracy Looked Upon as Advent of Great Nation," *Deming Graphic*, December 15, 1905.
105. "The Honor of the Post Office," *Evening World*, March 3, 1913.
106. "Privacy of the Mail Not Invaded," *San Francisco Call*, June 11, 1898.
107. "Writing—By the Card," *New York Times*, July 10, 1872.
108. Holbrook, *Ten Years Among the Mail Bags*; "Scrapbook of Circulars, Notices, Instructions, Regulations, and Newspaper Clippings, 1823–1871," USNA Record PI-168, 27; "Records Relating to Postal Devices for City Delivery, 12/1908–8/1911," USNA Record ID 194389; "Records Relating to Post Office Boxes (Lockboxes), 1894–1934," Box 2, USNA Record PI-168, 174.
109. Postal Bulletins, 1916. Also see Section 522 of the Postal Laws and Regulations of 1916 and Order 10142 of the Postmaster General.
110. "Letters to Santa Claus," *Evening Times*, December 18, 1900.
111. "Records of the Inspection Office at New York, 4/27/1907–10/7/1908," Box 1, Documents 55–57.
112. "Privacy of the Mail Not Invaded," *San Francisco Call*, June 11, 1898; "A Serious Charge," *Clinch Valley News*, August 23, 1912; "Plays in with Cliques," *Tacoma Times*, December 26, 1916.
113. *Ex parte Jackson*, 96 U.S. 727 (1878); *Abrams v. United States*, 250 U.S. 616 (1919). Also see Postal Laws and Regulations of 1887, Section 508.
114. "Records of the Inspection Office at New York, 4/27/1907–10/7/1908," Box 2.
115. "Records of the Censorship Board, 1917–1918," Box 3, USNA Record PI-168, 17.
116. Seipp, "The Right to Privacy in Nineteenth Century America."
117. Novak et al., "Democratic States of Unexception," 232.
118. For related discussions, see Stephen J. Collier, "Topologies of Power: Foucault's Analysis of Political Government Beyond 'Governmentality,'" *Theory, Culture and Society* 26, no. 6 (2009): 79; William Petersen, *Ethnicity Counts* (Transaction, 1997); Bowker and Star, *Sorting Things Out*; Margot Canaday, *The Straight State: Sexuality and Citizenship in Twentieth-Century America* (Princeton University Press, 2009); Caitlin Rosenthal, *Accounting for Slavery* (Harvard University Press, 2018).
119. James Bamford, "They Know Much More Than You Think," *New York Review of Books*, August 15, 2013, accessed September 22, 2022, https://www.nybooks.com/articles/2013/08/15/nsa-they-know-much-more-you-think.
120. Skowronek, *Building a New American State*; David Lyon, ed., *Surveillance as Social Sorting: Privacy, Risk, and Digital Discrimination* (Routledge, 2003). Michael Mann acknowledges that bureaucratic organizations store "a massive

amount of information about all of us," but this is commonly seen in studies of American political development as an ancillary feature of organizational capacity and thus denied standing as an independent object of inquiry. For example, two important scholars of the American state, Steven Skowronek and Brian Balogh, discuss the production of state knowledge primarily as a means of administrative bookkeeping—not as an instrumental part of the state's infrastructural power—or focus on the increasing visibility of state power to the American populace but without a corresponding discussion of the shifting visibility of that populace to the bureaucratic state. See Michael Mann, "The Autonomous Power of the State: Its Origins, Mechanisms, and Results," *European Journal of Sociology* 25, no. 2 (1984): 189; Skowronek, *Building a New American State*, 188; Balogh, *A Government out of Sight*.

121. Warren and Brandeis, "The Right to Privacy," 215–16.

122. Warren and Brandeis, "The Right to Privacy," 216.

123. Kim Scheppele, "Autocratic Legalism," *The University of Chicago Law Review* 85, no. 2 (2018): 545–84.

124. *Olmstead v. United States*, 277 U.S. at 478–79 (1928) (Brandeis, J., dissenting).

125. Colyvas and Jonsson, "Ubiquity and Legitimacy," 44; Elisabeth S. Clemens and James M. Cook, "Politics and Institutionalism: Explaining Durability and Change," *Annual Review of Sociology* 25, no. 1 (1999): 441–66; Orren and Skowronek, *The Policy State*; Paul Pierson, "Increasing Returns, Path Dependence, and the Study of Politics," *American Political Science Review* 94, no. 2 (2000): 251–67.

126. Fiske, "Surveilling the City"; Browne, *Dark Matters*; Brayne, "Big Data Surveillance"; Sabrina Alimahomed-Wilson, "When the FBI Knocks: Racialized State Surveillance of Muslims," *Critical Sociology* 45, no. 6 (2019): 871–87; Julia Angwin, *Dragnet Nation: A Quest for Privacy, Security, and Freedom in a World of Relentless Surveillance* (Times, 2014); Adriana C. Nuñez, "Collateral Subjects: The Normalization of Surveillance for Mexican Americans on the Border," *Sociology of Race and Ethnicity* 6, no. 4 (2020): 548–61; Anita L. Allen. "Dismantling the Black Opticon: Race Equity and Online Privacy and Data Protection Reform." *Yale Law Journal* 131 (2022): 907–59.

127. Anthony et al., "Toward a Sociology of Privacy"; Igo, *The Known Citizen*, 157.

128. Evan Perez, "Secret Court's Oversight Gets Scrutiny," *Wall Street Journal*, June 9, 2013, accessed December 7, 2023, https://www.wsj.com/articles/SB100014 24127887324904004578535670310514616.

129. See, for example, sections 1798.105(d) and 1798.145 of the California Civil Code.

130. See section 1798.99.80 of the California Civil Code.

CONCLUSION: PRIVACY IN AN AGE OF SURVEILLANCE

1. Solove, "Introduction: Privacy Self-Management and the Consent Dilemma"; Cohen, "What Privacy Is For"; Pilpel, "The Challenge of Privacy." See Dworkin,

"The Younger Committee Report on Privacy," for why privacy is difficult to define. Also see Day, "Perspectives on Privacy," for a list of competing definitions in the Anglo-American literature.

2. Hannah Arendt, *The Human Condition* (University of Chicago Press, 1958), 35; Regan, *Legislating Privacy*, xiv; Kasper, "Privacy as a Social Good."

3. This focus on specific struggles has conceptual similarities to John Dewey's emphasis on the concrete "situations" of life as objects of study and catalysts of social change. See John Dewey, *The Later Works (1925–1953)*, vol. 12 (Southern Illinois University Press, 1981), 72. For another theoretical treatment of this argument, also see Harrison White, *Identity and Control: How Social Formations Emerge* (Princeton University Press, 2008).

4. For related discussions of surveillance, see Marx, "What's New About the 'New Surveillance'?"; Cohen, "What Privacy Is For"; Samantha Barbas, "Saving Privacy From History," *DePaul Law Review* 61 (2011): 973–1048; Kirstie Ball, "Organization, Surveillance, and the Body: Towards a Politics of Resistance," in *Theorizing Surveillance*, ed. David Lyon (Routledge, 2006), 296–317.

5. Colyvas and Jonsson, "Ubiquity and Legitimacy," 39.

6. In Bourdieusian terms, privacy norms became "structuring structures" across different institutional contexts. See Pierre Bourdieu, *Distinction: A Social Critique of the Judgement of Taste* (Harvard University Press, 1984), 170.

7. David Lyon, "Surveillance: History, Technology, Culture," in *Histories of State Surveillance in Europe and Beyond*, ed. Kees Boersma et al. (Routledge, 2014), 32–45.

8. Colyvas and Jonsson, "Ubiquity and Legitimacy," 28–30.

9. For another analysis of legal emergence and institutionalization, see: Jenness, "The Emergence, Content, and Institutionalization of Hate Crime Law."

10. Richardson, *The Right to Privacy*; Helen Trouille, "Private Life and Public Image: Privacy Legislation in France," *The International and Comparative Law Quarterly* 49, no. 1 (2000): 199–208.

11. For a discussion of the Prussian sociopolitical and economic order, see Anthony Giddens, ed., "The Political Context of Weber's Sociology," in *Politics and Sociology in the Thought of Max Weber* (Polity, 1972): 28–39.

12. Still farther to the east, in the Ottoman Empire, Sultan Abdul Hamid II governed from 1876 to 1909 through an expansive network of secret police agents (to quell domestic opposition in a fracturing imperial state and to counter the influence of foreign imperial powers) but also defended the noninterference of the state in so-called family matters. See Priya Satia, *Spies in Arabia: The Great War and the Cultural Foundations of Britain's Covert Empire in the Middle East* (Oxford University Press, 2008); Yaron Ayalon, "Ottoman Urban Privacy in Light of Disaster Recovery," *International Journal of Middle East Studies* 43, no. 3 (2011): 513–28.

13. For a discussion of privacy as a differentiating feature during the Cold War, see Nelson, *Pursuing Privacy in Cold War America*.

14. Nicole A. Moreham, "The Right to Respect for Private Life in the European Convention on Human Rights: A Re-Examination," *European Human Rights Law Review* 44 (2008), Victoria University of Wellington Legal Research Paper No. 11/2019.

15. James Mahoney has argued that institutionalization is at the core of so-called path dependencies. See James Mahoney, "Path Dependence in Historical Sociology," *Theory and Society* 29, no. 4 (2000): 507–48. Also see Andrew Abbott, *Time Matters: On Theory and Method* (University of Chicago Press, 2001), 257.

16. Denenberg, "Privacy: Wanted but Vague." For a discussion of Nixon's legacy and the Privacy Act of 1974, also see Jerome J. Hanus and Harold C. Relyea, "A Policy Assessment of the Privacy Act of 1974," *American University Law Review* 25, no. 3 (1975): 555–93.

17. Sami Coll, "Power, Knowledge, and the Subjects of Privacy: Understanding Privacy as the Ally of Surveillance," *Information, Communication and Society* 17, no. 10 (2014): 1250–63.

18. Waldman, "Privacy Law's False Promise." Also see Cohen, *Between Truth and Power*.

19. See Ziegler, *Beyond Abortion*, 21, for the argument that privacy did not become a salient political issue until the mid-1960s. Also see Rule et al., *The Politics of Privacy*.

20. Westin, *Privacy and Freedom*; Rule et al., "Documentary Identification"; Igo, *The Known Citizen*.

21. Lyon, *The Electronic Eye*; Rule, *Private Lives and Public Surveillance*, 36.

22. *Griswold v. Connecticut*, 381 U.S. 479 (1965), *Roe v. Wade*, 410 U.S. 113 (1972). For an overview of abortion jurisprudence and privacy, see Ziegler, *Beyond Abortion*.

23. Rule, *Private Lives and Public Surveillance*.

24. Solove, "Introduction: Privacy Self-Management and the Consent Dilemma," 1880ff; Lyon, *The Culture of Surveillance*.

25. Westin, *Privacy and Freedom*, 7.

26. For a similar argument, focused on the limitations of a consent-based approach, see Solove, "Introduction: Privacy Self-Management and the Consent Dilemma."

27. Alfred W. McCoy, *Policing America's Empire: The United States, the Philippines, and the Rise of the Surveillance State* (University of Wisconsin Press, 2009); James K. Davis, ed., *Spying on America: The FBI's Domestic Counterintelligence Program* (Bloomsbury, 1992); Nelkin and Andrews, "Surveillance Creep in the Genetic Age," 108; David Lyon, "9/11, Synopticon, and Scopophilia: Watching and Being Watched," in *The New Politics of Surveillance and Visibility*, ed. Kevin Haggerty and Richard Ericson (University of Toronto Press, 2005), 35–54.

28. McCoy, *Policing America's Empire*; Jeffrey L. Vagle, "Tightening the OODA Loop: Police Militarization, Race, and Algorithmic Surveillance," *Michigan*

Journal of Race and Law 22 (2016): 101–37; Lynne M. Pochurek, "From the Battlefront to the Homefront: Infrared Surveillance and the War on Drugs Place Privacy Under Siege," *St. Thomas Law Review* 7 (1994): 137–68.

29. Dandeker, *Surveillance, Power and Modernity*; Koopman, *How We Became Our Data*; Igo, *The Averaged American*; Torpey, *The Invention of the Passport*; Rule et al., "Documentary Identification"; Scott, *Seeing Like a State*; Tooze, *Statistics and the German State*; Grommé and Scheel, "Doing Statistics, Enacting the Nation"; Foucault, *Security, Territory, Population*; Foucault, *The Birth of Biopolitics*; Nobles, *Shades of Citizenship*; Kertzer and Arel, *Census and Identity*; Loveman, *National Colors*.

30. Bouk, "The History and Political Economy of Personal Data"; Fourcade and Gordon, "Learning Like a State"; Mau, *The Metric Society*.

31. Westin, *Privacy and Freedom*; Zuboff, *The Age of Surveillance Capitalism*; Rule, *Private Lives and Public Surveillance*; Marion Fourcade, "Ordinalization: Lewis A. Coser Memorial Award for Theoretical Agenda Setting 2014," *Sociological Theory* 34, no. 3 (2016): 175–95.

32. Foucault, *The Birth of Biopolitics*; Frank Webster and Kevin Robins, *Information Technology: A Luddite Analysis* (Ablex, 1986); Rule, *Private Lives and Public Surveillance*.

33. Rob Kling, "The Struggles for Democracy in an Information Society," *The Information Society* 4, no. 1–2 (1986): 1–7; Zygmunt Bauman, *Liquid Modernity* (Polity, 2000); Bogard, *The Simulation of Surveillance*; Haggerty and Ericson, "The Surveillant Assemblage"; Brayne, "Big Data Surveillance."

34. Lyon, *Surveillance as Social Sorting*; Richard V. Ericson and Kevin D. Haggerty, *Policing the Risk Society* (University of Toronto Press, 1997); Fourcade and Healy, *The Ordinal Society*.

35. Lyon, *The Electronic Eye*; Lyon, *The Culture of Surveillance*; Josh Lauer and Kenneth Lipartito, *Surveillance Capitalism in America* (University of Pennsylvania Press, 2021); Carruthers, "From Uncertainty Toward Risk"; Fourcade and Healy, "Seeing Like a Market."

36. Foucault, *The Birth of Biopolitics*; Ivan Manokha, "Surveillance, Panopticism, and Self-Discipline in the Digital Age," *Surveillance and Society* 16, no. 2 (2018): 219–37; Fourcade and Healy, *The Ordinal Society*; Anthony et al., "Toward a Sociology of Privacy"; Igo, *The Known Citizen*.

37. Igo, *The Known Citizen*, 16; Barbas, "Saving Privacy from History"; John Naughton, "Is Privacy Dead?," *The New Statesman*, February 28, 2020; Whitaker, *The End of Privacy*.

38. Yuval Noah Harari, "Dataism Is Our New God," *New Perspectives Quarterly* 34, no. 2 (2017): 36–43.

39. Martin Enserink and Gilbert Chin, "The End of Privacy," *Science* 347, no. 6221 (2015): 491; John Naughton, "Slouching Towards Dystopia," *The New Statesman*, February 26, 2020, accessed May 5, 2022, https://www.newstatesman.com/2020/02/slouching-towards-dystopia-rise-surveillance-capitalism-and-death-privacy.

40. Shils, "Privacy."

41. Kling, "The Struggles for Democracy in an Information Society," 3.

42. Scott Skinner-Thompson, *Privacy at the Margins* (Cambridge University Press, 2020); Whitaker, *The End of Privacy*.

43. Simitis, "Reviewing Privacy in an Information Society," 733.

44. Calvin C. Gotlieb, "Privacy: A Concept Whose Time Has Come and Gone," in *Computers, Surveillance, and Privacy*, ed. David Lyon and Elia Zureik (University of Minnesota Press, 1996), 156–71. For a discussion of consumer attitudes, see chapter 8 in Igo, *The Known Citizen*, and Alastair R. Beresford et al., "Unwillingness to Pay for Privacy: A Field Experiment," *Economics Letters* 117, no. 1 (2012): 25–27. For a Marxist critique of privacy, see Neocleous, "Privacy, Secrecy, Idiocy."

45. Haggerty and Ericson, "The Surveillant Assemblage"; Lyon, "9/11, Synopticon, and Scopophilia"; Allen, "Dismantling the Black Opticon"; Raley, "Dataveillance and Countervailance"; Whitaker, *The End of Privacy*. For a critique of the panoptic metaphor, see David Lyon, "An Electronic Panopticon? A Sociological Critique of Surveillance Theory," *The Sociological Review* 41, no. 4 (1993): 653–78.

46. Jeremy Bentham, *Panopticon, or the Inspection House* (T. Payne, 1791), 1–4. Also see pp. 5–41 for a detailed discussion of different architectural and social aspects of panoptic penitentiaries. See Foucault, *Discipline and Punish*, especially 195ff, for a conceptualization of panopticism in modern society.

47. For a similar characterization, see Lyon, "An Electronic Panopticon?," 654ff.

48. Gilles Deleuze, "Postscript on the Societies of Control," in *Surveillance, Crime and Social Control*, ed. Clive Norris and Dean Wilson (Routledge, 2017), 35–39.

49. Vivian Aplin-Brownlee, "Ethical Questions Arise from Computers Biting Into Privacy: Computer Explosion Unearths New Questions of Ethics, Privacy," *Washington Post*, May 23, 1984. Also quoted in Kieran Healy, "The Performativity of Networks," *European Journal of Sociology* 56, no. 2 (2015): 188

50. Haggerty and Ericson, "The Surveillant Assemblage."

51. Giorgio Agamben, *Homo Sacer: Sovereign Power and Bare Life* (Stanford University Press, 1998), 104.

52. Bogard, *The Simulation of Surveillance*; Raley, "Dataveillance and Countervailance"; Steve Mann and Joseph Ferenbok, "New Media and the Power Politics of Sousveillance in a Surveillance-Dominated World," *Surveillance and Society* 11, no. 1–2 (2013): 18–34; Browne, *Dark Matters*, 18–20.

53. William Bogard, "Welcome to the Society of Control: The Simulation of Surveillance Revisited," in *The New Politics of Surveillance and Visibility*, ed. Kevin Haggerty and Richard Ericson (University of Toronto Press, 2005), 55–78.

54. Foucault traces this historical arc across several books and within an analytic framework that shifts slightly from his early emphasis on epistemes toward a subsequent focus on more specific techniques and technologies of rule. See Foucault, *Discipline and Punish*; Foucault, *Security, Territory, Population*; Foucault, *The Birth of Biopolitics*.

55. Steve Mann and Joseph Ferenbok, "New Media and the Power Politics of Sousveillance in a Surveillance-Dominated World," *Surveillance and Society* 11, no. 1/2 (2013): 18–34.

56. Thomas Pettitt, "The Privacy Parenthesis: Gutenberg, Homo Clausus, and the Networked Self," accessed June 24, 2021, http://web.mit.edu/comm-forum/mit8 /papers/TomPettitt%20Paper.pdf

57. Pettitt, "The Privacy Parenthesis."

58. Fourcade and Healy, *The Ordinal Society*, 260.

59. Marx, "What's New About the 'New Surveillance'?"; Browne, *Dark Matters*; Lauer and Lipartito, *Surveillance Capitalism in America*; Lauer, "Surveillance History and the History of New Media"; Dandeker, *Surveillance, Power, and Modernity*; David Lyon, "Surveillance Technology and Surveillance Society," in *Modernity and Technology*, ed. Thomas J. Misa et al. (MIT Press, 2003), 173.

60. Cora Currier, "The Kill Chain," *The Intercept*, accessed December 8, 2023, https:// theintercept.com/drone-papers/the-kill-chain.

61. Bruno Latour, *Science in Action: How to Follow Scientists and Engineers Through Society* (Harvard University Press, 1987), 235.

62. Gavison, "Privacy and the Limits of Law," 423.

63. Kevin Haggerty and Richard Ericson, eds., *The New Politics of Surveillance and Visibility* (University of Toronto Press, 2005), 6.

64. Fourcade and Healy, *The Ordinal Society*; Harcourt, "Against Prediction."

65. Lyon, "An Electronic Panopticon?," 675; Friedrich Nietzsche, *Human, All Too Human: A Book for Free Spirits* (Penguin Classics, 1994).

66. Goffman, *Asylums*; Anil Kalhan, "The Fourth Amendment and Privacy Implications of Interior Immigration Enforcement," *UC Davis Law Review* 41 (2007): 1137–1218; Eubanks, *Automating Inequality*. Also see Carol Warren and Barbara Laslett, "Privacy and Secrecy: A Conceptual Comparison," *Journal of Social Issues* 33, no. 3 (1977): 43–51.

67. Muhammad, *The Condemnation of Blackness*; Browne, *Dark Matters*.

68. Eubanks, *Automating Inequality*. Also see Carol A. Chase, "Privacy Takes a Back Seat: Putting the Automobile Exception Back on Track After Several Wrong Turns," *Boston College Law Review* 41 (1999): 71–102; Louise Amoore, "Security and the Claim to Privacy," *International Political Sociology* 8, no. 1 (2014): 108–12; Ioanna Tourkochoriti, "The Transatlantic Flow of Data and the National Security Exception in the European Data Privacy Regulation: In Search for Legal Protection Against Surveillance," *University of Pennsylvania Journal of International Law* 36 (2014): 459–524; Gina R. Bohannon, "Cell Phones and the Border Search Exception: Circuits Split Over the Line Between Sovereignty and Privacy," *Maryland Law Review* 78 (2018): 563–603.

69. Bridges, *The Poverty of Privacy Rights*.

70. Nippert-Eng, *Islands of Privacy*, 164; Oscar H. Gandy Jr., "Quixotics Unite! Engaging the Pragmatists on Rational Discrimination," in *Theorizing Surveillance*, ed. David Lyon (Routledge, 2006), 318–36; Neocleous, "Privacy,

Secrecy, Idiocy"; Kasper, "Privacy as a Social Good"; Anthony et al., "Toward a Sociology of Privacy"; Cohen, *Between Truth and Power.*

71. Neocleus, "Privacy, Secrecy, Idiocy," 103 and 105; Kasper, "Privacy as a Social Good," 166.

72. Mark Poster, "Hardt and Negri's Information Empire: A Critical Response," *Cultural Politics* 1, no. 1 (2005): 101–18; Pierre Bourdieu, *On the State: Lectures at the College of France, 1989–1992* (Polity, 2014), 6; Skowronek, *Building a New American State*; Morgan and Orloff, "The Many Hands of the State"; Skocpol, "State Formation and Social Policy in the United States"; Novak et al., "Democratic States of Unexception."

73. Keith Breckenridge and Simon Szreter, *Registration and Recognition: Documenting the Person in World History* (Oxford University Press, 2012), 299. Also see pp. 1–38.

74. Gary T. Marx, "Varieties of Personal Information as Influences on Attitudes Towards Surveillance," in *The New Politics of Surveillance and Visibility*, ed. Kevin Haggerty and Richard Ericson (University of Toronto Press, 2005), 79–110.

75. Igo, *The Known Citizen*; Simmel, "The Secret and the Secret Society"; Fuchs, "Towards an Alternative Concept of Privacy," 221; Etzioni, *The Limits of Privacy*; Nock, *The Costs of Privacy.*

76. Koopman, *How We Became Our Data.* Also see Calder, *Financing the American Dream*; Lauer, "From Rumor to Written Record."

77. George Hudson, "Traits of Trade—Laudable and Iniquitous," *The Merchants Magazine and Commercial Review* 29 (1853): 52. Also cited in Lauer, "From Rumor to Written Record."

78. Rob Aitken, "All Data Is Credit Data: Constituting the Unbanked," *Competition and Change* 21, no. 4 (2017): 274–300.

79. Igo, *The Known Citizen*, 98.

80. Franny Choi, "Unrequited Love Song for the Panopticon," *New York Times*, January 3, 2020, accessed February 15, 2020, https://www.nytimes.com/interactive/2020/01/03/opinion/franny-choi-privacy-poem.html.

81. Daniel Mendelsohn, "But Enough About Me," *New Yorker*, January 17, 2010, accessed November 22, 2022, https://www.newyorker.com/magazine/2010/01/25/but-enough-about-me-2. Also quoted in Igo, *The Known Citizen*, 344. Also see Lyon, *The Electronic Eye*, 76.

82. Walter Lionel George, "The Gentlest Art," *Harper's Magazine* (November 1918): 864–71; Huey, "A Social Movement for Privacy/Against Surveillance." But see Colin J. Bennett, *The Privacy Advocates: Resisting the Spread of Surveillance* (MIT Press, 2010); Emilio Lehoucq and Sidney Tarrow, "The Rise of a Transnational Movement to Protect Privacy," *Mobilization* 25, no. 2 (2020): 161–84; Skinner-Thompson, *Privacy at the Margins.*

83. For emerging challenges related to the increasing availability of genetic information, see Ellen Wright Clayton et al., "The Law of Genetic Privacy: Applications, Implications, and Limitations," *Journal of Law and the Biosciences* 6, no. 1 (2019): 1–36.

84. Coll, "Power, Knowledge, and the Subjects of Privacy"; James B. Rule, *Taking Privacy Seriously: How to Create the Rights We Need While We Still Have Something to Protect* (University of California Press, 2024).
85. Solove, "Conceptualizing Privacy," 1880.
86. For a similar argument—that the solution is not less technology but better politics—see Rule, *Taking Privacy Seriously.*
87. For a similar argument, see Samuel Moyn, *Liberalism Against Itself: Cold War Intellectuals and the Making of Our Times* (Yale University Press, 2023), 11.
88. Fourcade and Healy, *The Ordinal Society*, 187ff.
89. Nelson, *Pursing Privacy in Cold War America*, xx.

METHODOLOGICAL CODA

1. Damon Mayrl and Nicholas Hoover Wilson, "What Do Historical Sociologists Do All Day? Analytic Architectures in Historical Sociology," *American Journal of Sociology* 125, no. 5 (2020): 1345–94; Barkey, "Historical Sociology"; Merton, *Social Theory and Social Structure*; White, *Identity and Control: How Social Formations Emerge*; Mario L. Small, "How to Conduct a Mixed Methods Study: Recent Trends in a Rapidly Growing Literature," *Annual Review of Sociology* 37 (2011): 57–86; Lisa D. Pearce, "Mixed Methods Inquiry in Sociology," *American Behavioral Scientist* 56, no. 6 (2012): 829–48.
2. For fuller treatment of this approach, see Charles Tilly, "To Explain Political Processes," *American Journal of Sociology* 100, no. 6 (1995): 1594–610; Marshall Sahlins, *Islands of History* (University of Chicago Press, 1985); William H. Sewell, "Historical Events as Transformations of Structures: Inventing Revolution at the Bastille," *Theory and Society* 25, no. 6 (1996): 841–81; Barkey, "Historical Sociology." Also see Johan Goudsblom, *Sociology in the Balance* (Columbia University Press, 1977).
3. Norbert Elias, *What Is Sociology?* (Columbia University Press, 1978), 118. Also see Andrew Abbott, *Processual Sociology* (University of Chicago Press, 2016); George Herbert Mead, *The Philosophy of the Present* (University of Chicago Press, 1932).
4. Peter Hall, "Aligning Ontology and Methodology in Comparative Politics," in *Comparative Historical Analysis in the Social Sciences*, ed. James Mahoney and Dietrich Rueschemeyer (Cambridge University Press, 2003), 373–404.
5. Tilly, "To Explain Political Processes," 1605.
6. Colyvas and Jonsson, "Ubiquity and Legitimacy," 28.
7. The term "world-making" comes from Ian Hacking and Pierre Bourdieu, who saw the symbolic power of naming as one aspect of the political power to create social order. See Bourdieu, "The Force of Law," 838; Nelson Goodman, *Ways of Worldmaking* (Hackett, 1978).
8. Steven Ruggles et al., *IPUMS Ancestry Full Count Data: Version 3.0* [dataset] (IPUMS, 2021).

9. U.S. Bureau of the Census, *Historical Statistics of the United States: Colonial Times to 1970, Bicentennial Edition* (Government Printing Office, 1976); National Center for Education Statistics, *120 Years of American Education*.

10. *Chronicling America: Historic American Newspapers* [dataset] (Library of Congress, 2007), https://chroniclingamerica.loc.gov/; Mark Davies, *The Corpus of Historical American English: 400 Million Words, 1810–2009* [dataset] (Brigham Young University, 2010), https://www.english-corpora.org/coha.

11. *Google Books Corpus of American English: Version googlebooks-eng-us-20200217* [dataset] (Google, 2020), https://books.google.com/ngrams.

12. Ravi Illango, "Using NLP (BERT) to Improve OCR Accuracy," accessed January 20, 2022, https://www.statestitle.com/resource/using-nlp-bert-to-improve-ocr-accuracy; Ismet Zeki Yalniz and Raghavan Manmatha, "A Fast Alignment Scheme for Automatic OCR Evaluation of Books," in *2011 International Conference on Document Analysis and Recognition* (IEEE, 2011), 754–58.

13. Long Ma and Yanqing Zhang, "Using Word2Vec to Process Big Text Data," in *IEEE International Conference on Big Data (Big Data) 2015* (IEEE, 2015), 2895–97; Kenneth W. Church, "Word2Vec," *Natural Language Engineering* 23, no. 1 (2017): 155–62; Austin C. Kozlowski et al., "The Geometry of Culture: Analyzing the Meanings of Class Through Word Embeddings," *American Sociological Review* 84, no. 5 (2019): 905–49; Marc-Etienne Brunet et al., "Understanding the Origins of Bias in Word Embeddings," in *International Conference on Machine Learning 2019* (ICML, 2019), 803–11; Yoav Goldberg, *Neural Network Methods for Natural Language Processing* (Morgan & Claypool, 2017), 90–95; Pedro Rodriguez and Arthur Spirling, "Word Embeddings: What Works, What Doesn't, and How to Tell the Difference for Applied Research," *The Journal of Politics* 84, no. 1 (2021): 101–15.

14. Julie Weeds and David Weir, "Co-occurrence Retrieval: A Flexible Framework for Lexical Distributional Similarity," *Computational Linguistics* 31, no. 4 (2005): 439–75; Hamilton et al., "Cultural Shift or Linguistic Drift?"

15. Jiawei Han et al., *Data Mining: Concepts and Techniques* (Elsevier, 2011).

16. Nikhil Garg et al., "Word Embeddings Quantify 100 Years of Gender and Ethnic Stereotypes," *Proceedings of the National Academy of Sciences* 115, no. 16 (2018): E3635–44.

17. Thomas Hofmann, "Unsupervised Learning by Probabilistic Latent Semantic Analysis," *Machine Learning* 42, no. 1 (2001): 177–96.

18. Antoniak and Mimno, "Evaluating the Stability of Embedding-Based Word Similarities."

19. Rodrigo Pasti et al., "A Sensitivity and Performance Analysis of Word2Vec Applied to Emotion State Classification Using a Deep Neural Architecture," in *International Symposium on Distributed Computing and Artificial Intelligence 2019* (Avila, Spain, 2019), 199–206.

20. David M. Blei et al., "Latent Dirichlet Allocation," *The Journal of Machine Learning Research* 3 (2003): 993–1022; Daniel A. McFarland et al., "Differentiating Language Usage Through Topic Models," *Poetics* 41, no. 6 (2013): 607–25; Paul DiMaggio et al., "Exploiting Affinities Between Topic Modeling

and the Sociological Perspective on Culture: Application to Newspaper Coverage of U.S. Government Arts Funding," *Poetics* 41, no. 6 (2013): 570–606.

21. Hamilton et al., "Cultural Shift or Linguistic Drift?"; Wijaya and Yeniterzi, "Understanding Semantic Change of Words Over Centuries."

22. Norman P. Hummon and Patrick Dereian, "Connectivity in a Citation Network: The Development of DNA Theory," *Social Networks* 11, no. 1 (1989): 39–63; Evelien Otte and Ronald Rousseau, "Social Network Analysis: A Powerful Strategy, Also for the Information Sciences," *Journal of Information Science* 28, no. 6 (2002): 441–53; Linda S. Marion et al., "Social Network Analysis and Citation Network Analysis: Complementary Approaches to the Study of Scientific Communication," *Proceedings of the American Society for Information Science and Technology* 40, no. 1 (2003): 486–87.

23. Gabor Csardi and Tamas Nepusz, "The igraph Software Package for Complex Network Research," *InterJournal, Complex Systems* 1695, no. 5 (2006): 1–9.

24. Phillip Bonacich, "Some Unique Properties of Eigenvector Centrality," *Social Networks* 29, no. 4 (2007): 555–64.

25. Steven Manson et al., *IPUMS National Historical Geographic Information System: Version 16.0* [dataset] (IPUMS, 2021).

26. Barr and Ort, "Population Density Across the City"; Angel and Lamson-Hall, "The Rise and Fall of Manhattan's Densities, 1800–2010."

27. Geertz, *The Interpretation of Cultures*, 5.

28. National Conference on Social Welfare, *Official Proceedings of the Annual Meeting, 1874–1982*, University of Michigan Library Digital Collections, https://name.umdl.umich.edu/ACH8650.1957.001.

29. Mann, "The Autonomous Power of the State."

30. Mayrl and Wilson, "What Do Historical Sociologists Do All Day?," 1372; Andrew Abbott, "What Do Cases Do? Some Notes on Activity in Sociological Analysis," in *What Is A Case? Exploring the Foundations of Social Inquiry*, ed. Charles Ragin and Howard Becker (Cambridge University Press, 1992).

31. Matthew Gentzkow et al., *Congressional Record for the 43rd–114th Congresses: Parsed Speeches and Phrase Counts* (Stanford Libraries, 2018); *A Century of Lawmaking for a New Nation: U.S. Congressional Documents and Debates 1774 to 1875*, Library of Congress Digital Collections (Library of Congress), https://www.loc.gov/collections/century-of-lawmaking; *Congressional Record: Proceedings and Debates of the U.S. Congress*, https://www.congress.gov/congressional-record.

32. Lora Bex Lempert, "Asking Questions of the Data: Memo Writing in the Grounded Theory Tradition," in *The SAGE Handbook of Grounded Theory*, ed. Anthony Bryant and Kathy Charmaz (SAGE, 2007).

ACKNOWLEDGMENTS

1. Stephen Jay Gould, "A Triumph of Historical Excavation," *New York Review of Books*, February 27, 1986.

Bibliography

Abbott, Andrew. *Department and Discipline: Chicago Sociology at One Hundred.* University of Chicago Press, 1999.

Abbott, Andrew. "The Historicality of Individuals." *Social Science History* 29, no. 1 (2005): 1–13.

Abbott, Andrew. "History and Sociology: The Lost Synthesis." *Social Science History* 15, no. 2 (1991): 201–38.

Abbott, Andrew. *Processual Sociology.* University of Chicago Press, 2016.

Abbott, Andrew. *The System of Professions: An Essay on the Division of Expert Labor.* University of Chicago Press, 1988.

Abbott, Andrew. "Things of Boundaries." *Social Research* 62, no. 4 (1995): 857–82.

Abbott, Andrew. *Time Matters: On Theory and Method.* University of Chicago Press, 2001.

Abbott, Andrew. "What Do Cases Do? Some Notes on Activity in Sociological Analysis." In *What Is A Case?: Exploring the Foundations of Social Inquiry*, ed. Charles Ragin and Howard Becker. Cambridge University Press, 1992.

Abbott, Samuel W. *Past and Present Condition of Public Hygiene and State Medicine in the United States.* Wright and Potter, 1900.

Abrams, Philip. "Notes on the Difficulty of Studying the State (1977)." *Journal of Historical Sociology* 1, no. 1 (1988): 58–89.

Addams, Jane. *The Spirit of Youth and the City Streets.* University of Illinois Press, 1972.

Agamben, Giorgio. *Homo Sacer: Sovereign Power and Bare Life.* Stanford University Press, 1998.

Agamben, Giorgio. *State of Exception.* University of Chicago Press, 2005.

Aitken, Rob. "All Data Is Credit Data: Constituting the Unbanked." *Competition and Change* 21, no. 4 (2017): 274–300.

Alimahomed-Wilson, Sabrina. "When the FBI Knocks: Racialized State Surveillance of Muslims." *Critical Sociology* 45, no. 6 (2019): 871–87.

Allen, Amy. "Foucault and Enlightenment: A Critical Reappraisal." *Constellations* 10, no. 2 (2003): 180–98.

Allen, Anita L. "Dismantling the Black Opticon: Race Equity and Online Privacy and Data Protection Reform." *Yale Law Journal* 131 (2022): 907–59.

Allen, Anita L. "Surrogacy, Slavery, and the Ownership of Life." *Harvard Journal of Law and Public Policy* 13 (1990): 139–49.

Amoore, Louise. "Security and the Claim to Privacy." *International Political Sociology* 8, no. 1 (2014): 108–12.

Anderson, Margo J. *The American Census: A Social History*. Yale University Press, 1988.

Anderson, Margo, and William Seltzer. "Challenges to the Confidentiality of U.S. Federal Statistics, 1910–1965." *Journal of Official Statistics* 23, no. 1 (2007): 1–34.

Angel, Shlomo, and Patrick Lamson-Hall. "The Rise and Fall of Manhattan's Densities, 1800–2010." Marron Institute of Urban Management Working Paper 14. New York University, 2014.

Angwin, Julia. *Dragnet Nation: A Quest for Privacy, Security, and Freedom in a World of Relentless Surveillance*. Times, 2014.

Anthony, Denise, Celeste Campos-Castillo, and Christine Horne. "Toward a Sociology of Privacy." *Annual Review of Sociology* 43 (2017): 249–69.

Antoniak, Maria, and David Mimno. "Evaluating the Stability of Embedding-Based Word Similarities." *Transactions of the Association for Computational Linguistics* 6 (2018): 107–19.

Arendt, Hannah. *The Human Condition*. University of Chicago Press, 1958.

Arendt, Hannah. *On Revolution*. Penguin, 1963.

Armstrong, Gregory L., Laura A. Conn, and Robert W. Pinner. "Trends in Infectious Disease Mortality in the United States During the 20th Century." *Journal of the American Medical Association* 281, no. 1 (1999): 61–66.

Arora, Payal. "Decolonizing Privacy Studies." *Television and New Media* 20, no. 4 (2019): 366–78.

Auxier, Brooke, Lee Lainie, Monica Anderson, Andrew Perrin, Madhu Kumar, and Erica Turner. "Americans and Privacy: Concerned, Confused and Feeling Lack of Control Over Their Personal Information." Pew Research Center, 2019.

Ayalon, Yaron. "Ottoman Urban Privacy in Light of Disaster Recovery." *International Journal of Middle East Studies* 43, no. 3 (2011): 513–28.

Badie, Bertrand, and Pierre Birnbaum. *The Sociology of the State*. University of Chicago Press, 1983.

Baldwin, Robert, Martin Cave, and Martin Lodge. *Understanding Regulation: Theory, Strategy, and Practice*. Oxford University Press, 2011.

Balkin, Jack M. "How Social Movements Change (or Fail to Change) the Constitution: The Case of the New Departure." *Suffolk University Law Review* 39, no. 1 (2005): 27–66.

Ball, Kirstie. "Organization, Surveillance, and the Body: Towards a Politics of Resistance." In *Theorizing Surveillance*, ed. David Lyon. Routledge, 2006.

Balogh, Brian. *A Government Out of Sight: The Mystery of National Authority in Nineteenth-Century America*. Cambridge University Press, 2009.

Bamberger, Kenneth A., and Ariel Evan Mayse. "Pre-Modern Insights for Post-Modern Privacy: Jewish Law Lessons for the Big Data Age." *Journal of Law and Religion* 36, no. 3 (2021): 495–532.

Barabba, Vincent. "The Right of Privacy and the Need to Know." In *The Census Bureau: A Numerator and Denominator for Measuring Change*. Technical Paper 37, U.S. Bureau of the Census. Government Printing Office, 1975.

Barbas, Samantha. *Laws of Image: Privacy and Publicity in America*. Stanford Law, 2015.

Barbas, Samantha. "Saving Privacy from History." *DePaul Law Review* 61 (2011): 973–1048.

Barkey, Karen. "Historical Sociology." In *The Oxford Handbook of Analytical Sociology*, ed. Peter Bearman and Peter Hedström. Oxford University Press, 2011.

Barkhuus, Louise. "The Mismeasurement of Privacy: Using Contextual Integrity to Reconsider Privacy in HCI." In *Proceedings of the SIGCHI Conference on Human Factors in Computing Systems* (2012): 367–76.

Barr, Jason, and Teddy Ort. "Population Density Across the City: The Case of 1900 Manhattan." Working Paper. Rutgers University, 2013.

Barth, Gunther. *City People: The Rise of Modern City Culture in Nineteenth-Century America*. Oxford University Press, 1982.

Bates, Alan P. "Privacy—A Useful Concept?" *Social Forces* 42, no. 4 (1964): 429–34.

Bauman, Zygmunt. *Liquid Modernity*. Polity, 2000.

Bazzi, Samuel, Martin Fiszbein, and Mesay Gebresilasse. "Frontier Culture: The Roots and Persistence of 'Rugged Individualism' in the United States." *Econometrica* 88, no. 6 (2020): 2239–369.

Beaney, William M. "The Right to Privacy and American Law." *Law and Contemporary Problems* 31 (1966): 253–71.

Beaupre, Miles. "'What Are the Philippines Going to Do to Us?' E. L. Godkin on Democracy, Empire and Anti-imperialism." *Journal of American Studies* 46, no. 3 (2012): 711–27.

Becker, Howard. *Outsiders: Studies in the Sociology of Deviance*. Free Press, 1963.

Becker, Karin. "Photo-Journalism and the Tabloid Press." In *Journalism and Popular Culture*, ed. Peter Dahlgren and Colin Sparks. SAGE, 1992.

Behrent, Michael C. "Foucault and Technology." *History and Technology* 29, no. 1 (2013): 54–104.

Beisel, Nicola. "Class, Culture, and Campaigns Against Vice in Three American Cities, 1872–1892." *American Sociological Review* 55, no. 1 (1990): 44–62.

Bell, Colin, and Howard Newby, eds. *The Sociology of Community: A Selection of Readings*. Frank Cass, 1974.

Benjamin, Walter. *The Arcades Project*. Harvard University Press, 1999.

Benjamin, Walter. *Charles Baudelaire: A Lyric Poet in the Era of High Capitalism*. Verso, 1993.

Benjamin, Walter. "On the Concept of History." In *Selected Writings, Vol. 4: 1938–1940*, ed. Howard Eiland and Michael W. Jennings. Harvard University Press, 2003.

Benjamin, Walter. "Theses on the Philosophy of History." In *Critical Theory and Society: A Reader*, ed. Stephen Eric Bronner and Douglas MacKay Kellner. Routledge, 1989.

Benn, Stanley I. "Privacy, Freedom, and Respect for Persons." In *Privacy and Personality*, ed. Russell L. Ciochon. Routledge, 1971.

Bennett, Colin J. *The Privacy Advocates: Resisting the Spread of Surveillance*. MIT Press, 2010.

Bentham, Jeremy. *Panopticon, or the Inspection House*. T. Payne, 1791.

Beresford, Alastair R., Dorothea Kübler, and Sören Preibusch. "Unwillingness to Pay for Privacy: A Field Experiment." *Economics Letters* 117, no. 1 (2012): 25–27.

Berger, Peter, and Thomas Luckmann. *The Social Construction of Reality*. Anchor, 1966.

Biggs, Michael. "Putting the State on the Map: Cartography, Territory, and European State Formation." *Comparative Studies in Society and History* 41, no. 2 (1999): 374–405.

Blei, David M., Andrew Y. Ng, and Michael I. Jordan. "Latent Dirichlet Allocation." *The Journal of Machine Learning Research* 3 (2003): 993–1022.

Bloustein, Edward J. "Privacy as an Aspect of Human Dignity." *New York University Law Review* 39 (1964): 962–1007.

Bobbio, Norberto. *Democracy and Dictatorship: The Nature and Limits of State Power*. Polity, 1989.

Bogard, William. *The Simulation of Surveillance: Hypercontrol in Telematic Societies*. Cambridge University Press, 1996.

Bogard, William. "Welcome to the Society of Control: The Simulation of Surveillance Revisited." In *The New Politics of Surveillance and Visibility*, ed. Kevin Haggerty and Richard Ericson. University of Toronto Press, 2005.

Bohannon, Gina R. "Cell Phones and the Border Search Exception: Circuits Split Over the Line Between Sovereignty and Privacy." *Maryland Law Review* 78 (2018): 563–603.

Bohme, Frederick G., and David M. Pemberton. "Privacy and Confidentiality in the U.S. Censuses—A History." Paper Presented at the Annual Meeting of the American Statistical Association. Atlanta, GA, August 18–22, 1971.

Bok, Sissela. *Secrets: On the Ethics of Concealment and Revelation*. Pantheon, 1985.

Bolinger, Dwight. *Meaning and Form*. Longman, 1977.

Bonacich, Phillip. "Factoring and Weighting Approaches to Status Scores and Clique Identification." *Journal of Mathematical Sociology* 2 (1972): 113–20.

Bonacich, Phillip. "Some Unique Properties of Eigenvector Centrality." *Social Networks* 29, no. 4 (2007): 555–64.

Bouk, Dan. "The History and Political Economy of Personal Data Over the Last Two Centuries in Three Acts." *Osiris* 32, no. 1 (2017): 85–106.

Bouk, Dan. *How Our Days Became Numbered: Risk and the Rise of the Statistical Individual*. University of Chicago Press, 2015.

Bourdieu, Pierre. *Distinction: A Social Critique of the Judgement of Taste*. Harvard University Press, 1984.

Bourdieu, Pierre. "The Force of Law: Toward a Sociology of the Juridical Field." *Hastings Law Journal* 38 (1986): 814–53.

Bourdieu, Pierre. *On the State: Lectures at the College of France, 1989–1992*. Polity, 2014.

Bourdieu, Pierre. "Social Space and Symbolic Power." *Sociological Theory* 7, no. 1 (1989): 14–25.

Bowker, Geoffrey C., and Susan Leigh Star. *Sorting Things Out: Classification and Its Consequences.* MIT Press, 2000.

Boyer, Paul. *Urban Masses and Moral Order in America, 1820–1920.* Harvard University Press, 1978.

Brackett, Charles. "The Early Criminal Record on the Boundary of Entertainment: Thomas F. Byrnes' Professional Criminals of America and the Spectacle of Criminal Identification." *Surveillance and Society* 20, no. 2 (2022): 157–71.

Bradbury, Malcolm. *The History Man.* Picador, 2017.

Bratman, Benjamin. "Brandeis and Warren's The Right to Privacy and the Birth of the Right to Privacy." *Tennessee Law Review* 69 (2001): 623–52.

Braudel, Fernand. "History and the Social Sciences: The Longue Durée." In *On History.* Translated by Sarah Matthews, 27–38. University of Chicago Press, 1980.

Brayne, Sarah. "Big Data Surveillance. The Case of Policing." *American Sociological Review* 82, no. 5 (2017): 977–1008.

Brecht, Bertolt. *Geschichten vom Herrn Keuner.* Surhkamp, 2013.

Breckenridge, Keith, and Simon Szreter. *Registration and Recognition: Documenting the Person in World History.* Oxford University Press, 2012.

Breckinridge, Sophonisba P., and Edith Abbott. "Housing Conditions in Chicago." *American Journal of Sociology* 16, no. 4 (1911): 433–68.

Bremner, Robert H. "The Big Flat: History of a New York Tenement House." *The American Historical Review* 64, no. 1 (1958): 54–62.

Brenner, Neil, and Nik Theodore. "Cities and the Geographies of 'Actually Existing Neoliberalism.'" *Antipode* 34, no. 3 (2002): 349–79.

Brensinger, Jordan. "Identity Theft, Trust Breaches, and the Production of Economic Insecurity." *American Sociological Review,* 88, no. 5 (2023): 844–71.

Brenton, Myron. *The Privacy Invaders.* Coward-McCann, 1964.

Bridges, Khiara M. *The Poverty of Privacy Rights.* Stanford University Press, 2017.

Bristow, Nancy. *American Pandemic: The Lost Worlds of the 1918 Influenza Epidemic.* Oxford University Press, 2012.

Broun, Heywood, and Margaret Leech. *Anthony Comstock: Roundsman of the Lord.* Literary Guild of America, 1927.

Brown, Brendan F. "Natural Law and the Law-Making Function in American Jurisprudence." *Notre Dame Law Review* 15, no. 1 (1939): 9–25.

Browne, Simone. *Dark Matters: On the Surveillance of Blackness.* Duke University Press, 2015.

Brunet, Marc-Etienne, Colleen Alkalay-Houlihan, Ashton Anderson, and Richard Zemel. "Understanding the Origins of Bias in Word Embeddings." In *International Conference on Machine Learning 2019,* 803–811. ICML, 2019.

Bruno, Frank J. *Trends in Social Work.* Columbia University Press, 1948.

Bullard, Robert Doyle, Glenn Steve Johnson, and Angel O. Torres, eds. *Highway Robbery: Transportation Racism and New Routes to Equity.* South End, 2004.

Burchardt, Marian, Zeynep Yanasmayan, and Matthias Koenig. "The Judicial Politics of Burqa Bans in Belgium and Spain: Socio-legal Field Dynamics and the Standardization of Justificatory Repertoires." *Law and Social Inquiry* 44, no. 2 (2019): 333–58.

Byrd, W. Michael, and Linda A. Clayton. "Race, Medicine, and Health Care in the United States: A Historical Survey." *Journal of the National Medical Association* 93, no. 3 (2001): Suppl 11S.

Calder, Lendol. *Financing the American Dream: A Cultural History of Consumer Credit.* Princeton University Press, 1999.

Calkin, Homer L. "Pamphlets and Public Opinion During the American Revolution." *The Pennsylvania Magazine of History and Biography* 64, no. 1 (1940): 22–42.

Canaday, Margot. *The Straight State: Sexuality and Citizenship in Twentieth-Century America.* Princeton University Press, 2009.

Capozzola, Christopher. *Uncle Sam Wants You: World War I and the Making of the Modern American Citizen.* Oxford University Press, 2008.

Carpenter, Daniel. *The Forging of Bureaucratic Autonomy: Reputations, Networks, and Policy Innovation in Executive Agencies, 1862–1928.* Princeton University Press, 2002.

Carruthers, Bruce G. "From Uncertainty Toward Risk: The Case of Credit Ratings." *Socio-Economic Review* 11, no. 3 (2013): 525–51.

Chaddock, Robert E. "Sources of Information Upon the Public Health Movement." *Annals of the American Academy of Political and Social Science* 37, no. 2 (1911): 63–66.

Chase, Carol A. "Privacy Takes a Back Seat: Putting the Automobile Exception Back on Track After Several Wrong Turns." *Boston College Law Review* 41 (1999): 71–102.

Church, Kenneth W. "Word2Vec." *Natural Language Engineering* 23, no. 1 (2017): 155–62.

Citron, Danielle K. "Cyber Civil Rights." *Boston University Law Review* 89 (2009): 61–125.

Citron, Danielle K. *The Fight for Privacy: Protecting Dignity, Identity, and Love in the Digital Age.* Norton, 2022.

Clayton, Ellen Wright, Barbara J. Evans, James W. Hazel, and Mark A. Rothstein. "The Law of Genetic Privacy: Applications, Implications, and Limitations." *Journal of Law and the Biosciences* 6, no. 1 (2019): 1–36.

Clemens, Elisabeth S., and James M. Cook. "Politics and Institutionalism: Explaining Durability and Change." *Annual Review of Sociology* 25, no. 1 (1999): 441–66.

Cohen, Julie E. *Between Truth and Power: The Legal Constructions of Informational Capitalism.* Oxford University Press, 2019.

Cohen, Julie E. "Privacy, Visibility, Transparency, and Exposure." *The University of Chicago Law Review* 75, no. 1 (2008): 181–201.

Cohen, Julie E. "What Privacy Is For." *Harvard Law Review* 126, no. 7 (2012): 1904–33.

Cohen, Patricia C. *A Calculating People: The Spread of Numeracy in Early America*. University of Chicago Press, 1982.

Cohn, Morris E. "The Censorship of Radical Materials by the Post Office." *Washington University Law Review* 17, no. 2 (1932): 95–119.

Cole, Robert H., and Lon Mishler. *Consumer and Commercial Credit Management*, 11th ed. McGraw-Hill, 1998.

Coll, Sami. "Power, Knowledge, and the Subjects of Privacy: Understanding Privacy as the Ally of Surveillance." *Information, Communication and Society* 17, no. 10 (2014): 1250–63.

Collier, Stephen J. "Topologies of Power: Foucault's Analysis of Political Government Beyond 'Governmentality.'" *Theory, Culture and Society* 26, no. 6 (2009): 78–108.

Collins, Patricia Hill. *Black Feminist Thought: Knowledge, Consciousness, and the Politics of Empowerment*. Routledge, 2002.

Collins, Paul. *The Murder of the Century: The Gilded Age Crime That Scandalized a City and Sparked the Tabloid Wars*. Broadway, 2011.

Colomina, Beatriz. *Privacy and Publicity: Modern Architecture as Mass Media*. MIT Press, 1996.

Colyvas, Jeannette A., and Stefan Jonsson. "Ubiquity and Legitimacy: Disentangling Diffusion and Institutionalization." *Sociological Theory* 29, no. 1 (2011): 27–53.

Commons, John R. *Legal Foundations of Capitalism*. Transaction, 1995.

Comte, Auguste. *Social Physics: From the Positive Philosophy of Auguste Comte*. Calvin Blanchard, 1856.

Constant, Benjamin. *Constant: Political Writings*, ed. Biancamaria Fontana. Cambridge University Press, 1988.

Cooley, Thomas M. *A Treatise on the Law of Torts or the Wrongs Which Arise Independent of Contract*. Callaghan and Co., 1879.

Cooley, Thomas M. *A Treatise on the Law of Torts or the Wrongs Which Arise Independent of Contract*, 3rd ed., vol. 1, ed. John Lewis. Callaghan and Co., 1906.

Coontz, Stephanie. *The Social Origins of Private Life: A History of American Families, 1600–1900*. Verso, 1988.

Copestake, Ann, and Ted Briscoe. "Semi-Productive Polysemy and Sense Extension." *Journal of Semantics* 12 (1995): 15–67.

Cortada, James W. *All the Facts: A History of Information in the United States Since 1870*. Oxford University Press, 2016.

Coser, Rose Laub. "Insulation from Observability and Types of Social Conformity." *American Sociological Review* 26, no. 1 (1961): 28–39.

Cott, Nancy F. "Eighteenth Century Family and Social Life Revealed in Massachusetts Divorce Records." *Journal of Social History* 10, no. 1 (1976): 20–43.

Cotter, David A., Joan M. Hermsen, and Reeve Vanneman. "Women's Work and Women Working: The Demand for Female Labor." *Gender and Society* 15, no. 3 (2001): 429–52.

Coyle, Erin K. "E. L. Godkin's Criticism of the Penny Press: Antecedents to a Legal Right to Privacy." *American Journalism* 31, no. 2 (2014): 262–82.

Craddock, Susan. *City of Plagues: Disease, Poverty, and Deviance in San Francisco.* University of Minnesota Press, 2004.

Cromley, Elizabeth C. "A History of American Beds and Bedrooms." *Perspectives in Vernacular Architecture* 4 (1991): 177–86.

Crouthamel, James L. *Bennett's New York Herald and the Rise of the Popular Press.* Syracuse University Press, 1989.

Csardi, Gabor, and Tamas Nepusz. "The igraph Software Package for Complex Network Research." *InterJournal, Complex Systems* 1695, no. 5 (2006): 1–9.

Dandeker, Christopher. *Surveillance, Power and Modernity: Bureaucracy and Discipline from 1700 to the Present Day.* St. Martin's, 1990.

Danielian, Nooba R. *AT&T: The Story of Industrial Conquest.* Arno, 1974.

Danielson, Caroline. "The Gender of Privacy and the Embodied Self: Examining the Origins of the Right to Privacy in U.S. Law." *Feminist Studies* 25, no. 2 (1999): 311–44.

Daston, Lorraine. "Calculation and the Division of Labor, 1750–1950." *Bulletin of the German Historical Institute* 62 (2017): 9–30.

Davis, James K., ed. *Spying on America: The FBI's Domestic Counterintelligence Program.* Bloomsbury, 1992.

Day, Katherine J. "Perspectives on Privacy: A Sociological Analysis." PhD diss., University of Edinburgh, 1985.

de Tocqueville, Alexis. *Democracy in America.* Penguin, 2003.

De Wolf, Ralf. "Contextualizing How Teens Manage Personal and Interpersonal Privacy on Social Media." *New Media and Society* 22, no. 6 (2020): 1058–75.

Debatin, Bernhard, Jennette P. Lovejoy, Ann-Kathrin Horn, and Brittany N. Hughes. "Facebook and Online Privacy: Attitudes, Behaviors, and Unintended Consequences." *Journal of Computer-Mediated Communication* 15, no. 1 (2009): 83–108.

DeForest, Robert W. "A Brief History of the Housing Movement in America." *The Annals of the American Academy of Political and Social Science* 51, no. 1 (1914): 8–16.

Deleuze, Gilles. "Postscript on the Societies of Control." In *Surveillance, Crime and Social Control,* ed. Clive Norris and Dean Wilson. Routledge, 2017.

Demos, John. *A Little Commonwealth: Family Life in Plymouth Colony.* Oxford University Press, 2000.

Demos, John. *Past, Present, and Personal: The Family and the Life Course in American History.* Oxford University Press, 1986.

Desai, Anuj C. "Wiretapping Before the Wires: The Post Office and the Rebirth of Communications Privacy." *Stanford Law Review* 60 (2007): 553–94.

Desrosières, Alain. *The Politics of Large Numbers: A History of Statistical Reasoning.* Harvard University Press, 1998.

Deutsch, Sarah. *Women and the City: Gender, Space, and Power in Boston, 1870–1940.* Oxford University Press, 2000.

Devine, Warren D. "From Shafts to Wires: Historical Perspective on Electrification." *The Journal of Economic History* 43, no. 2 (1983): 347–72.

Dewey, John. *The Later Works (1925–1953), Volume 12*. Southern Illinois University Press, 1981.

Dewey, John. *The Public and Its Problems*. Holt and Co., 1927.

Dezalay, Yves, and Mikael Rask Madsen. "The Force of Law and Lawyers: Pierre Bourdieu and the Reflexive Sociology of Law." *Annual Review of Law and Social Science* 8 (2012): 433–52.

Dienlin, Tobias, and Sabine Trepte. "Is the Privacy Paradox a Relic of the Past? An In-Depth Analysis of Privacy Attitudes and Privacy Behaviors." *European Journal of Social Psychology* 45, no. 3 (2015): 285–97.

Dill, William A. *Growth of Newspapers in the U.S.: A Study of the Number of Newspapers, of the Number of Subscribers, and of the total Annual Output of the Periodical Press, from 1704 to 1925, with Comment on Coincident Social and Economic Conditions*. Bulletin of the Department of Journalism of the University of Kansas, 1928.

DiMaggio, Paul. "Culture and Cognition." *Annual Review of Sociology* 23 (1997): 263–87.

DiMaggio, Paul, Manish Nag, and David Blei. "Exploiting Affinities Between Topic Modeling and the Sociological Perspective on Culture: Application to Newspaper Coverage of U.S. Government Arts Funding." *Poetics* 41, no. 6 (2013): 570–606.

Dixon, Robert G. "The Griswold Penumbra: Constitutional Charter for an Expanded Law of Privacy?" *Michigan Law Review* 64, no. 2 (1965): 197–218.

Dolkart, Andrew S. *Biography of a Tenement House in New York City: An Architectural History of 97 Orchard Street*. University of Virginia Press, 2006.

Douglas, Mary. *How Institutions Think*. Syracuse University Press, 1986.

Du Boff, Richard B. "Business Demand and the Development of the Telegraph in the United States, 1844–1860." *Business History Review* 54, no. 4 (1980): 459–79.

Du Bois, W. E. B. *The Philadelphia Negro: A Social Study*. University of Pennsylvania Press, 2023.

Du Bois, W. E. B. *The Souls of Black Folk*. Oxford World's Classics, 2007.

Dubois, Vincent. *The Bureaucrat and the Poor: Encounters in French Welfare Offices*. Routledge, 2016.

Duffy, Mignon. "Doing the Dirty Work: Gender, Race, and Reproductive Labor in Historical Perspective." *Gender and Society* 21, no. 3 (2007): 313–36.

Dunaway, Wilma A. "Diaspora, Death, and Sexual Exploitation: Slave Families at Risk in the Mountain South." *Appalachian Journal* 26, no. 2 (1999): 128–49.

Durkheim, Emile. *The Division of Labor in Society*. Free Press, 1964.

Durkheim, Emile. *Professional Ethics and Civic Morals*. Free Press, 1958.

Dwivedi, Divya, and Viswanathan Sanil, eds. *The Public Sphere from Outside the West*. Bloomsbury, 2015.

Dworkin, Gerald. "The Younger Committee Report on Privacy." *The Modern Law Review* 36, no. 4 (1973): 399–406.

Eiermann, Martin. "The Process of Legal Institutionalization: How Privacy Jurisprudence Turned Towards the U.S. Constitution and the American State." *Law and Social Inquiry* 49, no. 1 (2024): 537–68.

Eiermann, Martin, Elizabeth Wrigley-Field, James J. Feigenbaum, Jonas Helgertz, Elaine Hernandez, and Courtney E. Boen. "Racial Disparities in Mortality During the 1918 Influenza Pandemic in United States Cities." *Demography* 59, no. 5 (2022): 1953–79.

Eisinger, Peter K. "The Conditions of Protest Behavior in American Cities." *American Political Science Review* 67, no. 1 (1973): 11–28.

Elias, Norbert. *The Civilizing Process: Sociogenetic and Psychogenetic Investigations.* Blackwell, 2000.

Elias, Norbert. *What Is Sociology?* Columbia University Press, 1978.

Emigh, Rebecca J., Dylan Riley, and Patricia Ahmed. *Antecedents of Censuses from Medieval to Nation States: How Societies and States Count.* Palgrave Macmillan, 2016.

Epp, Charles R. *The Rights Revolution: Lawyers, Activists, and Supreme Courts in Comparative Perspective.* University of Chicago Press, 1998.

Ericson, Richard V., and Kevin D. Haggerty. *Policing the Risk Society.* University of Toronto Press, 1997.

Eskridge, William N. "Some Effects of Identity-Based Social Movements on Constitutional Law in the Twentieth Century." *Michigan Law Review* 100, no. 8 (2002): 2062–407.

Espeland, Wendy N., and Mitchell L. Stevens. "A Sociology of Quantification." *European Journal of Sociology* 49, no. 3 (2008): 424.

Etzioni, Amitai. *The Limits of Privacy.* Basic, 1999.

Eubanks, Virginia. *Automating Inequality: How High-Tech Tools Profile, Police, and Punish the Poor.* St. Martin's, 2018.

Evans, Robin. "Figures, Doors, and Passages." In *Translations from Drawing to Building and Other Essays,* 55–92. Architectural Association Publications, 1997.

Ewick, Patricia, and Susan S. Silbey. *The Common Place of Law: Stories from Everyday Life.* University of Chicago Press, 1998.

Fair, Freda L. "Surveilling Social Difference: Black Women's 'Alley Work' in Industrializing Minneapolis." *Surveillance and Society* 15, no. 5 (2017): 655–75.

Fairchild, Amy L., Ronald Bayer, and James Colgrove. *Searching Eyes: Privacy, the State, and Disease Surveillance in America.* University of California Press, 2007.

Farber, Bernard. *Guardians of Virtue: Salem Families in 1800.* Basic, 1972.

Farber, Daniel A. "Lincoln, Presidential Power, and the Rule of Law." *Northwestern University Law Review* 113, no. 3 (2018): 667–700.

Feigenbaum, James J., Christopher Muller, and Elizabeth Wrigley-Field. "Regional and Racial Inequality in Infectious Disease Mortality in U.S. Cities, 1900–1948." *Demography* 56, no. 4 (2019): 1371–88.

Felstiner, William L. F., Richard L. Abel, and Austin Sarat. "The Emergence and Transformation of Disputes: Naming, Blaming, Claiming." In *Theoretical and Empirical Studies of Rights,* ed. Laura Beth Nielson. Routledge, 2017.

Field, Alexander J. "Newspapers and Periodicals: Number and Circulation by Type, 1850–1967." In *Historical Statistics of the United States: Earliest Times to the Present, Millennial Edition.* Cambridge University Press, 2006.

Fields, Barbara J., and Karen E. Fields. *Racecraft: The Soul of Inequality in American Life.* Verso, 2012.

Fischer, Claude S. "The Revolution in Rural Telephony, 1900–1920." *Journal of Social History* 21, no. 1 (1987): 5–26.

Fischer, David H. *Albion's Seed: Four British Folkways in America.* Oxford University Press, 1989.

Fiske, John. "Surveilling the City: Whiteness, the Black Man and Democratic Totalitarianism." *Theory, Culture and Society* 15, no. 2 (1998): 67–88.

Flaherty, David H. *Privacy in Colonial New England, 1630–1776.* University of Virginia Press, 1972.

Fligstein, Neil, and Doug McAdam. *A Theory of Fields.* Oxford University Press, 2015.

Ford, Larry R. *Cities and Buildings: Skyscrapers, Skid Rows and Suburbs.* Johns Hopkins University Press, 2005.

Foster, George G. *New York Naked.* DeWitt & Davenport, 1852.

Foucault, Michel. *The Birth of Biopolitics: Lectures at the Collège de France, 1978–1979.* Picador, 2008.

Foucault, Michel. *Discipline and Punish: The Birth of the Prison.* Vintage, 1995.

Foucault, Michel. *A History of Sexuality: Volume 1.* Vintage, 1990.

Foucault, Michel. *The Order of Things.* Routledge, 2002.

Foucault, Michel. "Of Other Spaces." *Diacritics* 16, no. 1 (1986): 22–27.

Foucault, Michel. *Security, Territory, Population: Lectures at the Collège de France, 1977–78.* Picador, 2007.

Foucault, Michel. "The Subject and Power." *Critical Inquiry* 8, no. 4 (1982): 777–95.

Fourcade, Marion. "Ordinalization: Lewis A. Coser Memorial Award for Theoretical Agenda Setting 2014." *Sociological Theory* 34, no. 3 (2016): 175–95.

Fourcade, Marion, and Jeffrey Gordon, "Learning Like a State: Statecraft in the Digital Age." *Journal of Law and Political Economy* 1, no. 1 (2020): 78–108.

Fourcade, Marion, and Kieran Healy. *The Ordinal Society.* Harvard University Press, 2024.

Fourcade, Marion, and Kieran Healy. "Seeing Like a Market." *Socio-Economic Review* 15, no. 1 (2017): 9–29.

Fraser, Nancy. "Foucault on Modern Power: Empirical Insights and Normative Confusions." *Praxis International* 1, no. 3 (1981): 272–87.

Freeden, Michael. *Ideologies and Political Theory: A Conceptual Approach.* Clarendon, 1996.

Fried, Charles. "Privacy." *Yale Law Journal* 77, no. 3 (1968): 482–83.

Friedman, Lawrence M. "Name Robbers: Privacy, Blackmail, and Assorted Matters in Legal History." *Hofstra Law Review* 30, no. 4 (2002): 1039–132.

Fuchs, Christian. "Political Economy and Surveillance Theory." *Critical Sociology* 39, no. 5 (2013): 671–87.

Fuchs, Christian. "Towards an Alternative Concept of Privacy." *Journal of Information, Communication and Ethics in Society* 9, no. 4 (2011): 220–37.

Gaebler, Ralph F. "Is There a Natural Law Right to Privacy?" *American Journal of Jurisprudence* 37 (1992): 319–36.

Gajda, Amy. *The First Amendment Bubble: How Privacy and Paparazzi Threaten a Free Press*. Harvard University Press, 2015.

Gajda, Amy. *Seek and Hide: The Tangled History of the Right to Privacy*. Penguin, 2022.

Gajda, Amy. "What if Samuel D. Warren Hadn't Married a Senator's Daughter: Uncovering the Press Coverage That Led to the Right to Privacy." *Michigan State Law Review* (2008): 35–60.

Gallagher, Winifred. *How the Post Office Created America: A History*. Penguin, 2016.

Gandy Jr., Oscar H. *The Panoptic Sort: A Political Economy of Personal Information*, 2nd ed. Oxford University Press, 2021.

Gandy Jr., Oscar H. "The Preference for Privacy: In Search of the Social Locations of Privacy Orientations." Paper presented at the Annual Meeting of the Speech Communication Association, San Francisco, CA, November 18–21, 1989.

Gandy Jr., Oscar H. "Quixotics Unite! Engaging the Pragmatists on Rational Discrimination." In *Theorizing Surveillance*, ed. David Lyon. Routledge, 2006.

Garb, Margaret. "Health, Morality, and Housing: The 'Tenement Problem' in Chicago." *American Journal of Public Health* 93, no. 9 (2003): 1420–30.

Garg, Nikhil, Londa Schiebinger, Dan Jurafsky, and James Zou. "Word Embeddings Quantify 100 Years of Gender and Ethnic Stereotypes." *Proceedings of the National Academy of Sciences* 115, no. 16 (2018): E3635–44.

Gavison, Ruth. "Privacy and the Limits of Law." *Yale Law Journal* 89, no. 3 (1980): 421–71.

Geertz, Clifford. *The Interpretation of Cultures*. Basic, 1973.

Gerety, Tom. "Redefining Privacy." *Harvard Civil Rights-Civil Liberties Law Review* 12, no. 2 (1977): 234.

Gerstein, Robert S. "Intimacy and Privacy." *Ethics* 89, no. 1 (1978): 76–81.

Geuss, Raymond. *Public Goods, Private Goods*. Princeton University Press, 2001.

Gibson, Campbell, and Kay Jung. "Historical Census Statistics on the Foreign-Born Population of the United States: 1850–2000." Working Paper 81, U.S. Bureau of the Census Population Division, 2006.

Gibson, Otis. *The Chinese in America*. Hitcock and Walden, 1877.

Giddens, Anthony. "The 'Individual' in the Writings of Emile Durkheim." *European Journal of Sociology/Archives Européennes de Sociologie* 12, no. 2 (1971): 210–28.

Giddens, Anthony, ed. "The Political Context of Weber's Sociology." In *Politics and Sociology in the Thought of Max Weber*. Polity, 1972.

Giedion, Siegfried. *Mechanization Takes Command: A Contribution to Anonymous History*. Oxford University Press, 1970.

Gieryn, Thomas F. "Boundary-Work and the Demarcation of Science from Non-Science." *American Sociological Review* 48, no. 6 (1983): 781–95.

Gieryn, Thomas F. "A Space for Place in Sociology." *Annual Review of Sociology* 26 (2000): 475–99.

Gimpel, James G., Nathan Lovin, Bryant Moy, and Andrew Reeves. "The Urban–Rural Gulf in American Political Behavior." *Political Behavior* 42, no. 4 (2020): 1343–68.

Glancy, Dorothy J. "The Invention of the Right to Privacy." *Arizona Law Review* 21 (1979): 1–39.

Glancy, Dorothy J. "Privacy and the Other Miss M." *Northern Illinois University Law Review* 10 (1989): 401-440.

Gleick, James. *The Information: A History, a Theory, a Flood*. Pantheon, 2011.

Goffman, Erving. *Asylums: Essays on the Social Situation of Mental Patients and other Inmates*. Anchor, 1961.

Goffman, Erving. *The Presentation of Self in Everyday Life*. Allen Lane, 1959.

Goldberg, Yoav. *Neural Network Methods for Natural Language Processing*. Morgan & Claypool, 2017.

Goldman, Joanne Abel. *Building New York's Sewers: Developing Mechanisms of Urban Management*. Purdue University Press, 1997.

Gonzalez, George A. *The Politics of Air Pollution: Urban Growth, Ecological Modernization, and Symbolic Inclusion*. SUNY Press, 2005.

Goodman, Nelson. *Ways of Worldmaking*. Hackett, 1978.

Goodwin, Doris Kearns. *The Bully Pulpit: Theodore Roosevelt, William Howard Taft, and the Golden Age of Journalism*. Simon and Schuster, 2013.

Gordon, Robert. *Taming the Past: Law in History and History in Law*. Cambridge University Press, 2017.

Gorman, Thomas J. *Growing Up Working Class: Hidden Injuries and the Development of Angry White Men and Women*. Palgrave Macmillan, 2017.

Gormley, Ken. "One Hundred Years of Privacy." *Wisconsin Law Review* (1992): 1335–441.

Gotlieb, Calvin C. "Privacy: A Concept Whose Time Has Come and Gone." In *Computers, Surveillance, and Privacy*, ed. David Lyon and Elia Zureik. University of Minnesota Press, 1996.

Goudsblom, Johan. *Sociology in the Balance*. Columbia University Press, 1977.

Gould, Elgin R. L. "The Housing Problem in Great Cities." *Quarterly Review of Economics* 14, no. 3 (1900): 378–93.

Gould, Roger V. *Insurgent Identities: Class, Community, and Protest in Paris from 1848 to the Commune*. University of Chicago Press, 1995.

Graham, Mary. *Presidents' Secrets: The Use and Abuse of Hidden Power*. Yale University Press, 2017.

Granovetter, Mark, and Patrick McGuire. "The Making of an Industry: Electricity in the United States." *The Sociological Review* 46, no. 1 (1998): 147–73.

Grommé, Francisca, and Stephan Scheel. "Doing Statistics, Enacting the Nation: The Performative Powers of Categories." *Nations and Nationalism* 26, no. 3 (2020): 576–93.

Gusfield, Joseph R. "Social Structure and Moral Reform: A Study of the Woman's Christian Temperance Union." *American Journal of Sociology* 61, no. 3 (1955): 221–32.

Habermas, Jürgen. *The Structural Transformation of the Public Sphere*. MIT Press, 1991.

Hacking, Ian. "Kinds of People: Moving Targets." *Proceedings of the British Academy* 151, no. 1 (2007): 285–317.

Hacking, Ian. *The Social Construction of What?* Harvard University Press, 1999.

Hacking, Ian. *The Taming of Chance.* Cambridge University Press, 1990.

Haggerty, Kevin D., and Richard V. Ericson, eds. *The New Politics of Surveillance and Visibility.* University of Toronto Press, 2005.

Haggerty, Kevin D., and Richard V. Ericson. "The Surveillant Assemblage." *British Journal of Sociology* 51, no. 4 (2000): 61–78.

Haiman, John. *Natural Syntax: Iconicity and Erosion.* Cambridge University Press, 1985.

Hall, David D. *Worlds of Wonder, Days of Judgment: Popular Religious Belief in Early New England.* Harvard University Press, 1990.

Hall, Peter. "Aligning Ontology and Methodology in Comparative Politics." In *Comparative Historical Analysis in the Social Sciences*, ed. James Mahoney and Dietrich Rueschemeyer. Cambridge University Press, 2003.

Halliday, Terence C., and Lucien Karpik, eds. *Lawyers and the Rise of Western Political Liberalism: Europe and North America from the Eighteenth to Twentieth Centuries.* Clarendon, 1998.

Halpern, Sue. *Migrations to Solitude.* Vintage, 2011.

Halttunen, Karen. *Confidence Men and Painted Women: A Study of Middle-class Culture in America, 1830–1870.* Yale University Press, 1982.

Hamilton, Gary G., and John R. Sutton. "The Problem of Control in the Weak State: Domination in the United States, 1880–1920." *Theory and Society* 18, no. 1 (1989): 1–46.

Hamilton, William L., Jure Leskovec, and Dan Jurafsky. "Cultural Shift or Linguistic Drift? Comparing Two Computational Measures of Semantic Change." In *Proceedings of the 2016 Conference on Empirical Methods in Natural Language Processing*, 2116–21. Association for Computational Linguistics, 2016.

Hamilton, William L., Jure Leskovec, and Dan Jurafsky. "Diachronic Word Embeddings Reveal Statistical Laws of Semantic Change." arXiv preprint, arXiv:1605 .09096. 2016.

Han, Jiawei, Jian Pei, and Micheline Kamber. *Data Mining: Concepts and Techniques.* Elsevier, 2011.

Hand, Augustus N. "Schuyler Against Curtis and the Right to Privacy." *The American Law Register and Review* 45, no. 12 (1897): 745–59.

Handlin, David P. *The American Home: Architecture and Society, 1815–1915.* Little, Brown, 1979.

Hansen, Karen V. "Rediscovering the Social: Visiting Practices in Antebellum New England and the Limits of the Public/Private Dichotomy." In *Public and Private in Thought and Practice*, ed. Jeff A. Weintraub and Krishan Kumar. University of Chicago Press, 1997.

Hanus, Jerome J., and Harold C. Relyea. "A Policy Assessment of the Privacy Act of 1974." *American University Law Review* 25, no. 3 (1975): 555–93.

Harari, Yuval Noah. "Dataism Is Our New God." *New Perspectives Quarterly* 34, no. 2 (2017): 36–43.

Haraway, Donna. "Situated Knowledges: The Science Question in Feminism and the Privilege of Partial Perspective." *Feminist Studies* 14, no. 3 (1988): 575–99.

Harlow, Alvin F. *Old Wires and New Waves: The History of the Telegraph, Telephone, and Wireless.* D. Appleton-Century Company, 1936.

Harris, Louis, and Alan F. Westin. *The Dimensions of Privacy: A National Opinion Research Survey of Attitudes Toward Privacy.* Garland, 1981.

Hartog, Hendrik. "Pigs and Positivism." *Wisconsin Law Review* 1985, no. 4 (1985): 934–35.

Harvard Law Review Association. "The Right to Privacy Today." *Harvard Law Review* 43, no. 2 (1929): 297–302.

Harvey, David. "The Right to the City." *International Journal of Urban and Regional Research* 27, no. 4 (2003): 939–41.

Haveman, Heather A. *Magazines and the Making of America: Modernization, Community, and Print Culture, 1741–1860.* Princeton University Press, 2015.

Hayes, Sharon, and Laura Miller. "Informed Control: Dun & Bradstreet and the Information Society." *Media, Culture and Society* 16, no. 1 (1994): 117–40.

Healy, Kieran. "The Performativity of Networks." *European Journal of Sociology* 56, no. 2 (2015): 175–205.

Heise, David. "Understanding Social Interaction with Affect Control Theory." In *New Directions in Sociological Theory*, ed. J. Berger and M. Zelditch. Rowman & Littlefield, 2002.

Higham, John. *Hanging Together: Unity and Diversity in American Culture.* Yale University Press, 2001.

Hirschman, Charles, and Elizabeth Mogford. "Immigration and the American Industrial Revolution from 1880 to 1920." *Social Science Research* 38, no. 4 (2009): 897–920.

Hixson, Richard F. *Privacy in a Public Society: Human Rights in Conflict.* Oxford University Press, 1987.

Hochfelder, David. *The Telegraph in America, 1832–1920.* Johns Hopkins University Press, 2012.

Hofmann, Thomas. "Unsupervised Learning by Probabilistic Latent Semantic Analysis." *Machine Learning* 42, no. 1 (2001): 177–96.

Hofstadter, Richard. *The Age of Reform.* Vintage, 1955.

Hofstadter, Samuel H., and George Horowitz. *The Right to Privacy.* Central Book Company, 1964.

Holbrook, James. *Ten Years Among the Mail Bags.* H. Cowperthwait and Co., 1855.

Holcombe, Randall G. "The Growth of the Federal Government in the 1920s." *The Cato Journal* 16 (1996): 175–99.

Hollinger, David. *In the American Province: Studies in the History and Historiography of Ideas.* Indiana University Press, 1985.

Homer Bates, David Homer. *Lincoln in the Telegraph Office: Recollections of the United States Military Telegraph Corps during the Civil War.* University of Nebraska Press, 1995.

Hoofnagle, Chris Jay, and Jennifer M. Urban. "Alan Westin's Privacy Homo Economicus." *Wake Forest Law Review* 49 (2014): 261–317.

Hopper, Paul J., and Elizabeth Closs Traugott. *Grammaticalization*. Cambridge University Press, 2003.

Horwitz, Morton J. *The Transformation of American Law, 1870–1960: The Crisis of Legal Orthodoxy*. Oxford University Press, 1992.

Howe, John R. *Language and Political Meaning in Revolutionary America*. University of Massachusetts Press, 2004.

Huey, Laura. "A Social Movement for Privacy/Against Surveillance: Some Difficulties in Engendering Mass Resistance in a Land of Twitter and Tweets." *Case Western Reserve Journal of International Law* 42 (2009): 699–709.

Hummon, Norman P., and Patrick Dereian. "Connectivity in a Citation Network: The Development of DNA Theory." *Social Networks* 11, no. 1 (1989): 39–63.

Hurley, Mikella, and Julius Adebayo. "Credit Scoring in the Era of Big Data." *Yale Journal of Law and Technology* 18 (2016): 148–216.

Hurty, John N. "The Bookkeeping of Humanity." *Journal of the American Medical Association* 55, no. 14 (1910): 1157–60.

Igo, Sarah E. *The Averaged American: Surveys, Citizens, and the Making of a Mass Public*. Harvard University Press, 2007.

Igo, Sarah E. *The Known Citizen: A History of Privacy in Modern America*. Harvard University Press, 2018.

Jackman, Mary R., and Kimberlee A. Shauman. "The Toll of Inequality: Excess African American Deaths in the United States Over the Twentieth Century." *DuBois Review* 16, no. 2 (2019): 291–340.

Jacobs, Jane. *The Death and Life of Great American Cities*. Vintage, 1992.

Jacobs, Margaret D. *White Mother to a Dark Race: Settler Colonialism, Maternalism, and the Removal of Indigenous Children in the American West and Australia, 1880–1940*. University of Nebraska Press, 2009.

Jagodzinski, Cecile M. *Privacy and Print: Reading and Writing in Seventeenth-Century England*. University of Virginia Press, 1999.

Jasanoff, Sheila. "Ordering Knowledge, Ordering Society." In *States of Knowledge: The Co-Production of Science and Social Order*, 13–45. Routledge, 2004.

Jenness, Valerie. "The Emergence, Content, and Institutionalization of Hate Crime Law: How a Diverse Policy Community Produced a Modern Legal Fact." *Annual Review of Law and Social Science* 3 (2007): 141–60.

Jentzsch, Nicola. "The Regulation of Financial Privacy: The United States vs. Europe." ECRI Research Report no. 5, 2003.

Jerolmack, Colin, and Iddo Tavory. "Molds and Totems: Nonhumans and the Constitution of the Social Self." *Sociological Theory* 32, no. 1 (2014): 64–77.

John, Richard R. *Spreading the News: The American Postal System from Franklin to Morse*. Harvard University Press, 1998.

Johnson, Charles W., and Scott P. Beetham. "The Origin of Article I, Section 7 of the Washington State Constitution." *Seattle University Law Review* 31 (2007): 431–67.

Johnson, David K. *The Lavender Scare: The Cold War Persecution of Gays and Lesbians in the Federal Government*. University of Chicago Press, 2006.

Jouvenet, Morgan. "Contexts and Temporalities in Andrew Abbott's Processual Sociology." *Annales. Histoire, Sciences Sociales-English Edition* 71, no. 3 (2016): 361–92.

Kalhan, Anil. "The Fourth Amendment and Privacy Implications of Interior Immigration Enforcement." *UC Davis Law Review* 41 (2007): 1137–1218.

Kalven Jr., Harry. "Privacy in Tort Law: Were Warren and Brandeis Wrong?" *Law and Contemporary Problems* 31, no. 2 (1966): 326–41.

Kasinitz, Philip, ed. *Metropolis: Centre and Symbol of Our Times.* Macmillan, 1995.

Kasper, Debbie V. S. "The Evolution (or Devolution) of Privacy." *Sociological Forum* 20, no. 1 (2005): 69–92.

Kasper, Debbie V. S. "Privacy as a Social Good." *Social Thought and Research* 28 (2007): 165–89.

Katz, James E., and Annette R. Tassone. "Public Opinion Trends: Privacy and Information Technology." *The Public Opinion Quarterly* 54, no. 1 (1990): 125–43.

Kertzer, David, and Dominique Arel, eds. *Census and Identity: The Politics of Race, Ethnicity, and Language in National Censuses.* Cambridge University Press, 2002.

Keulen, Sjoerd, and Ronald Kroeze. "Privacy From a Historical Perspective." In *The Handbook of Privacy Studies: An Interdisciplinary Introduction*, ed. Bart van der Sloot and Aviva de Groot. Amsterdam University Press, 2018.

Kinley, David. *The Use of Credit Instruments in Payments in the United States (National Monetary Commission).* Augustus M. Kelley, 1910.

Kling, Rob. "The Struggles for Democracy in an Information Society." *The Information Society* 4, no. 1–2 (1986): 1–7.

Knight, Carly R. "Classifying the Corporation: The Role of Naturalizing Analogies in American Corporate Development, 1870–1930." *Socio-Economic Review* 21, no. 3 (2023): 1629–55.

Konvitz, Milton R. "Privacy and the Law: A Philosophical Prelude." *Law and Contemporary Problems* 31, no. 2 (1966): 272–80.

Koopman, Colin. *How We Became Our Data: A Genealogy of the Informational Person.* University of Chicago Press, 2019.

Koselleck, Reinhart. *Futures Past: On the Semantics of Historical Time.* Columbia University Press, 2004.

Koselleck, Reinhart. *The Practice of Conceptual History.* Stanford University Press, 2002.

Kozlowski, Austin C., Matt Taddy, and James A. Evans. "The Geometry of Culture: Analyzing the Meanings of Class Through Word Embeddings." *American Sociological Review* 84, no. 5 (2019): 905–49.

Kramer, Howard D. "The Beginnings of the Public Health Movement in the United States." *Bulletin of the History of Medicine* 21 (1947): 352–76.

Kramer, Irwin P. "The Birth of Privacy Law: A Century Since Warren and Brandeis." *Catholic University Law Review* 39, no. 3 (1990): 703–24.

Kumaraguru, Ponnurangam, and Lorrie Faith Cranor. "Privacy Indexes: A Survey of Westin's Studies." Carnegie Mellon University Institute for Software Research Working Paper, 2005.

Lake, Jessica. *The Face That Launched a Thousand Lawsuits: The American Women Who Forged a Right to Privacy.* Yale University Press, 2016.

LaMay, Craig L. "America's Censor: Anthony Comstock and Free Speech." *Communications and the Law* 19, no. 3 (1997): 1–59.

Landrum, Shane. "Registering Race, Policing Citizenship: Delayed Birth Registration and the Virginia Racial Integrity Act, 1924–1975." Working Paper, Policy History Conference, Columbus, 2010.

Lane, Frederick S. *American Privacy: The 400-Year History of Our Most Contested Right.* Beacon, 2009.

Lange, Bettina. "Sociology of Regulation." In *Research Handbook on the Sociology of Law*, ed. Jiří Přibáň. Edward Elgar, 2020.

Laslett, Barbara. "The Family as a Public and Private Institution: An Historical Perspective." *Journal of Marriage and Family* 35, no. 3 (1973): 480–92.

Latour, Bruno. *The Pasteurization of France.* Harvard University Press, 1993.

Latour, Bruno. *Science in Action: How to Follow Scientists and Engineers Through Society.* Harvard University Press, 1987.

Lauer, Josh. *Creditworthy: A History of Consumer Surveillance and Financial Identity in America.* Columbia University Press, 2017.

Lauer, Josh. "From Rumor to Written Record: Credit Reporting and the Invention of Financial Identity in Nineteenth-Century America." *Technology and Culture* 49, no. 2 (2008): 301–24.

Lauer, Josh. "Surveillance History and the History of New Media: An Evidential Paradigm." *New Media and Society* 14, no. 4 (2012): 566–82.

Lauer, Josh, and Kenneth Lipartito. *Surveillance Capitalism in America.* University of Pennsylvania Press, 2021.

Lefebvre, Henri. *The Production of Space.* Blackwell, 1991.

Lehoucq, Emilio, and Sidney Tarrow. "The Rise of a Transnational Movement to Protect Privacy." *Mobilization* 25, no. 2 (2020): 161–84.

Leigh, Robert D. *Federal Health Administration in the United States.* Harper, 1927.

Lempert, Lora Bex. "Asking Questions of the Data: Memo Writing in the Grounded Theory Tradition." In *The SAGE Handbook of Grounded Theory*, ed. Anthony Bryant and Kathy Charmaz. SAGE, 2007.

Leonard, Devin. *Neither Snow nor Rain: A History of the United States Postal Service.* Grove, 2016.

Lepore, Jill. "The Prism: Privacy in an Age of Publicity." *The New Yorker*, June 24, 2013.

Lessig, Lawrence. "The Architecture of Privacy." *Vanderbilt Journal of Environmental Law and Practice* 1, no. 1 (1999): 56–65.

Lévi-Strauss, Claude. *Structural Anthropology.* Basic, 1963.

Levitsky, Steven, and Daniel Ziblatt. *How Democracies Die.* Broadway, 2018.

Levy, Jonathan. *Freaks of Fortune: The Emerging World of Capitalism and Risk in America.* Harvard University Press, 2012.

Lieberson, Stanley, and Freda B. Lynn. "Barking Up the Wrong Branch: Scientific Alternatives to the Current Model of Sociological Science." *Annual Review of Sociology* 28, no. 1 (2002): 1–19.

Link, Vernon. "A History of Plague in the United States of America." *Public Health Monograph* 26, *Publication 392*. Government Printing Office, 1955.

Lipsky, Michael. *Street-Level Bureaucracy: Dilemmas of the Individual in Public Services*. Russell Sage Foundation, 1980.

Little, Daniel. *New Contributions to the Philosophy of History*. Springer Netherlands, 2009.

Lomawaima, Tsianina. "Domesticity in the Federal Indian Schools: The Power of Authority Over Mind and Body." *American Ethnologist* 20, no. 2 (1993): 227–40.

Lopez, Russ. *Building American Public Health: Urban Planning, Architecture, and the Quest for Better Health in the United States*. Palgrave Macmillan, 2012.

Loveman, Mara. *National Colors: Racial Classification and the State in Latin America*. Oxford University Press, 2014.

Lubove, Roy. "Lawrence Veiller and the New York State Tenement House Commission of 1900." *The Mississippi Valley Historical Review* 47, no. 4 (1961): 659–77.

Lubove, Roy. *The Progressives and the Slums: Tenement House Reform in New York City, 1890–1917*. University of Pittsburgh Press, 1963.

Lukes, Steven, and Andrew Scull, eds. *Durkheim and the Law*. Palgrave Macmillan, 2013.

Lynch, John F. "Truthful Libel and Right of Privacy in Wyoming." *Wyoming Law Journal* 11, no. 3 (2019): 184–88.

Lyon, David. "9/11, Synopticon, and Scopophilia: Watching and Being Watched." In *The New Politics of Surveillance and Visibility*, ed. Kevin Haggerty and Richard Ericson. University of Toronto Press, 2005.

Lyon, David. *The Culture of Surveillance: Watching as a Way of Life.* Polity, 2018.

Lyon, David. *The Electronic Eye: The Rise of Surveillance Society*. University of Minnesota Press, 1994.

Lyon, David. "An Electronic Panopticon? A Sociological Critique of Surveillance Theory." *The Sociological Review* 41, no. 4 (1993): 653–78.

Lyon, David, ed. *Surveillance as Social Sorting: Privacy, Risk, and Digital Discrimination*. Routledge, 2003.

Lyon, David. "Surveillance: History, Technology, Culture." In *Histories of State Surveillance in Europe and Beyond*, ed. Kees Boersma, Rosamunde Van Brakel, Chiara Fonio, and Pieter Wagenaar. Routledge, 2014.

Lyon, David. "Surveillance Technology and Surveillance Society." In *Modernity and Technology*, ed. Thomas J. Misa, Philip Brey, and Andrew Feenberg. MIT Press, 2003.

Lystra, Karen. *Searching the Heart: Women, Men, and Romantic Love in Nineteenth-Century America*. Oxford University Press, 1992.

Ma, Long, Yanqing Zhang. "Using Word2Vec to Process Big Text Data." In *IEEE International Conference on Big Data (Big Data) 2015*, 2895–97. IEEE, 2015.

Machiavelli, Niccolo. *The Prince and Other Writings*. Simon and Schuster, 2014.

Madden, Mary, Amanda Lenhart, Sandra Cortesi, et al. "Teens, Social Media, and Privacy." *Pew Research Center* 21, no. 1055 (2013): 2–86.

Madison, James H. "The Evolution of Commercial Credit Reporting Agencies in Nineteenth-Century America." *Business History Review* 48, no. 2(1974): 164–86.

Mahoney, James. "Path Dependence in Historical Sociology." *Theory and Society* 29, no. 4 (2000): 507–48.

Mann, Michael. "The Autonomous Power of the State: Its Origins, Mechanisms, and Results." *European Journal of Sociology* 25, no. 2 (1984): 185–213.

Mann, Steve, and Joseph Ferenbok. "New Media and the Power Politics of Sousveillance in a Surveillance-Dominated World." *Surveillance and Society* 11, no. 1–2 (2013): 18–34.

Mannheim, Karl. *Ideology and Utopia*. Routledge, 1964.

Manokha, Ivan. "Surveillance, Panopticism, and Self-Discipline in the Digital Age." *Surveillance and Society* 16, no. 2 (2018): 219–37.

Margulis, Stephen T. "Conceptions of Privacy: Current Status and Next Steps." *Journal of Social Issues* 33, no. 3 (1977): 5–21.

Margulis, Stephen T. "Privacy as a Social Issue and Behavioral Concept." *Journal of Social Issues* 59, no. 2 (2003): 243–61.

Marion, Linda S., Eugene Garfield, Lowell L. Hargens, Leah A. Lievrouw, Howard D. White, and Concepción S. Wilson. "Social Network Analysis and Citation Network Analysis: Complementary Approaches to the Study of Scientific Communication." *Proceedings of the American Society for Information Science and Technology* 40, no. 1 (2003): 486–87.

Markel, Howard. *Quarantine! East European Jewish Immigrants and the New York City Epidemics of 1892*. Johns Hopkins University Press, 1999.

Marshall, Anna-Maria. "Injustice Frames, Legality, and the Everyday Construction of Sexual Harassment." *Law and Social Inquiry* 28, no. 3 (2003): 659–90.

Marshall, Edward. "New York Tenements." *The North American Review* 157, no. 445 (1893): 753–56.

Marske, Charles E. "Durkheim's 'Cult of the Individual' and the Moral Reconstitution of Society." *Sociological Theory* 5, no. 1 (1987): 1–14.

Martin, Brian. *Information Liberation. Challenging the Corruptions of Information Power*. Freedom Press, 1998.

Martin, Jessica, and Alec Ryrie, eds. *Private and Domestic Devotion in Early Modern Britain*. Ashgate, 2012.

Marwick, Alice E., and danah boyd. "Networked Privacy: How Teenagers Negotiate Context in Social Media." *New Media and Society* 16, no. 7 (2014): 1051–67.

Marx, Gary T. "Varieties of Personal Information as Influences on Attitudes Towards Surveillance." In *The New Politics of Surveillance and Visibility*, ed. Kevin Haggerty and Richard Ericson. University of Toronto Press, 2005.

Marx, Gary T. "What's New About the 'New Surveillance'? Classifying for Change and Continuity." *Surveillance and Society* 1, no. 1 (2002): 9–29.

Marx, Gary T. *Windows Into the Soul: Surveillance and Society in an Age of High Technology*. University of Chicago Press, 2016.

Marx, Karl. *Capital: Volume 1: A Critique of Political Economy*. Penguin Classics, 1992.

Marx, Karl. "The Eighteenth Brumaire of Louis Bonaparte." In *The Marx-Engels Reader*, ed. Robert C. Tucker. Norton, 1978.

Marx, Karl. "The German Ideology." In *The Marx-Engels Reader*, ed. Robert C. Tucker. Norton, 1978.

Marx, Karl. "On the Jewish Question." In *The Marx-Engels Reader*, ed. Robert C. Tucker. Norton, 1978.

Marx, Karl. "Speech at the Anniversary of the People's Paper." In *The Marx-Engels Reader*, ed. Robert C. Tucker. Norton, 1978.

Massey, Douglas S. "American Apartheid: Segregation and the Making of the Underclass." *American Journal of Sociology* 96, no. 2 (1990): 329–57.

Mathews, Donald G. "The Second Great Awakening as an Organizing Process, 1780–1830: An Hypothesis." *American Quarterly* 21, no. 1 (1969): 23–43.

Mau, Steffen. *The Metric Society: On the Quantification of the Social*. Wiley, 2019.

May, Elaine T. *Homeward Bound: American Families in the Cold War Era*. Basic, 2008.

Mayrl, Damon, and Nicholas Hoover Wilson. "What Do Historical Sociologists Do All Day? Analytic Architectures in Historical Sociology." *American Journal of Sociology* 125, no. 5 (2020): 1345–94.

McAdam, Doug. *Political Process and the Development of Black Insurgency, 1930–1970*. University of Chicago Press, 1999.

McCann, Michael. "Law and Social Movements: Contemporary Perspectives." *Annual Review of Law and Social Science* 2 (2006): 17–38.

McCarthy, John D., and Mayer N. Zald. "Resource Mobilization and Social Movements: A Partial Theory." *American Journal of Sociology* 82, no. 6 (1977): 1212–41.

McClain, Charles. "Of Medicine, Race, and American Law: The Bubonic Plague Outbreak of 1900." *Law and Social Inquiry* 13, no. 3 (1988): 447–513.

McCoy, Alfred W. *Policing America's Empire: The United States, the Philippines, and the Rise of the Surveillance State*. University of Wisconsin Press, 2009.

McFarland, Daniel A., Daniel Ramage, Jason Chuang, Jeffrey Heer, Christopher D. Manning, and Daniel Jurafsky. "Differentiating Language Usage Through Topic Models." *Poetics* 41, no. 6 (2013): 607–25.

McGerr, Michael. *A Fierce Discontent: The Rise and Fall of the Progressive Movement in America*. Oxford University Press, 2003.

McKeon, Michael. *The Secret History of Domesticity: Public, Private, and the Division of Knowledge*. Johns Hopkins University Press, 2006.

McKinney, William M., ed. *Ruling Case Law* 21. Edward Thompson, 1918.

McMath, Robert C. *American Populism: A Social History, 1877–1898*. Macmillan, 1993.

Mead, George H. *The Philosophy of the Present*. University of Chicago Press, 1932.

Meagher, Thomas Francis. *The Commercial Agency "System" of the United States and Canada Exposed. Is The Secret Inquisition a Curse or a Benefit?* New York, 1876.

Melosi, Martin C. *The Sanitary City: Urban Infrastructure in America from Colonial Times to the Present*. Johns Hopkins University Press, 2000.

Mencken, Henry L. *Newspaper Days, 1899–1906*. Johns Hopkins University Press, 1996.

Mensel, Robert E. "'Kodakers Lying in Wait': Amateur Photography and the Right of Privacy in New York, 1885–1915." *American Quarterly* 43, no. 1 (1991): 24–45.

Merton, Robert K. "Social Structure and Anomie." *American Sociological Review* 3, no. 5 (1938): 672–82.

Merton, Robert K. *Social Theory and Social Structure*. Free Press, 1968.

Merton, Robert K. *The Sociology of Science: Theoretical and Empirical Investigations*. University of Chicago Press, 1979.

Mertz, Elizabeth. "A New Social Constructionism for Sociolegal Studies." *Law and Society Review* 28, no. 5 (1994): 1243–66.

Merwood-Salisbury, Joanna. "Architecture as Model and Standard: Modern Liberalism and Tenement House Reform in New York City at the Turn of the Twentieth Century." *Architectural Theory Review*, 23, no. 3 (2019): 345–62.

Meyer, David S., and Debra C. Minkoff. "Conceptualizing Political Opportunity." *Social Forces* 82, no. 4 (2004): 1457–92.

Michel, Jean-Baptiste, Yuan Kui Shen, Aviva Presser Aiden, et al. "Quantitative Analysis of Culture Using Millions of Digitized Books." *Science* 331, no. 6014 (2011): 176–82.

Mill, John Stuart. *On Liberty and Other Essays*. Oxford University Press, 1998.

Miller, Arthur R. *The Assault on Privacy: Computers, Data Banks, and Dossiers*. University of Michigan Press, 1971.

Mitchell, Timothy. "Everyday Metaphors of Power." *Theory and Society* 19 (1990): 545–77.

Moore, Barrington. *Privacy: Studies in Social and Cultural History*. Routledge, 1984.

Moreham, Nicole A. "Privacy in Public Places." *The Cambridge Law Journal* 65, no. 3 (2006): 606–35.

Moreham, Nicole A. "The Right to Respect for Private Life in the European Convention on Human Rights: A Re-Examination." *European Human Rights Law Review* 44 (2008), Victoria University of Wellington Legal Research Paper No. 11/2019.

Moreland, Roy. "The Right of Privacy To-Day." *Kentucky Law Journal* 19, no. 2 (1931): 101–38.

Morgan, Edmund S. *The Puritan Family: Religion and Domestic Relations in Seventeenth-Century New England*. Harper, 1944.

Morgan, Kimberly J., and Ann Shola Orloff, eds. *The Many Hands of the State: Theorizing Political Authority and Social Control*. Cambridge University Press, 2017.

Morton, George W. *Laws and Ordinances Relative to the Preservation of Public Health*. Edmund Jones and Co., 1860.

Moudry, Roberta. *The American Skyscraper: Cultural Histories*. Cambridge University Press, 2005.

Moyn, Samuel. *Liberalism Against Itself: Cold War Intellectuals and the Making of Our Times*. Yale University Press, 2023.

Mueller, Milton. "Universal Service in Telephone History: A Reconstruction." *Telecommunications Policy* 17, no. 5 (1993): 352–69.

Muhammad, Khalil Gibran. *The Condemnation of Blackness: Race, Crime, and the Making of Modern Urban America*. Harvard University Press, 2010.

Muller, Christopher. "Freedom and Convict Leasing in the Postbellum South." *American Journal of Sociology* 124, no. 2 (2018): 367–405.

Müller, Jan-Werner. "On Conceptual History." In *Rethinking Modern European Intellectual History*, ed. Darrin M. McMahon and Samuel Moyn. Oxford University Press, 2014.

Myrdal, Gunnar. *An American Dilemma: The Negro Problem and Modern Democracy*. Harper, 1944.

Naipaul, Vidiadhar S. *The Enigma of Arrival*. Vintage, 1988.

Negley, Glenn. "Philosophical Views on the Value of Privacy." *Law and Contemporary Problems* 31, no. 1 (1966): 319–25.

Nelkin, Dorothy, and Lori Andrews. "Surveillance Creep in the Genetic Age." In *Surveillance as Social Sorting*, ed. David Lyon. Routledge, 2005.

Nelson, Deborah. *Pursuing Privacy in Cold War America*. Columbia University Press, 2001.

Neocleous, Mark. "Privacy, Secrecy, Idiocy." *Social Research* 69, no. 1 (2002): 85–110.

Newman, Mark E. "Modularity and Community Structure in Networks." *Proceedings of the National Academy of Sciences* 103, no. 23 (2006): 8577–82.

Nicholls, David. "Positive Liberty, 1880–1914." *American Political Science Review* 56, no. 1 (1962): 114–28.

Nietzsche, Friedrich. *Human, All Too Human: A Book for Free Spirits*. Penguin Classics, 1994.

Nietzsche, Friedrich. "On the Uses and Disadvantages of History for Life." In *Untimely Meditations*, ed. Daniel Breazeale. Cambridge University Press, 1997.

Nippert-Eng, Christena E. *Islands of Privacy*. University of Chicago Press, 2010.

Nissenbaum, Helen. "A Contextual Approach to Privacy Online." *Daedalus* 140, no. 4 (2011): 32–48.

Nissenbaum, Helen. "Privacy as Contextual Integrity." *Washington Law Review* 79 (2004): 119–158.

Nissenbaum, Helen. *Privacy in Context: Technology, Policy, and the Integrity of Social Life*. Stanford University Press, 2010.

Nissenbaum, Helen. "Protecting Privacy in an Information Age: The Problem of Privacy in Public." *Law and Philosophy* 17 (1998): 559–96.

Nissenbaum, Helen. "Toward an Approach to Privacy in Public: Challenges of Information Technology." *Ethics and Behavior* 7, no. 3 (1997): 207–19.

Nobles, Melissa. *Shades of Citizenship: Race and the Census in Modern Politics*. Stanford University Press, 2000.

Nock, Steven L. *The Costs of Privacy: Surveillance and Reputation in America*. De Gruyter, 1993.

Nock, Steven L. "Too Much Privacy?" *Journal of Family Issues* 19, no. 1 (1998): 101–18.

Norris, James D. *R. G. Dun & Co. 1841–1900: The Development of Credit-Reporting in the Nineteenth Century*. Greenwood, 1978.

Novak, William J. "The Myth of the 'Weak' American State," *The American Historical Review* 113, no. 3 (2008): 752–72.

Novak, William J., Stephen W. Sawyer, and James T. Sparrow. "Democratic States of Unexception: Toward a New Genealogy of the American Political." In *The Many Hands of the State: Theorizing Political Authority and Social Control*, ed. Kimberly J. Morgan and Ann Shola Orloff. Cambridge University Press, 2018.

Nugent, Rolf. *Consumer Credit and Economic Stability*. Russell Sage Foundation, 1939.

Nuñez, Adriana C. "Collateral Subjects: The Normalization of Surveillance for Mexican Americans on the Border." *Sociology of Race and Ethnicity* 6, no. 4 (2020): 548–61.

Oberg, Barbara B., ed. *The Papers of Thomas Jefferson, vol. 39, 13 November 1802–3 March 1803*. Princeton University Press, 2012.

Orren, Karen, and Stephen Skowronek. *The Policy State: An American Predicament*. Harvard University Press, 2017.

Orwell, George. *Nineteen Eighty-Four*. Signet Classics, 1961.

Ostrander, Gilman M. *American Civilization in the First Machine Age, 1890–1940*. Harper Collins, 1970.

Otte, Evelien, and Ronald Rousseau. "Social Network Analysis: A Powerful Strategy, Also for the Information Sciences." *Journal of Information Science* 28, no. 6 (2002): 441–53.

Pagano, Marco, and Tullio Jappelli. "Information-Sharing in Credit Markets." *Journal of Finance* 48, no. 5 (1993): 1693–718.

Painter, Nell Irvin. *Standing at Armageddon: A Grassroots History of the Progressive Era*. Norton, 2008.

Palmer, Vernon L. "Three Milestones in the History of Privacy in the United States." *Tulane European and Civil Law Forum* 26 (2011): 67–97.

Parent, William A. "Recent Work on the Concept of Privacy." *American Philosophical Quarterly* 20, no. 4 (1983): 341–55.

Parenti, Christian. *The Soft Cage: Surveillance in America, from Slavery to the War on Terror*. Basic, 2007.

Park, Robert. *On Social Control and Collective Behavior*. University of Chicago Press, 1997.

Parsons, Talcott. "Age and Sex in the Social Structure of the United States." *American Sociological Review* 7, no. 5 (1942): 604–16.

Pasquale, Frank. *The Black Box Society*. Harvard University Press, 2015.

Pasquale, Frank. "Privacy, Antitrust, and Power." *George Mason Law Review* 20, no. 4 (2012): 1009–24.

Pastalan, Leon A. "Privacy as a Behavioral Concept." *Social Science* 45, no. 2 (1970): 93–97.

Pasti, Rodrigo, Fabrício G. Vilasbôas, Isabela R. Roque, and Leandro N. de Castro. "A Sensitivity and Performance Analysis of Word2Vec Applied to Emotion State Classification Using a Deep Neural Architecture." In *International Symposium on Distributed Computing and Artificial Intelligence 2019*, 199–206. Avila, Spain, 2019.

Patterson, Orlando. "Making Sense of Culture." *Annual Review of Sociology* 40 (2014): 1–30.

Patton, Jason W. "Protecting Privacy in Public? Surveillance Technologies and the Value of Public Places." *Ethics and Information Technology* 2 (2000): 181–87.

Patton, Paul. "MetamorphoLogic: Bodies and Powers in a Thousand Plateaus." *Journal of the British Society for Phenomenology* 25, no. 2 (1994): 157–69.

Paul, James C. N., and Murray L. Schwartz. "Obscenity in the Mails: A Comment on Some Problems of Federal Censorship." *University of Pennsylvania Law Review* 106 (1957): 214–53.

Pearce, Lisa D. "Mixed Methods Inquiry in Sociology." *American Behavioral Scientist* 56, no. 6 (2012): 829–48.

Pedersen, Dahrl M. "Psychological Functions of Privacy." *Journal of Environmental Psychology* 17, no. 2 (1997): 147–56.

Peirce, Charles S. *Collected Papers of Charles Sanders Peirce, Volumes I and II: Principles of Philosophy and Elements of Logic*, ed. Charles Hartshorne, Paul Weiss, and Arthur W. Burks. Harvard University Press, 1932.

Peters, Guy B., Jon Pierre, and Desmond S. King. "The Politics of Path Dependency: Political Conflict in Historical Institutionalism." *The Journal of Politics* 67, no. 4 (2005): 1275–300.

Petersen, William. *Ethnicity Counts*. Transaction, 1997.

Peterson, Dawn. *Indians in the Family: Adoption and the Politics of Antebellum Expansion*. Harvard University Press, 2017.

Phillips, Scott, and Ryken Grattet. "Judicial Rhetoric, Meaning-Making, and the Institutionalization of Hate Crime Law." *Law and Society Review* 34, no. 3 (2000): 567–606.

Pierson, Paul. "Increasing Returns, Path Dependence, and the Study of Politics." *American Political Science Review* 94, no. 2 (2000): 251–67.

Piketty, Thomas, and Emmanuel Saez. "Inequality in the Long Run." *Science* 344, no. 6186 (2014): 838–43.

Pilpel, Harriet F. "The Challenge of Privacy." In *The Price of Liberty*, ed. Alan Reitman. Norton, 1969.

Pindek, Shani, Winny Shen, and Stephanie Andel. "Finally, Some 'Me Time': A New Theoretical Perspective on the Benefits of Commuting." *Organizational Psychology Review* 13, no. 1 (2023): 44–66.

Plunz, Richard. *History of Housing in New York City*. Columbia University Press, 1990.

Pochurek, Lynne M. "From the Battlefront to the Homefront: Infrared Surveillance and the War on Drugs Place Privacy Under Siege." *St. Thomas Law Review* 7 (1994): 137–68.

Polelle, Michael J. "The Unconstitutionality of the Qualified Truth Defense to Libel Actions." *UIC Law Review* 11, no. 2 (1978): 259–81.

Poole, Deborah. *Vision, Race, and Modernity: A Visual Economy of the Andean Image World*. Princeton University Press, 1997.

Popenoe, David. *Private Pleasure, Public Plight: Urban Development, Suburban Sprawl, and the Decline of Community*. Routledge, 2001.

Porter, Theodore M. *Trust in Numbers: The Pursuit of Objectivity in Science and Public Life*. Princeton University Press, 1995.

Post, Robert C. "Three Concepts of Privacy." *Georgetown Law Journal* 89 (2001): 2087–98.

Poster, Mark. "Hardt and Negri's Information Empire: A Critical Response." *Cultural Politics* 1, no. 1 (2005): 101–18.

Pound, Roscoe. *Law and Morals*. University of North Carolina Press, 1924.

Prasad, Monica. *The Land of Too Much American Abundance and the Paradox of Poverty*. Harvard University Press, 2012.

Pressly, Lowry. *The Right to Oblivion: Privacy and the Good Life*. Harvard University Press, 2024.

Preston, Samuel H., and Michael R. Haines. *Fatal Years: Child Mortality in Late Nineteenth-Century America*. Princeton University Press, 2014.

Prosser, William L. "Privacy." *California Law Review* 48, no. 3 (1960): 383–423.

Quill, Lawrence. *Secrets and Democracy*. Palgrave Macmillan, 2014.

Rabban, David M. *Free Speech in Its Forgotten Years*. Cambridge University Press, 1997.

Raley, Rita. "Dataveillance and Countervailance." In *Raw Data Is an Oxymoron*, ed. Lisa Gitelman. MIT Press, 2013.

Rana, Aziz. *The Constitutional Bind: How Americans Came to Idolize a Document That Fails Them*. University of Chicago Press, 2024.

Rana, Aziz. "Constitutionalism and the Foundations of the Security State." *California Law Review* 103, no. 2 (2015): 335–85.

Redford, Bruce. *The Converse of the Pen: Acts of Intimacy in the Eighteenth-Century Familiar Letter*. University of Chicago Press, 1986.

Regan, Priscilla M. *Legislating Privacy: Technology, Social Values, and Public Policy*. University of North Carolina Press, 1995.

Regan, Priscilla M. "Privacy as a Common Good in the Digital World." *Information, Communication and Society* 5, no. 3 (2002): 382–405.

Reich, Charles A. "Police Questioning of Law Abiding Citizens." *Yale Law Journal* 75 (1966): 1161–72.

Reidenberg, Joel R. "Privacy in Public." *University of Miami Law Review* 69 (2014): 141–59.

Reilly, Philip, and Margery Shaw. "The Virginia Racial Integrity Act Revisited: The Plecker-Laughlin Correspondence: 1928–1930." *American Journal of Medical Genetics* 16, no. 4 (1983): 483–92.

Reiman, Jeffrey H. "Privacy, Intimacy, and Personhood." In *Privacy*, ed. Eric Barendt. Routledge, 2001.

Rheinstein, Max, ed. *Max Weber on Law in Economy and Society*. Simon and Schuster, 1967.

Rice, Thurman B. *The Hoosier Health Officer: A Biography of Dr. John N. Hurty*. Indiana State Board of Health, 1946.

Richards, Neil M. "The Puzzle of Brandeis, Privacy, and Speech." *Vanderbilt Law Review* 63, no. 5 (2010): 1295–352.

Richards, Neil M., and Daniel J. Solove. "Prosser's Privacy Law: A Mixed Legacy." *California Law Review* 98, no. 6 (2010): 1887–924.

Richardson, Meagan. *The Right to Privacy: Origins and Influence of a Nineteenth-Century Idea*. Cambridge University Press, 2017.

Riis, Jacob. *How the Other Half Lives: Studies Among the New York Tenements*. Charles Scribner's Sons, 1890.

Riis, Jacob. *The Making of an American*. The Macmillan Company, 1901.

Risse, Guenter. *Plague, Fear, and Politics in San Francisco's Chinatown*. Johns Hopkins University Press, 2012.

Roberts, Samuel. *Infectious Fear Politics, Disease, and the Health Effects of Segregation*. University of North Carolina Press, 2009.

Rodriguez, Pedro, and Arthur Spirling. "Word Embeddings: What Works, What Doesn't, and How to Tell the Difference for Applied Research." *The Journal of Politics* 84, no. 1 (2021): 101–15.

Roosevelt, Theodore. *Theodore Roosevelt: An Autobiography*. The Macmillan Company, 1913.

Rose, Nikolas, Pat O'Malley, and Mariana Valverde. "Governmentality." *Annual Review of Law and Social Science* 2 (2006): 83–104.

Rosen, David, and Aaron Santesso. "Inviolate Personality and the Literary Roots of the Right to Privacy." *Law and Literature* 23, no. 1 (2011): 1–25.

Rosen, Jeffrey. *The Unwanted Gaze: The Destruction of Privacy in America*. Vintage, 2011.

Rosenthal, Caitlin. *Accounting for Slavery*. Harvard University Press, 2018.

Rossiter, Clinton L. *Constitutional Dictatorship: Crisis Government in the Modern Democracies*. Princeton University Press, 1948.

Roth, Louise Marie. "The Right to Privacy is Political: Power, the Boundary Between Public and Private, and Sexual Harassment." *Law and Social Inquiry* 24, no. 1 (1999): 45–71.

Rothschild-Elyassi, Gil, Johann Koehler, and Jonathan Simon. "Actuarial Justice at a Quarter Century." In *The Handbook of Social Control*, ed. Mathieu Deflem. Wiley, 2019.

Rothstein, Richard. *The Color of Law: A Forgotten History of How Our Government Segregated America*. Liveright, 2017.

Rubenfeld, Jed. "The Right of Privacy." *Harvard Law Review* 102, no. 4 (1989): 737–807.

Rubin, Zick, Charles T. Hill, Letitia Anne Peplau, and Christine Dunkel-Schetter. "Self-Disclosure in Dating Couples: Sex Roles and the Ethic of Openness." *Journal of Marriage and the Family* 42, no. 2 (1980): 305–17.

Rule, Alix, Jean-Philippe Cointet, and Peter S. Bearman. "Lexical Shifts, Substantive Changes, and Continuity in State of the Union Discourse, 1790–2014." *Proceedings of the National Academy of Sciences of the United States of America* 112, no. 35 (2015): 10837–44.

Rule, James B. *Privacy in Peril*. Oxford University Press, 2009.

Rule, James B. *Private Lives and Public Surveillance: Social Control in the Computer Age*. Schocken, 1974.

Rule, James B. *Taking Privacy Seriously: How to Create the Rights We Need While We Still Have Something to Protect*. University of California Press, 2024.

Rule, James B., Doug McAdam, Linda Stearns, and David Uglow. "Documentary Identification and Mass Surveillance in the United States." *Social Problems* 31, no. 2 (1983): 222–34.

Rule, James B., Doug McAdam, Linda Stearns, and David Uglow. *The Politics of Privacy: Planning for Personal Data Systems as Powerful Technologies*. Elsevier, 1980.

Ruppenthal, Jacob C. "Criminal Statutes on Birth Control." *Journal of Criminal Law and Criminology* 10 (1919): 48–61.

Sadowski, Jathan. *Too Smart: How Digital Capitalism Is Extracting Data, Controlling Our Lives, and Taking Over the World*. MIT Press, 2020.

Sadowski, Jathan. "When Data Is Capital: Datafication, Accumulation, and Extraction." *Big Data and Society* 6, no. 1 (2019): 1–12.

Sahlins, Marshall. *Islands of History*. University of Chicago Press, 1985.

Satia, Priya. *Spies in Arabia: The Great War and the Cultural Foundations of Britain's Covert Empire in the Middle East*. Oxford University Press, 2008.

Sawers, Brian. "The Poll Tax Before Jim Crow." *American Journal of Legal History* 57, no. 2 (1997): 166–97.

Schattschneider, Elmer E. *The Semisovereign People: A Realist's View of Democracy in America*. Holt, Rinehart, and Winston, 1960.

Scheppele, Kim. "Autocratic Legalism." *The University of Chicago Law Review* 85, no. 2 (2018): 545–84.

Schlabach, Elizabeth. "The Influenza Epidemic and Jim Crow Public Health Policies and Practices in Chicago, 1917–1921." *The Journal of African American History* 104, no. 1 (2019): 31–58.

Schmitt, Carl. *Die Diktatur*. Duncker & Humblot, 1921.

Schmitt, Carl. *Political Theology*. MIT Press, 1985.

Schumpeter, Joseph. *The Economics and Sociology of Capitalism*, ed. Richard Swedberg. Princeton University Press, 1991.

Schwartz, Barry. "The Social Psychology of Privacy." *American Journal of Sociology* 73, no. 6 (1968): 741–52.

Sciama, Lidia. "The Problem of Privacy in Mediterranean Anthropology." In *Women and Space: Ground Rules and Social Maps*, ed. Shirley Ardener. Routledge, 1993.

Scott, James. *Seeing Like a State: How Certain Schemes to Improve the Human Condition Have Failed*. Yale University Press, 1998.

Seipp, David J. "The Right to Privacy in American History." Harvard University Program on Information Resources Policy Publication P-78-3 (1978).

Seipp, David J. "The Right to Privacy in Nineteenth Century America." *Harvard Law Review* 94, no. 8 (1981): 1892–910.

Sennett, Richard. *The Fall of Public Man.* Norton, 1974.

Seo, Sarah A. "The New Public." *Yale Law Journal* 125 (2016): 1616–71.

Sevignani, Sebastian. "The Commodification of Privacy on the Internet." *Science and Public Policy* 40, no. 6 (2013): 733–39.

Sewell, William H. *Logics of History: Social Theory and Social Transformation.* University of Chicago Press, 2005.

Sewell, William H. "Historical Events as Transformations of Structures: Inventing Revolution at the Bastille." *Theory and Society* 25, no. 6 (1996): 841–81.

Sewell, William H. "Three Temporalities: Toward an Eventful Sociology." In *The Historic Turn in the Human Sciences*, ed. Terrence McDonald. University of Michigan Press, 1996.

Shapiro, Fred R., and Michelle Pearse. "The Most-Cited Law Review Articles of All Time." *Michigan Law Review* 110, no. 8 (2012): 1483–520.

Shils, Edward. "Privacy: Its Constitution and Vicissitudes." *Law and Contemporary Problems* 31, no. 2 (1966): 281–306.

Shlapentokh, Vladimir. *Public and Private Life of the Soviet People: Changing Values in Post-Stalin Russia.* Oxford University Press, 1989.

Shoeman, Ferdinand D., ed. *Philosophical Dimensions of Privacy: An Anthology.* Cambridge University Press, 1984.

Shryock, Richard H. "The Early American Public Health Movement." *American Journal of Public Health* 27, no. 10 (1937): 965–71.

Simitis, Spiros. "Privacy—An Endless Debate?" *California Law Review* 98, no. 6 (2010): 1989–2005.

Simitis, Spiros. "Reviewing Privacy in an Information Society." *University of Pennsylvania Law Review* 135, no. 3 (1987): 707–46.

Simmel, Georg. "Bridge and Door." *Theory, Culture and Society* 11 (1994): 5–10.

Simmel, Georg. "The Metropolis and Mental Life." In *The Sociology of Georg Simmel*, ed. Kurt H. Wolff. Free Press, 1950.

Simmel, Georg. "The Secret and the Secret Society." In *The Sociology of Georg Simmel*, ed. Kurt H. Wolff. Free Press, 1950.

Simmel, Georg. "The Sociology of Secrecy and of Secret Societies." *American Journal of Sociology* 11, no. 4 (1906): 441–98.

Simmel, Georg. *Soziologie: Untersuchungen über die Formen der Vergesellschaftung.* Duncker & Humblot, 1908.

Simmel, Georg. "The Stranger." In *Georg Simmel on Individuality and Social Forms*, ed. Donald N. Levine. University of Chicago Press, 1971.

Simson, Henry L., and McGeorge Bundy. *On Active Service in Peace and War.* Harper & Brothers, 1948.

Skinner-Thompson, Scott. *Privacy at the Margins.* Cambridge University Press, 2020.

Sklansky, David A. "'One Train May Hide Another': Katz, Stonewall, and the Secret Subtext of Criminal Procedure." *U.C. Davis Law Review* 41 (2008): 875–934.

Sklansky, David A. "Too Much Information: How Not to Think About Privacy and the Fourth Amendment." *California Law Review* 102, no. 5 (2014): 1069–122.

Skocpol, Theda. *Protecting Soldiers and Mothers: The Political Origins of Social Policy in the United States.* Harvard University Press, 1995.

Skocpol, Theda. "State Formation and Social Policy in the United States." *American Behavioral Scientist* 35, nos. 4–5 (1992): 559–84.

Skowronek, Stephen. *Building a New American State: The Expansion of National Administrative Capacities, 1877–1920.* Cambridge University Press, 1982.

Small, Mario L. "How to Conduct a Mixed Methods Study: Recent Trends in a Rapidly Growing Literature." *Annual Review of Sociology* 37 (2011): 57–86.

Small, Mario L., and Laura Adler. "The Role of Space in the Formation of Social Ties." *Annual Review of Sociology* 45 (2019): 111–32.

Smelser, Neil. *Social Change in the Industrial Revolution.* University of Chicago Press, 1959.

Smillie, Wilson. "The Basis of Communicable Disease Control." *Public Health Reports* 67, no. 3 (1952): 289–92.

Smith, Adam. *The Wealth of Nations.* Bantam Classics, 2003.

Smith, Janna Malamud. "Privacy and Private States." In *The Private I: Privacy in a Public World,* ed. Molly Peacock. Graywolf, 2001.

Smith, Neil. *The New Urban Frontier: Gentrification and the Revanchist City.* Routledge, 1996.

Smith, Robert Ellis. *Ben Franklin's Web Site: Privacy and Curiosity from Plymouth Rock to the Internet.* Privacy Journal, 2000.

Smith, Stephen Smith. *The City That Was.* Frank Allaben, 1911.

Smith, Timothy L. *Revivalism and Social Reform in Mid-Nineteenth Century America.* Abingdon, 1957.

Solove, Daniel J. "Conceptualizing Privacy." *California Law Review* 90, no. 4 (2002): 1087–155.

Solove, Daniel J. "Introduction: Privacy Self-Management and the Consent Dilemma." *Harvard Law Review* 126, no. 1 (2012): 1880–903.

Solove, Daniel J. *Understanding Privacy.* Harvard University Press, 2010.

Solove, Daniel J., Marc Rotenberg, and Paul M. Schwartz. *Privacy, Information, and Technology.* Aspen, 2006.

Solzhenitsyn, Aleksandr. *Cancer Ward.* Penguin, 1974.

Spacks, Patricia Meyer. *Privacy: Concealing the Eighteenth-Century Self.* University of Chicago Press, 2003.

Spain, Daphne. "Gender and Urban Space." *Annual Review of Sociology* 40 (2014): 195–205.

Spencer, David R. *The Yellow Journalism: The Press and America's Emergence as a World Power.* Northwestern University Press, 2007.

Srnicek, Nick. *Platform Capitalism.* Polity, 2017.

Stage, Sarah. "The Greening of Suburbia." *American Quarterly* 37, no. 5 (1985): 749–54

Sternberg, William P. "Natural Law in American Jurisprudence." *Notre Dame Lawyer* 13, no. 2 (1938): 89–100.

Stimpson, Catharine R., Elsa Dixler, Martha J. Nelson, and Kathryn B. Yatrakis, eds. *Women and the American City.* University of Chicago Press, 1981.

Stinchcombe, Arthur L. "Institutions of Privacy in the Determination of Police Administrative Practice." *American Journal of Sociology* 69, no. 2 (1963): 150–60.

Streitmatter, Rodger. *Mightier Than the Sword: How the News Media Have Shaped American History.* Routledge, 2018.

Sundstrom, Eric, Robert E. Burt, and Douglas Kamp. "Privacy at Work: Architectural Correlates of Job Satisfaction and Job Performance." *The Academy of Management Journal* 23 (1980): 101–17.

Susman, Warren I. *Culture as History: The Transformation of American Society in the Twentieth Century.* Pantheon, 1973.

Sunstein, Cass. *After the Rights Revolution: Reconceiving the Regulatory State.* Harvard University Press, 1993.

Swidler, Ann. "Culture in Action: Symbols and Strategies." *American Sociological Review* 51, no. 2 (1986): 273–86.

Swire, Peter P. "The System of Foreign Intelligence Surveillance Law." *George Washington Law Review* 72 (2003): 1306–72.

Taylor, Charles. *Philosophical Papers: Volume 2, Philosophy and the Human Sciences.* Cambridge University Press, 1985.

Terry, Henry T. "Constitutionality of Statutes Forbidding Advertising Signs on Property." *Yale Law Journal* 24, no. 1 (1915): 1–11.

Tester, Keith, ed. *The Flâneur.* Routledge, 1994.

Thompson, Francis M. L. *The Rise of Respectable Society: A Social History of Victorian Britain, 1830–1900.* Harvard University Press, 1990.

Thompson, Guy H. "The Right of Privacy as Recognized and Protected in Law and in Equity." *Central Law Journal* 47, no. 8 (1898): 148–58.

Thompson, Robert. *Wiring a Continent.* Princeton University Press, 1947.

Thomson, Judith J. "The Right to Privacy." *Philosophy and Public Affairs* 4, no. 4 (1975): 295–314.

Tilly, Charles. "Contentious Repertoires in Great Britain, 1758–1834." *Social Science History* 17, no. 2 (1993): 253–80.

Tilly, Charles. "To Explain Political Processes," *American Journal of Sociology* 100, no. 6 (1995): 1594–610.

Tipple, John. "Big Businessmen and a New Economy." In *The Gilded Age: A Reappraisal,* ed. H. Wayne Morgan. Syracuse University Press, 1970.

Tobey, James A. *Public Health Law.* Williams & Wilkins, 1926.

Tooze, Adam. *Statistics and the German State, 1900–1945: The Making of Modern Economic Knowledge.* Cambridge University Press, 2001.

Torpey, John. *The Invention of the Passport: Surveillance, Citizenship and the State.* Cambridge University Press, 2000.

Tourkochoriti, Ioanna. "The Transatlantic Flow of Data and the National Security Exception in the European Data Privacy Regulation: In Search for Legal

Protection Against Surveillance." *University of Pennsylvania Journal of International Law* 36 (2014): 459–524.

Trauner, Joan. "The Chinese as Medical Scapegoats in San Francisco, 1870–1905." *California History* 57, no. 1 (1978): 70–87.

Tribe, Laurence H. *American Constitutional Law*, 2nd ed. Foundation Press, 1988.

Trodd, Zoe. "In Possession of Space." In *Representing Segregation: Toward an Aesthetics of Living Jim Crow, and Other Forms of Racial Division*, ed. Brian Norman and Piper Kendrix Williams. SUNY Press, 2012.

Trouille, Helen. "Private Life and Public Image: Privacy Legislation in France." *The International and Comparative Law Quarterly* 49, no. 1 (2000): 199–208.

Vagle. Jeffrey L. "Tightening the OODA Loop: Police Militarization, Race, and Algorithmic Surveillance." *Michigan Journal of Race and Law* 22 (2016): 101–37.

Vaisey, Stephen. "Motivation and Justification: A Dual-Process Model of Culture in Action." *American Journal of Sociology* 114, no. 6 (2009): 1675–715.

Vasquez-Tokos, Jessica, and Priscilla Yamin. "The Racialization of Privacy: Racial Formation as a Family Affair." *Theory and Society* 50, no. 5 (2021): 717–40.

Veiller, Lawrence. "The Housing Problem in American Cities." *The Annals of the American Academy of Political and Social Science* 25, no. 2 (1905): 46–70.

Veldhuis, Niek. "Exploring Ancient Networks." *H2D Revista de Humanidades Digitais* 3, no. 1 (2021).

Vidmar, Neil, and David H. Flaherty. "Concern for Personal Privacy in an Electronic Age." *Journal of Communication* 35, no. 2 (1985): 91–103.

Violette, Zachary J. *The Decorated Tenement: How Immigrant Builders and Architects Transformed the Slum in the Gilded Age*. University of Minnesota Press, 2019.

Waldman, Ari Ezra. *Industry Unbound: The Inside Story of Privacy, Data, and Corporate Power*. Cambridge University Press, 2021.

Waldman, Ari Ezra. *Privacy as Trust: Information Privacy for an Information Age*. Cambridge University Press, 2018.

Waldman, Ari Ezra. "Privacy Law's False Promise," *Washington University Law Review* 97 (2019): 773–834.

Waldo, James, Herbert S. Lin, and Lynette I. Millett, eds. *Engaging Privacy and Information Technology in a Digital Age*. National Academies Press, 2007.

Walker, Nathaniel R. "American Crossroads: General Motors' Midcentury Campaign to Promote Modernist Urban Design in Hometown USA." *Buildings and Landscapes: Journal of the Vernacular Architecture Forum* 23, no. 2 (2016): 89–115.

Warner, Michael. *The Letters of the Republic: Publication and the Public Sphere in Eighteenth-Century America*. Harvard University Press, 2009.

Warner Jr., Sam B. *Streetcar Suburbs: The Process of Growth in Boston (1870–1900)*. Harvard University Press, 1962.

Warr, Deborah, and Lynne Hillier. "'That's the Problem with Living in a Small Town': Privacy and Sexual Health Issues for Young Rural People." *Australian Journal of Rural Health* 5, no. 3 (1997): 132–39.

Warren, Carol, and Barbara Laslett. "Privacy and Secrecy: A Conceptual Comparison." *Journal of Social Issues* 33, no. 3 (1977): 43–51.

Warren, Samuel D., and Louis D. Brandeis. "The Right to Privacy." *Harvard Law Review* 4, no. 5 (1890): 193–220.

Webb, Diana. *Privacy and Solitude in the Middle Ages.* Hambledon Continuum, 2007.

Weber, Max. *Economy and Society, Volume 1.* University of California Press, 1978.

Weber, Max. *The Protestant Ethic and the Spirit of Capitalism.* Routledge Classics, 2005.

Webster, Frank, and Kevin Robins. *Information Technology: A Luddite Analysis.* Ablex, 1986.

Weeds, Julie, and David Weir. "Co-occurrence Retrieval: A Flexible Framework for Lexical Distributional Similarity." *Computational Linguistics* 31, no. 4 (2005): 439–75.

Weinrib, Laura. "Freedom of Conscience in War Time: World War I and the Limits of Civil Liberties." *Emory Law Journal* 65, no. 4 (2016): 1051–137.

Weintraub, Jeff, and Krishan Kumar, eds. *Public and Private in Thought and Practice: Perspectives on a Grand Dichotomy.* University of Chicago Press, 1997.

Welter, Barbara. "The Cult of True Womanhood." *American Quarterly* 18, no. 2 (1956): 151–74.

Westin, Alan F. *Privacy and Freedom.* Athenum, 1967.

Westin, Alan F. *Whistleblowing! Loyalty and Dissent in the Corporation.* McGraw-Hill, 1981.

Wexler, Rebecca. "Privacy as Privilege: The Stored Communications Act and Internet Evidence." *Harvard Law Review* 134 (2020): 2721–92.

Whitaker, Reg. *The End of Privacy: How Total Surveillance Is Becoming a Reality.* New Press, 2000.

White, G. Edward. *The Constitution and the New Deal.* Harvard University Press, 2002.

White, G. Edward. *Tort Law in America: An Intellectual History.* Oxford University Press, 2003.

White, Harrison. *Identity and Control: How Social Formations Emerge.* Princeton University Press, 2008.

Whitman, James Q. "The Two Western Cultures of Privacy: Dignity Versus Liberty." *Yale Law Journal* 113 (2004): 1151–221.

Wiebe, Robert H. *The Search for Order, 1877–1920.* Hill and Wang, 1967.

Wiecek, William. *The Lost World of Classical Legal Thought.* Oxford University Press, 2001.

Wijaya, Derry Tanti, and Reyyan Yeniterzi, "Understanding Semantic Change of Words over Centuries." In *Proceedings of the 2011 International Workshop on DETecting and Exploiting Cultural DiversiTy on the Social Web—DETECT.* ACM Press, 2011.

Williamson, Bess. "The People's Sidewalks: Designing Berkeley's Wheelchair Route, 1970–1974." *Boom: A Journal of California* 2, no. 1 (2012): 49–52.

Wilson, William H. *The City Beautiful Movement*. Johns Hopkins University Press, 1989.

Winter, Bodo, Graham Thompson, and Matthias Urban, "Cognitive Factors Motivating the Evolution of Word Meanings: Evidence from Corpora, Behavioral Data and Encyclopedic Network Structure." In *Evolution of Language: Proceedings of the 10th International Conference (EVOLANG10)*. 2014.

Witt, John Fabian. *American Contagions: Epidemics and the Law from Smallpox to COVID-19*. Yale University Press, 2020.

Wittgenstein, Ludwig. *The Blue and Brown Books*. Basil Blackwell, 1958.

Wittgenstein, Ludwig. *Philosophical Investigations*, 4th ed. Ed. Joachim Schulte. Wiley-Blackwell, 2009.

Wright, Benjamin F. *American Interpretations of Natural Law: A Study in the History of Political Thought*. Russell and Russell, 1962.

Wright, Gwendolyn. *Building the Dream: A Social History of Housing in America*. MIT Press, 1983.

Wuthnow, Robert. *Meaning and Moral Order: Explorations in Cultural Analysis*. University of California Press, 1987.

Yalniz, Ismet Zeki, and Raghavan Manmatha. "A Fast Alignment Scheme for Automatic OCR Evaluation of Books." In *2011 International Conference on Document Analysis and Recognition*. IEEE, 2011.

Yunxiang, Yan. *Private Life Under Socialism: Love, Intimacy, and Family Change in a Chinese Village, 1949–1999*. Stanford University Press, 2003.

Zelizer, Viviana A. *Pricing the Priceless Child. The Changing Social Value of Children*. Basic, 1985.

Zemans, Frances K. "Legal Mobilization: The Neglected Role of Law in the Political System." *American Political Science Review* 77, no. 3 (1983): 690–703.

Zerubavel, Eviatar. "Lumping and Splitting: Notes on Social Classification." *Sociological Forum* 11, no. 3 (1996): 421–33.

Zerubavel, Eviatar. *Social Mindscapes: An Invitation to Cognitive Sociology*. Harvard University Press, 1999.

Zhao, Dingxin. "Ecologies of Social Movements: Student Mobilization During the 1989 Prodemocracy Movement in Beijing." *American Journal of Sociology* 103, no. 6 (1998): 1493–529.

Ziegler, Mary. *Beyond Abortion: Roe v. Wade and the Battle for Privacy*. Harvard University Press, 2018.

Zimmerman, Diane L. "Requiem for a Heavyweight: A Farewell to Warren and Brandeis's Privacy Tort." *Cornell Law Review* 68, no. 3 (1982): 291–367.

Zuboff, Shoshana. *The Age of Surveillance Capitalism: The Fight for a Human Future at the New Frontier of Power*. Public Affairs, 2019.

Zukin, Sharon. *Landscapes of Power: From Detroit to Disney World*. University of California Press, 1991.

PRIMARY DATASETS AND ARCHIVAL COLLECTIONS

A Century of Lawmaking for a New Nation: U.S. Congressional Documents and Debates 1774 to 1875. Library of Congress Digital Collections. https://www.loc.gov/collections/century-of-lawmaking/.

Chronicling America: Historic American Newspapers. Library of Congress. https://chroniclingamerica.loc.gov/.

Congressional Record: Proceedings and Debates of the U.S. Congress. U.S. Congress. https://www.congress.gov/congressional-record.

Davies, Mark. *The Corpus of Historical American English: 400 Million Words, 1810–2009* [dataset]. Brigham Young University, 2010. https://www.english-corpora.org/coha.

Gentzkow, Matthew, Jesse M. Shapiro, and Matt Taddy. *Congressional Record for the 43rd–114th Congresses: Parsed Speeches and Phrase Counts.* Stanford Libraries, 2018.

Google Books Corpus of American English: Version googlebooks-eng-us-20200217 [dataset]. Google, 2020. https://books.google.com/ngrams.

Manson, Steven, Jonathan Schroeder, David Van Riper, Tracy Kugler, and Steven Ruggles. *IPUMS National Historical Geographic Information System: Version 16.0* [dataset]. IPUMS, 2021.

National Conference on Social Welfare Collection of Conference Proceedings. University of Michigan Library Digital Collections. University of Michigan, Ann Arbor. https://name.umdl.umich.edu/ACH8650.1957.001.

Postal bulletins and postal laws and regulations. U.S. Postal Bulletin Consortium. http://www.uspostalbulletins.com/.

Public Health Reports Collection. University of California Berkeley Bioscience, Natural Resources, and Public Health Library, Berkeley.

Record Group 28: Records of the Post Office Department. U.S. National Archives.

Record Group 29: Records of the Bureau of the Census. U.S. National Archives.

Record Group 90: Records of the Public Health Service. U.S. National Archives.

Reports of the Tenement House Department of the City of New York, 1903–1937. New York Public Library.

Ruggles, Steven, Catherine A. Fitch, Ronald Goeken, J. David Hacker, Matt A. Nelson, Evan Roberts, Megan Schouweiler, and Matthew Sobek. *IPUMS Ancestry Full Count Data: Version 3.0* [dataset]. IPUMS, 2021.

U.S. Bureau of the Census. *Historical Statistics of the United States: Colonial Times to 1970, Bicentennial Edition.* Government Printing Office, 1976.

Index

Page numbers in *italics* indicate figures or tables.

Abbott, Andrew, 23
abortion access, 9, 193, 194
Abrams, Philip, 174
ACB. *See* Associated Credit Bureaus of America
access, 9, 13, 16, 31; contraceptive, 134–35, 137, 193, 194; exposure and, 36; privacy norms for, 11; spatial, 6–7, 17, 189–90; visibility relation to, 19
Act for the Suppression of Trade in, and Circulation of, Obscene Literature and Articles of Immoral Use (1873), 177
Adams, John, 30, 31, 112
Addams, Jane, 92
administration, 166, 184; in Early Information Age, 2–3; personal data relation to, 130; Postal, 176, 177, 179, 181; public, 127, 159, 161–62, 185, 204; regulations for, 183
administrative practice, 166–67
adolescent sociability, online presence relation to, 7–8
advertisements, 103–4; classified, 58–59, *60*, 148; photography for, 152
advertising agencies, 149
Agamben, Giorgio, 165, 198
"age of reform," 78–79
algorithmic risk scoring models, 164
"alters," 216–17

"American creed," U.S. Constitution as, 158
American Medical Association, 3
American Telephone and Telegraph Company (AT&T), 4, 114
American Weekly Mercury, The (newspaper), 43–44
analytical sociology, 207
anomie, 105
antebellum America, 17–18
antiobscenity legislation, moral panic relation to, 130
antislavery legislation, 67
antitotalitarian principles, of liberal societies, 108
antitrust legislation, 75
API. *See* application programming interfaces
application programming interfaces (API), 204
arcana imperii, 44
archival records, 220
Arizona, 154–55
Arrears of Pension Act (1879), 163
assemblages, 198–99
assimilationist policies, 33
Associated Credit Bureaus of America (ACB), 118
at-home manufacturing, 71–72
Atlanta Georgian, The (newspaper), 114

Atlantic Monthly (magazine), 8, 31, 43, 49, 146; on publicity, 120; on public opinion, 125; on tenement dwellings, 86
atomistic societies, 13, 26
AT&T. *See* American Telephone and Telegraph Company
audience expansion, 44
authoritarianism, 166, 192
autocratic legalism, 185
automation, 9, 196
automobiles, 13–14
autonomy: informational, 159; of private citizens, 108–9

Bailey, James, 61
Bailey, Joseph W., 72, 73–74
Balogh, Brian, 281n120
Baltimore, 172
Baltimore Sun, The (newspaper), 70
banks, 49, 59
Barnaby Rudge (Dickens), 5
Barnum, P. T., 148
BART. *See* Bayesian additive regression trees
bathroom facilities: in tenement dwellings, 89, 98, 99; in Tenement House Act, 98, 99
Bayard, Mabel, 121–22
Bayard, Thomas F., 122
Bayesian additive regression trees (BART), 212
Beauchampe (Simms), 44
Beecher, Charles, 123–24
behavioral data, 8, 163–64, 201
Belknap, William, 68
Benjamin, Walter, 85, 165
Bentham, Jeremy, 197
Bertillon records, 163
Better Housing League, 92
Bible, 12
Big Data surveillance, 27
Biggs, Hermann, 174
Bill of Rights, 143

biopolitical governance, 200
birth certificates, 3, 168
Birth Registration Area, 168
Black Americans, 33–34, 77, 168–69
Black Chamber, 183–84
Black enslaved people, 18, 33
Bloustein, Edward, 107
boards of health, 163, 167–68; Indiana, 2; infectious diseases relation to, 170; Kansas, 128; *salus populi* doctrine relation to, 174; San Francisco, 172–73
Bolshevik revolution, 179
Bonaparte, Charles, 179
Borah, William, 75
Bossier Banner, The (newspaper), 64
Boston, 170
Boyd v. United States, 142
Bradbury, Malcolm, ix
Brandeis, Louis, 9, 109; in *Harper's Weekly*, 114; in *Harvard Law Review*, 107, 121–23, 125–26, 134, 136, 184–85; *Olmstead v. United States* relation to, 138, 156, 183
breadth, durability and, 229n27
Brecht, Bertolt, 264n106
Brents v. Morgan, 151
Bridges, Khiara, 202
Brigham Young University, 211
Brooklyn Daily Eagle, The (newspaper), 113, 119
Browning Ruling, 18
Brown University, 229n18
bubonic plague, 172
Building Code Commission, 94
building codes, 78
building inspectors, 258n95
Buildings Department, of New York City, 93
built environments, 80–81, 132
Bundesdatenschutzgesetz, 192
bureaucracy, 8, 281n120
Bureau of Prohibition, 143
Burleson, Albert S., 182

business correspondence, 45
Byrnes, Thomas, 3

CA. *See Chronicling America*
Calder, Lendol, 118
California Consumer Privacy Act
    (CCPA), 187
Calvinist church, 39
capitalism: consumer, 118, 203;
    monopoly, 108; retail, 58;
    surveillance, 9–10, 27, 131, 159–60
Carlton, Newcomb, 184
Cartier-Bresson, Henri, 111
case law, 145, 150, 153; jurisprudence
    and, 143; legal institutionalization
    relation to, 138
caste, in homes, 40
"Castles in the Air" (libretto), 147
casual gaze, of community, 63
CBOW. *See* continuous bag-of-words
CCPA. *See* California Consumer
    Privacy Act
celebrity culture, 113
cellulose nitrate film, 106
censorship, 177–80, 280n99
Censorship Board, War Department,
    179
"Census, The," *Harper's Weekly*, 73
Census Bureau, 3–4, 67, 161, 169,
    209; discretionary authority of, 74;
    financial records relation to, 72
Census of Telephones, 261n43
charitable organization movement, in
    Philadelphia, 89
Charity Organization Society (COS),
    93–94
Chattanooga News, The
    (newspaper), 60
Chicago Daily Tribune (newspaper), 5,
    49, 112–13, 154, 196
Chicago World's Fair, 48–49, 51–52
Child, Lydia Maria, 30
childhood development, 87–88
childhood education, 1

child labor, 168
children, 31–32, 33
Children's Bureau, 168
Chinese-born population, 172–73
Choi, Franny, 203
Chronicling America (CA), 34, 125,
    125, 211, 240n31, 268n32
Church, William Conant, 65
church attendance, 39
cipher bureau, 183–84
citizenship, 78, 94–95, 203, 255n42
"City Beautiful" movement, 81, 88
Civic League, in Yonkers, 102–3
Civil Rights Law (1902), 155, 158
clan-based societies, 26
Clarksburg Daily Telegram, The
    (newspaper), *60*
classification, of social phenomena,
    52–53
classified advertisements, *60*; in
    newspapers, 58–59; photography
    in, 148
Cleveland, Grover, 48
coalition-building, 135
coastal inspections, 167
coded language, 45, 69
codification, 16
COHA. *See* Corpus of Historical
    American English
COINTELPRO program, 195
collective conscience, 15
Columbus, Christopher, 48
Colyvas, Jeannette, 208, 229n27
commercial agencies, 117
commodification, of personal
    information, 121
common law, 37, 122–23, 133, 143,
    144, 155; jurisprudence and,
    151–52, 192; lower-court judges
    relation to, 137
"common scold," 37
communal living, 38–40
community, 44, 55; casual gaze of, 63;
    privacy norms relation to, 12

competition, 135, 145, 153, 160
computational data processing, 138, 197, 221
computational text analysis, 20, 23, 53–54
Comstock, Anthony, 176–78
Comstock laws, 177, 185
conceptual expansion, 158
confidentiality, 195; consumer credit ratings relation to, 119–20; in doctor-patient interactions, 165
Congressional Globe, 209
Congressional Record, 209, 221
Conkling, Roscoe, 71
Constant, Benjamin, 12, 108
constitutional guardrails, 155
constitutional revolution, in jurisprudence, 155
consumer capitalism, 118, 203
consumer credit ratings, 4, 117–18, 119–20, 203
consumer economy, personal data relation to, 106
consumer-focused legislation, 187
consumer privacy laws, 160
consumer rights, 9
consumers, 8–9, 109, 196–97
Continental Congress, 176
continuity, 123
continuous bag-of-words (CBOW), 213–14
contraceptive access, 134–35, 137, 193, 194
Cooke, Jay, 68
Cooley, Thomas M., 107, 126–27
copyright, 212
corporate records, 75–76
corporate strategists, 8–9
corporations, 75–76, 109
Corpus of Historical American English (COHA), 211, 219, 240n31
corruption, 152
COS. *See* Charity Organization Society

cosine similarity score, 46, 47, *47*, 55, *58*
"countervailance," 199
Court of Appeals, 103, 151–52, 156, 173
COVID-19 pandemic, 186
Cowles, William H. H., 71
Craddock, Ida, 130
creditworthiness, 106, 118
crime, 152
criminal justice system, 168
cultivation, of self, 25, 26, 27, 47
"cult of the individual," 4–5, 85
cultural customs, social norms and, 146
cultural norms, 5, 27, 43–44, 52, 92, 106
cuneiform texts, 22–23, 112
Customs and Border Protection, 9

Dana, Malcolm, 90
data aggregation, 7, 9
databases, 1–2
data brokers, 160, 187
data collection, 73–74, 184, 186, 194–95, 204–5; consumers relation to, 8–9; immigrants relation to, 201–2; income, 67; language of privacy and, 54–55; mass, 7, 197; regulations for, 17; rules for, 51; social stratification relation to, 19; state-level, *162*, 163–65; for U.S. Census, 167
data processing, geography of, 200
Data Protection Directive, of European Union, 192–93
"dataveillance," 198
death certificates, 3, 168–69
defamation, 119, 122, 150
DeForest, Robert W., 91, 95–96
Deleuze, Gilles, 198
democratic oversight, 69
density calculations, 217–19
Department of Commerce, 3

Department of Defense, Census
 Bureau relation to, 74
Department of Education, 49
Department of Government Efficiency
 (DOGE), 197
Department of Tenements, 89, 91, 98,
 99, 209, 218–19
Dependent Pension Act (1890), 163
Detroit Free Press (newspaper), 180
developer lobby, 94
developers, spatial subdivisions
 relation to, 99
Devonia, SS, 24
Dewey, John, 130
diabolus in machina, 202
diaries, 29, 31, 45
Dickens, Charles, 5
dictionary definitions, 52
Dictionary of the English Language
 (Johnson), 44
diffusion, institutionalization and, 208,
 229n27
digital collections, 208–9
digital communications, 159
digital economy, 160
digitization, of historical data, 23
digitized historical data, 211–12
Diogenes, 12
disciplinary power, 199
disciplinary societies, 198
discretionary authority, of Census
 Bureau, 74
discretionary powers, of police, 13–14
discrimination, 163
distributional similarity, 34
doctor-patient interactions,
 confidentiality in, 165
DOGE. *See* Department of
 Government Efficiency
domain formation, 133, 135
domesticity, 33, 54, 62, 80, 91,
 241n45; common law and, 123;
 moral purity relation to, 64; women
 relation to, 65

domestic life, 30, 31–32, 41, 64
domestic relations, 16, 123
domestic servants, 32
domestic space, 12, 38, 54, 241n45
doors, access and, 31
dragnet collection, of geolocated data,
 133, 186
duality, of self, 124
Du Bois, W. E. B., 163, 169
dumbbell tenements, 82, *83*, 88
durability, breadth and, 229n27
Durkheim, Emile, 5, 105, 124

Early Information Age, x, 10, 13–14,
 15, 146, 190–91; in administration,
 2–3; jurisprudence in, 134; language
 of privacy in, 54–55; social
 phenomena in, 47
Eastman, George, 110
Eastman Kodak Company, 110
eavesdropping, 5–6, 36–37, 43, 51,
 113, 153
Ecclesiastes, 12
ecclesiastical authorities, 39–40
École des Beaux-Arts, 91
e-commerce systems, 187
economic activity, 65
economic constraints, spatial
 subdivisions relation to, 32
economy, 33, 106, 159, 160
education officials, 168
"egos," 216–17
eigenvector centrality, 216–17
Eighteenth Amendment, to U.S.
 Constitution, 129–30, 144, 154
electoral fraud, 69
electromechanical calculating
 machines, 53
electronic databases, 137
electronic surveillance, of personal
 data, 157
Elias, Norbert, 13, 26–27, 207
elites, 112–13, 121–22, 158
Emancipation Proclamation, 18

emergencies, public health, 165
Emerson, Ralph Waldo, 45
"enigma of arrival," 27–28
entrepreneurs, moral, 92, 104
e pluribus unum, 14–15
Equifax, 118
"era of publicity," ix, 120
Ericson, Richard, 198
Espionage Act (1917), 129, 154,
    179, 180
European Convention on Human
    Rights, 192
European General Data Protection
    Regulation (GDPR), 160
European Union, 192–93, 200
Evening World, The (newspaper), 180
exceptions, 167, 182–83, 186, 187–88,
    194; for governance, 7, 152, 184,
    195; informational power through,
    190; for regulations, 185; during
    wartime, 165, 166
executive power, 128–29, 156, 183,
    200, 204
Experian, 118
exposure, 15, 36, 63, 109, 204–5;
    involuntary, 21, 85–86; publicity
    and, 27, 203; self, 7, 120
expressio unius est exclusiu alteriu, 74
extralegal debates, on social
    relations, 148

familial privacy, in urban society, 66
family life, 33, 36
family reputation, 122
FAPP. *See* floor area per person
federal bureaucracy, 8, 161
federalism, 67
Federal Register, 221
Federal Trade Commission, 9
financial records, 49, 55, 59, 72,
    117–18, 155
FISC. *See* Foreign Intelligence
    Surveillance Court
Flagg, Ernest, 79–80, 81, 88

"flâneur," 85
flexible photographic film, 110
floor area per person (FAPP), 99, 102,
    102, 217–18
food safety, regulations for, 71–72
Foreign Intelligence Surveillance Court
    (FISC), 186–87
formal rights, in social relations, 137
Foucault, Michel, 164, 197, 198, 199,
    252n15
Founding Fathers, 112, 191
Fourcade, Marion, 199
Fourteenth Amendment, to U.S.
    Constitution, 75, 133
Fourth Amendment, to U.S.
    Constitution, 22, 69, 138, 142,
    156, 175
France, 169, 191–92
Franklin, Benjamin, 28, 43–44, 69
fraud prevention, 128–29
Freeden, Michael, 18
freedom, 112, 124
French, Alice, 41
Friedman, Lawrence, 133
frontier individualism, 42–43
"Fruits of Solitude," 42

GAI. *See* general artificial intelligence
Gajda, Amy, 28, 146
Galaxy (magazine), 63
Gandy, Oscar H., Jr., 7
GDPR. *See* European General Data
    Protection Regulation
gender bias, 64, 65–66, *66*
gendered problems, 162
gender equality, 194
general artificial intelligence
    (GAI), 204
General Data Protection Regulation, of
    European Union, 192–93, 200
genocidal violence, 192
geography, of data processing, 200
geolocated data, dragnet collection of,
    133, 186

Georgia Supreme Court, 150, 151–52
Germany, 169, 179
Gibbons v. Ogden, 174–75
Gilded Age, 77
Gilman, Charlotte Perkins, 40
Godkin, Edwin Lawrence, 83, 105–6,
107, 121, 124, 147
Goffman, Erving, 25–26
"golden age," of privacy, 8, 10
good life, 234n88
gossip, 44, 121
Gould, Elgin, 89–90, 99
governance, 18–19, 37, 38, 130, 166,
199; biopolitical, 200; exceptions
for, 7, 152, 184, 195; mass data
collection for, 197; personal data
relation to, 108–9, 198, 201–3;
personal information relation to,
182–83; of risk, 196, 202; *salus
populi* doctrine relation to,
173–74; social order and, 15;
during wartime, 67–68
governmental overreach, 22, 72, 73
governmental searches, 144
government officials, 52, 132
Great Depression, 163, 203
Greece, 12
Green Bag (journal), 148–49
Griswold v. Connecticut, 134–35, 137,
159, 194

habeas corpus, 166
Haggerty, Kevin, 198
Halpern, Sue, 42
Hamid, Abdul, II, 283n12
Harding, Warren G., 113
Harper's Weekly (magazine), 73, 114,
204
Harris, Kamala, 159
Harvard Law Review (journal), 107,
121–23, 125–26, 134, 136, 184–85
Hawaiian Star (newspaper), 115
Hawthorne, Nathaniel, 5
Hayes, Rutherford B., 69

Health Department, 49
Healy, Keiran, 199
Hearst, William Randolph, 4, 105
Hein Online, 220
Hepburn Act, 75
Herald and News (newspaper), 111
Higginson, Thomas Wentworth, 65
historical data, digitization of, 23
historical magazines, 55
historical social science, 23
historicism, teleology and, 20
History of Man, The (Bradbury), ix
Hofstadter, Richard, 78–79
Hollerith, Herman, 3–4
Holmes, Oliver Wendell, Jr., 157
Holmes, Oliver Wendell, Sr., 31
"home economics" movement, 41
home intruders, 37
homes, 40, 52, 54, 62, 64, 126; "islands
of privacy" in, 86; single-family, 90;
spatial subdivisions in, 31–32, 41;
women relation to, 64–65
homo clausus, 13
homosexual relationships, 186
houseguests, 39–40
household (*oikos*), 12
Howard Kirk (fictional character), ix–x
How the Other Half Lives (Riis), 77–78
human dignity, 234n88
human-interest stories, 110
Hunt's Merchant Magazine, 203
Hurty, John, 2–3, 5, 16
Hurty, Josiah, 1–2
Hurty, Julia, 1
hygiene, 32, 81, 88, 89
hypercontrol, 198–99

IBM. *See* International Business
Machines
"I-Cards," 258n95
Igo, Sarah, 15–16
illicit liquor, 130, 142, 143
Illinois, 150
illiteracy rates, 29

immaterial properties, 149
immigrants, 4, 32, 110; data collection relation to, 201–2; sentinel surveillance of, 172–73, 186
immunization, 49
income data collection, 67
income tax system, 74
independent self, 107–8
Indiana, 2, 151
Indian Removal campaigns, 33
"Indian schools," 33
Indigenous children, 33
individualism, 42–43, 107, 135; liberal, 108–9, 126, 128, 131, 191; logic of privacy relation to, 21
individuality, 26, 85
individuation, 26, 124
industrialization, urbanization and, 81
Industrial Revolution, 53
inequalities, 15, 77, 163, 198
infectious diseases, 2–3, 7, 167, 175; boards of health relation to, 170; confidentiality relation to, 165; reporting forms for, 170, *171*; *salus populi* doctrine relation to, 174, 186; in tenement dwellings, 82; in urban society, 64
Information Age, 19, 203–4
informational autonomy, 159
informational persons, 21, 106–7, 195, 203
informational power, 4, 10, 52, 189, 190, 199; social control and, 200; of sysadmins, 204
informational privacy, 46, 233n73
informational self-determination, 6–7
informational society, 103
information-sharing networks, 29
initial judicialization, 135, 145
inquisitorial powers, 75
institutional invasions, 21
institutionalization, 11, 80, 104, 220–21; diffusion and, 208, 229n27; legal, 107, 133–34, 135, 137, 138,

157, 158, 216; of logic of privacy, 189, 191; moral, 79, 91, 103
institutional power, x, 15, 27, 47, 201
institutional suspicion, obscurity relation to, 19
insurance companies, 159
interannual continuity, 23
interdecadal change, 55
intergenerational transfer, 44
Internal Revenue Service, 67, 71, 74, 169
International Business Machines (IBM), 4
interpretation, of U.S. Constitution, 145
interracial marriage, 168
Interstate Commerce Act (1887), 75
interstitial spaces, 34
intralegal competition, 135, 145, 153
investigative committees, of U.S. Congress, 68–69
inviolate personality, 122–23, 125, 190
involuntary exposure, 21, 85–86
IPUMS USA, 209, 218, 229n18
Irish Standard (newspaper), 147
"islands of privacy," 16, 86
isolation, 25, 38, 42

Jefferson, Thomas, 112
Jeffersonian, The (newspaper), *60*
Jim Crow era, 168
John M. Bradstreet Company, 117
Johnson, Andrew, 68, 69
Johnson, Samuel, 44
Jonsson, Stefan, 208, 229n27
journalism, 58, 110, 264n106; secrecy relation to, 114; yellow, 111, 133
judgment, 11–12, 25
judicial consolidation, 135, 145
judicial interventions, 27, 103
judicialization, initial, 135, 145
Jungle, The (Sinclair), 71
juridical regimes, 166–67

jurisprudence, 6, 21–22, 28, 125, 133, 136; case law and, 143; common law and, 151–52, 192; constitutional revolution in, 155; in Early Information Age, 134; governance and, 130; logic of privacy in, 21; Michigan Supreme Court and, 147; Prosser relation to, 266n18; public consciousness relation to, 148; *stare decisis* principle of, 138; state-centric turn of, 156–57, 158–59; temporality of, 145

Kansas, 128
Katz v. United States, 135, 137, 194
Kelly, James K., 69–70
Kenosha Telegraph, The (newspaper), 64
Kentucky Court of Appeals, 151
Klug v. Sheriffs, 149–50
Knights of Labor, 87
knowledge, 6, 50
Known Citizen, The (Igo), 15–16
Koopman, Colin, 106–7

labor, 50, 53, 85, 87, 168
labor contributions, 39
labor statistics, 163
landlines, 55, 261n43
landlords, 153
language, of privacy, 54–55, *56–57*, 58, 59, 62, 65–66
latent Dirichlet allocation (LDA), 215
legal citations, 138
legal elites, 158
legal institutionalization, 107, 133–34, 135, 137, 158, 216; case law relation to, 138; social order relation to, 157
legal periodicals, 219–20
legal reasoning, 28, 145, 147
legislation, 6, 27, 67, 75, 130, 132; consumer-focused, 187; logic of privacy in, 21; sectoral, 22, 192, 193; for social organization, 79;

social reform movements relation to, 93–94; state-level, 149; during wartime, 185. *See also* Tenement House Act
Lewis, John, 127
libel, 37, 112, 122, 192; consumer credit ratings relation to, 119; truthful, 28, 150
liberal individualism, 108–9, 126, 128, 131, 191
liberal societies, 10, 108
Library of Congress, 34, 208–9
Lincoln, Abraham, 67, 166
liquid societies, 200
liquor, 71, 130, 142, 143
liquor laws, 155–56
literary fiction, 29, 55, 58
logic, of privacy, 6, 9, 10, 47, 50; individualism relation to, 21; institutionalization of, 189, 191; in legislation, 21; as modern legal fact, 138; political interests relation to, 17; social order and, 16; social problems and, 20, 51; social reform movements and, 79; social relations and, 46; visibility relation to, 104
Loi informatique et libertés, 192
long-distance communication, 4, 61, 114, 115, 121, 145–46
Los Angeles, 172
lower-court judges, 21–22, 137, 138, 148

mail fraud, 128, 177, 178
mail-order catalogues, 58
Mann, Michael, 281n120
Mannheim, Karl, 50
Manola, Marion, 147–48
marital privacy, 38–39, 134–35
Martinsburg Daily Gazette (newspaper), 111
Marx, Gary, 164
Marx, Karl, 77
Massachusetts, 129, 153, 170

Massachusetts Institute of Technology, School of Architecture and Planning at, 91
mass data collection, 7, 197
mass relocation, 90
Mayrl, Damon, 207
McKelway, St. Clair, 113, 114
mechanized production, 40
media empires, 145–46
media saturation, 112
medical examinations, 55
medical information, 159, 170, 175
menstrual histories, 186
Merchant's Credit Association, 118
Mesopotamia, 112
Mexican workers, 172
mezzo-social phenomena, 16
mezzo-spatial concentration, 88, 90, 98
Michigan, 147, 150, 220
micro-spatial layouts, 88, 98
Middle Ages, 12
middle-class apartments, 80, 89, 92
middle-class people, 36, 90–91
military armament campaigns, 129
military recruitment, data collection for, 167
minority populations, 164, 172, 186, 202
Mississippi Court of Appeals, 156
mobility, social, 113, 119
modernity, 64, 77
modern legal fact, 136, 138
modularity, 216–17
monopoly capitalism, 108
Moore, Barrington, 25
moral crises, 104
moral crusade, 83, 84
moral cultivation, of self, 47
moral decay, 21, 86, 87–88
moral development, 42
moral entrepreneurs, 92, 104
moral faculties, 29
moral ills, 78, 80, 84, 86, 87–88

moral innocence, 147
moral institutionalization, 79, 91, 103
morality code, night-watch patrols for, 39
moral order, 162, 190
moral panic, x, 6, 22, 78–79, 176–77, 190; antiobscenity legislation relation to, 130; exceptions relation to, 184
moral purity, 64
moral rejuvenation, 123
moral virtue, 21, 46, 86
Morse, Sidney, 124
muckraking journalists, 110
Muhammad, Khalil Gibran, 163, 202
municipal corruption, 95
municipal sanitary committee, 170, 172
mutual trust, 26

Naipaul, V. S., 27–28
Napoleonic Code, 191–92
Nation, The (newspaper), 105, 147
National Archives, 23, 208
National Association of Retail Credit Agencies, 118
National Board of Trade, 127–28
National Center for Education Statistics, 209
National Conference on Social Welfare (NCSW), 87, 90, 102, 208–9, 220
National Digital Newspaper Program, 211, 212
National Health Board, 167–68
National Historical Geographic Information System (NHGIS), 99, 218
National Monetary Commission, 118
National Quarantine Act (1878), 167–68
national security, 7, 67, 182
National Security Agency (NSA), 183–84
Native Americans, 18, 32–33

natural law, 133, 143, 144, 150, 151–52, 155

NCSW. *See* National Conference on Social Welfare

negative space, 11

Nelson, Deborah, 50

network visualization, 139, *140*

"New law" tenements, Tenement House Act, *97, 98*

New Republic, The (newspaper), 130

newspaper industry, *110*

newspaper publishers, 149

newspapers, 29, 54, 55, 104, 146, 240n31; classified advertisements in, 58–59; personal information in, 143, 153; postal delivery relation to, 109; tabloid, 21, 105–6, 110–11, 147

New Statesman (magazine), 196

Newsweek (magazine), 196

New York City, 77–78, 80, 81, 82, *82*, 83; boards of health, 172; Buildings Department of, 93; Department of Tenements of, 89, 91, 98, 99, 209, 218–19; FAPP in, 99, 102, *102*, 217–19; mass relocation in, 90; municipal sanitary committee in, 170, 172; population density in, 229n18; sectoral legislation in, 193; Sherry Building, 94; social reform movements in, 86; Tenement Commission of, 88; Tenement House Committee of, 103

New York Court of Appeals, 103, 151–52

New York Public Library (NYPL), 209, 219

New York Society for the Suppression of Vice, 176–77

New York State, Civil Rights Law of, 155, 158

New York Stock Exchange (NYSE), 128–29

New York Times, The (newspaper), 49, 68, 115, 178; on tenement dwellings, 84, 85–86; on U.S. Census, 72

New York Tribune, The (newspaper), *60*, 69, 139, 142, 152

New York World (newspaper), 105

Nexis Uni database, 216

NHGIS. *See* National Historical Geographic Information System

Nietzsche, Friedrich, 201

night-watch patrols, 34, 39

Nineteen Eighty-Four (Orwell), 164, 275n19

Nippert-Eng, Christena, 16

Nixon, Richard, 193

nomadic tribes, 33

NSA. *See* National Security Agency

nuclear family, 26–27, 32–33, 39, 41, 86, 186

NYPL. *See* New York Public Library

NYSE. *See* New York Stock Exchange

obscurity, institutional suspicion relation to, 19

observability, cultural norms for, 27

OCR. *See* optical character recognition

Odell, Benjamin, Jr., 96

oikos (household), 12

Olmstead v. United States, 134, 136, 138, 156, 183

online presence, adolescent sociability relation to, 7–8

optical character recognition (OCR), 211

ordinal ranks, 201

organizational practice, 132

Orwell, George, 164, 275n19

Orwellian state, 198

Ottoman Empire, 283n12

overcrowding, in tenement dwellings, 81, 89–90

overpolicing, 202

oversight, democratic, 69

Palace of Mechanic Arts, 48
Panic of 1873, 68
panopticism, 197–99
panoptic prison, 164
"panoptic sort," 7
park beautification, 255n42
partisan agendas, 50, 68
patriarchy, 40, 66
Patriot Act (2001), 166, 186
Paul Pry (fictional character), 43,
    44, 68
*Pavesich v. New England Life Insurance
    Co.*, 150, 152
pawn brokers, 49
paying lodgers, working-class people
    relation to, 40
Penn, William, 42
"penny press," 4, 105
performance, of private family life, 36
personal checks, 118
personal data, 13, 22, 52, 130, 132,
    191; consumer economy relation
    to, 106; electronic surveillance of,
    157; governance relation to, 108–9,
    198, 201–3; public administration
    relation to, 204; social order
    relation to, 164; surveillance
    capitalism relation to, 159–60
personal information, 48–49, 115–117,
    120, 169, 187; commodification of,
    121; governance relation to, 182–83;
    in newspapers, 143, 153; protection
    of, 61, 62
personality, 85, 122–23, 124, 125, 190
personally identifiable information
    (PII), 169
personal space, 31
personhood, 33, 107–8
Pew Research Center, 9
Philadelphia, 89, 178
Philadelphia Negro, The,
    (Du Bois), 169
Philippine-American War, 195
philosophical arguments, 234n88

Philothea (Child), 30
*Photographic Times and American
    Photographer* (publication),
    146–47
photography, 106, 110–11, 114, 146,
    152; public sentiment relation to,
    147–48; "rogue gallery," 142, 153; of
    yellow journalism, 133
physical privacy, 233n73
physical space, 81, 252n15
PII. *See* personally identifiable
    information
Planned Parenthood v. Casey, 108
plantation economy, 33
Plecker, Walter A., 168
PLUTO. *See* Primary Land Use Tax
    Lot Output
police, 3, 154, 163, 170, 283n12;
    boards of health relation to, 173;
    discretionary powers of, 13–14;
    minority populations relation to,
    202; prison authorities relation to,
    153; during Prohibition, 130, 142,
    143; water management relation to,
    70–71; wiretapping by, 132–33
polis (community), 12
political climate, 10
political corruption, "penny press"
    and, 4
political imagination, 14
political interests, 17
political negotiations, 67
political order, 162
politicians, 68, 69
poll taxes, 74
population density, 99, *100–101*,
    229n18
population-level statistics, 229n18
populist agitation, 105
pornography, 177–78
positive empirical case, 220–21
Postal administration, 176, 177,
    179, 181
postal delivery, 29, 45, 109, 114, 176

Postal Inspection Service, 128, 177–79, 181–82, 221
postal regulations, 45–46, 181
postcards, 165, 177–78, 179, 180, 182
Post Office Department, 22, 45–46, 165, 177, 181, 182
power dynamics, formal rights in, 137
prejudice, 18
presentation, of self, 25–26, 27, 84–85, 120
press, freedom of, 112
press syndicates, 29
preventative health campaigns, 167
primary datasets and data sources, *210*
Primary Land Use Tax Lot Output (PLUTO), 218
print industry, 58–59
printing technologies, 29
prison authorities, 153
privacy. *See specific topics*
Privacy Act (1974), 193
Privacy for America, 9
privacy laws, 9
privacy norms, 11, 12, 19
"privacy of the individual," 125, *125*
"privacy paradox," 8
Privacy Protection Agency, 187
private citizens, autonomy of, 108–9
private detectives, consumer credit ratings relation to, 119
private investment, 78
private-sector organizations, 51
probabilistic topic models, 215
probably cause, 175
professional associations, 104
Professional Criminals of America, 3
professional training programs, 91
Progressive Era, 3, 87, 255n42; monopoly capitalism in, 108; women in, 65
progressivism, 191
Prohibition, 129–30, 142, 143, 144, 155–56
property claims, 149–50, 266n18

property rights, 144, 192
Prosser, William, 134, 143, 266n18
protection: of personal information, 61, 62; of single-family homes, 90; from social obligations, 65
Protestant Ethic, The (Weber), 39
Prussia, 192
psychoanalysis, 124
psychogenesis, sociogenesis and, 27
public administration, 127, 159, 161–62, 185, 204
public benefits, 163
public consciousness, 148
public discourse, 52–53, 215; classified advertisements relation to, 59; language of privacy in, 62
public health, 2–3, 83, 128, 162, 170, 172; emergencies, 165; *salus populi* doctrine relation to, 174–75; tenement dwellings relation to, 77–78
Public Health and Marine Hospital Service, 167–68
Public Health Service, 22, 165, 167–68, 175, 221
public interest, 114, 121–22, 129, 152
publicity, 63; era of, ix, 120; exposure and, 27, 203; "right to be let alone" relation to, 127; ruthless, 121
public morals, x, 22, 176–77, 190
public opinion, 125, 134
public/private dichotomy, 12
public prominence, 49
public records, 22, 169
public safety, 114
public scrutiny, 15, 30, 31, 146
public sector, 44
public sentiment, photography relation to, 147–48
Public Service Act, 186
Public Service Commission, of Massachusetts, 129
public spaces, 255n42
public warning systems, 170

public welfare programs, 53
Publikum, 59
Pulitzer, Joseph, 4, 105
Puritan communities, 39
Puritanism, 39–40
Python WordNet lemmatizer, 212

racial data revolution, 163
racial inequality, 163
Racial Integrity Act, 168
racialized problems, 162
racial purity laws, 168, 169
racism: in sentinel surveillance, 172–73; in social reform movements, 255n42
Radical, The (newspaper), 124
radical libertarians, 130
Radio Communications Act, 184
rail industry, 75
railroad tenements, 81, 82, 88
Randolph, Thomas Mann, Jr., 5–6
Real Estate Record and Builders Guide (publication), 85
rearguard actions, 132
Recluse, The (Wordsworth), 42
Reconstruction era, 77
Regan, Priscilla, 131
regulations, 7, 16, 22, 45–46; for administration, 183; for data collection, 17; exceptions for, 185; for food safety, 71–72; General Data Protection, 192–93, 200; governance through, 199; of tenement dwellings, 78; U.S. Postal Rules and, 181
religion, 39–40, 124
religious orthodoxy, 123
Renaissance era, 12
reporting forms, for infectious diseases, 170, *171*
reproductive decision-making, 137
Republican Party, 95
reputation, 122, 150
respect, for personality, 124

retail capitalism, 58
Retail Credit Company, 118
"revivalists," 40
R.G. Dun & Company, 117–18
Rhode Island Supreme Court, 151
Richards, Neil, 133
Richmond, Mary Ellen, 89
Richmond Times-Dispatch (newspaper), 113
rights-bearing individuals, 109
rights consciousness, 137
rights revolution, 21
"right to be let alone," 9–10, 107, 126–27
"right to privacy" cases, 139, *140–41*, 142, *144*, 149
Riis, Jacob, 77–78, 83, 89, 94–95, 255n42
risk, governance of, 196, 202
Roberson v. Rochester Folding Box Co., 103, 142–43, 152, 153
Roebuck, Alvah C., 58
Roe v. Wade, 157, 159, 186, 194
"rogue gallery" photographs, 142, 153
Roosevelt, Theodore, 80, 93, 94–95, 179
Royall, Anne, 37
rules: for access, 16–17, 189; for data collection, 51
Ruling Case Law (legal guide), 151
rural communities, 84
Russell Sage Foundation, 89
Russia, 180. *See also* Bolshevik revolution
ruthless publicity, 121

Saint-Just, Louis Antoine de, 13
salus populi doctrine, 173–75, 186
same-sex marriage, 157, 159
Sanborn, Benjamin, 146
sanctuary, 31, 34, 36
San Francisco, 172–73
San Francisco Call, The, (newspaper), 115, *116*

sanitary police, 170
sanitation, 87
Santa Claus, 181
Scarlet Letter, The (Hawthorne), 5
Schattschneider, Elmer Eric, 104
Schmitt, Carl, 165–66
School of Architecture and Planning, at Massachusetts Institute of Technology, 91
Schroeder, Theodore, 130
Schumpeter, Joseph, 20
Schumpeterian creed, 23
Schuyler v. Curtis, 142–43, 151
Science (journal), 196
Scribner's Magazine, 41, 43, 64, 106
Sears, Richard W., 58
Sears Corporation, 58
Second Great Awakening, 40
second-order effects, of privacy norms, 19
secrecy, 15–16, 39, 44, 114
secret police, 283n12
"secrets of state," 161–62
sectoral legislation, 22, 192, 193
security forces, 204
Sedition Act (1918), 129
self, 47, 190; duality of, 124; independent, 107–8; presentation of, 25–26, 27, 84–85, 120; solitude relation to, 30; spatial arrangements relation to, 80–81
self-actualization, 42, 196
self-contained territory, 89
self-determination, 17, 27; informational, 6–7; sexual, 157, 159
self-exposure, 7, 120
self-expression, 63, 84
self-interest, of politicians, 68
self-promotion, 8, 15–16
self-regulating economy, 159
semantic neighborhoods, 34, 35, 36, 46, 47
semantic similarity, 34

sentinel surveillance, 2, 170, 186; racism in, 172–73; *salus populi* doctrine relation to, 174
sewer networks: in New York City, 81; for tenement dwellings, 98
sexual intimacy, 32, 41
sexual orientation, 13
sexual revolution, 137, 138
sexual self-determination, 157, 159
Sherman, John, 70
Sherry Building, 94
Shils, Edward, 8
Simitis, Spiros, 197
Simmel, Georg, 11, 16–17, 26, 31, 85
Simms, William Gilmore, 44
simplification, 207–8
Sinclair, Upton, 71
single-family homes, protection of, 90
Skowronek, Steven, 281n120
slander, 37, 126; in newspapers, 146; reputation relation to, 150
Smith, Adam, 108
Smith, Charles Emory, 180–81
Smith, Robert Ellis, 8, 233n73
social atomization, 105
social control, 34, 39, 131, 197–98; informational power and, 200; visibility and, 19
social custom, 11
social dislocation, 17, 52, 190–91
social expectations, 25
social inclusion, 203
social inequality, 15
social integration, 80
social interdependence, 5
socialism, 161
sociality, 11, 26, 81
socialization, individuation and, 26
social life, tenement dwellings relation to, 91
social mobility, 113, 119
social movement activism, 134, 136–37, 194
social network analysis, 216

social norms, 51, 147; cultural customs and, 146; for domestic relations, 16; for solitude, 20

social obligations, 38, 54, 65

social order, 17, 80, 185, 190, 194, 208; governance and, 15; legal institutionalization relation to, 157; logic of privacy and, 16; mass data collection for, 197; personal data relation to, 164; rearguard actions for, 132

social organization, 14, 79

social phenomena: classification of, 52–53; in Early Information Age, 47

social physics, 161–62

social problems, ix–x, 44, 157–58, 190; cultural norms relation to, 106; of Industrial Revolution, 53; logic of privacy and, 20, 51; as moral crises, 104; NCSW relation to, 87

social question, 21, 77, 103, 114

social reform movements, 21, 76, 89, 91–92; legislation relation to, 93–94; logic of privacy and, 79; of NCSW, 87; in New York City, 86; racism in, 255n42

social relations, 16–17, 25, 26, 85, 199; extralegal debates on, 148; formal rights in, 137; governance and, 38; logic of privacy and, 46; spatial arrangements relation to, 80–81

social safety valve, 25

social science, 23, 205

Social Security numbers, 163, 203

social stigmatization, 36, 84

social stratification, 19, 131

social valuation, 33, 41, 203

societal function, 15

sociogenesis, psychogenesis and, 27

"sociologist as historian," 207

sociology, analytical, 207

solidarity, social, 26

solitude, 15–16, 25, 29, 33–34, 36, 42; self relation to, 30; social norms for, 20

Solove, Daniel, 133

soul, 123–24

"sousveillane," 199

southern plantations, 33–34

sovereign power, 166

Spanish-American War, 180–81

spatial access, 6–7, 17, 189–90

spatial arrangements, social relations relation to, 80–81

spatial subdivisions, 31–32, 41, 99

special-interest publications, 110

specialized knowledge, 50

special knowledge, 6

Spiritual Manifestations (Beecher), 123–24

spiritual rejuvenation, 25, 42

"spiritual welfare," 53

stare decisis principle, of jurisprudence, 138

state-centric turn, of jurisprudence, 156–57, 158–59

state constitutions, 150, 154–55

state-level data collection, *162*, 163–65

state-level legislation, 149

state power, 22, 128, 156, 167, 187–88, 281n120

Stevenson, Robert Louis, 24–25, 27

stigmatization, social, 36

Stimson, Henry L., 92

St. Johnsbury Caledonian, The (newspaper), *60*

street-level bureaucrats, 98

stress responses, 37

suffragette movement, 65

Supreme Court: Georgia, 150, 151–52; Massachusetts, 153; Michigan, 147, 150; Rhode Island, 151; U.S., 108, 134–35, 136, 139, 142, 156–57; Wisconsin, 149–50

surveillance. *See specific topics*
surveillance capitalism, 9–10, 27, 131, 159–60
surveillance creep, 163
"surveillance of blackness," 34
surveillance slack, 164
suspicion, 34, 72
Swidler, Ann, 37
sysadmins, 204

tabloid newspapers, 21, 105–6, 110–11, 147
Tabulating Machine Company, 4
Tappan's Mercantile Agency, 117
taxation, 71, 74, 167
technological changes, 20, 48–49, 196
technology, 8, 29, 48–49, 60–61
telegrams, 67–68, 69, 128–29
telegraph, 60–61, *61*, 62, 68–69, 114, 153
Telegrapher, The (publication), 61
teleology, historicism and, 20
telephones, 4, *61*, 114, 154; Census of, 261n43; eavesdropping on, 153; wiretapping of, 106, 115, 130, 132–33
temporality, of jurisprudence, 145
Tenement Commission, 88, 95–96
tenement dwellings, 21, 63, 82, *82*, 83; bathroom facilities in, 89, 98, 99; citizenship relation to, 94–95; involuntary exposure in, 85–86; middle-class apartments in, 80, 92; moral ills relation to, 84, 87–88; municipal sanitary committee in, 170, 172; overcrowding in, 81, 89–90; public health relation to, 77–78; social life relation to, 91
Tenement House Act (1901), 78, 79, 96, 102, 104, 158; bathroom facilities in, 98, 99; "New law" tenements, *97, 98*

Tenement House Committee, of New York City, 103
Tenement House Exhibition, 94
Tesla, Nikola, 115
"There are purchasable spies in many households," *116*
Thirteenth Census Act (1909), 74
Thomson, Judith Jarvis, 15
Thoreau, Henry David, 42
Thurman, Allen G., 67
Tilden, Samuel, 69
Time Magazine, 196
Tocqueville, Alexis de, 13, 108
torts, 133, 143, 266n18
transcendentalist thinkers, 42–43, 123–24
translocal communities, 55
transparency, 15–16
Treatise on Torts (Cooley), 126–27
Treaty of Versailles, 179
Tribe, Laurence, 132
trust, mutual, 26
truthful libel, 28, 150
tuberculosis, 170, 172
Tufts, James H., 87–88
typhoid fever, 172

"überveillance," 198
Union Pacific Railroad, 59
United States v. Lefkowitz et al., 138, 156
University of Michigan, 220
urban centers, middle-class people in, 90–91
urbanization, 79, 81
urban life, 21, 78, 80, 102
urban planners, 90–91
urban reform, 94–95
urban society, 63; familial privacy in, 66; infectious diseases in, 64
Urban Transition Historical GIS Project, at Brown University, 229n18
U.S. Census, 72, 73, 99, 167. *See also* Census Bureau

U.S. Congress, 52, 67, 75–76; food safety relation to, 71–72; investigative committees of, 68–69; Western Union relation to, 69–70

U.S. Constitution, 193; as "American creed," 158; Eighteenth Amendment to, 129–30, 144, 154; Fourteenth Amendment to, 75, 133; Fourth Amendment to, 22, 69, 138, 142, 156, 175; interpretation of, 145

U.S. Postal Rules and Regulations, 181

U.S. Postal Service, 3, 69, 128, 193. *See also* Post Office Department

U.S. Supreme Court, 108, 134–35, 136, 139, 142, 156–57. *See also specific cases*

U.S. urban populations, 62, *62*, 63

Vallandigham, Clement, 67–68
Vandegrift, Fanny, 24
Veiller, Lawrence, 80, 93–94, 95, 96
venereal diseases, 175
violations, of privacy, 123, 142
Virginia, 186
virtue, 21, 40–41, 46, 86
visibility, 200–201; access relation to, 19; exposure and, 109; logic of privacy relation to, 104; management of, 27; moral decay relation to, 21; moral panic relation to, 22; social control and, 19; of state power, 281n120
vital statistics, 3, 168–69, 175
Volkszählungsgesetz, 169
Voorhees, Daniel W., 70–71

wage information, 153
Walden Pond, 42
Waldman, Ari Ezra, 194
Wall Street Journal, The (newspaper), 187
War Department, 179
warfare, 53

warrantless searches, 67
warrants, 156, 175
Warren, Samuel, 107, 121–23, 125–26, 134, 136, 184–85
wartime, 180, 195; exceptions during, 165, 166; governance during, 67–68; legislation during, 185
Washington, DC, 70–71
Washington, George, 30–31
Washington Herald, The (newspaper), 63
Washington Post (newspaper), 9
Washington State, 153, 154–55
Washington Times, The (newspaper), 63, 119, 196
Watergate scandal, 193
water management, 70–71
Watkins v. United States, 159
Waves, The (Woolf), 30
Wealth of Nations, The (Smith, A.), 108
Weber, Max, 39
Weeks v. United States, 137–38
Weimar Republic, 165, 192
"welfare of nations," 53
welfare services, 186
Western Union, 61, 69–70
Westin, Alan, 195
White, Alfred T., 91
White, Richard Grant, 31
Wilson, Nicholas Hoover, 207
Wilson, Woodrow, 183–84
"wire fence" society, 7
wiretapping, 61, 68, 106, 115, 130, 132–33
Wisconsin Supreme Court, 149–50
Wittgenstein, Ludwig, 14
womanhood, 147–48
women, 29–30, 40–41, 64–65
Woolf, Virginia, 30
Word2Vec models, 212–13, 214, *214*
word embedding models, 214
Wordsworth, William, 42

working-class people, 32, 40, 255n42
World War I, 53, 179, 184, 195
World War II, 192
Wright, Carroll D., 161
Wyman, Walter, 173

xenophobia, in sentinel surveillance,
    172–73

Yale Law Journal, 125–26, 155
Yardley, Herbert O., 183–84
yellow journalism, 111, 133
Yonkers, Civic League in, 102–3
Young Men's Christian Association, 176

Ziegler, Mary, 136
"zones of indistinction," 198

GPSR Authorized Representative: Easy Access System Europe, Mustamäe tee
50, 10621 Tallinn, Estonia, gpsr.requests@easproject.com